Understanding Contemporary India
Critical Perspectives

DELHI UNIVERSITY READER

Edited by
Achin Vanaik
and
Rajeev Bhargava

Orient BlackSwan

UNDERSTANDING CONTEMPORARY INDIA

ORIENT BLACKSWAN PRIVATE LIMITED

Registered Office
3-6-752 Himayatnagar, Hyderabad 500 029, Telangana, India
email: centraloffice@orientblackswan.com

Other Offices
Bangaluru, Chennai, Guwahati, Hyderabad, Kolkata,
Mumbai, New Delhi, Noida, Patna, Visakhapatnam

First published 2010
Reprinted 2012, 2014, 2021

The Editors on behalf of the Department of Political Science, University of Delhi thank the University Grants Commision for their support in bringing out this volume.

ISBN 978 81 250 3989 1

Typeset in Adobe Garamond 11/13
by Eleven Arts, Delhi

Printed in India at
Glorious Printers
Delhi

Published by
Orient Blackswan Private Limited
3-6-752 Himayatnagar, Hyderabad 500 029, Telangana, India
Email: info@orientblackswan.com

Contents

Acknowledgements

For permission to reproduce copyright material in this Reader, the volume editors and publishers wish to make the following acknowledgements.

RAJEEV BHARGAVA, 'India's Secular Constitution'. Originally published in E. Sreedharan, Zoya Hasan, R. Sudarshan (ed.), *India's Living Constitution*, Delhi: Permanent Black, 2002.

NEERA CHANDHOKE, 'Putting Civil Society in Its Place'. Originally published in *Economic and Political Weekly*, Vol. 40, No. 7, 14–20 February, 2009.

GOPAL GURU, 'How Egalitarian Are the Social Sciences in India'. Originally published in *Economic and Political Weekly*, Vol. 37, No. 51, 14 December, 2002.

MANORANJAN MOHANTY, 'Social Movements in Creative Society: Of Autonomy and Interconnection'. Originally published in Manoranjan Mohanty, Partha Mukherji with Olla Tormsquist (ed.), *People's Rights: Social Movements and the State in the Third World*, New Delhi: SAGE Publications India Pvt. Ltd., 1993.

Abbreviations

AIADMK	All India Anna Dravida Munnetra Kazhagam
AIFODR	All India Federation of Organisations of Democratic Rights
APC	Agricultural Prices Commission
APCLC	Andhra Pradesh Civil Liberties Committee
APDPIP	Andhra Pradesh District Poverty Initiative Project
APRPRP	Andhra Pradesh Rural Poverty Reduction Programme
ASAFLA	Asia Africa Latin America
BC	Benefit-Cost analysis
BPL	Below Poverty Line
CABE	Central Advisory Board of Education
CAG	Comptroller and Auditor General
CENTO	Central Treaty Organisation
CMEY	Chief Minister Employment Yojana
DWACRA	Development of Women and Children in Rural Area
ESIA	Economic Survey of Indian Agriculture
FCI	Food Corporation of India
FMS	Foreign Military Sales
GATT	General Agreement on Tariffs and Trade
GHQ	General Headquarters
HYV	High Yield Variety
ICSSR	Indian Council of Social Science Research
IMC	Indian Middle Class

IRDP	Integrated Rural Development Programme
ISI	Inter-Services Intelligence
JKLF	Jammu and Kashmir Liberation Front
LTTE	Liberation of Tamil Tigers Eelam
NAFTA	North American Free Trade Agreement
NAM	Non-Aligned Movement
NAS	New Agricultural Strategy
NCERT	National Council of Educational Research and Training
NCF	National Curriculum Framework
NEP	New Economic Policy
NMML	Nehru Memorial Museum and Library
NPC	National Planning Committee
NWFP	North-West Frontier Province
PAC	Public Accounts Committee
PDO	Peoples' Democratic Organisations
PDS	Public Distribution System
PRO	People's Rights Organisation
PUCL	People's Union for Civil Liberties
PUDR	People's Union for Democratic Rights
REC	Rural Electrification Corporation
SEATO	Southeast Asia Treaty Organisation
SERP	Society for Elimination of Rural Poverty
SHG	Self-Help Groups
UGC	University Grants Commission
WTO	World Trade Organisation

A Collective Vision

Achin Vanaik and Rajeev Bhargava

EDUCATION

Education, without a doubt, has an important functional, instrumental and utilitarian dimension. This is revealed when one asks questions such as 'what is the purpose of education?' The answers, too often, are 'to acquire qualifications for employment/upward mobility', 'wider/higher (in terms of income) opportunities', 'to meet the needs for trained human power in diverse fields for national development'. But in its deepest sense education is not instrumentalist. That is to say, it is not to be justified outside of itself because it leads to the acquisition of formal skills or of certain desired psychological-social attributes. It must be respected in itself.

Education is thus not a commodity to be acquired or possessed and then used, but a process of inestimable importance to individuals and society, although it can and does have enormous use value. Education then, is a process of expansion and conversion, not in the sense of converting or turning students into doctors or engineers, but the widening and turning out of the mind—the creation, sustenance and development of self-critical awareness and independence of thought. It is an inner process of moral-intellectual development.

Education is not so much a 'preparation for life', but in the final analysis the finding of a way of life.

Therefore, education must not be confused with training which is at most a subset of what constitutes education. Those who are highly trained are not necessarily highly educated or even reasonably educated. It is precisely the confusion and lack of sensitivity to the distinction between formal skill development and educational development that allows the widespread acceptance of the ridiculous, insulting and arrogant term 'brain drain' when what is meant is a drain of no doubt valuable formal skills, but nothing more and nothing less. One should not underestimate the importance of formal skill formation in a developing society, but it is vital that this be put in a proper perspective. There must be the deepest respect for the poor and illiterate, a recognition of what can be learnt from those who are not formally skilled in the ways provided by the formal academic system, but who are in their own ways educated. A formal education system which even at its highest level is unable or unwilling to inculcate in its students a respect for the educated, though they may be illiterate, and therefore an understanding of the truer meaning of education is itself seriously deficient.

The conceptual understanding of education as the 'finding of a way of life' carries an important implication. It implies that there should always be an expansion, deepening and enriching of education, the sharpening of critical, analytical and learning capacities and the widening and changing of norms and values because education is a process, a constant finding and not a final find. One of the great differences between the natural sciences on the one hand, and the social sciences and humanities on the other hand, is the dominance of positivism as the underlying philosophical attitude in the teaching and learning patterns of the former. The social sciences and humanities are certainly not immune from this positivism but the very nature of the social sciences and the humanities is that it must deal with values and their connection to knowledge rather than take easy refuge in the notion of a value-free or value-neutral 'science'. This makes the social sciences and humanities more amenable in key respects to recognising and respecting the distinction between formal skill training and education and also the connection between ethics and knowledge acquisition.

Political science teaching must then be guided by a sense of balance between promoting 'skill' formation and education, and between credentialising and humanising. The sole purpose of a post-graduate department of political science is not to become more 'practical', i.e., to prepare students to 'fit better' into a market society outside the academy. Yes, it is important to help students of political science get employment in the civil services, the corporate sector, the media world, the academic institutions and the NGOs. This is the functionalist dimension of academic training and it is necessary, but not at all sufficient. A political science department fails itself if it is not able to promote the development of self-critical and independent-minded students who are also humane and decent, i.e., the inculcation and exposure to good and progressive values. That is why a holistic curriculum is absolutely vital, one that goes well beyond, and indeed seeks to counter the pressures imposed by modernising societies. These are the pressures related to the vast expansion of knowledge that push ever more strongly for the functionalisation and specialisation of knowledge, i.e., knowing more and more about less and less. Indeed, one must not make the mistake of thinking that interdisciplinarity of courses by itself is a counterweight to this, when in fact it is all too often simply a more refined expression of precisely this compartmentalisation and functionalisation of knowledge. What then are the roles and responsibilities of the academic?

ROLES OF A UNIVERSITY ACADEMIC

Every profession exists within a broader ethical horizon that it shapes, and which in turn is shaped by it. Every profession also generates an ideal for itself, a model and a particular set of role-expectations. What are the expectations from a person who joins the faculty of a university? In our view there are at least three.

Teaching

The first and most obvious expectation is that the person be a good teacher. A good teacher equips students with skills to deliberate on an issue both on their own and with others. This kind of critical and collective deliberation requires not only the ability to think analytically, to grasp concepts and to see connections between otherwise disparate things, but also to have virtues, such as open-mindedness, the ability to engage with and listen to others, a willingness to change one's attitude and position. For teaching, it is particularly important to have the ability to sympathise with those who are ready to learn, who are not yet intellectually the equal of their teachers, but must be gently guided to be so. Patience and empathy are other crucial qualities of a teacher.

The most important requirement of teachers, however, is that they continually learn from their own teaching. Only such teachers can get others to learn. Rabindranath Tagore made this point almost a century ago. To inspire students, to give them the spark necessary for original thought, Tagore argued, 'a teacher must be still learning himself. A lamp can never light another lamp unless it continues to burn its own flame. A teacher with no living traffic with his knowledge can only load the minds of students, he cannot quicken them'. Unfortunately, as Tagore remarked, 'the greater part of our learning in schools and universities is wasted because for most of our teachers, their subjects are like dead specimens of once living things with which they have learned acquaintance but no communication of life and love'. But the learning process can also be easily obstructed by a flawed misunderstanding of one's role as that of an informant or worse as someone who has to initiate the student to a particular ideology of the good life. Instructors, preachers and ideologues are enemies of higher learning. This tendency within the academia to confuse teaching with the transmission of a particular ideological tool-kit, what can be called the 'over-ideologisation of the mind', is extremely destructive for teaching. In modern societies, the relationship between the academics and the 'people' is indirect and somewhat fractured. Confronted and baffled by this distance, the academic has a tendency to forsake open-ended deliberation, replacing it by new dogma and prefabricated solutions. Instead of a dispassionate search for a solution to the many problems at hand, academics may busy themselves with closing each other's minds and ultimately their own. Nothing undermines learning and teaching more.

Research

The second expectation from faculty members is that they pursue their own research. This research is done largely individually, but may also be done collectively. Research is increasingly becoming perhaps the most important aspect of what is required of university academics. This is the most important change that has occurred within the ethos of the Indian university in the last quarter of the century. Till the 1980s university academics could legitimately claim to have fulfilled social expectations by merely being good teachers. Many academics who started their careers in the late seventies or early eighties would remember that one thought one's day's job was done when one gave what one believed was a good lecture, one that elicited high praise from the students. It was truly satisfying to find ourselves surrounded by a group of students brimming with ideas they received in the classroom and who seemed eager to take them forward. Or those who gravitated towards us because something that we discussed in the classroom had gently shaken their settled outlook, and who therefore were eager to either collectively prove teachers wrong or compelled to probe the issue deeper. Good teaching continues to be a very important ingredient of university activity but more and more teachers now realise that their academic life is woefully incomplete without research publications. It is no longer enough for academics to reach out to their students or to discuss ideas within a small circle of friendly colleagues. Through their ideas, they want to reach out to a larger academic audience, perhaps even to a wider public. And for this to happen they need time for themselves, outside and beyond the classroom. One is not suggesting that Indian academics have taken publications seriously only now. Great scholars have existed in the past and their scholarly reputation has travelled world-wide. What one is suggesting is that it is increasingly becoming a part of the academic ethos of good Indian universities. Many more academics today are keen to publish. And why not? This is how it should be.

We have spoken of research as if it has a single unambiguous meaning. But research can be of two kinds. The first type is typical of the modern university but is found outside it also. This research is aligned closely to the productive and industrial requirements of society, directly concerned with solving the immediate problems that arise from our productive interaction with the natural world and from sustained interaction with one another. However, there is another kind of research, reminiscent more of classical schools of learning, which is also a feature of modern universities. One should really call it higher learning but in keeping with its current designation, let us call it research, though to distinguish it from the first kind we will call it foundational research.

Higher Learning or Foundational Research

Foundational research is closely linked to what we might call a love of ideas for their own sake. This research is different from the first kind because it discourages us from seeing ideas purely from an instrumental or pragmatic point of view. To be sure, they are not without relevance. Yet relevance cannot become their sole criteria of evaluation. After all, only omniscient beings with full clairvoyance can know all their possible and future relevance. It is of course true that they perform a social function. Yet, their social function cannot be fixed a priori for posterity. Again, ideas may become political forces. Yet, an obsession to turn them into a political force is self defeating. Ideas are relevant and irrelevant simultaneously, and as a natural home for ideas, the value of the university also lies in its simultaneous relevance and irrelevance to society.

The best universities in the world provide a home to the strangest, the weirdest, the least understood, and the most perplexing of ideas. If there is one place where ideas *must* live, it is surely the modern university; not just ideas about the good, but even ideas about the bad, if only to remind ourselves what makes something evil and why. It is one of the functions of the university to ensure, at least within its own confines, the survival of all kinds of ideas. For this purpose, it must be hospitable to restless and open, questioning and uncertain minds, minds that dare to go further and deeper than others. In short, a university must be liberal in the best sense of the term. It is, however, a mistake to think that the best society is one in which all its institutions have a liberal orientation. There are many stages and spheres in our personal and social life where to act as a liberal or to develop predominantly liberal institutions would be mistaken. There are many dimensions of a common institutional life where classical liberal values are either undesirable or simply not feasible. However, a good society on any definition must have two institutions with a predominantly liberal character: first, the media, and second the university. Both these institutions must not only be open enough to sustain free discussion and debate on just about anything, but also try to respect as best as it can the grey line separating free speech from hate speech.

Every good university must have space to learn and celebrate the irrelevant, and no person who enters the university should leave it without, at least once, experiencing the joy and excitement of partaking of this space. Every good scholar, without necessarily and self-consciously being a good teacher, is able to transmit an intellectual enthusiasm to all those who come to her/him. If one is truly immersed in the pursuit of learning then one is able to communicate its joy even to those who lack the ambition to become scholars. Arguably the articulation of original ethical visions and the discovery of imaginative solutions to some of our most pressing problems are conditional upon a healthy distrust of the demand for relevance.

What holds for good universities is automatically true of departments that make it up. Any good department must have scholars engaged in foundational research who by work and example prepare students for more research of the same kind. A department that confuses these two kinds of research and emphasises instrumentally-oriented research at the expense of foundational research may be able to secure for its faculty members and students all kinds of external goods but will deprive them of goods internal to academic life.

However, no amount of good teaching or good research can substitute for another very crucial function that must also be performed by university academics. Let us call it the institutional function. Students and perhaps young faculty members may get the impression that the function of academics is exhausted by teaching and research. After all, this is the visible part of an academic's life. This is what shows, and this is what counts. Students are impressed by good teaching and occasionally by good research. Our academic peers may know little about our teaching but they think well of us by virtue of the quality of our academic work. A department's reputation is built around the quality of teaching it offers, its collective research profile and the research of its individual members, by books and articles that they publish in good academic journals.

Institutional Role

However, some of us do not realise that good teaching and research presupposes a larger institutional context. This institutional context is not sustained by an invisible hand. Nor is it the work of God. There are three ways in which it can be sustained and each of these can be evaluated from an ethical point of view. In the first, the work required to sustain it is shared equally by all faculty members. There is a fair division of labour—each person, in addition to teaching and conducting his research, puts in his share in sustaining and building the institution. The incentive to perform this work comes from the participation of each faculty member in the decision-making process. Rewards and burdens, in this system or approach are distributed by a rough criterion of fairness endorsed by almost every member. In the second approach the fruits of the institutional system are shared by everybody—by virtue largely of the fact that most institutional goods are irreducibly collective. But the burdens are not equally shared. Some faculty members always find an excuse not to perform the work assigned to them. Occasionally and sadly some of them may precisely be those faculty members who are good at teaching and who assiduously pursue their own research. More often they happen to be the ones who are generally alienated from academic life, have lost interest in academics or are distracted by things other than academics. They are too busy elsewhere to find time for institutional work. The consequence of this is a wholly unjust division of labour. Some people get by with very little work while others with better scruples, or better understanding of the importance of institutions or simply because of their habit of shouldering everybody's burdens—and many in our society possess these nearly saintly qualities—are compelled to or voluntarily perform much greater work. For shirkers and free riders even democracy is a burden because it requires from them too much commitment and work. To be sure, this is one way in which institutions can be run and run well, but ethically speaking this is not how our institutions should be run.

There is yet another way in which institutions are run. The quickest way to understand this third mode of institutional functioning is to contrast it with the second. In the second, some people voluntarily exclude themselves from the work of the institutions. They reap benefits but are not prepared to share the burdens. In this third mode, academics wish to be included in the larger life of the institution, they are prepared to work and share the burdens of institutional life, but either an individual or a faction takes control of the institution and excludes willing faculty members from institutional processes and rewards. Those who concentrate power within themselves may do so because they are habitually hierarchical or because they view institution as a tool to further their own personal ends, and the ends of those who possess a similar attitude towards the institution. They view it as their own personal property or the property of a small exclusive group, not as a collective good.

EXTERNAL AND INTERNAL GOODS

The distinction between external and internal goods is borrowed from Alasdair Macintyre. We can get a handle on this distinction by taking an example. Consider filmmaking. People make films for all kinds of reasons. Some for money, others for instant fame, still others for 'self-realisation' or bravura, still others for effect, because they want to get across a message to large numbers of people. Filmmaking is an efficient way by which these goods are achieved. But the relation between these goods and the art of filmmaking is extrinsic and contingent. Wealth, fame, power can be gained by other means and not all filmmakers are wealthy, famous or powerful. So, these goods are external to the practice of filmmaking. Hence, they are external goods.

But some goods are such that they can only be had by participating in the practice of filmmaking. More significantly, the greater the skill, the larger is your procurement of these goods. These goods, because they are internal to each practice, are internal goods. Consider the art of French filmmaker Bresson. Bresson seeks a controlled and rigorous narrative of cinema, which is distinct from the narrative structure of life as also from forms of narrative found in other art forms like novels, theatres and paintings. He wishes to liberate cinema even from the visual form of storytelling. This anti-dramatic, deeply reflective and austere form of cinema that he seeks and succeeds in producing is a goods unavailable to those who are outside cinema or to those who make bad films. A bad filmmaker—who is narcissistically self-indulgent, who seeks money or speedy popularity, or does not fully understand one's medium—can obtain external goods in plenty. But only a good filmmaker who shuns the temptations of external goods can achieve internal goods.

Bresson unhesitatingly cut 45 minutes of the *Diary of the Country Priest* to hit the right spiritual rhythm. Of another of his films, *A Man Escaped*, Truffaut said, 'there is not a single spoilt shot in the film; it conforms to the author's intentions from beginning to end.' He added, 'It is one of those films which can be said not to contain a single useless shot or scene that can be cut or shortened.' What Bresson is trying to get right and what he may have achieved in his films is an internal good. The sketch books of painters and the notebooks of poets and novelists demonstrate that they too strive hard 'to get it just right', that trying to achieve something better is crucial to their practice.

Much the same is true of academics. We can acquire fame by appearing frequently on television or power by becoming academic administrators and members of politically powerful think-tanks, perhaps even money by being consultants for international organisations and wealthy industrial houses. But the quality of academics is judged by the kind of students they produce and by the enduring value of their research. We look in academics for an original insight, for good arguments, for complex and nuanced perspectives, for conceptual grasp and for the breadth and depth of their vision. We look for these qualities in academics because these, precisely the internal goods of academic life, are what the best among them are trying to achieve. Since institutional context is a condition for realisation of these goods, intellectual leadership within the institution may also be included as an internal good. All others, power, fame and money are simply external goods.

FACTORS UNDERMINING ACADEMIC LIFE

The academic life of institutions is undermined if not ruined by several interrelated factors. The first of which has already been mentioned above, namely a tendency amongst many of us to look at institutions purely instrumentally as a means to accumulate external goods, including realisation of certain kinds of non-academic personal goals such as personal ambition, power, fame, patronage and personal favours. If the conduct of the members of a university is guided solely by such ends causing persistent neglect of internal goods, of leading a life of the mind, then the academic life of the university is ruined.

A second factor is factionalism. A department is faction-ridden if it is divided into two or more rival camps which fight for external goods of institutional life. There are many rewards in academic institutional life that appear to be academic but are not, or at best are only marginally related to them. Here are some examples. Every department must hold seminars, invite people for talks, recruit students to their various degree programmes, conduct examinations, hold vivas, allocate students to supervisors and update and restructure courses. Each of these can be done on the basis of clearly laid down procedures devised to promote academic excellence or be done keeping in mind considerations that have little to do with academic merit. If these are done without considerations of academic merit then the academic life of the institution degenerates. Secondly, all of this may be done by including all faculty members in the process or factionally, i.e., by excluding all members of the rival faction so that all decisions pertaining to such issues rest exclusively in the hands of one faction. Many academic departments suffer because the distribution of decision-making power is done purely on factional considerations. When one faction takes over power in the department, all members of the other faction are excluded. But what it might be argued is that if one faction upholds academic standards and the other does not, would it not be better if the academically-oriented faction takes control of the department? For what might happen if the non-academic faction has all the power? Surely this would ruin any department. Our own view is that factionalism is nearly as bad as non-compliance with academic standards. Put differently, academic standards may thrive for a while if the academically-oriented faction controls the department, but it will not flourish for long enough to become a constitutive part of the institutional life of the department. And unless that happens the short tenure of academic excellence can only be called an adventure, great fun while it lasts but of no real significance in the long run. Somehow, therefore, we must work towards minimising factionalism in academic institutions. We believe we can contribute to its reduction by ensuring within departments installation of norms of minimal decency which no one is allowed to cross. Among such norms is the inclusion of everyone, regardless of personal and ideological differences, in the decision-making process and a fair distribution of rewards and burdens among all. Alas, this is easier said than done! It is extremely difficult if there are people in the department who are already prejudiced, have closed their minds and carry a permanent mark of bitter factional struggles of the past. It is almost impossible to achieve anything if matters which must be settled within the department are taken outside it.

The assumption that self-interest is identical with the pursuit of external goods is mistaken. Some personal goals are worthy, and yet may come into conflict with an institutional role. Internal goods come into conflict not only with external goods but also with one another. For example, if a teacher spends an enormous amount of time in the preparation of her/his lectures or has an obsession with a research problem, she/he may continually neglect an important institutional function that she/he is also morally required to perform. Such goals may somewhat mitigate the inappropriate institutional conduct of good academics but they do not completely absolve them of their institutional irresponsibility, especially if this neglect is a continuous, almost permanent feature. Free-riding, even if it is for the sake of another worthy cause, is a problem and is the third factor in the decline of institutional life. When internal goods conflict with one another, the solution is not to ride roughshod over any one of them. No internal goods must be bypassed or neglected. The only sensible resolution of the conflict is to find a proper balance between them. For example, an academic may decide to forego some of the less important seminars in order to focus on teaching or on fulfilling an institutional function. Or suppose an academic needs some extra time to finish her/his manuscript, or if she/he takes leave, it is bound to put some of her/his colleagues under additional pressure of teaching. A sensible compromise would be to ensure that leave be given to her/him for this important work now on the understanding that later, after the manuscript is finished, she/he will teach additional courses to lessen the burden of those teachers who likewise need time for their own research.

Another internal threat to academic institutional life, the fourth factor, flows from the deficiencies of a wider societal culture in India that lie too deep to quickly dissipate. Tocqueville warned of the tendency of nascent democracy, in its passionate anti-feudal mood of general social levelling, to breed mediocrity and to catapult envy as the dominant sentiment in society. This has an obvious and particularly pernicious effect on academic practice. Envy erases qualitative distinctions and drags the qualitatively better down to the level of the mediocre. This de-recognises work of proven worth. Indeed, the greater the worth the stronger is the campaign for its erasure from the wider academic domain, a subterranean pretence that the work does not even exist grips the collective mind. Over a period of time, the persistent non-recognition of her/his work also induces in the author a doubt about its worth. In the end, it is a no-win situation for everyone because the very sense of internal goods and standards vital to a free academic life is lost.

A fifth factor is endemic to large metropolises such as Delhi. Indeed, it might be a very specific problem of Delhi University, which has witnessed a remarkable decline of real campus life. This is partly due to the way Delhi has expanded and commuting to the university has become difficult. Students and faculty members come to the campus only to attend or take classes and to leave immediately thereafter, giving rise to what is widely called the 'U-special' culture. This is extremely detrimental to a vibrant intellectual life because students learn from teachers as much inside the classroom as outside it, and they learn from each other even more than they learn from teachers and books. By learning here we mean making ideas integral to one's worldview and sometimes one's practice. This happens only after we discuss the ideas threadbare, over long periods. And this prolonged engagement with ideas is possible more among fellow students than between teachers and students. Of course, better transport alone will not improve this intellectual interaction. There must be many more public spaces for students to meet one another.

A final sixth factor contributing to the problems of academic life stems from vestiges of a pre-democratic feudal era. For example, merit-based institutions are customarily converted into little fiefdoms run by tin gods doling out petty patronage to loyal supporters and creating suffocating tyrannies for others. In such contexts, ideas are applauded or condemned with a view not to their intrinsic worth but to those who articulate them. This is no doubt part of a larger malaise of a knee-jerk personalisation of every issue, a deeper inability to imagine and sustain impersonal institutional structures. Sometimes even factions within university departments, as mentioned above, are based on personal loyalty rather than on principle or ideology. Intra-group cooperation also depends on personal loyalty to a leader, often to whoever happens to be the chairperson. Within impersonal situations of equality, as in large rule-governed universities, cooperation then quickly gives way to intense rivalry, atrophy and isolation. Therefore, projects that require sustained team effort are difficult to execute. Such habits of the mind are hardly conducive to the growth of stable traditions of scholarly work.

THE HEAD OF THE DEPARTMENT

How do we curb concentration of power, or prevent turning a position of legitimate authority into a mini-feudal tyranny? Over the years good universities throughout the country have devised methods to check the tyrannical tendencies of academic administrators. For example, the term of heads of departments has been limited to two or three years; good universities no longer have permanent heads of departments. At this point it might be complained that chairpersonship by rotation can create a problem of continuity. But the obvious response here is that continuity must be made dependent on institutional rules and the collective ethos generated by teachers, scholars, students and the non-academic staff and should not depend on particular individuals. If such institutional checks exist and if decision is taken by consultation in the appropriate forum, i.e., the meeting of the faculty then should it matter who the chairperson is? Yet, just as no college can do without the principal, no department can do without a chairperson.

Day-to-day Administration, Coordination and Conflict-management

What is then the role of the chairperson? We believe a chairperson must perform at least four functions, two of which are clearly burdensome which is why no academic worth his salt would like to stick to this office beyond a specified time period. The first is day-to-day management of routine administrative matters, for example to prepare teaching schedules, arrange facilities and equipment for teaching, acquire teaching materials such as books and journals, conduct tutorials and examinations, set question papers, check answers, and recruit new students. Others include financial decisions related to infrastructural facilities, acquisition of books for departmental library if there is one, representation of the centre on various academic and non-academic bodies mostly within the university and sometimes outside it. These issues arise not just periodically, but are present as part of the daily life of an academic institution. Any person who works seriously in an academic institution knows this. The second has to do with coordination and, if and when the need arises, conflict management. In any large and complex institutions the activities of all its members need proper coordination. Any institution inhabited by living people will run into problems arising out of diverse, competing and sometimes conflicting perceptions and understandings of the situation, conflicting interpretation of relevant rules and competing views on how best to resolve conflicts that arise when the interests of one group, say students, clash with the interests of other groups, say teachers and non-academic staff. A conflict may arise between the interests of a group and the common ideals of the institution. To resolve, settle and manage all these conflicts, we need someone to take the initiative even if all relevant persons participate in the process of deliberation and conflict resolution. Both these jobs of daily administration and management of competing interests are very demanding and exhausting, and take away a lot of one's personal time. Yet, someone has to perform them, and chairpersonship by rotation is a splendid procedure to share this burden. It ensures fairness because it distributes the burden of leadership equally amongst all those who are willing or required to take it up.

Recruitment

The recruitment of faculty members is absolutely crucial in any college or university, and the role of heads of departments is pivotal in it. It is particularly so in large centralised universities in which university departments play a crucial role in the selection of college teachers. How should such recruitment be done? On what basis should they be done? What are the values and principles in which they should be grounded? In order to answer these questions it is best to construct a worst-case scenario. We need to do this not because this is necessarily an accurate description of how teachers are recruited. One is sure this is not the case. This thought experiment is significant only because what we wish to focus on is best illuminated when contrasted with its exact opposite. What then is the worst possible context of recruitment, at least from the point of view of most aspirants for an academic job, say, that of a college teacher?

The worst scenario for most candidates is when a candidate is already selected outside the proceedings of the selection committee and the selection itself is based on largely non-academic criteria. Here key members of the selection committee have either already selected one person or come to the selection committee meeting with names of their own respective candidates whose case they relentlessly push. In such cases, the interview is bound to turn into a farce. Questions are asked to deliberately trump or confuse the candidate. No time is given to warm up. The shortest possible time is spent on candidates whose failure is preordained. Some candidates may even be humiliated, leading to a loss of self-confidence, an important prerequisite for good performance. After the interviews no reasons are offered as to why a particular candidate is preferred over others. If the selection of an undeserving candidate is contested, votes are taken and the majoritarian principle is invoked to defend a pre-determined choice. If the selection committee is split over a candidate, a deal is struck that either supports a compromise candidate—one who still fails to satisfy the criterion of academic merit—or the candidate of one faction is chosen this time on the understanding that the candidate of the other faction is selected at the next selection meeting in some other college. These are descriptions of a possible situation in which bad candidates are chosen by manipulation and power-play.

However, bad candidates may also be chosen out of sheer boredom, negligence, or carelessness. Mindless questions are asked. No thought is given to select the best from among the good. After all, it is not only the candidates who need to prepare for interviews, but members of selection committees too must spend time to prepare themselves for it. If necessary, members should also be prepared to spend more time on interviews than is formally scheduled. Nor should they shun long discussions after the interview is over. How can long discussions be avoided if there are too many good candidates? The violation of procedures and academic norms has a profoundly adverse impact on not only the mental condition of the candidates, but also on how they approach future interviews. Bad selection committee meetings invariably breed cynicism, insecurity, paranoia and bitterness. If young job-seekers begin their adult life with such an attitude and disposition, they will neither do justice to themselves nor to society. If they happen to get teaching jobs later in their lives, they are unlikely to make good teachers or scholars.

Any reasonable interviewer would then wish to keep in mind the following while selecting college teachers.

- The interviewer should give some thought to questions she would ask and the answers she expects from candidates.
- Questions must be asked in a certain order. In order to get the best out of candidates, the first couple of questions must get the right pitch. Subsequent questions should be raised in an ascending order of quality.
- Questions must be asked in such a way that they enable us not only to distinguish the good from the bad, but also the best from the good.
- Roughly the same amount of time should be spent on each candidate in order to ensure that no one feels that she/he was treated unfairly.
- Every candidate must be treated with respect. No one should feel humiliated at the end of the interview. We can probably get the best out of them by putting ourselves in their shoes.
- Confidence and proficiency of language must not be seen as a substitute for thought. The candidate must know that it is not only important to have a correct position or even a point of view of an issue, but it is also necessary to be able to think cogently. In short, it is not enough for a candidate to be quick and smart and ready with sound bytes. Instead, what is needed is evidence of reflection. Besides, it must be recognised that different people have different manners and styles. This pluralism must be taken into account at the time of interviews.
- A tendency exists among interviewers to imagine that their job is done at the end of the process of interviews. A hasty decision is then taken by deploying the majoritarian principle. Reasoned debate on good candidates is frequently avoided. This should be prevented.

- Decisions of the committee must not be influenced by diktats or by claims of some special knowledge that nobody else possesses, for example, 'I have known this candidate for a long time' or that 'I have a better understanding of the needs of the college.' What are the other interviewers to do in the face of such claims, especially if they come from outside or are newcomers? Claims about every candidate must be publicly defended.
- There should not be any deals. Choosing a candidate is not equivalent to bargain in a business. An impartial set of criteria must be applied for all. We must learn to accept that our own students are not always the best or the most suitable.

There is a fourth function, however, which is perhaps the most important—to provide intellectual leadership. Here too the idea should not be to have one leader who is followed for two to three years by all teachers and students. Leadership should be minimal in this sense that any collective good can only be realised by team effort. As far as possible, the chairperson should try to build a consensus in the meeting rather than outside it. Usually, two modes of functioning exist. Firstly, decisions are already taken and only presented before the faculty. Secondly, all faculty members are involved in the process of decision making. The second one is democratic and the first one is not. Therefore, the chairperson must avoid the first one, and implement the second one. Yet someone must take responsibility to initiate discussion on the collective vision of the centre, on what its teaching programmes are, what should its research profile be, the areas in which the research of the students be directed, and on how to enhance the intellectual strength of its faculty members. A chairperson who foregoes all these functions does disservice to her department.

AN IDEAL DEPARTMENT?

What then is an ideal university department? The list is almost certainly going to be a set of truisms which no one would deny, but may be very difficult to realise in practice. They are as follows:

- To uphold standards of academic excellence in teaching of courses, recruit students and faculty members, induct students in MPhil, and particularly in PhD programmes, mark scripts and appoint external examiners, select visiting scholars and lecturers, and select themes and participants for seminars;
- To eschew factionalism, both personal and ideological;
- To ensure strict compliance with institutional norms of basic minimum decency;
- To settle differences and disputes by discussion and negotiation within the department, rather than politicising them in a wrong way; and
- To sustain an institutional life of the department in such a way that it is not dependent on particular persons.

None of the above should change with any change, for example, that of the chairperson.

A real transformation can be brought about in university departments only, if we follow rules, procedures, norms and ethical precepts. This transformation would be evident when:

- Every student feels that she/he has learnt something by being in the department,
- Students get attracted to academic work, into the world of scholarship,
- There is good quality research by students and faculty,
- Teachers have a national and international standing, and
- University departments begin to possess the capacity to make themselves relevant to the rest of the society, and a scholar who comes from outside the university begins to feel that it will be an honour to be invited by the department.

Achieving all these require decades of sustained labour by a group of committed academics who build on the work of their predecessors, who learn from their own mistakes, and are inspired by each other to take scholarly traditions forward.

Introduction

Achin Vanaik and Rajeev Bhargava

Amidst the plethora of books that in one way or the other bring together essays by academics, in what way can this volume claim to be distinctive and useful? This is the challenge that we have sought to address. For the first time the postgraduate Department of Political Science, Delhi University, has brought out a collection of contributions from those who teach or have taught in this department. Besides the editors of this volume, there are contributions from three other former heads of the department.[1] This is, to say the least, unusual and might seem to bespeak of a certain sense of self-aggrandising arrogance. But it is not, and there is another purpose why we resorted to this particular format.

An edited volume can be unified by the common purpose it is intended to serve. This could be to provide a textbook of sorts to students, undergraduate or post-graduate, in one or other area of the overall syllabus that needs to be covered. Or an edited collection might wish to address not just students, researchers, scholars or fellow academics in the field, but also to reach out to a wider, more general, yet informed readership and be so structured as to meet this objective. Either way such books look outside of their specific institutional-departmental confines to bring in others who can make relevant contributions to the particular theme or themes that are to be articulated. Or if the aim is simply to showcase the talents of a particular faculty, then given the various sub-disciplines and areas of specialisation of individual teachers, what would emerge is almost certainly going to be something of a hodge-podge, no matter how worthy or thought-provoking each or every chapter might be. This is certainly not what our department wanted to do.

The Department of Political Science of Delhi University has a two-year MA course in which students must take exams in sixteen course papers. It also takes in MPhil and PhD students who have to complete their course work, and with the help of appointed supervisors prepare and eventually submit dissertations. The requirements of MA are such that all its six sub-disciplinary areas must be covered by the teaching faculty who are thus appointed keeping these sub-disciplinary requirements in mind. What are these six areas? They are 'Politics in India', 'Political Theory', 'Comparative Politics', 'Indian Political Thought', 'Public Administration', and 'International Relations'. Each of these sub-disciplines in turn covers a range of topics.

When we as fellow departmental colleagues discussed the proposal to bring out this collective volume, we had to answer the questions why, how and what for? All this in the background of a great diversity of courses and themes taught and absorbed, itself made possible only by an equal diversity of scholarly aptitudes and interests. Could there be some unifying vision behind this intra-departmental diversity? And if we discovered that there was, and needed to be such a collective vision, then could we or should we seek to publicly articulate it? We answered 'yes' to both these questions and this book is the product of our effort to flesh out that response. It has been a quest for 'unity' in two important respects. First, for all the diverse formal skills and research interests of colleagues we were able to come to a broad convergence of thematic purpose. Our many intellectual pathways, diverse and meandering though they are, have nonetheless had not one but repeated meeting points. Whether our concerns are more general or theoretical, whether they are more empirical or descriptive, whether they tread the terrain of the national or that of the regional-global, we return time and again to the contemporary Indian reality which we seek in some way or the other to better explain and understand. This imparted a definite coherence to the structure of this book. What follows in this introduction will say something about this and about the individual chapter presentations even as we have largely eschewed the common practice to provide proper summaries. There is no substitute and much reward, after all, for reading each contribution with the thoroughness that each deserves.

Second, we have sought to elucidate a collective vision of the department regarding the meaning and purpose of education, and thereby relate the formal academic system of higher, postgraduate teaching in political science to this overarching perspective and understanding. This naturally required clarification of the roles and responsibilities of a university academic in the context of India generally, and of Delhi University specifically. Our collective vision has been spelt out in the chapter preceding this Introduction. Though that chapter has been written jointly by a former head of the department and by the current head, we wish to state that we are much indebted to the introspection and discussion that so many members of the faculty undertook. Not everything we two say there will have the assent of all our colleagues. But after all allowances are made for qualifications and reservations, we do believe it represents broadly and faithfully the commitments and values of our contributors with whom we have, at one time or the other, had the honour and pleasure of professional and collegial association in the department. Let us now turn to the contributions.

Towards the end of the first decade of the new millennium there is a revived and sharply growing interest worldwide in India because it is, as the new buzz phrase has it, an 'Emerging Power'. The major reasons for this transformation of image are not that difficult to discern. First, the collapse of the USSR automatically raised the relative status of other 'significant' powers such as Japan, Germany, China, India and Brazil.

Second, an Indian shift, in economical and political terms, towards what was widely considered admirable in the West resulted in an altogether more favourable and sympathetic attitude towards India in circles of influence—governments, elites, high-ranking academia and leading media outlets. Politically, India had abandoned its strategic tilt towards Russia, increasingly giving only lip service to the Non-Aligned Movement (NAM) of which it had been a leader, and is now seeking to establish and consolidate a strategic partnership with the USA. Economically, the new policies (NEP), introduced by the Indian Government in 1991, represented an ideological shift towards acceptance and endorsement of the post- and anti-Keynesianism that from the beginning of the 1980s had started to reshape the economies of the advanced capitalist countries. Suddenly, the high and steady average annual growth rates of the Indian economy—consistently touching just under 6 per cent from the early 1980s right up to 2003, after which the average growth rate increased to around 8 per cent per year—were recognised and lauded. In the face of the 'Great Recession' of 2007–9, the average annual growth rate fell to the norm of the nineties, but even this showed that India, along with China, was much better able to tide over this global economic storm than the advanced industrialised countries of the West and Japan. India is now perceived as a new economic giant.

Third, in 1998 India became in effect a nuclear power following its overt conduct of a number of controversial underground nuclear tests. The USA and other Western nations and Japan initially opposed, but eventually accepted this new status. In becoming a nuclear power, India effectively defied the rest of the world, including the dominant powers, and paid no serious or lasting price in doing so. Leaving aside the merits or demerits and dangers or consequences of what it had carried out, India's successful defiance enhanced its status as a major power—a power that could set new global rules of behaviour (as the Indo-US Nuclear Deal and its aftermath showed) that others would eventually follow.

So how significant a power is India going to be? And does this not crucially depend on how adequately it is able to cope with its immense internal contradictions and tensions? How well is it equipped, through its institutions, its Constitution and its governmental practices and routines, to address these challenges? The India that will emerge is as yet undecipherable since it will be the result of an ongoing process of conflicting economic, social, political, cultural and ideological forces, pressures and tendencies. There are different understandings of what India is, what it will be, or should be. That is to say, there are different national imaginings and hopes which are themselves linked to different political-normative projects and social actors. All this, ultimately, is what this book is about, hence its title *Understanding Contemporary India: Critical Perspectives.*

THE CONTRIBUTIONS

State and Constitution

We start with the contributions by Rajeev Bhargava and Ashok Acharya, and appropriately enough, about what they have to say about the Indian Constitution, the template which is to guide the ongoing project of building a more humane and decent India. No country compares with the incredible cultural, religious and social diversity of India. At its very inception its Constitution sought to reflect and protect the diversity as well as provide legal-institutional correctives to address its equally multifarious evils. The Indian Constitution is a remarkable one and the Indian experience in the decades since independence provides remarkable lessons for even the advanced democracies in how to handle issues for which they thought they had the best answers, but did not—matters of secularism and multiculturalism. The gravamen of Bhargava's case is that the Indian Constitution, in its effort to legitimise and promote an understanding of secularism as 'principled distance' between religion and the state, makes a distinctive contribution to both the theory and practice of what it means to be a secular and democratic society and polity. Sensitivity to group and minority rights has meant that the Indian state has, at its best, justifiably intervened in religious matters in order to defend principles of religious liberty and equality of citizenship. Western conceptions of secularism, which emerged in a different historical context, were based on a uniform, indeed homogenised, and abstract notion of what constitutes individual dignity and self-respect across societies and cultures. This is both its strength and its weakness. Better liberalism requires a reasonable communitarianism through deeper understanding of the beliefs and practices which shape behaviour both within and between religious communities, and between them and the state. Strict exclusion rather than principled distance between the state and religion will be the enemy of a truly respectful multiculturalism.

The issue of respecting difference and institutionalising minority rights is the central focus of Acharya's chapter. More than in any other democracy, the Constituent Assembly debates in India that led to the framing of the Constitution took this up with unmatched seriousness and depth of thought. This Constitution is the longest and in many respects the most sophisticated document of its kind anywhere. It is far from perfect and is a 'living' document subject to amendments and reflects the contemporary interplay of various forces and their power relationships. Indeed, the fierce debates of that assembly continue to have relevance and reflect a tussle between two views of citizenship: the common citizenship model that takes the individual as the unit of the political community and the group-differentiated position that approves protection and rights for communities. Interestingly, Acharya argues that the Constitution is paradoxically both a deviation from and a derivation of the colonial model. It explicitly rejects the colonial model of balance between various groups but then recognises the need to treat differences differently in the form of special representation rights to disadvantaged groups. Second, as a compendium of various difference sensitive rights that coexist with a common citizenship model, India's Constitution anticipated what is known as multiculturalism in contemporary liberalism.

Matters of Governance

Whether and to what extent the current global downturn will lead to a rejection of neo-liberal economics and the right-wing politics necessarily associated with it, remains an open matter. But the neo-liberal turn worldwide of the last twenty-five to thirty years, which in India was accelerated after the 1991 reforms, has significantly altered political discourse and structural realities. The notion of 'good governance' introduced by the World Bank and the new theories of public management which emerged from the beginning of the 1990s were aimed at reducing the role and significance of the state in favour of market-based structures and processes, primarily in the name of greater efficiency. For all the problems associated with the socially-biased character of even democratic states, it remains the case that its political institutions must legitimise themselves through some degree of public accountability. The turn to neo-liberalism then necessarily involves a reshaping of ideas and practices of citizenship, a re-jigging of the relationship between state and civil society, indeed re-configurations in the connections between various civil society bodies themselves. Neo-liberalisation of the economy has meant a neo-liberalisation of politics and the 'pluralisation' (Neera Chandhoke's term) of the state even as this takes variable forms in different societies and democracies. There has been both a disciplinary neo-liberalism and a compensatory neo-liberalism somewhat more concerned with softening the impact of rising inequalities of wealth and power. In both the cases the aim is to delegate responsibilities for welfare and even justice to non-state structures which by their nature will be segmented and compartmentalised, and thus far less publicly accountable.

All this has had profound implications for the principle of democratic citizenship and in a wide-ranging theoretical critique Chandhoke explores all these developments. Amidst the widespread celebration of civil society and its agents, Chandhoke points out the limitations of civil society and its agents even as she recognises its importance and distinctive strengths. The contracting out of public functions to willing state agents such as NGOs can be both positive and negative. NGOs can be closer, and therefore more sensitive to those on the ground. But it also means the easy abnegation of state responsibilities in various welfare domains, functions it should not be allowed to discard. Civil society agencies have become more important in India because they have had to fill in a space vacated by the 'unresponsiveness of the state', the 'indifference of the bureaucracy' and the 'pulverization of the party system'.

Nevertheless, NGOs as one of the key agencies in civil society cannot substitute for the state. Policymaking and implementation are the domain of the state, and the citizenry knows this. Hence in India, there is the clear preference of the ordinary public for a strong governmental role in the public provision of health, education, jobs and social security. Civil society activism is thus the crucial stimulus for the exercise of responsible power not the substitute for the state in democratic politics.

Where Chandhoke leaves off is where Satyajit Singh begins. Equally disturbed by neo-liberal notions of governance, he looks at the irrigation and water policies of the Indian government over the past decades. It is the social and political relations in which the technologies of water supply and distribution, e.g., large dams, are inserted that prove decisive. It is these that determine the scale and pattern of distribution of benefits which are not really captured by the technical cost-benefit analyses that the government resorts to in order to justify and rationalise its various irrigation projects. Indeed, sociologists, political scientists and environmental experts could provide additional considerations that are usually omitted in cost-benefit analyses in the assessment of whether to go ahead with large and medium irrigation projects. But even at the level of standard economic accounting there is all too often a gross underestimate of the true costs which must factor in the impact of uncertainties over time as well as being sensitive to the importance of 'energy accounting'. Social relations of power prevailing since independence determined that equitable land reforms on a major scale would not take place and that a technological approach—green revolution—would need to be adopted to reinforce inequitable forms of social stratification. The latter was also to emphasise the pursuit of large and medium irrigation projects as well as subsidisation of tubewells with very damaging consequences on groundwater resources. The Indian government or more precisely, the irrigation bureaucracy has had a vested interest in deflecting serious criticism of its plans and actions which have included heavy displacement of oustees and flooding of forest cover on a scale that is grossly underestimated by the bureaucracy and thus hidden from its technical-economic accounting. There is a real case to respect traditional irrigation science and to recognise the many strengths and cheapness of small-scale irrigation projects. Even as he is strongly critical of the Indian government, Satyajit Singh is careful not to go overboard and reject all large projects and is not calling for a return to the past. Rather he is calling for a newer and more sensible mix of the old and the new, the large and the small, as well as a more careful and many-sided approach to the accounting of all projects, large and small. Singh makes an important case to separate hydraulic property rights from the existing pattern of highly unfair land-owning rights. He acknowledges that institutionalisation of an egalitarian system of water rights does not mean that more egalitarian forms of land redistribution are not required. Both these property structures crucially shape the character and composition of agricultural production and hence the generation and distribution of rural incomes. Befitting contemporary concerns, he also explores the ecological implications of such skewed water policies.

N. Sukumar attends to that dimension of research that all serious macro-generalisations are founded upon—solid, scrupulously carried out and empirically rich micro-studies. There can be no convincing claim that neo-liberalism and its related practices of governance have all too frequently made matters worse in terms of poverty and inequality in many parts of India without such evidential verification. Sukumar shows how even in Andhra Pradesh—whose state government was internationally lauded as a model of far-sighted and good governance that would deliver its citizens from poverty, ill-health, inequality and unemployment-underemployment—the reality does not quite match up to the rhetoric. In a most detailed and comprehensive micro-study of four mandals in AP, Sukumar reveals how Panchayati Raj Institutions (PRIs) have either been suborned or bypassed through other kinds of state-society networks to serve the interests of dominant castes and classes rather than those at the bottom to whom the PRIs were supposed to help empower. Here again, one sees exemplified at the level of the concrete, the dangers and problems that Chandhoke has warned of at a more abstract analytical level.

National Re-imaginings

Modernity brings with it newer, sharper and more self-reflexively revisable identities, among which the national identity has acquired a distinctive power. The nation-state too has become a more important political unit than ever before and has remained so even over the last three to four decades in what is widely referred to as the era of globalisation. Discussing from different angles and with different purposes Nivedita Menon, Pradip Kumar Datta and Navnita C. Behera interrogate the making of an Indian national identity—the manner in which it is done and its relationship to other identities. Veena Kukreja looks at the 'identity crisis' of Pakistan and how its 'national self' is seemingly inextricably tied to hostility towards India because of the enduring domination of the armed forces over the Pakistan polity.

The controversy over history textbook writing and re-writing emerged when the BJP-led NDA coalition government first came to power in 1999. The Indian nation as an imagined political community strives to establish cultural foundations of one sort or the other for itself, themselves legitimised by particular readings of history. Hence history-writing could not but be a crucial part of the *Hindutva*-secular debate and a conflict that continues to wrack Indian society to this day. Taking up this issue Menon goes on to address the more fundamental philosophical question of the relationship between history and truth since the demand to raise historical awareness is now considered vital for strengthening nationhood and national loyalties. For Menon the search for a 'truer' history, national or otherwise, is essentially fruitless. There is no universally acceptable criterion for comparative judgement. What counts are the interests of the interrogator and the values of the discursive universe to which he or she is aligned. Values clash, therefore histories clash. But one cannot and should not abstain from the necessary struggle to defend one's values and one's history.

P. K. Datta warns us not to assume that the undeniably accelerating process of economic interconnectedness (which can marginalise as well as integrate), which is what most people have in mind when they talk of globalisation, implies that the nation-state is becoming more irrelevant. The nation-state remains part of the crucial conduit through which globalisation proceeds, and therefore the latter has to operate through and with cultural nationalisms. So at one level expanding commodification and the successful marketisation of even 'foreign' goods must take place through the manipulation of domestic and ethnic cultural symbols and idioms. As long as contemporary nationalism expresses itself through the assertion of cultural pride and not in attempts to reclaim an economic sovereignty, it is quite compatible with the sustenance and deepening of a neo-liberal global order. Datta goes on from here to explore, through the writings of Tagore, what an alternate more humane global order might require with respect to the juxtapositioning and interaction of multiple identities. This will have to take place at both the terrains of the national and global. It is about democratising the 'national' identity so that different collectivities, while retaining pride in their own communities of belonging, can also want to belong to an encompassing national community because it is positively meaningful to do so, and because it reinforces the sense of individual and group dignity. What can be done at the national level can also be done at the global level. What Datta draws from Tagore is the notion of a 'processual identity' of multiple levels with varying degrees of heterogeneity that through interaction with others is constantly open to revision and self-transformation.

In her own way Navnita C. Behera also makes a strong plea for the construction of a generous national identity, one that is open and democratic. She posits that in doing so, the Indian identity then becomes truly meaningful and therefore acceptable to sub-national groupings. This requires that the state, still the key locus of power and the point of attraction for 'national sentiment', be genuinely respectful, appreciative and materially and culturally helpful to its minorities. This is easier said than done. In modern times stable group identities are political in ways that pre-modern group identities were not, and part of this process of politicisation has often enough meant the sharpening of boundaries against 'others' through forms of mobilisation that have involved violence. Behera worries that insofar as the nation-state tends to prioritise one identity it tends to deny sufficient autonomy to other group identities. When a nation-state is also a liberal democratic state, the logic of numbers becomes important. That is to say, groupings which at lower spatial levels can become majorities, assert themselves as such, creating other kinds of uneasy majority-minority relationships. And once again the processes of majoritarian assertion at different levels can and does lead to violence.

Behera's more specific focus is on Kashmir, on the clash of competing nationalisms. There is the official nationalism of the Indian state whereby Kashmir's accession is taken as proof of India's secular character, and therefore independence of Kashmir is effectively ruled out. But then there is the further erosion of Kashmir's earlier autonomy, the rise of an Islamist identity that opposed Kashmiriat and then a Muslimisation of Kashmiriat itself that alienates Jammu and Ladakh. Instead of 'unity in diversity', what has emerged is a dangerous project of attempted 'unification of diversity'. A possible way out might be a much more confederational approach to the Indian Union and forms of power devolution that eventually make the base units stronger relative to the Centre. Conceptually, one no longer talks of federalism, no matter how loose, but of radically new ways to envision the architecture of the Indian nation-state.

The US invasion of Afghanistan in 2001 did not end with the elimination of the Taliban either in Afghanistan or in Pakistan. In fact, after the invasion the fates of the two neighbouring countries have become more closely tied than ever before. With President Obama shifting US imperial emphasis away from the 'bad war' of Iraq to what he would like others to think as the 'good war' of Afghanistan, the US has increased its military aggression in Pakistan. This has further legitimised Islamist forces there enabling them to adopt the mantle of nationalist anti-imperialism in comparison to the more collaborationist elements of the Pakistan polity. At the same time, following the emergence of the Lawyers' Movement, the retirement of former President Musharraf, and the re-establishment of civilian rule in 2008, the forces which promoted democratisation have also received a certain fillip. Nevertheless, the armed forces remain the dominant actor in Pakistan politics.

Identitywise, Pakistani nationalism remains a fragile entity which seems unable to base itself on a sense of territorial pride in the way that Persia or Egypt do. For them there is no problem whatsoever to accommodate, indeed glorify their pre-Islamic heritage and past. For Pakistan, its sense of nationalism relies to a considerable degree on hostility to an 'unIslamic' Indian other. Since nationalism is an ongoing project and since democratisation cannot hope to be consolidated without a decisive weakening of the Pakistan army, the forces which pushed for democracy in Pakistan have always been much more concerned to transform relations between Pakistan and India than has been the case with Indian supporters of domestic democracy. In Pakistan the army remains the key barrier to the emergence of a newer more democratic and tolerant Pakistan state and a more relaxed Pakistani nationalism. Veena Kukreja has provided a detailed and thorough analysis of the nature of Pakistan's armed forces, of its ethnic make-up and its 'mentalite', for which we can be particularly grateful. For without a decisive transformation of this army and of its relationship to the civilian apparatuses of governance, there will be no decisive and long-standing democratisation of the Pakistan polity, nor any decisive transformation of relations with India. This is not to say that responsibility for such poor relations between the two countries is Pakistan's alone. The dangers of a growing Indian hubris accompanied by the rise and institutionalisation of Hindutva in Indian society are important contributory factors which shaped the larger context.

New Explorations

The contributions by Gopal Guru and Manoranjan Mohanty are the most passionately partisan in the volume. The reader can have no doubts about where they stand—on the side of the downtrodden and oppressed—in an Indian society and polity that for all its democratic claims is seen as quite unacceptable because of its casteist and capitalist character. For Guru there is an epistemological imperialism in the practice of the social sciences whereby theory is largely the preserve of caste and class elites. Both the social structure and the structures of intellectual production and dissemination are so organised as to discourage if not exclude dalit and *shudra* scholars from long and serious theoretical work as distinct from empirically oriented research. Guru calls on the current intellectual doyens and gate-keepers of the social science disciplines to examine their own practices, to reform their institutions in a spirit of real egalitarianism and modesty even as he also calls on dalits and subalterns to exhibit the moral stamina to enter into the theoretical domain and to sustain their efforts therein regardless of the difficulties, institutional or otherwise.

Mohanty has no time for those who would defend existing capitalism even in its liberal democratic form. This is contra Fukuyama, not the 'end of history'. What he calls the creative society emerges from a creative politics that always strives to make India progressively better through the never-ending struggle of those most subordinated and oppressed. The great problem in such efforts at a transformative politics is how to unite sectoral social movements in India with each other, and with mass organisations that remain controlled by political parties. In Mohanty's terms this is the 'dialectics of autonomy and interconnection'. For all the difficulties to achieve this dialectic he takes heart from the successes in this respect that have shaped the whole of the twentieth century. The three principal forms taken by a politics of the universal that has sometimes succeeded in attracting and incorporating the politics of the particular to the immense benefit of both, have been nationalism, socialism and democracy, either separately or in combination. The successes of the past—the emergence of a socialist challenge to the injustices of capitalism thereby causing the latter's partial self-reform, the heroic defeat of fascism, the victories of de-colonisation for all their subsequent tribulations—provide a promise for the future, a reassurance that the struggle for betterment continues and can advance in steps—both large and small, sudden and gradual.

The Indian Polity

The final two contributions by Mahendra Pratap Singh with Kyoung-Hee Koh and by Achin Vanaik provide an overview of the Indian polity and aim to assess where this polity might be heading. Both contributions recognise that this polity entered into a period of deep flux from the late sixties-early seventies. For Singh and Koh the most prominent concern is the shift towards a fragmented multi-partyism that currently expresses itself in coalition governments at the Centre, belying incidentally Duverger's law that majoritarian electoral systems produce, in contrast to proportional representation electoral systems, stable two-party competitive politics. Singh and Koh give a lucid narrative of this shift and end with proposals aiming to redress the 'pathology' of the current party system in India. Vanaik, in his contribution, surveys the Indian scene through the elucidation of thirteen 'paradoxes' that, according to him, sum up the peculiarities of Indian society and polity. It is a characteristic of this most diverse and complex country with its turbulent politics, its extremes, its unexpected turns and shifts that nothing is ever quite as bad or as good as it might seem initially. This is source for both optimism and pessimism about the future, reminding us that India will be what we and coming generations make of it.

ENDNOTES

[1] The contribution by Mahendra Pratap Singh, also a former head of the department, is the one exception since it was written along with a post-doctoral student from South Korea, Dr Hyoung-Hee Koh.

STATE AND CONSTITUTION
INDIAN PECULIARITIES

1

India's Secular Constitution

Rajeev Bhargava

Secularism is a beleaguered doctrine in India. Only someone with a blinkered vision can deny its crisis today. An ideal like secularism can be threatened because of two broad categories—either its core values or the interpretations thereof are themselves flawed, or because the form of doctrine is such that it cannot fit into conceptual spaces available within the culture where it is meant to work. Such reasons are internal to the doctrine. External reasons need not question the internal coherence or validity of the doctrine, but seek explanation in the political, economic or socio-psychological domain. Here is an example: the demise of the one-party dominant system opened up a fresh power struggle among the new and the older elites. In this ensuing conflict, traditional elites found a handy resource in communalism with which to reassert hegemony. Since secularism and communalism are believed to be antithetical, the rise of one necessarily entailed the decline of the other.

Inclined as I am to believe that the current crisis of secularism is due largely to external factors, I know that this view is not shared by most contemporary writers on secularism.[1] My principle

Originally published in E. Sreedharan, Zoya Hasan, R. Sudarshan (ed.), *India's Living Constitution*, Delhi: Permanent Black, 2002.

objective in this chapter is to show that internalist explanations of the crisis of secularism are mistaken. Elsewhere, I have argued that such explanations misidentify the background cultural conditions of modern secularism and misrecognise the model of secularism embedded in the best practice of the secular state in India. In this chapter, I contend that such critics misunderstand the form secularism takes in the Indian Constitution. In addition, I show that the best judicial practice of the Indian state is consistent with my interpretation of secularism.

I

THEOCRACY, ESTABLISHMENT, MULTIPLE ESTABLISHMENT

I wish to begin with the distinction between a state that establishes religion and a theocratic state. A theocratic state is governed by divine laws directly administered by a priestly order claiming a divine commission. The Islamic Republic of Iran run by the Ayatollahs is an obvious example. On the other hand a state that establishes religion, grants it official and legal recognition. Here, religion benefits from a formal alliance with government. The sacerdotal order does not govern a state where religion is established.

Establishment of religion takes two forms. In the classical European view, it means that a single Church or religion enjoys formal, legal, official monopolistic privilege through a union with the government of the state (Levy 1994: 7). The phrase 'establishment' has been used for centuries to describe the established Protestant Churches of England, Scotland and Germany, and the Catholic Churches in Italy and Spain. Thus, if in preference to all other religions the state recognises a particular religion as the official religion, compels individuals to congregate for only one religion, punishes them for failing to profess a particular set of religious beliefs, levies taxes in support of one particular religion or makes instruction in one religion mandatory in educational institutions or in the media, then it is known as the establishment of religion. Where a particular religion is established, equality among religions is non-existent, and while members of the established religion may enjoy a modicum of religious liberty, those belonging to unestablished religions enjoy no liberty at all.

This classical European view of establishment of religion is to be distinguished from one where the state respects more than one religion, recognises, and perhaps nurtures all religions without preferring one over the other. This might be termed 'multiple establishment' or 'establishment without a name' (ibid.: 12). Such a state may levy a religious tax on everyone, and yet grant the freedom to remit the tax money to a Church or religious organisation of their choice. It may financially aid schools run by religious institutions but on a non-discriminatory basis. It may also punish people for disavowing or disrespecting religion; though not compel them to profess the beliefs of a particular religion. A state that respects multiple establishments treats all religions non-preferentially. It gives liberty to each group to conduct its religious affairs but is indifferent to the freedom of members within the group. The state of New York in the mid-seventeenth century which allowed every Church of the Protestant faith to be established furnishes perhaps the earliest example of 'multiple establishment'. The colonies of Massachusetts, Connecticut and New Hampshire show a similar pattern (ibid.: 11). Related examples abound in India too. The Vijayanagar kingdom granted official recognition to the Shaivites, the Vaishnavites, and perhaps even the Jains in the fourteenth century AD. Arguably, the British Empire gave de facto legitimacy to multiple establishments.

SECULAR STATE: DISESTABLISHMENT

A secular state is to be distinguished not only from theocracy but also from a state where religion is established. It is a state in which religion has been disestablished. The disestablishment of religion means the separation of state not merely from one, but from all religions. I shall call it feature a. A secular state is not anti-religious but exists and survives only when religion is no longer hegemonic. It admits a more general equality between believers and unbelievers. It allows freedom for all religions but is itself free from religion. Thus, in a secular state, a formal or legal union between state and religion is impermissible.

No official status is given to any religion. Persons are as free to disavow religion as they are to profess one. No one is compelled to pay tax for religious purposes or to receive religious instruction. No automatic grants to religious institutions are available.

VALUES OF A SECULAR STATE

So, a secular state is constitutively tied to the value of religious liberty that has three dimensions. The first refers to the liberty of members of any one religious group (feature b). It is a fact that in most religious communities, one or two interpretations of its core beliefs and practices come to dominate. Given this dominance, it is important that every individual or sect within the group be given the right to criticise, revise or challenge these dominant interpretations. The second aspect of this important liberty in a secular state (feature c) is that it is granted non-preferentially to all members of all religious communities. It is entirely possible that non-preferential treatment by the state that accords religious liberty to its members is also found in states which respect multiple establishments. But religious liberty is not part of the core principles of multiple establishments. However, it is a constitutive feature of the secular state. The third dimension of religious liberty (feature d), unthinkable in states with multiple establishments, is that individuals are free not only to criticise the religion into which they are born, but at the very extreme, to reject it and further, given ideal conditions of deliberation, to freely embrace another religion or to remain without one.

Religious liberty, when understood broadly, is one feature of a secular state. To understand its other crucial ingredient, it is necessary to grasp the point that liberty and equality in the religious sphere are all of a piece with liberty and equality in other spheres. It is not a coincidence that the disestablishment clause in the first amendment to the American Constitution institutes not only religious freedom, but also the more general freedom of speech, of peaceful assembly and political dissent. It is entirely possible that a state which respects multiple establishments permits religious liberty and equality, but forbids other forms of freedom and equality. For instance, a person may challenge the authority of the religious head of his own denomination, but not be free to challenge the authority of the state. This is impossible in a secular state which is committed to a more general freedom and equality. Thus, the second value to which a secular state is constitutively linked is the equality of free citizenship.

The value of equal citizenship has two dimensions that require elaboration. Members of any political society always occupy two distinct roles: they are both the makers and the matter of government; its producers and one might say its consumers (Hobbes). To put the point differently, citizenship has two aspects to it, one active, and the other passive. It is a feature of democratic polities that these two roles of citizens coincide and therefore a democratic government must be continuously justifiable from both points of views (Beitz 1989). To be a passive citizen is to be entitled to physical security, a minimum of material well-being and a sphere of one's own in which others ought not to interfere. Although a part of this idea of passive citizenship goes back to ancient Rome, the radical emphasis on material well-being and on privacy is a result of a profound transvaluation of values that has taken place under conditions of modernity (Taylor 1989). This lies at the root of the idea of right to life, liberty, material welfare and perhaps, education. A citizen is entitled to these benefits. This is partly an extension of the point implicit in the defence of religious liberty, but in part it adds something substantial of its own. The benefits of citizenship must be available to everyone and there is no room here for discrimination on grounds of religion (feature e). This equal treatment is entailed by equal (passive) citizenship. State agencies and the entire system of law must not work in favour of one religious group. If the state works to protect the security and well-being of some individuals or groups but fails to secure these meagre but important benefits to others, then the principle of equal (passive) citizenship is violated. Likewise, since the full exercise of citizenship depends upon education, no one must be denied admission to educational institutions, solely on grounds of religion (feature f).

The active dimension of citizenship involves the recognition of citizens as equal participants in the public domain. Such active citizenship rights can be denied in two ways. Either when they are brutally excluded from the political domain (they are politically dead)[2] (Beitz 1989: 109), or when their recognition in the public domain betrays the social acceptance of a belief in the intrinsic superiority of one group as when there is communally weighed voting or efforts to dilute the votes of religious minorities through the use of gerrymandering techniques (ibid.: 110). Groups singled out as less worthy are demeaned and insulted, encouraged to feel that patterns of disrespect existing in society at large enjoy official sanction. In contrast to this, equality of citizenship to which secularism is tied conveys a community-wide acknowledgement of equal respect for everyone in the political domain (feature g).

MISCONCEPTIONS OF SECULARISM

The core idea of secularism then is this: separation of religion and state for the sake of religious liberty and equality of free citizenship. From what I have said above, some alleged conceptions of secularism are ruled out as conceptions of secularism. First, the point about the constitutive links between a secular state and the values of liberty and equality removes a widespread misunderstanding that the only thing required for a state to be secular is its separation from religions. On this, the purely instrumentalist view of secularism is that, whether or not any substantive value is realised even when some key values are undermined; a state is secular if religious and political institutions of the society are separated, and the neater and stricter the separation, the more secular it is. But I have argued that mere separation of religion and politics does not create a secular state. Second, a non-instrumental view that overburdens secularism is equally mistaken. This view identifies secularism with rationalism, individualism, disenchantment, scientisation, indeed with a particular extremely partial, prejudiced understanding of the whole process of modernisation (Nandy 1998). Secularism is not a comprehensive doctrine laden with every single substantive value in the empire of modernity nor is it merely a strategy with instrumental significance. Rather, it seeks separation, for the sake of specific values. Third, secularism is not a single value doctrine. Suppose we have a state that prevents religious conflict, then this feature alone does not make it secular. Although every secular state prevents barbarism, not every state that manages to prevent evil is secular. For example, some states bring about religious peace by undermining religious liberty and such states cannot be deemed secular. Moreover, a state that permits even promotes religious liberty but violates the principle of equal citizenship, either in its passive or its active dimension, is not secular. Indeed, even a 'tolerant state' is not a secular one. To tolerate is to refrain from interfering in the affairs of any individual or group, however disagreeable or morally repugnant, despite the fact that one has the power to do so. Given this definition of tolerance a tolerant attitude, particularly of the state, certainly engenders a truce between warring religious groups. Tolerance is compatible with, though, not the same as religious liberty. But it does not encourage respect and equality between two groups. At any rate it is fully compatible with inequality. A tolerant state does not necessarily encourage an attitude of equal respect. And certainly a tolerant state need not have any truck with political equality and the idea of equal citizenship. However, in the view outlined above, a state that does not show equal respect to all religious groups and its members, and more particularly, a state that does not grant equal citizenship rights is not a secular state. It follows that tolerance and secularism are two different, quite incompatible ideals.

STATE IN THE INDIAN CONSTITUTION: IS IT SECULAR?

The state in the Indian Constitution appears to possess all the features (features a–g) of a secular state. Feature a is specified in Article 27 which rules out public funding of religion and Article 28(1) under which 'no religious instruction is to be provided in any educational institution wholly maintained out of state funds'.

Articles 25, 27 and 28 guarantee religious liberty and meet the conditions specified by features b, c and d. Under Article 25(1), 'all persons are equally entitled to freedom of conscience and the right freely to profess, practice and propagate religion' (feature b and c). The phrase 'freedom of conscience' is meant to cover the liberty of persons without a religion (feature d). Under Article 27, 'no person is compelled to pay any taxes, the proceeds of which are specifically appropriated in payment of expenses for the promotion or maintenance of any particular religion or religious denomination'. Finally, under Article 28(3), 'no person attending any educational institution ... shall be required to take part in any religious instruction or to attend any religious worship that may be conducted in such institution'.

Equality of citizenship is guaranteed by Articles 14, 15(1) and 29(2) of the Indian Constitution. Article 15(1) states that the state shall not discriminate against any citizen on grounds only of religion, race, caste, sex, place of birth or any of them (feature e). Article 29(2) declares that no citizen shall be denied admission into any educational institution maintained by the state on grounds only of religion, race, etc. (feature f). Article 16(1) and (2) of Indian Constitution affirm equal opportunity for all citizens in matters relating to employment or appointment of any office under the state. It further affirms that no citizen, on grounds of religion or race be eligible for or discriminated against in respect of any employment or office under the state. The clause on universal franchise as well as Article 325 declares a general electoral roll for all constituencies and states that no one shall be ineligible for inclusion in this roll or claim to be included in it on grounds only of religion, etc., embodies the value of equal active citizenship. Thus feature g is specified in the articles on equality of active citizenship.

To accept that the state in the Indian Constitution is meant to possess features a–g, has some implications that are not always spelt out. First, the Constitution rules out theocracy and the establishment of religion. The term 'secular state' is usually contrasted simply with theocracy. This is misleading, if not false, because the absence of theocracy is compatible with the establishment of religion. The secular credentials of the state cannot be derived from the mere absence of theocracy. Second, the secularism of the Indian Constitution is neither purely procedural nor hyper-substantive. But it is a complex, multivalue doctrine. Third, the Indian state is not merely a tolerant state (in the sense specified above). Indian secularism must not be confused with a generally professed Hindu tolerance. It is frequently claimed that Indians have a natural, traditional affinity with secularism. In view of our traditional obsession with subtle and not so subtle hierarchies, this claim is an exaggeration. It is of course true that tolerance, even within a hierarchical framework, forms an important background condition for the development of modem secularism and elements of this background condition can certainly be found within India.

FORMS OF SECULARISM: THE INDIVIDUALIST, WALL OF SEPARATION THESIS

A further point to note concerns the precise form of secularism to be found in the Constitution. Broadly, secularism is the view that religion must be separated from the state for the sake of extensive religious liberty and equality of citizenship. This view can be differently interpreted. For Donald Smith the secular state involves three distinct but interrelated relations concerning the state, religion and the individual (Smith 1963). The first relation concerns individuals and their religion, from which the state is excluded. Individuals 'are thereby free to decide the merits of the respective claims of different religions without any coercive interference by the state'—the libertarian ingredient in secularism. The second concerns the relation between individuals and the state, from which religion is excluded. Thus, all individuals are entitled to the same citizenship rights irrespective of the religious beliefs held by them—the egalitarian component in secularism. Finally, for Smith, the integrity of both these relations is dependent on the third relation between the state and different religions. Here he argues that secularism entails the mutual exclusion of state and religion. Just as political power is outside the scope of religion's legitimate objectives, just so it is not the function of the state to promote, regulate, direct or interfere in religion. This interpretation is in line with the dominant American interpretation of secularism as erecting 'a wall of separation' between religion and state. On the classical American view of disestablishment, there can be no support for religion even on a non-preferential basis. Even partial aid to educational institutions run by religious organisations will constitute some form of establishment. Moreover, a state that disestablishes all religions is one that has no power to interfere in the affairs of religious institutions. For better or for worse, the state is powerless to bring about changes in religion. So for Smith, secularism means the strict exclusion of religion from the state for the sake of the religious liberty and equal citizenship of individuals.

Does Indian secularism erect a similar 'wall of separation' for the sake of individualistically construed values? Articles 15, 16, 25, 29(2) and 325 support the 'wall of separation' interpretation. Though there is no direct reference to disestablishment, Articles 27 and 28(1) imply strict separation. By giving the President of the Republic the option of not taking oath in the name of god, Article 60 confirms the strictly neutral character of the Indian Constitution. Thus far, it appears that the state in India is constitutionally bound to follow Smith's model of secularism. However, further examination of the Constitution reveals this impression to be mistaken. To begin with, Article 30(1) recognises the rights of religious minorities which, unlike other articles applicable to citizens qua individuals, are group specific. Indeed, another group-specific right granting political representation to all religious minorities was almost granted and was removed from the Constitution only at the last minute. Second, Article 30(2) commits the state to give aid to educational institutions established and administered by religious communities. Also permitted is religious instruction in educational institutions partly funded by the state. These are significant departures from the 'wall of separation' view of the secular state. Even more significant are Articles 17 and 25(2) that require the state to intervene in religious affairs. Article 25(2)(b) states that 'nothing in Article 25(1) prevents the state from making a law providing for social welfare and reform or the throwing open of Hindu religious institutions of a public character to all classes, and sections of Hindus'. Article 17 is an uninhibited, robust attack on the caste system, arguably the central feature of Hinduism, by abolishing untouchability, and by making the enforcement of any disability arising out of it an offence punishable by law. Both appear to contravene Article 26 and take away the individual freedom of religion granted under Section I of Article 25.

These features of the Indian Constitution depart from the strict separation view in two ways. First, unlike the strict separation view that renders the state powerless in religious matters, they enjoin the state to interfere in religion. Second, more importantly, by giving powers to the state in the affairs of one religion, they necessitate a departure from strict neutrality or equidistance. This power of interference may be interpreted to undermine or promote Hinduism. Either way it appears to strike a powerful blow to the idea of non-preferential treatment.

In short, some articles in the Indian Constitution support an individualist interpretation and others a non-individualist one. Some conceive separation as exclusion, others as non-preferential treatment, and finally some depart altogether from separation understood as exclusion or neutrality. At the end of the day, a confusing somewhat contradictory picture on secularism emerges from a reading of the Constitution. Critics could hardly fail to notice this, and therefore for many Articles 17, 25(2), 30(1 and 2) compromise the secularity of the Indian state. For Donald Smith, any intervention in Hinduism, for example the legal ban on the prohibition of dalit entry into temples or any protection of the rights of communities seriously compromises secularism. For others, like Madan and Chatterjee, the presence of these features in the Indian Constitution shows why the Indian state cannot be really secular. The Indian Constitution does not give an unambiguous criterion to maintain the secularity of the state and, quite simply, given Indian conditions, it could never have.

In the rest of the chapter, I oppose this view and argue that the core principles of secularism do not dictate the particular model of secularism advocated by Smith and implicitly accepted, though not endorsed, by Madan and Chatterjee. I argue that the conception of secularism embodied in the Indian Constitution is not as ambiguous or contradictory as is made out by these critics. Though different from the standard, individualistically grounded 'wall of separation' model, the conception of secularism in the Indian Constitution is a defensible version of secularism because it does not depart from the appropriately interpreted, core principles of secularism. Most critiques of secularism on the ground that it is conceptually unsound or culturally inadaptable in India appear to me to be unsuccessful. Therefore an internalist, rather than an externalist, explanation for its crisis must be pursued. In what follows, I try to defend my claim by discussing two issues integral to the critique of Indian secularism: a) intervention by the state in the affairs of Hindus, b) group-specific minority rights.[3]

II

MODERN INDIAN SECULARISM

State Interference in Religion: The Idea of Principled Distance

The Constitution sanctions interference in Hinduism by the state. Does that mean that Articles 25(2) and 17 violate Articles 15(1) and 26 of the Constitution? Let us take the examples of Hindu Bigamous Marriages Act, 1946, and the Hindu Marriage Act, 1955. Does the fact that monogamy is enforced on the Hindus and not on Muslims constitute discrimination against the former? Or for that matter against the Muslims? More importantly, does it not breach the 'wall of separation', and by implication, secularism? Such interference violates secularism only if separation is taken to mean exclusion or poorly understood neutrality. It does not compromise secularism if separation is taken to mean what elsewhere I call 'principled distance' (Bhargava 1998).

It is important to understand that the idea of separation within value-based secularism cannot only mean exclusion. Recall the ties of secularism with the value of equal citizenship. Equal citizenship rights challenge hierarchical religions which are particularly insensitive to the vital interest of some of its members—those at the bottom of a sanctioned hierarchy. To ensure equal treatment, to uphold the value of equal citizenship, and therefore secularism, the state must interfere in hierarchically organised religions.

It is equally important to grasp the point that principled distance is not mere equidistance. In the strategy of principled distance, whether or not the state intervenes or refrains from action depends on what really strengthens religious liberty and equality of citizenship for all. If this is so, the state may not relate to every religion in exactly the same way, intervene to the same degree, or in the same manner. All it must ensure is that the relation between religious and political institutions be guided by non-sectarian principles that remain consistent with a set of values constitutive of a life of equal dignity for all—what I have elsewhere called principled distance (Bhargava 1998: 492–4, 515–16). Principled distance builds upon two ideas, at least one of which derives from a distinction drawn by the American philosopher, Ronald Dworkin (Dworkin 1978: 125) between equal treatment, and treating everyone as an equal. The principle of equal treatment, in the relevant political sense, requires that the state treat all its citizens equally in the relevant respect, for example in the distribution of a resource of opportunity. The principle of treating people as equals entails that every person is treated with equal concern and respect. This second principle may sometimes require equal treatment, say equal distribution of resources, but it may also occasionally dictate unequal treatment. Differential treatment is entirely consistent with treating people as equals. To take a familiar example, permitting Sikhs to wear turbans in the armed forces does violate the principle of equality. This idea is the second ingredient in what I have called principled distance. To say that a state keeps principled distance from religion is to claim that it intervenes or refrains from interfering in religion, depending entirely upon whether or not some values (liberty and equality) are protected or advanced. Moreover, it is to admit that a state may interfere in one religion more than in others, depending once again on the historical and social condition of all relevant religions. For the promotion of a particular value constitutive of secularism; some religion relative to other religions, may require more interference from the state. On this interpretation of separation, a secular state neither mindlessly excludes all religions nor is blindly neutral towards them.

Consider once again laws that constitute interference within Hinduism. The relevant consideration in their evaluation is not whether they immediately encompass all groups but whether or not they are just and consistent with the values undergirding secularism. Three reasons exist for why all social groups need not be covered by these laws. First, they may be relevant only to Hindus. Take the abolition of child marriage and *devadasi* dedication or the introduction of the right to divorce. Before deciding whether it was necessary to enact a special provision for Hindus, the legislature took into account their social customs and beliefs. Similar laws for Muslims were simply redundant. Second, laws in liberal democracies require legitimacy; the consent of at least the representatives of communities is vital. If consent has indeed been obtained from the representatives of only one community, it is sometimes prudent to enact community-specific laws. It is wise to apply the general principle in stages, rather than not have it at all. Finally, it is perfectly within the competence of the legislature to take account of the degree of evil which is prevalent under various circumstances and the legislature is not bound to legislate for all evils at the same time. Therefore, an act passed by legislature cannot be attacked merely because it tackles only some of the evils in society and does not tackle other evils of the same or worse kind which may be prevalent. Thus acting on these considerations if the legislature wanted to enact a special provision with regard to bigamous marriages among Hindus, it cannot be said that the legislature was discriminating against Hindus only on the ground of religion (AIR 1952). A state interfering in one religion more than in others does not automatically depart from secularism.

Secularism and Minority Rights

Does the recognition of rights for religious minorities violate the core principles of secularism? A cursory reading of the assembly debates might give out an impression that some members at least found the recognition of any community-specific rights morally and politically disturbing. The grant of community-specific rights was seen to encourage a spiralling estrangement between social groups, what elsewhere I have called the minority-majority syndrome (Bhargava 1999). For these members of the Constituent Assembly, the very words 'minority' or 'minority-interest' were an anathema. Deshmukh, a member from C.P. and Berar, found 'no more monstrous word in the history of Indian politics than the word "minority"'. He claimed it to be 'a demon that hampered the progress of the country' (CAD 1947: 201). Sidhwa, a Parsi from C.P. and Berar, wanted 'the phrase "minorities" to be wiped out from history' (CAD 1947: 209). Closer readings of the debates reveal that this venom is directed not against the idea of minorities per se, but specifically against the notion of religious minorities. They claimed that to grant religious minorities a social right to establish their own educational institutes 'will block the way to national unity, promote communalism and a narrow anti-national outlook'. It was further contended that 'in a secular state, minorities based on religion is the very negation of secularism. Only minorities based on language deserve recognition' (CAD 1948: 899).[4] A more detailed examination of the debates shows that even this objection to religious minorities was limited to a few members. Most members justified the grant of social rights not only to linguistic minorities but also to minority religious communities. In other words, they willingly endorsed what might in contrast to the syndrome be called a majority-minority framework. Their principal objection was directed at community-specific political rights, in particular against the demand for separate electorates. For them, separate electorates were outside the acceptable framework and could not but help generate a syndrome. Their quarrel was not with religious minorities per se, but with the specific political form of their demands. The demand for separate electorates was seen to be inherently anti-secular.

Why did they think so? And what was the argument put forth for separate electorates. The debate in the assembly over separate electorates is illuminating. Pocker Sahib Bahadur, an advocate of separate electorates, began his argument with the premise that human beings identify themselves with particular communities and since such communities cannot be numerically equal, there are bound to be minorities in every land (CAD 1947: 211). For him, there was little use regretting or wishing away this fact. Minorities could not be 'erased out of existence'. Therefore coming to terms with them entails reconciling with the fact that complete unity or harmony between communities or the total eradication of differences among them is impossible, while on the other hand, the minimisation of difference is possible. And this can occur only if minorities are satisfied with the overall political framework which they abide by. A condition of such satisfaction, Bahadur argued, was that their views and grievances be given an effective voice in the deliberations of the legislature. Since all members of the minority community cannot bring their own voices in the deliberative assembly, attempts must be made to induct their authentic representatives, and 'to lay down a procedure by which the best man who can represent that community and voice forth the feelings of that community is elected to the legislature' (CAD 1947: 212).

Many premises of this argument were acceptable to opponents of separate electorates. For example, Govind Ballabh Pant began by agreeing that in a free and democratic state citizens would satisfy not only their material wants but also 'a spiritual sense of self-respect'. This self-respect, he assumed, was linked to their community-based identity. It was linked also with their recognition as equals by other communities. This requirement entailed that the majority be 'informed and inspired by genuine feelings of regard for the minorities and for all its decisions to be actuated by a real sense of understanding and sympathy'. Therefore, he thought it incumbent upon the majority to examine the issue of separate electorates from the point of view of the minorities. Implicit in much of what he said was a deep understanding of the active dimension of citizenship. Active participation does not mean a mere presence in the political domain or the possession of the right to vote, but more importantly a right to participate in public deliberation. Citizens are not treated as equals in the public domain if despite a formal right to vote, they are excluded from public deliberations by informal mechanisms. As a result, they begin to have a persistent feeling that they are inadequately heard, that their views are not properly taken into deliberation, that they have no real say in public matters. They then begin to assume a 'shrill and discordant voice'. For Pant, the Muslim voice in the legislatures must be 'powerful', not shrill or discordant (CAD 1947: 212).

Bahadur conceded that these premises were shared by some of the best Congressmen. Differences arose over the procedure to put them into effect, over how adequate representation for Muslims could be achieved. For the Congress, initially, the best procedure for this was a system of community-based reservations of a certain number of seats based on joint electorates. This was consistent with the view that Muslims have a better practical knowledge of the needs of their own community. But Bahadur saw defects in this procedure because it could elect a person favoured solely by the majority, one who fails to represent the real views and interests of Muslims. He insisted that real interests of Muslims can be understood only by Muslims themselves. Furthermore, even the fact of belonging to a community was not sufficient for proper representation. The elected person must be the right one from the community and this, he argued, could be ensured only by separate electorates.[5] To elect the best man, only Muslims must choose their Muslim representative. For this requirement to be met, separate electorates were essential. Separate electorates were fiercely opposed by all members except those who belonged to the League. Four arguments were put forward against separate electorates, all quite convincing, but only two of which addressed the issues raised by Bahadur. First, inherent in the logic of distributing political rights on a purely religious basis was the installation of a theocratic state which in the Indian context could only be a Hindu state. This was clearly against the interests of the minorities. Second, under separate electorates, religion was mixed freely with the desire for profit, for office and for the encroachment on other's properties, and this led directly to communal crimes and massacres. More important were arguments that accepted the initial premises of Bahadur's argument but rejected his conclusion. The argument from democratic accountability put forward by Pant appealed to the best interests of Muslims themselves. Pant argued that under a system of separate electorates both majority and minority representatives would be chosen separately by their respective communities. When this happens, representatives of the majority will not be accountable to the minority community. In the absence of general accountability, and despite the formal presence of minority representatives in the deliberative assembly, they could easily take decisions against the interests of the minority. If this were to occur, the chosen representatives of the minority will have been reduced in the legislature to play the role of mere advocates, with little power to affect decision-making. The price of guaranteed representation in the legislature may be reduced representation in the most effective decision-making body, the cabinet and that Pant insightfully argued was a heavy price indeed. Pant concluded that it was dangerous for the minorities to be segregated from the rest of the community, to keep aloof in an airtight compartment 'where they would have to rely on others even for the air they breathed'. To have a powerful, rather than a shrill and discordant voice the Muslims must, he pleaded, reject separate electorates. In short, Pant agreed that if people are excluded from or discriminated against within the deliberative assembly solely on the ground that they belong to a particular religion then the principle of equal citizenship and core values of secularism is violated. But he argued that separate electorates force this exclusion, and by implication breach the core principles of secularism.

A related argument was made by Gopalaswamy Ayyangar who distinguished between religious difference and communal division and argued that though religious difference was inevitable, communal division was not. By making cross-communal political representation impossible, separate electorates congealed communal divisions. Here Ayyangar was alluding to the very real possibility opened up by communal political representation of a future society in which citizens remain permanently alienated from each other, never address the needs of one another or share a common destiny. This is a mockery of the very idea of citizenship that presupposes shared membership in a political community. It is clear from this discussion that it was not community-based difference that was unacceptable to the best of the Congressmen. Nor, going by their initial acceptance of reservations for Muslims based on joint electorates, did they entirely reject what is frequently called, 'mirror representation', namely the view that a legislature is representative only if it mirrors the ethnic, religious or gender characteristics of the public. Rather, they unequivocally rejected the sufficiency of mirror representation. For them, separate electorates embodied a generalised mirror representation. Muslims could represent members of their own community, but it was argued they need not by law have monopoly over such representation (Sheikh 1993: 81–101).[6]

Also important to note is that separate electorates were rejected not because they fostered communal difference as such or because they endangered a simple, undifferentiated notion of immediate national unity, but because, as Vallabhbhai Patel put it, 'they had in the past sharpened communal difference to a *dangerous extent* and had proved one of the main stumbling blocks to the development of a healthy national life' (emphasis mine). I wish to stay with this point because by stressing the compatibility of communal difference and a healthy national life, it shows the anti-assimilationist streak in even Patel. It also indicates the kind of assimilation a nation-state requires, and why.

Liah Greenfield has recently drawn attention to a change in the semantics of the term 'nation' (Greenfield 1992). In the late thirteenth century, the term 'nation' meant a community of opinion where the constituents of the said community were representatives of cultural and political authority. In short, a nation was a group of social elites. In the sixteenth century, however, the reference of 'nation' changed, it began to be applied to the entire population of a country and became synonymous with the word 'people'. This change in meaning signalled the symbolic elevation of the rabble into an elite, its move from irrelevance to relevance, from the wings onto centre-stage. Henceforth, every member of the population could partake of this superior, elite quality (Taylor 1998).[7]

This effected yet another change in their self-understanding, the nation exists prior to and independent of the political organisation of society, which has the power to give itself a constitution. This idea that the basic rules of society stem from the common action of a people, of a nation, is identical with the democratic idea that sovereignty is located within a people with a fundamentally equal status. As Greenfield puts it 'nationalism was the form in which democracy appeared in the world, contained in the idea of the nation as a butterfly in a cocoon' (Taylor 1998: 10). Now, I wish to argue that underlying the anxious talk of national unity and the almost obsessive attack on communal division lay the very real need to create and sustain, what one assembly member called 'the unadulterated identity of people, a democracy' (CAD 1947: 219). This is of a piece with a point recently made by political philosopher Charles Taylor that unlike other political systems, democratic states need cohesion, a common identity, a common personality and a common agency. In other words, democracy is not just a procedural but also an identity-related communitarian issue. It allows for differences but it cannot stomach divisions which are 'sharpened to a dangerous extent'. It was precisely for this reason that a 'suffrage based on religious affiliation was ridiculous (CAD 1947), and that is why in the end religion in India had to be separated from a democratic state. This explains why eventually community-differentiated political rights were not granted in the Constitution. This of course is entirely a contextual issue. The exclusion of religion from politics was necessary in India not because such exclusion is necessarily required by every form of secularism, but because religion-based divisions had become too dangerous here. Indeed, the rejection of community-specific political rights was entirely consistent with the acceptance of community-specific social rights. The rights granted under Article 30 were as necessary for a democratic state as the rejection of separate electorates under Article 325. The reason for their inclusion is also found in the debates. Members believed that even if the majority-minority framework was subject to 'historical process of assimilation', 'the minorities must be dissolved into the majority by justice'. As Hridaya Nath Kunzru put it, 'if this elementary justice is not given to minorities, we may open up the dangerous path of fanatical nationalism'. The principle of elementary justice, and the very same principles of liberty and equality that ruled community-differentiated political rights out, necessitated community-differentiated social rights. Ambedkar's riposte to Mahavir Tyagi is very telling on this issue. Tyagi asked him if the grant of cultural and educational rights to minorities in India should not wait till the fate of minorities residing in Pakistan was more clearly known. Ambedkar replied firmly that the rights of minorities are not relative or conditional upon the decision of other states but were absolute. He said, 'No matter what others do, we ought to do what is right in our own judgement and, therefore, every minority, irrespective of any other consideration, is entitled to the right to use their language, script and culture and the right not to be precluded from establishing any educational institution that they wish to establish' (CAD 1947).

Forms of Secularism: Group-sensitivity and Principled Distance

I shall now address the issue raised at the end of part I. By accepting community-specific rights for religious minorities and endorsing state-intervention in Hinduism, did the Constitution depart from secular principles? I do not think it did. Rather, it developed its own modern variant. This distinctiveness of Indian secularism can be understood only when one can grasp the cultural background and social context in India. At least four such features of this socio-cultural context call for attention. First, there exists a mind-boggling diversity of religious communities in India. Such diversity may coexist harmoniously but it invariably generates conflicts, the most intractable of which, I believe, are deep conflicts over values. Second, within Hinduism in particular, and in South Asian religions more general, a greater emphasis is placed on practice rather than belief. A person's religious identity and affiliation are defined more by what she or he does with and in relation to others, than by the content of beliefs individually held by them. Since practices are intrinsically social, any significance placed on them brings about a concomitant valourisation of communities. Together, these two features entail inter-community conflicts which are further exacerbated if fuelled by competing conceptions of democracy and nationalism. Third, many social practices sanctioned by religion are oppressive by virtue of their illiberal and inegalitarian character, and deny a life of dignity and self-respect. Therefore, from a liberal and egalitarian standpoint, they desperately need to be reformed. Such practices frequently have a life of their own, independent of consciously held beliefs, and possess a causal efficacy that remains unaffected by the presence of conscious beliefs. Furthermore, a tendency to fortify and insulate them from reflective critique makes them resistant to easy change and reform. It follows that an institution vested with enormous social power is needed to transform their character. Fourth, in Hinduism, the absence of an organised institution such as the Church has meant that the impetus for effective reform cannot come exclusively from within. Reform within Hinduism can hardly be initiated without help from powerful external institutions such as the state.

In such a context, India needed a coherent set of intellectual resources to tackle inter-religious conflict, and to struggle against oppressive communities not by disaggregating them into a collection of individuals or by de-recognising them, but by somehow making them more liberal and egalitarian. A political movement for a united, liberal, democratic India had to struggle against hierarchical and communal conceptions of community, but without abandoning a reasonable communitarianism. Besides, the state had an important contribution to make in the transformation of these communities, and for this reason a perennial dilemma was imposed on it. The state in India walked a tightrope between the requirement of religious liberty that frequently entails non-interference in the affairs of religious communities, and the demand for equality and justice which necessitates intervention in religiously sanctioned social customs. Secularism in India simply had to be different from the classical liberal model that does not recognise groups, and dictates strict separation between religious and political institutions.

If we abandon the view, such as Donald Smith's, that political secularism entails a unique set of state policies valid under all conditions which provide the yardstick by which the secularity of any state is to be judged, then we can better understand why despite 'deviation' from the ideal, the 'state in India continues to embody a model of secularism' (Galanter 1998: 234–67).[8] This can be shown even if we stick to Smith's working definition of secularism as consisting of three relations. Smith's first relation embodies the principle of religious liberty construed individualistically, i.e. pertaining to the religious beliefs of individuals. However, it is possible to make a non-individualistic construal of religious liberty by speaking not of the beliefs of individual but rather of the practices of groups. Here religious liberty would mean distancing the state from the practices of religious groups. The first principle of secularism can then be seen to also grant the right to a religious community to its own practices. Smith's second relation embodies the value of equal citizenship. But this entails—and I cannot substantiate my claim—that we tolerate the attempt of radically differing groups to determine the nature and direction of society as they best see it. In this view then, the public presence of the religious practices of groups is guaranteed and entailed by the recognition of community-differentiated citizenship rights. Smith's version of secularism entails a charter of uniform rights. But it is clear that the commitment of secularism to equal citizenship can dictate community-specific rights, and therefore differentiated citizenship. In principle, this could easily accommodate a reasonable demand for community-specific political rights. In India, for reasons outlined above, it meant community-specific social rights, such as the right to administer and maintain educational institutions. Smith's third principle pertain to non-establishment, and therefore to a strict separation of religion from state, under which religion and the state both have the freedom to develop without interfering with each other. Separation, however, need not mean strict non-interference, mutual exclusion or equidistance, as in Smith's view. Instead, it could be a policy of principled distance, which entails a flexible approach on the question of intervention or abstention, combining both, dependent on the context, nature or current state of relevant religions.

It was largely this group-sensitive conception of secularism of the principled distance variety that legitimised the practices of the state wherein religion was excluded and included as an object of state policy. By its refusal to allow (i) separate electorates, (ii) reserved constituencies for religious communities; (iii) reservations for jobs on the basis of religious classification, and (iv) the organisation of states on religious basis, the Indian state excluded religion from its purview on the ground that its inclusion would inflame religious and communal conflict and produce another Partition-like scenario. However, the very principles that excluded religion from state-institutions also influenced its inclusion in policy matters of cultural import. For example, a uniform charter of rights was not considered absolutely essential for national integration. Separate rights were granted to minority religious communities to enable them to live with dignity. Integration was not seen as identical to complete assimilation. Similar liberal and egalitarian motives compelled the state to undertake reforms within Hinduism. By making polygamy illegal, introducing the right to divorce, abolishing child marriage, legally recognising inter-caste marriages, regulating the activities of criminals masquerading as holy men, introducing temple entry rights for dalits and reforming temple administration, the state intervened in religious matters to protect the ordinary but dignified life of its citizens.

To sum up (a) modern secularism is fully compatible with, indeed sometimes even dictates a defence of, differentiated citizenship; and (b) the secularity of the state does not necessitate strict intervention, non-interference or equidistance but rather any or all of these, as the case may be. If this is so, the criticism that the Constitution envisages a state that cannot be secular because it explicitly abandons equidistance is mistaken. A secular state need not be equidistant from all religious communities and may interfere in one religion more than another. A critique of constitutional secularism on the ground that it acknowledges group rights or that it gives up on neutrality simply does not wash.

POSTSCRIPT: THE PRACTICE OF SECULARISM

How successful has the Indian state been in implementing the principles of the secular state? Which principles has it implemented anyway? It is obvious to any observer that the practice of secularism by the Indian state has at best been inconsistent. To assess the performance of all the institutions of the Indian state over the past fifty years is hardly easy. To make my task manageable, in this chapter, I focus on the Supreme Court only. By looking at the judgment of 1995 on Prabhoo vs. Kunte, I hope to show that the judiciary has understood the principles of secularism in much the same way as I have interpreted them in this chapter. Put differently, the best practice of the Indian state conforms to my interpretation of constitutional secularism.

The judgment pertains to the inflammatory speeches made by Shiv Sena supremo Bal Thackeray while canvassing for Ramesh Prabhoo, an independent candidate for the Maharashtra State Legislative Assembly. A sample of speeches cited by the judgment is given below:

'We are fighting this election for the protection of Hinduism. Therefore, we do not care for the votes of the Muslims. This country belongs to the Hindus and will remain so.... You will find Hindu temples underneath if all the mosques are dug out. Anybody who stands against the Hindus should be showed or worshipped with shoes. Prabhoo should be led to victory in the name of Hindu. Though this country belongs to Hindus, Ram and Krishna are insulted. We do not want Muslim votes. A snake like Shahabuddin is sitting in the Janata Party. So, the voters should bury this party.'

The election of Prabhoo was declared void by the Bombay High Court on the ground that Thackeray had appealed for votes on the basis of the returned candidate's religion. Moreover, Thackeray's election speeches promoted feelings of enmity and hatred among the citizens of India on grounds of religion and community. Both Thackeray and Prabhoo appealed to the Supreme Court and claimed that their acts did not constitute a violation of the Representation of the Peoples Act, 1951 which prohibits only a direct appeal for votes on the ground of religion of the candidate. They also argued that their public speeches did not amount to appeal for votes on the ground of their religion because Hindutva means Indian culture, and not merely Hindu religion. The court accepted this view. This judgment exemplifies a combination of the best and worst practice of the Indian judiciary. Their counsel argued that since they violated the fundamental right to free speech under Article 19(I)(a) of the Constitution, sub-sections 3 and 3A of Section 123 of the act are also unconstitutional.

The Supreme Court rejected the arguments of the appellants, particularly their contention that sub-section 3 of Section 123 is violated only when an election speech makes a direct appeal for votes on the ground of the candidate's religion. According to the court, the nature of the speech is determined by its substance as well as by the manner in which it is meant to be understood by the audience within a particular social setting, and if a reasonable interpretation of the speech leads to the same conclusion as a direct appeal, then the speech violates the relevant sub-section of the act. The purpose to enact the provision, the court argued, was to ensure that no candidate at an election gets or is denied votes only because of his religion.

Is this judgment consistent with the principle of secularism? More specifically, which version of secularism does it endorse? As one goes through the judgment one arrives at the unambiguous conclusion that the court contends that it is part of the meaning of secularism that the state has no religion (feature a). The judgment claims that a secular state guarantees all its citizens the right to follow their religion according to their own convictions. It further clarifies that secularism is one facet of the right to equality, for it means equality in matters of religion to all individuals and groups (features b and c). In several passages, the court also endorses equality of citizenship (features f and g). However, in the opinion of the court, secularism cannot allow religion and politics to mix. Its professed goal is violated when a candidate appeals for votes on the ground of his religion. Does it mean that the court understands separation to mean the exclusion of religion from politics? If so, then its understanding of secularism is indeed different from the one outlined above.

Fortunately, the court clarifies that this secular principle must not be understood simplistically. The mere mention of religion in an election speech is not forbidden by the act. Religion may figure in an election speech as long as its introduction does not amount to an appeal to vote on the ground of the candidate's religion or an appeal not to vote for the opponent on the ground of his religion. For example, an election speech made in conformity with the fundamental right to freedom of religion guaranteed under Articles 25–30 of the Constitution cannot be treated as anti-secular. Similarly, if a speech refers to discriminatory acts against any particular religion and promises removal of this imbalance, then because its objective is promotion rather than denial of equality and justice, the speech is entirely consistent with secularism. This means that the court endorses Articles 25–30 where every group is protected from discrimination on grounds of religion and is granted the right to obtain funds from the state for educational purposes on a non-preferential basis. Only when an electoral or political speech promotes enmity between religious communities, thereby trying to alienate the electorate from a candidate on the ground of his religion or when the candidate wants to gain political mileage for himself simply on the ground of his own religion, that mixing of religion with politics is inappropriate and anti-secular. Thus when the use of religion in political or electoral speeches creates alienation among citizens instead of encouraging solidarity, when it violates the principle of equal citizenship, only then is the principle of secularism violated. It was to uphold the principle of equal citizenship and to prevent political alienation among citizens that, according to the court, the makers of the Constitution rejected separate electorates. Forbidding use of religion to gain votes is of a piece with the rejection of separate electorates. Both mix religion and politics in an inappropriate manner. This distinction between appropriate and inappropriate mixing of religion and politics is at the heart of the idea of principled distance. Since this distinction is accepted or presupposed by the judgment, it follows unambiguously that separation is understood not as exclusion of religion but in terms of the idea of principled distance.

FEATURES OF SECULARISM

- Disestablishment of religion.
- Religious liberty to any religious group.
- Religious liberty granted non-preferentially to members of every religious group.
- The liberty to embrace a religion other than the one into which a person is born and to reject all religions.

- No discrimination by the state on grounds of religion to entitlements provided by the state.
- No discrimination in admission to educational institutions on grounds of religion.
- Equality of active citizenship with no discrimination on grounds of religion.

SECULARISM IN THE INDIAN CONSTITUTION

Feature a: Articles 27, 28(1)
Features b, c and d: Articles 25, 27, 28
Feature e: Article 15(1)
Feature f: Article 29(2)
Feature g: Articles 16(1) and (2), Article 325
Articles that support the individualist, wall of separation thesis: Articles 15, 16, 25, 29(2), 325, 27, 28(1), 60
Articles that depart from the individualist, wall of separation thesis: Articles 30(1), 30(2), 17, 25(2), 25(2)(B)

ENDNOTES

[1] I have in mind the writings of T. N. Madan, Ashis Nandy and Partha Chatterjee (See Bhargav 1998).

[2] This idea is closely related to the notion of social death to be found in Oscar Patterson's writings (See Beitz 1989: 109).

[3] In this chapter, I do not deal with the third fascinating issue concerning religious instruction in state-aided educational institutions.

[4] Therefore it was argued that only minorities based on language should be recognised (CAD December 1948: 899).

[5] The casteist overtones of Bahadur's demand could hardly go unnoticed. He was anxious that hegemonic considerations may compel members of the majority community to strategically vote for a lower caste Muslim candidate, 'some illiterate sweeper or scavenger', who may not be capable of understanding the real needs of the community and whose selection, therefore, could be detrimental to its long term interests!

[6] Farzana Sheikh who claims that the Congress categorically assumed that the unit of representation simply had to be the individual is mistaken, for the Congress did not completely rule out community-based political representation (See Sheikh 1993: 81–101).

[7] The transformation of a rabble into a people and of the people into an elite, presupposes a profound change in the way societies are imagined, i.e., from hierarchical communities to networks consisting of free and equal individuals (See Taylor 1998: 10).

[8] For an interesting critique of Smith's interpretation of Indian secularism as derived from the American model with an 'extra dose of separation' (See Galanter 1998: 234–67).

REFERENCES

Beitz, Charles. 1989. *Political Equality*. Princeton: Princeton University Press. Chapter 5.

Bhargava, Rajeev (ed.). 1998. *Secularism and Its Critics*. New Delhi: Oxford University Press.

Bhargava, Rajeev. 1998. 'What is Secularism For?', in Rajeev Bhargava (ed.), *Secularism and Its Critics*. New Delhi: Oxford University Press.

Bhargava, Rajeev. 1999. 'Should We Abandon the Majority-minority Framework?', in D. L. Sheth and Gurpreet Mahajan (ed.), *Nation State and Minorities*. Delhi. Oxford University Press.

Constituent Assembly Debates (CAD). 1947. Delhi: Lok Sabha Secretariat. 27 August. 201

Constituent Assembly Debates (CAD). 1948. Delhi: Lok Sabha Secretariat. 8 December. 899.

Constituent Assembly Debates. 1947. Delhi: Lok Sabha Secretariat. 27 August. 219

Dworkin, Ronald. 1978. 'Liberalism', in Stuart Hampshire (ed.), *Public and Private Morality*. Cambridge: Cambridge University Press. 125.

Galanter, Marc. 1998. 'Secularism, East and West', in Rajeev Bhargava (ed.), *Secularism and Its Critics*. New Delhi: Oxford University Press. 234–67.

Greenfield, Liah. 1992. *Nationalism: Five Roads to Modernity*. Cambridge and London: Harvard University Press. Introduction.

Levy, Leonard W. 1994. *The Establishment Clause*. Chapel Hill, North Carolina: University of North Carolina Press. 7.

Nandy, Ashis. 1998. 'The Politics of Secularism and Recovery of Religious Tolerance', in Rajeev Bhargava (ed.), *Secularism and Its Critics*. New Delhi: Oxford University Press.

Sheikh, Farzana. 1983. 'Muslims and Political Representation in Colonial India: The Making of Pakistan', in Mushirul Hasan (ed.), *India's Partition: Process, Strategy and Mobilisation*. Delhi: Oxford University Press. 81–101.

Smith, Donald. 1963. *India As a Secular State.* Princeton and Oxford: Princeton University Press.

Taylor, Charles. 1989. *Sources of the Self.* Cambridge: Cambridge University Press.

Taylor, Charles. 1998. 'Modes of Secularism', in Rajeev Bhargava (ed.), *Secularism and Its Critics*. New Delhi: Oxford University Press.

The State of Bombay vs. Narasn Appa. AIR. 1852. Bom. 74.

2

Constitutionalising Difference: The Indian Experiment

Ashok Acharya

Ideally, constitutions are understood as expressions of the shared political values of a political community. However, in plural and deeply divided multinational[1] states there is no consensus as to what properly constitutes the shared space, and the understanding of political values (Hanafin and Williams 1999). Given the nature of irreconcilable differences most of the time, constructing a common space is a task laden with hazards: minority groups in many multinational states rightfully object to the dominant majority's role in arbitrarily defining and filling up the shared space with the latter's own cultural symbols. In the absence of institutional protections, especially a constitution that does not at the least define the shared space that all citizens enjoy and secure some guarantees to protect their rights, minorities are at risk in many societies. How does a country of India's diversity constitutionally define citizenship that is fair to its minorities?

With regard to India, this essay attempts a study of two dimensions: the historical and the normative. The historical review is necessary to give us a glimpse of how group rights in the Indian context acquired political coinage; and the normative analysis will probe the justifications of such rights in relation to recent discussions on multiculturalism in contemporary liberalism. Essentially, two questions are addressed: First, how did the founders of India's Constitution negotiate questions of diversity? Second, how does the Indian model measure up to contemporary liberal and multicultural interventions in securing recognition for identities? Much of the discussion below will explore how questions of difference, particularly of caste and religion, were constitutionally treated during the making of the Constitution, keeping in view constitutional developments in the colonial period. With helpful insights on how such questions were raised, addressed, and justified in policies of accommodation, the concluding section juxtaposes the final outcome of the constitution-making process to the multicultural character of liberal constitutionalism. In contrast to rival views that group-sensitive provisions may not be entrenched in a liberal constitution, the Indian constitutional experiment offers an alternative in accommodating various claims of identity. As interest in constitutional engineering related to issues of diversity increases, the Indian model offers an experiment worth emulating.

ORDERING DIFFERENCE: THE COLONIAL BACKGROUND

The Cabinet Mission, led by Lord Pethick-Lawrence, Secretary of State for India and senior member of the mission, visited India in 1946 to bring about an understanding between the Congress and the Muslim League. The outcome of the mission's proposals, called the Cabinet Mission Plan, was one of the last-ditch attempts on the part of the colonial government to bring about political reconciliation between the Congress and the Muslim League. As a political understanding between the two parties was not possible, the mission advocated a federation within which provinces would have complete autonomy subject to federal powers such as foreign affairs, defence and communications. The federation would include both British India and the princely states. The mission's proposal was a watered-down version of a tighter federation envisaged by the Congress. In a continuation of past colonial practice of according political recognition to groups who conceived their interests to be at variance with the Hindu majority, the mission wanted adequate safeguards to be put in place for other minorities.

It proposed the setting up of a Constituent Assembly to draft a constitution for India. In forming this assembly to decide a new constitutional structure, the mission felt the first problem was to obtain as broad-based and accurate representation of the whole population as was possible. After debating the desirable method of adult franchise to elect members to the assembly, the plan endorsed a second-best practicable solution of utilising the recently elected Provincial Legislative Assemblies as electing bodies to the assembly. However, as the elected provincial assemblies did not reflect proportionately the sizes of their assemblies to the population, the mission concluded that each province ought to be allotted a total number of seats proportional to its population, in the ratio of one to one million. Second, it found it fair to divide this provincial allocation of seats between the main communities in each province in proportion to their population. And, third, it provided for representatives to be elected by the members of their community from the legislative assembly. In what is believed to be a very crucial decision with regard to future constitutional deliberations on matters of importance to minorities, the mission recognised three communities—'general', Muslim, and Sikh, the general community including all those who were not Sikhs or Muslims.

The plan was a culmination of a series of political experiments undertaken in the past to acknowledge, recognise and order social and cultural differences in India. The method of selection of Indian representation during the colonial period broadly followed the principle of representation of communities, not individuals. For purposes of representation through much of the pre-Independence period, the British viewed India as 'essentially a congeries of widely separated classes, races, and communities with divergences of interest and hereditary sentiment, which could be properly represented only by those, who knew and shared their sectional opinions' (Coupland 1944: 24). This view of a corporate India had political consequences, most notably group preferences in matters of political representation. Separate representation accorded by the colonial government covered class, religion, and economic interest. This pre-modern approach to India conflicted with the modern perceptions of the latter-day nationalist elites who championed notions of equality, individuality and national unity.

Although the Government of India Act of 1909 introduced separate electorates[2] for the first time, the roots of such a policy were already visible in the Indian Councils Acts of 1861 and 1892. The 1861 Act is generally credited with the introduction of the representative principle into the Indian Constitution by requiring that at least half of the new or additional members of the Governor General's Executive Council and the Provincial Legislative Councils be filled from outside the ranks of the civil service which effectively meant inclusion of natives. The 1892 Councils Act, however, was more specific in requiring that for the majority of the positions so filled, recommendations were to be made by the local bodies or corporations such as religious communities, municipalities, universities, and chambers of commerce. Although the process of representation was not secured through direct election, the effective representation of candidates recommended on the basis of group membership meant that in the British-established councils seats were reserved for commercial interests, large landowners, university faculties, Anglo-Indians, and Muslims among others.

The Government of India Act, 1909, continued the tradition of separate representation of the 1892 Act with two differences: 1) the process was formalised, and 2) the scope of representation was enhanced and separate electorates provided for Muslims for the first time. The 1909 Act, however, needs to be seen against the backdrop of the Morley-Minto reforms and the partition of Bengal into Hindu- and Muslim-concentrated territories (Menon 1957: 6).[3] The 1909 Act is pertinent to the extent of unfolding an official policy that recognised by way of introducing separate electorates that the two communities, Hindus and Muslims, could not be anticipated to vote together for their common good.[4]

The Government of India Act of 1919, following the Montagu-Chelmsford Reforms, not only advocated the continuation of separate electorates for Muslims on the basis of the Lucknow Pact between Congress and the Muslim League, but also extended the same principle to Sikhs in Punjab and more generally to Europeans, Anglo-Indians, and Indian Christians, while a certain proportion of non-Mohammedan seats were reserved for non-Brahmins and Mahrattas in the provinces of Madras and Bombay, respectively. All this ran coterminous to the provision of special representation to landholders, universities, commercial, and landed interests and to any other community or class that may have failed to secure adequate representation on the councils (Menon 1957: 23).

Following the politics of bargaining and the stiffening of attitudes by the Muslim League, which had a different vision than the Congress on the future of self-government and the place of Muslims in post-colonial India, Mohammed Ali Jinnah, the leader of the Muslim League, proposed his 'fourteen points', of which a few deserve mention. Jinnah in consultation with other Muslim leaders argued that:

- All legislatures in the country and other elected bodies shall be constituted on the definite principle of adequate and effective representation of minorities in every province without reducing the majority in any province to a minority or even equality (point 3).
- Representation of communal groups shall continue to be by separate electorates provided that it shall be open to any community at any time to abandon its separate electorate in favour of joint electorates (point 5).
- Full religious liberty, that is liberty of belief, worship, and observance, propaganda, association and education, shall be guaranteed to all communities (point 7).
- No Bill or Resolution or any part thereof shall be passed in any legislature or any other elected body if three-fourths of the members of any community in that particular body oppose it as being injurious to the interests of that community (point 8).
- Provision should be made in the Constitution giving Muslims an adequate share along with the other Indians in all the services of the State and in local self-governing

bodies having due regard to the requirements of efficiency (point 11).

- The Constitution should embody adequate safeguards for the protection of Muslim culture, and for the protection and promotion of Muslim education, language, religion, personal laws, and Muslim charitable institutions and for their due share in grants-in-aid (point 12).
- No Cabinet, either central or provincial, should be formed without there being at least of one-third of Muslim ministers (point 13) (Menon 1957: 36–7).

Jinnah's demands of 28 March 1929 are to be seen against the backdrop of an activist colonial policy that was intent on satisfying demands of groups for rights of representation. For reasons of national unity the Congress took an entirely different view. Flailing the colonial process of dividing the nationalist front on lines of group segmentation, the Congress opposed the British initiatives and refused to cooperate with the authorities. The Congress recalcitrance on the one hand, and the Muslim League's uncompromising intransigence for retention of the separate electorates on the other, meant that the British had to engage all actors in attaining a negotiated settlement towards self-government.

During the 1930s the British invited members of the Congress, the Muslim League, and leaders of other groups to a series of Round Table Conferences with the ostensible purpose of finding a just settlement of disputes regarding self-government and the constitutional status of the minorities. It was hoped that the ensuing deliberations would pave the way for a workable Indian Constitution that would be fair to the groups.

Although the First Round Table Conference (convened in late 1930) failed owing to the refusal of the Congress to participate in its proceedings, the Second Round Table Conference (in which all parties, including the Congress, participated) dwelt at length on questions of minority representation. However, the proceedings were by and large inconclusive on the central issue that plagued the deliberations. All minorities, except the Sikhs, demanded separate electorates. To Gandhi's surprise and chagrin, what was most troubling was the demand by the untouchables, or the Depressed Classes, for separate electorates. B. R. Ambedkar, who represented the latter category, had joined hands with other minorities to enlarge the scope of separate electorates. Although Gandhi was sympathetic to the demands of religious minorities and harped on the necessity of a commonly agreed formula of minority representation, he was far from conceding similar treatment to the untouchables. Gandhi argued that the untouchables were a part and parcel of the Hindu community and need not be granted separate electorates. Gandhi's was an emotive appeal. As the matter remained unresolved, British Prime Minister, Ramsay MacDonald, who was also chairing the Minorities Committee, assumed responsibility for finding a suitable solution acceptable to all at a later date.

A few months later, on 16 August 1932, the Communal Award was proclaimed. The award not only granted separate electorates to Muslims, Europeans, Sikhs, Indian Christians, and Anglo-Indians, with some reserved seats for Mahrattas in selected general constituencies in Bombay: it also extended the benefits to the untouchables, or the Depressed Classes. The untouchables were granted both general voting rights and special and reserved seats. The Communal Award followed unsuccessful attempts in the Round Table Conferences held in London between British colonial administrators on the one hand, and other communities representing British India on the other, to hammer out a workable solution towards representation of minorities in Indian legislatures. The award was a unilateral imposition of the British view of what sort of representation different communities in India would require. The Indian communities themselves were divided on the acceptable basis of power-sharing arrangement in legislatures. While the Muslims found common cause with the Depressed Classes or the untouchables, the Anglo-Indians, a section of the Indian Christians, the Congress, the Hindu Mahasabha, and the Sikhs remained opposed to demands of Muslims and untouchables.

The award sought to break this impasse between communities. It created separate electorates for both communal and non-communal groups: for the general (mostly Hindu), Muslim, Sikh, Indian Christian, Anglo-Indian, European, untouchables, and tribal and backward areas belonging to the first category, and labour, commerce, landholders, and universities belonging to the latter category with a few reserved seats for women as well (Retzlaff 1960: 24).[5] In effect, the idea of separate electorates was expanded to include all minorities and brought the untouchables under its ambit. Gandhi was strongly opposed to granting of separate electorates to the Depressed Classes or the untouchables on grounds that the untouchables formed an indivisible part of the Hindu community and this representational schema would further alienate them from the larger community. In protest, he went on a fast unto death. Following Gandhi's fast and his negotiations with the leader of the untouchables, Ambedkar, in what is historically referred to as the Poona Pact, it was agreed to do away with the system of separate electorates for untouchables. Having lost the separate electorates, the Depressed Classes were compensated by an increase in reserved seats to be elected from joint or undifferentiated electorates, more in number than what was originally stipulated in the Communal Award (Galanter 1984: 32).[6] The pact basically established an enduring pattern for the representation of the Scheduled Castes (SCs) and Scheduled Tribes (STs), one that continues until today. The historic understanding also unleashed a series of Congress-sponsored efforts to abolish the practice of untouchability and secure their inclusion within the Hindu community through legal and social reformist means.

The Government of India Act, 1935, a bulky and exhaustive document detailing provisions for a federal government that encompassed British India and the Indian princely states, not only retained much of the representational scheme unfolded by the Communal Award of 1932 in relation to the minorities, but also included within its ambit more safeguards for different communities, one of which led to the Instrument of Instructions issued to the Governors in 1937 requiring them to secure a due proportion of official positions to the several communities.

Despite a long list of safeguards for minorities instituted by the colonial administration, the political history of the sub-continent in the 1940s led many to accept the inevitability of Partition. In particular, the failure of the Congress and the Muslim League to enter into genuine and workable power-sharing arrangements in the provincial governments that came to life for a brief spell between 1937–9 made a united India seem implausible.

In 1940 the Muslim League adopted the famous Pakistan resolution, which stated that 'no constitutional plan would be workable or acceptable to the Muslims unless it recognized the basic principle that geographically contiguous units should be demarcated into regions so constituted that the areas in which Muslims were numerically in a majority were grouped to constitute "Independent States"' (Rao Vol. V 1967: 744).

Between 1940 and 1947, the inevitability of Partition was increasingly felt to be unstoppable with the Muslim League's demands of a separate and territorially organised Muslim nation remaining uncompromising and the lack of flexibility and creative thinking on the Congress side jettisoning any remaining scope for rapprochement. During negotiations between the Congress and the League with the helpful intervention by the British to arrive at a mutually agreed self-government formula, it was clear that the only important item remaining on the agenda, short of a workable power-sharing arrangement, was to work out the modalities of transfer of power with a continued focus on the protection of the interests of minorities, one that eventually formed the hub of the Cabinet Mission Plan outlining in detail the structure and goals of the Constituent Assembly.

The brief historical sketch outlined above provides us with a few insights in constitutional engineering and patterns of claims-making by groups during the pre-independence period. The colonial trends vis-à-vis the issue of minorities clearly show that the question of adequate representation, especially that of separate electorates, formed the primary demand of minority identities. At later stages this demand was expanded to include other safeguards such as reservation of positions in government jobs and the provincial and federal executive (Retzlaff 1960: 29). The British, on their part, kept insisting on the need to arrive at a just solution of the 'minority problem' prior to any constitutional settlement of the transfer of power. In this insistence the British largely viewed themselves as playing the role of an impartial and arbitral authority (Rao Vol. V 1967: 744).

The gradual broadening of the definition of minorities and the steady widening of the scheme of representation to include new minorities was strategically designed to divide the nationalist front. However, for much of the first half of the twentieth century, this also meant satisfying the elites among the minorities. The colonial model of negotiating the politics of difference, designed to act as a balance between competing communities or interests, was a top-down power-sharing model. This model, however, continues to be an enduring feature in defining identity and ordering the politics of difference. As per the terms of reference of the Constituent Assembly outlined in the Cabinet Mission Plan, the pre-constitutional requirement that minorities' interests be protected in post-British India became an effective precondition to define the nature of rights in the constitutional document. Even after Partition of British India, the prerequisite of minority protection remained in effect during constitutional deliberations. But the reality of Partition was used as a political foil by the Congress, the dominant political actor in the Constituent Assembly, to mute 'immoderate' demands of minorities in trying to achieve national unity.

DELIBERATING DIVERSITY

While the Cabinet Mission Plan had already guaranteed the representation of Muslims and Sikhs in the Constituent Assembly, members of the Parsi, Anglo-Indian, Indian Christian, scheduled caste, scheduled tribe groups were brought into the assembly as representatives of the Congress Party. The Constituent Assembly came into existence on 9 December 1946 and for roughly three years it sat in session deliberating on the different aspects of the Constitution that was finally adopted. Following the Muslim League's initial boycott, subsequent enrolment, and cessation of responsibility caused by Partition and creation of Pakistan, the total membership of the assembly and the minority communities within it kept varying. Of the initial 235 seats allotted to the provinces (barring the princely states) where indirect elections were first held to fill up the Constituent Assembly, 88 of them, or 37 per cent of the total membership, were derived from the minority communities. In mirroring India's diversity, representatives of the Nepali, Sikh, Parsi, Christian, Anglo-Indian, Backward Tribe, Muslim, and scheduled caste communities found places in the Constituent Assembly. Keeping in view the need to ensure adequate representation to minorities, Dr H. C. Mookerjee, an Indian Christian from Bengal, was elected the Vice-President of the Constituent Assembly. He later served as Chair of the Minorities Sub-committee that worked under the larger structure of the Advisory Committee on Fundamental Rights, Minorities and Tribal and Excluded and Partially Excluded Areas to the Constituent Assembly. Similarly, Dr B. R. Ambedkar, the Indian untouchable leader, was entrusted with the historic responsibility of preparing the draft of the Constitution in his capacity as the Chairman of the Drafting Committee.

CONSTITUENT ASSEMBLY: MINORITY PROTECTIONS

The overall philosophy of the Constitution was contained in the Objectives Resolution, moved by Jawaharlal Nehru on the floor of the Constituent Assembly on the fourth day of its first session. Among its objectives, Clause 6 of the resolution reiterated that 'adequate safeguards shall be provided for minorities, backward and tribal areas, and depressed and other backward classes' (Rao Vol. II 1967: 4).

Realising the need to deliberate upon the minorities question, Govind Ballabh Pant moved a resolution to set up an Advisory Committee on Fundamental Rights, Minorities and Tribals, and Excluded and Partially Excluded Areas on the floor of the assembly on 24 January 1947. He argued:

> The question of minorities everywhere looms large in constitutional discussions. Many a constitution has foundered on this rock. A satisfactory solution of questions pertaining to minorities will ensure the health, vitality and strength of the free state of India that will come into existence as a result of our discussions here. The question of minorities cannot possibly be overrated. It has been used so far for creating strife, distrust and cleavage between

> the different sections of the Indian Nation. Imperialism thrives on such strife. It is interested in fomenting such tendencies. So far, the minorities have been incited and have been influenced in a manner that has hampered the growth of cohesion and unity. But now it is necessary that a new chapter should start and we should all realize our responsibility. Unless the minorities are fully satisfied, we cannot make any progress: we cannot even maintain peace in an undisturbed manner (CAD Vol. II 1967: 310–11).

For much of the deliberations that took place on the floor of the Constituent Assembly, during various stages in the meetings of its different committees and sub-committees, the issue of what constitutes the rights and protections of minorities was weighted against the demands of national unity. It is interesting to observe that the fear of balkanisation loomed heavily in the minds of the founders, especially those representing the Congress party, and accordingly a necessity was felt to justify granting of any rights and protections to minorities in accordance with, and in particular consideration to, its possible impact on the unity and integrity of the nation.

If the threat of balkanisation created caution in the minds of the Congress leaders, the lure of a common citizenship as a way out of the impasse held out an alternative workable aspiration. This aspiration would also foster common bonds and nationalist sentiments among Indians irrespective of community differences. It had held irresistible appeal back in 1931 when the Congress in its Karachi session had adopted a resolution on fundamental rights applicable to all citizens, majority and minority alike. Underlying the Congress-sponsored views and provisions on common fundamental rights were a central uniting strand of protection against discrimination, notwithstanding group differences among citizens. 'The minorities for their part,' Retzlaff appropriately notes, 'regarded this (i.e., mere protection against discrimination) as insufficient, and demanded additional constitutional safeguards, as well as other special arrangements in such things as employment in the public services' (Retzlaff 1963: 60).

To fulfill the aspirations of the minorities and in accordance with the stipulations of the Cabinet Mission Plan, the Advisory

Committee of the Constituent Assembly set up the Minority Rights Sub-committee on 27 February 1947. The sub-committee set itself the task of formulating responses individually and collectively to a set of questions that K. M. Munshi had prepared. Munshi's questionnaire asked:

- What should be the nature and scope of the safeguards for a minority in the new Constitution?
- What should be the political safeguards for a minority
  (a) in the Centre;
  (b) in the Provinces?
- What should be the economic safeguards for a minority
  (a) in the Centre;
  (b) in the Provinces?
- What should be the religious, educational, and cultural safeguards for a minority?
- What machinery should be set up to ensure that the safeguards are effective?
- How is it proposed that the safeguards should be eliminated, in what time and under what circumstances?

Partly as response to this questionnaire and the deliberations in the Minority Rights Sub-committee and the floor of the Constituent Assembly, members' views on rights of minorities were divergent. The divergence can be traced as a model of intersecting axes between two views of citizenship: the common citizenship model that takes the individual as the unit of political community, and the group-differentiated position that approves protections and rights for communities. Figure 2.1 further explains this.

Responses to Munshi's questionnaire depended on which minority one was speaking for. For those who spoke from the lower caste perspective, the emphasis was on non-discrimination and a strong version of legal and political equality among citizens. It was also not uncommon for representatives of untouchables to align their political voices in favour of an egalitarian but well-integrated and assimilated society. However, in terms of what it requires to be

Figure 2.1: Mapping Divergence in Founders' Attitude Towards Citizenship

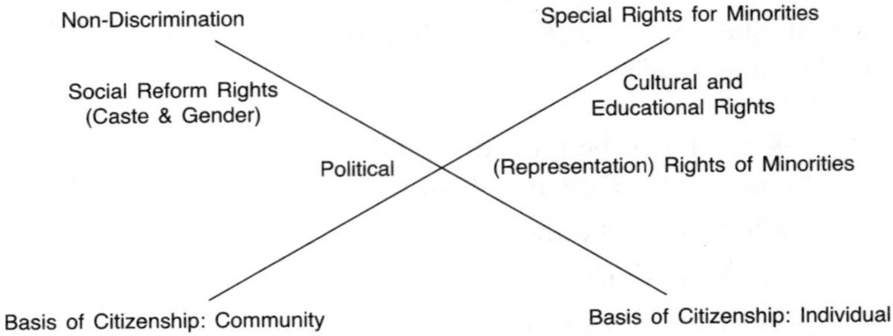

politically equal, such a perspective marshalled support for special representation rights of untouchables. To those who expressed views on behalf of religious and cultural communities, the choice was clear: to desire both cultural autonomy and political rights of representation. Following the colonial model, and encouraged by the Cabinet Mission's promises of using minority rights as some sort of a constitutional trump card even before actual deliberations on the Constitution took place, all the minorities, with the exception of the Parsis, found a common meeting ground in demanding separate representation rights as a necessary political safeguard in post-independence India (denoted by the intersection of the axes in Figure 2.1).

The idea that the principle of representation should be sociologically based, or descriptive in nature, mirroring the diversity of the population, found favour with most members representing minorities throughout the deliberations. Rajkumari Amrit Kaur, a member of the sub-committee, was one among few exceptions, who advanced a crude form of Burkean virtual representation as a remedy to the conundrum of the more popular descriptive representation (Rao Vol. II 1967: 310–1).[7]

In April 1947, the Minority Rights Sub-committee decided first of all to consider the Fundamental Rights Sub-committee Report in detail to ascertain whether any of its recommended provisions required amplification or alteration for the specific purpose of safeguarding minority rights. Having examined the interim proposals of the Report of the Fundamental Rights Sub-committee from the minorities' point of view, it recommended:

- Reservation of public offices for the classes that were not adequately represented in government services,
- Freedom to 'practise' and 'propagate' as well as to profess religion,
- Education through one's mother tongue and script,
- Protection of language, script and culture of minority groups,
- Free admission of all the minorities in state-funded schools and other educational institutions,
- Equal state funding to the institutions of minorities,
- Abolition of discrimination in places of public use, and
- Restriction of the right of residence and possession of land in tribal areas.

A few days later the sub-committee met to consider the political safeguards of the minorities and the issues identified for further deliberation were of four types:

- Representation in the legislatures—joint vs. separate electorates and weightage,
- Reservation of seats in the cabinets,
- Reservation in public services, and
- Administrative machinery to ensure protection of minority rights partly covered by making certain fundamental rights justiciable (ibid.: 392).

Working on the agenda, the sub-committee could not muster unanimity on any one item listed above. In partisan voting, where views differed from one item to another, the working group voted by a majority to do away with the colonial scheme of separate electorates but chose to retain a common scheme of reserved seats in joint electorates for all sizeable minorities for a period of 10 years. Similarly, in relation to item no. 2, the group voted to do away with reservation of seats for minorities in the cabinet. On item 3, i.e., reservations in services, or affirmative action quotas, the sub-committee voted to ensure quotas for scheduled castes, Muslims, Sikhs, Plain tribes in Assam, and Anglo-Indians. The Parsis and the Indian Christians did not claim any quotas. On item 4, two proposals were accepted: (i) An independent officer appointed by the executive reporting to the legislature about the working of the safeguards provided for the minorities, and (ii) A statutory commission to investigate into the conditions of the socially and educationally backward classes and reporting remedial measures (ibid.: 396–400).

However, when deliberating over the specific recommendations of the Minority Rights Sub-committee, the Advisory Committee, to which the sub-committee report was submitted, held the view that some proposals needed to be rejected on the grounds that rigid constitutional provisions would make parliamentary democracy unworkable and that it was important to harmonise the special claims of minorities with the development of a healthy national life (ibid.: 416–17).

In the immediate aftermath of the country's Partition, the reports of the Advisory Committee on Minority Rights were placed before the Constituent Assembly. Sardar Vallabhbhai Patel, a prominent Congress leader and President of the Advisory Committee, tabled the Report on Minority Rights, as it came to be called. While fully conscious of the tragic and violent post-Partition political environment surrounding the nation and mass migrations triggered between India and Pakistan, Patel stressed how the agreement surrounding the document was arrived at in a consensual manner between the minorities and the majority. Responding to a few minority members' concerns and amendment motions that sought to reclaim separate electorates for Muslims, Patel, mindful of the majority support in the assembly and the members' strong nationalist sentiments, rejected it on the grounds of national unity. A representation system that entrenched minority constituencies would, in his opinion, pave the way for another Pakistan, or further division of the country. Barring the discussions on joint vs. separate electorates, the assembly adopted the report without any alterations and the latter was incorporated into the draft constitution presented to the assembly much later.

Steering a middle course between strong entrenchment of minority rights and the equally crucial task of acknowledging majority interests, Ambedkar reasoned that a lot of the safeguards for minorities depended for their success on the goodwill and the sense of duty among the majority community to not discriminate against minorities. Ambedkar asserted:

> [T]he Constituent Assembly has done wisely in providing such safeguards for minorities as it has done. In this country both the minorities and the majorities have followed a wrong path. It is wrong for the majority to deny the existence of minorities. It is equally wrong for the minorities to perpetuate themselves. A solution must be found which will serve a double purpose. It must recognize the existence of minorities to start with. It must also be such that it will enable majorities and minorities to merge some day into one ... [Minorities in India] have loyally accepted the rule of the majority which is basically a communal majority and not a political majority. It is for the majority to realize its duty not to discriminate against minorities ... The moment the majority loses the habit of discriminating against the minority, the minorities can have no ground to exist. They will vanish (CAD Vol. VII 1967: 39).

In the fast-changing political landscape of a partitioned India, however, the growing divide between the majority and the minority communities fuelled by Mahatma Gandhi's assassination in 1948 led to a growing intolerance toward political safeguards for minorities. The Congress reflected the changed mood of the nation in the assembly. Between the seventh session of the assembly in November 1948 and the conclusion of constitution-making in November 1949, several debates within the assembly and the Advisory Committee led towards a gradual process of whittling down the political safeguards of the minorities.

Although the provision of separate electorates for minorities was done away with, it figured in the discussions of the House during deliberations on the draft constitution. When the majority in the House vehemently rejected this, the idea of proportional representation was also brought up for discussion by representatives of the Sikh and the Muslim communities (Retzlaff 1963).[8] The Congress did not see any difference between the demands for separate electorates and proportional representation, and the latter too was rejected on grounds that it would have a divisive impact on the polity with the potential to balkanise the nation further.[9]

Of the three choices for minority political safeguards—separate electorates, proportional representation, and joint electorates with reserved seats—it was the third one that applied uniformly to all minorities and was part of the Minority Rights Sub-committee recommendations to the assembly. But even this provision was withdrawn by the Advisory Committee for minorities other than the scheduled castes, which now included lower castes from the Sikh community, and Tribes. In a new report submitted to the assembly on May 11, 1949, Sardar Patel remarked:

> (that under vastly changed circumstances) it was no longer appropriate ... that there should be reservation of seats for Muslims, Christians, Sikhs or any other religious minority. Although the abolition of separate electorates had removed much of the poison from the body politic, the reservation of seats for religious communities, it was felt, did lead to a certain degree of separatism and was to that extent contrary to the conception of a secular democratic state (Rao Vol. IV 1967: 600).

Later, the same principle was applied to reservations of jobs; except for the scheduled castes and tribes, every other minority community during the conclusion of the constitution-making was excluded from this other important safeguard.

In a nutshell, then, with regard to representation rights of minorities, or the political safeguards, a gradual process of attenuation marked the constitutional deliberations. From an initial consideration of caste-, tribe-, and religion-based minorities, special representation rights (of reserved seats in joint electorates) were granted only to scheduled caste and scheduled tribe communities with an added provision to nominate two members from the Anglo-Indian community to the popular house (Lok Sabha) in Parliament. In denying special representation rights to religious minorities, the founders used the argument of national unity and nation building. The same model applied to the reservation of jobs, too, with slight modification, in this case, of allowing lower caste members of the Sikh community inclusion in the scheduled caste list. In a definite but partial break from the colonial model, the Indian Constitution considered it useful and necessary to recognise caste and tribal identities for special representation and affirmative action (job reservations by way of quotas) rights on a temporary basis, to be renewed every ten years.

It is also useful to recapitulate here that in the making of the Indian Constitution, there were differences of opinion between representatives of different communities on who deserves rights of representation and affirmative action. The final outcome of the deliberations suggest anything but complete unanimity, although by some stretch of logic one may claim arithmetical consensus as a way of resolving the issue of minority representation. However, while Granville Austin, the Indian constitutional guru, waxes eloquently on the quintessential Indian virtue of consensus displayed in the deliberative process (Austin 1966: 311–17), he also admits to the pressures exerted on religious minorities by Congress leaders, especially Sardar Patel, to relinquish colonial privileges[10] (ibid.: 151).

Cultural Rights

If a departure from the colonial model was made in the case of representation rights, such a departure or break from the tradition did not inform the founders during deliberations on the appropriate religious, educational, and cultural safeguards for minorities. Although the safeguards contemplated by the Minority Rights Sub-committee and the larger Constituent Assembly included a vast array of subjects for consideration and discussion, the essential issues revolved around how identity-bearing individuals and groups needed recognition. Some protections and safeguards pertained to clarifying the meaning, implication and amplification of fundamental rights that all citizens would enjoy at an individual level. These covered areas were commonly grouped together under the categories of freedom of religion, which aroused highly interesting debates on certain religious practices such as *sati*, devadasi (dedication of girls to temples), child marriage and on the ever more contentious issues of the freedom to propagate religion and religious instruction in educational institutions. In different ways these issues brought to the fore questions about the role of the secular Indian state, especially about its responsibility for taking appropriate initiatives to trigger social reform in community practices and questions about the public-private distinction.

To the question of how the state would maintain its relationship with religion, the common overwhelming approach was that the state would be secular, which in the Indian case meant that there would be no state religion, but the state would allow religious freedom, including the right to practise and propagate religion. Indian secularism, a feature implicit in the original document but made explicit by way of an amendment to the Preamble by the 42nd Constitutional Amendment Act, 1974, was never contemplated to approximate the American model of the 'wall of separation' between the Church and state. The secular state, most founders concurred, was to allow room for both neutral involvement and pursuing a policy of equidistance between religions. Some involvement in religion was considered necessary for a progressive welfare state that sought appropriate legal reforms. What exactly these reforms would mean and how precisely the state would involve itself in cultural or religious matters was never specified in detail, but the state received ample scope within a democratic governance model to act as it deemed necessary. As a general policy this approach was both compatible with democracy and protective of religious freedom.

In terms of how the question of one's cultural or religious identity affected one's status as a citizen, the major divide in the assembly and the pertinent committees, focused on the question of who was a legitimate bearer of rights in the newly-formed political community—the individual or the group—and how this would shape other protections guaranteed to minorities. For example, during discussions in the meetings of the Fundamental Rights Sub-committee, there was a disagreement about what a right to practise religion meant which separated those who believed that the Constitution need only spell out a few broad non-discrimination principles together with a common citizenship model and those who advocated explicit constitutional recognition of the rights of cultural and religious minorities.

That citizenship is granted only to individuals was the common refrain of those who were opposed to religious practices and customs such as purdah (the practice of veil common to most Muslim and some Hindu women), child marriage, polygamy, unequal laws of inheritance, prevention of inter-caste marriages, and devadasi. Spearheading the cause of social reform in opposition to some of these traditional practices were women representatives such as Rajkumari Amrit Kaur and Hansa Mehta, with support from A.K. Ayyar (Rao Vol. II 1967: 65–198).[11]

On a different plane, whether the right to religion encompasses rights of propagation has been, and still continues to be a highly contested issue. Although the final outcome of the constitutional deliberations included the right of an organisation or a group to propagate its religious tenets, the matter was put to a severe test due to the views of some members that Hinduism, unlike Islam or Christianity, did not believe in proselytisation. In the Minority Rights Sub-committee, M. Ruthnaswami maintained that since Islam and Christianity were essentially proselytising religions, the purview of religious freedom should encompass the right to propagate religion (ibid.: 201). In spite of several attempts made by the assembly members to curtail this right by seeking to prohibit certain forms of conversion and treat them as illegal, such a move was abandoned as a result of a political conciliation reached between community representatives largely as a concession to the Christian (Catholic) community.

In the last fifty years, especially with a phenomenal increase of violence in recent times caused by an ascendant Hindu nationalism, the question of conversion threatens to endanger harmony between the Christian and Hindu communities. Despite legal wrangles and political controversies that impinge on the reality of religious conversions and re-conversions of lower caste groups and tribals today, K. M. Munshi's broad defence of the principle of conversion made on the floor of the Constituent Assembly,[12] is still reflective of the Indian Constitution's general approach to the issue.

Of the non-discriminatory basis of the cultural and religious objects the assembly found it useful to allow the state to intervene to throw open 'religious institutions with a public character' and disallow compulsory religious instructions, with reasonable exceptions, in educational institutions that are maintained or are receiving aid wholly out of public funds.

Long before the constitutional discussions, the subject of personal laws was a matter of prime concern to religious minorities, especially Muslims. As a cultural right or safeguard, the issue of personal laws had figured in successive demands made by the Muslim League and was part of even Jinnah's fourteen-point demand made in 1929. However, the practice of religious communities having their own separate personal laws dates back to Warren Hastings' 1772 Judicial Plan under the East India Company's judicial directive to its new civil courts, or diwani adalats, to ensure, 'that in all suits regarding Inheritance, Marriage, Caste, and all other religious Usages or Institutions, the Laws of the Koran with respect to Mahometans, and those of the Shaster with respect to Gentoos, shall be invariably adhered to ...' (Conrad 1995: 306). For the entire duration of the colonial administration, the institution of personal laws was left completely untouched. During the nationalist movement, the Muslim League rallied around this issue and claimed it to be a core component of its distinctive identity. Deliberations on this issue in the Minority Rights and Fundamental Rights Sub-committees and the Constituent Assembly evoked great deal of heat and passion.

Although Rajkumari Amrit Kaur, Hansa Mehta, and Minoo Masani were insistent in demanding a uniform civil code in conformity with their strong views on common citizenship and making the individual the sole bearer of rights, many Muslim representatives in the assembly took strong exception to this idea, and even to mentioning the prospect of a uniform civil code in the non-justiciable section of the Constitution. They regarded this as an infringement upon their collective right.

Speaking for most religious minorities and drawing on appropriate European examples of minority accommodations, Mohd. Ismail Sahib, a Muslim representative, contended that personal laws constituted an inviolable fundamental right of religious minorities on grounds that they were an intrinsic part of their religion and culture (CAD Vol. VII 1967: 540–1). Different members gave different reasons for the preservation of personal laws. Mohd. Ismail Sahib defended it as the ethical choice of the community. Other Muslim members gave various reasons—historical, pragmatic, contextual, and democratic—to justify the continued existence of the personal laws. All defenders agreed, however, that personal laws closely reflected the religious practices of the community. To that extent the definition of secularism was reinterpreted to mean non-religiosity, not irreligiosity or anti-religiosity. It was important to define the secular state as non-religious to make a distinction between a form and attribute of neutrality that a non-interfering secular state ought to display and the anti-religiosity of an apparent secularism that an interventionist state uses to legislate uniformity over and against distinctive ways of life.

In line with this reasoning, Mahboob Ali Baig Sahib Bahadur and Hussain Imam argued that secularism should not mean having common laws, but that a secular state can, and ought to, respect diverse religious practices (ibid.: 543–5). B. Pocker Sahib Bahadur asserted that interference in religious practices is tantamount to tyranny. Following the well-known Millian argument, he stressed that a majority is not tyrannical if it respects the rights of the minorities. To objections based on European and American practices, Pocker Sahib responded that it did not matter how other constitutions dealt with this issue. In underscoring that constitutions differ in their approaches to accommodate diversity, Pocker Sahib accentuated the contextual foundations of constitutionalism. However, not all members who supported the idea of retaining personal laws saw a necessary correlation between protection of minority interests and state interference in religious matters. To some, especially Naziruddin Ahmed, certain interventions by the secular state could be in order and legitimate. In fact Ahmed suggested that a future uniform civil code with the consent of all concerned might look attractive under ideal conditions but claimed that pragmatism demanded continuation of the present arrangement (ibid.: 541).

In reaction to these views, K. M. Munshi and Alladi Krishnaswami Ayyar made a case for a uniform civil code, highlighting how it remains a future democratic option that could effectively imply the consent of all communities affected by such an outcome. Munshi argued that any future civil code could not ignore the views of the minority, but insisted that the idea of a civil code was not tyrannical per se. Moreover, he suggested that tyranny could take other forms than an imposed secularism or a uniform civil code. For instance, he pointed out, Khojas and Cutchi Memons, despite being Muslim communities, had largely followed Hindu practices in relation to personal laws until they were brought, against their wishes, within the ambit of Muslim personal laws. If the prospect of civil code is tyrannical to Muslims, Munshi argued, then Khojas and Cutchi Memons, minorities within a minority, already suffer from the tyranny of a personal law imposed upon them. Expanding upon this example, Ambedkar observed later that personal laws were neither immutable nor uniform throughout India and until 1939 most of the North-West Frontier Province (presently part of Pakistan) and many Muslims in the southern cone of the subcontinent followed respectively Hindu laws and laws that had regional moorings.[13] More generally, Ambedkar suggested, 'It is perfectly possible that the future parliament may make a provision by way of making a beginning that the Code shall apply only to those who make a declaration that they are prepared to be bound by it, so that in the initial stage the application of the Code may be purely voluntary. Parliament may feel the ground by some such method' (ibid.: 545).

Playing the familiar chords of unity, both Munshi and Ayyar argued that a uniform civil code could act as a catalyst for national unity and that rather than create a schism between the communities, it might actually help bridge communal divides (ibid.).

The supporters and detractors of the civil code remained unconvinced of each other's views on what brings about unity. When Mohd. Ismail Sahib had first moved an amendment to the non-justiciable provision of Uniform Civil Code in the Directive Principles of State Policy, he had maintained that harmony is best upheld by a respect for diverse practices, not by uniform legal 'regimentation' (ibid.: 541).

The question of whether or not religious instruction could be imparted in state-funded schools also led to a debate about the secular basis of the Constitution. While acknowledging the fact that a secular state need not compel students to study religion, Mohd. Ismail Sahib also affirmed that it was not necessary for the secular state to ban religious instruction in public schools especially if parents or their wards wanted religious instruction in conformity to their own religions in the public schools. Such a fact need not be construed further as a violation of the neutrality of the secular state (ibid.: 867). Reacting to this view and offering a narrower version of the secular state, Tajamul Husain, the most 'liberal' of Muslim representatives, argued against religious instruction in schools that were maintained wholly by the state' (ibid.: 871). K. T. Shah further extended Husain's argument to include even those schools that were partially maintained by the state's finances.

In response to these positions, Ambedkar pointed out that the draft version for this particular clause 'strikes a mean' whose implication was that (contrary to Ismail Sahib's views) religious instruction could be barred in public schools but in deference to the cultural claims of religious communities, institutions operated by the communities would continue to enjoy full liberties in imparting religious education regardless of whether or not they received aid.[14]

Whatever the scope for public funding for religious communities, the Constituent Assembly agreed that both religious and linguistic minorities should have the right to establish educational institutions of their choice. Drawing reference to an analogous provision in the old Estonian Constitution, Harnam Singh in clause 15 of his draft presentation to the Sub-committee on Fundamental Rights in March, 1947, had typically brought to members' attention that:

> Religious minorities in the country shall have a right to establish autonomous institutions for the preservation and development of their culture and to maintain special organization with powers to levy taxes for the maintenance and welfare of such institutions (CAD Vol. II 1967: 82).

In the Sub-committee on Minority Rights, M. Ruthnaswami, responding to Munshi's questionnaire, dwelt at length on the theme of cultural protections of minorities. Central to his arguments was the distinction he sought to make between political minorities and national or religious minorities. For political minorities that were essentially non-permanent in nature, Ruthnaswami believed, institutional mechanisms of checks and balances, division of powers, rule of law, decentralisation, and federal properties, would suffice' (ibid.: 313–14). However, for national or religious minorities, such as Muslims, Sikhs, Indian Christians, and Anglo-Indians, who constituted 'permanent' minorities, certain constitutionally entrenched rights, would be in order. 'It is as a permanent minority,' he said, 'never able or hoping to be able to influence and carry the government of any day that they require certain rights to be asserted and safeguarded' (ibid.: 314). Among his suggestions for rights of permanent national minorities were: 1) grants-in-aid to schools and educational institutions maintained by religious communities; 2) special grants toward enhancement of education of educationally backward minorities; and 3) schools for minorities, where their religion and culture would be preserved and cultivated, which the government ought to maintain especially in those areas where such minorities are majorities in a demographic sense (ibid.: 315). Largely conforming to Ruthnaswami's suggestions, S. P. Mookerjee in his Memorandum on Minorities made a similar case for the educational rights of minorities to preserve their culture, language, and script (ibid.: 337–41).

As the foregoing account suggests, the justification for cultural rights varied. Founders who narrowly defined citizenship clustered rights in favour of individuals; others prioritised the needs and interests of different communities. The balance sheet is captured best by Lloyd and Susanne Rudolph's general observation that the Indian constitution makes 'simultaneous commitment to communities and to equal citizenship' (Rudolph and Rudolph 1987: 39–9). What is pertinent to note in this context is how such simultaneous commitments pervade the domain of cultural rights as well. As Figure 2.1 illustrates, such simultaneous commitments are to be best understood as reflecting conflicting perspectives of Founders on the sources of citizenship. As a result of a series of compromises made between the members of the Constituent Assembly, political safeguards for minorities, i.e., representation rights and promises of state-mandated reservation policies, were confined only to the scheduled castes and tribes while other religious, cultural, and educational safeguards were extended to religious and ethnic minorities. This compromise prompts some to critique the process by which the religious minorities were deprived of their share of political safeguards (Retzlaff 1963; Chaube 1974; Ansari 1999; Chirkandiath 1999; Bajpai 2000).[15] While the dominant role of the Congress in the assembly, the changing political realities and compulsions, and the newly-discovered accent and rhetoric of national unity all help to explain the lack of support for political rights of religious minorities, the constitutional model that ultimately evolved, also jettisoned the colonial model on principled grounds. Committing themselves to a new beginning and a new chapter, the Founders rejected the top-down model of elite power-sharing between communities that had shaped colonial policies.

IDENTITY AND RIGHTS IN THE INDIAN CONSTITUTION

Considered to be the longest written constitution in the world, with features and principles compatible with Indian thought but 'nevertheless almost entirely of non-Indian origin' the Constitution was, as Granville Austin notes, 'perhaps the greatest political venture since that originated in Philadelphia in 1787' (Austin 1966: 308). India's age-old civilisation and modern democratic political institutions were never thought to be working at cross-purposes. Indeed, it was the Constitution itself, more than anything else, which honed diverse social aspirations to a refurbished and fine-tuned Westminster-style representative form of government. The underlying Indian mantra that achieved this in large measure was 'Unity in Diversity'.

As 'the charter of Indian unity', the Constitution is all-encompassing in providing a wide institutional and normative framework within which questions of diversity have been, and continue to be, negotiated and accommodated (ibid.: 309).[16] The Constitution responds to issues of identity and difference with varied nuances of equality. The Fundamental Rights of the Constitution, contained in Part III, are complemented by principles of social legislation in Part IV called the Directive Principles of State Policy. Together these two account for the egalitarian mode that the liberal democratic system of India aspires to achieve in relation to both individuals and groups. Depending on the context, equal treatment carries varying connotations.

Originally, the Constitution guaranteed seven sets of justiciable rights: Right to Equality, Right to Freedom, Right against Exploitation, Right to Freedom of Religion, Cultural and Educational Rights, Right to Property, and the Right to Constitutional Remedies.[17] In general, all these 'Rights lay down that the state is to deny no one equality before law' (ibid.: 51).

The Directive Principles, on the other hand, are non-justiciable but lay down the parameters and goals for future legislation. The principles are broadly culled from Gandhian precepts and socialist values; in sum, a charter intended for social progress. If some of the rights in the Constitution reflect formal equality, a major part of the Directive Principles gave concrete shape to substantive equality. But the Principles, some of which bore a distinctively Indian and Gandhian essence, also pointed towards a higher good, the telos of an ethical-cum-socialist communitarianism. However, the fundamental rights in the Constitution do also balance considerations of formal or difference-blind equality on the one hand, and considerations of substantive equality informed by sensitivities to group differences on the other.

Articles 14–16 contain different expressions of the right to equality and equal protection of laws. Although the said articles contain the crux of formal equality considered important to do away with caste-, gender-, and religion-based social discrimination, they are circumscribed by provisions of state-mandated affirmative action for disadvantaged groups. Article 17, making a direct reference to the ritual and social discrimination of the 'untouchable' castes, seeks to abolish the practice of untouchability.

By widespread opinion Articles 29 and 30—introduced together as Cultural and Educational Rights in the chapter on Fundamental Rights—are the crux of special rights for minorities. Titled 'Protection of Interests of Minorities,' Article 29 (1) states, 'Any section of the citizens residing in the territory of India or any part thereof having a distinct language, script or culture of its own shall have the right to conserve the same.' Article 30 on right of minorities to establish and administer educational institutions categorically emphasises, 'All minorities, whether based on religion or language, shall have the right to establish and administer educational institutions of their choice.' Clause 2 of the same reads, 'The State shall not, in granting aid to educational institutions, discriminate against any educational institution on the ground that it is under the management of a minority, whether based on religion or language.'

Although both the articles protect the special interests of minorities, Article 29 can also be extended to apply to other communities, including the majority community, as well. As Massey (1999) argues, although Article 29 provides 'protection to the interests of minorities, it does not refer specifically to the minorities whose numerical strength is less'. In referring to 'any section of the citizens,' who may have a distinct language, script or culture, it may effectively 'belong even to the majority community'. As an example, Massey critically observes that even 'members of the Hindu community living in Punjab or Nagaland will receive protection for their linguistic or cultural rights, by virtue of being "so-called minorities" in these States' (Massey 1999: 83).

By common consent, however, both these articles stipulate respect for the religious and cultural autonomy of the minorities. The recognition of the minorities' cultural autonomy is justified on grounds of equality as evidenced in Justice Khanna's observation in The Ahmedabad St. Xavier's College Society vs. State of Gujarat, 1974:

> The idea of giving some special rights to the minorities is not to have a kind of privileged or pampered section of the population, but to give to the minorities a sense of security and a feeling of confidence.... Special rights for minorities were designed not to create inequality. Their real effect was to bring about equality by ensuring the preservation of the minority institutions and by guaranteeing to the minorities autonomy in the matter of the administration of these institutions. The differential treatment for the minorities by giving them special rights is intended to bring about an equilibrium,

> so that the ideal of equality may not be reduced to a mere abstract idea, but should become a living reality and result in true, genuine equality, an equality not merely in theory, but in fact... (AIR 1974: SC 1389).

However, Article 44 in the Directive Principles of State Policy stands in tension with the cultural autonomy of religious minorities with regard to personal laws. In conformity to the idea of common citizenship, it relates to the provision of a uniform civil code or secular law for citizens cutting across religious boundaries. A controversial stipulation, it enjoins upon the state to try 'secure for the citizens a uniform civil code throughout the territory of India'.

In Part XVII (Artists 343–51) the Constitution dwells upon the status of languages and provisions for linguistic minorities. While Article 347 creates a special proviso for official recognition of a language spoken by a section of the population throughout or in any part of a state or province, Article 350A stipulates that the state shall endeavour 'to provide adequate facilities for instruction in the mother-tongue at the primary stage of education to children belonging to linguistic minority groups'.

MULTICULTURAL CONSTITUTIONALISM

The Constitution of independent India is paradoxically both a deviation from, and a derivation of, the colonial model. It rejects explicitly the policy of balance between groups and avoids a full-fledged microcosmic view of representation[18] in legislatures and services. However, like the colonial model, it retains some aspects of the principle of microcosmic representation, or group representation in the form of quotas, especially for the scheduled castes and tribes, and by symbolic extension to the Anglo-Indian community. One of the major thrusts of disparity between the colonial and post-colonial constitutional systems, however, lies in how the latter model treats difference. Equal treatment in the post-colonial constitution required that dissimilar forms of difference be differently treated. In other words, caste and tribal differences, according to the Founders, merited special representation rights, whereas religious and linguistic differences acquired cultural and educational autonomy. Cutting across this dichotomy, however, were territorial self-government rights for tribes and linguistic groups and a special status for Kashmir in an asymmetrical federal association.

As the foregoing discussion on the constitution-making process in the late 1940s amply demonstrates, it is clear how religious minorities were outvoted on the question of political safeguards, a synonym for special representation rights. From the perspective of religious minorities, cultural and educational autonomy granted to religious groups, of which personal laws was an important facet, was a second best outcome of the deliberative process, especially for Muslims who lost a privileged position in the transition to post-independence situation.

The final outcome in the Constitution regarding provisions for different groups almost exhausts the taxonomical list on cultural rights prepared by Jacob T. Levy (1997) where each category of cultural right-claims constitutes a cluster of entitlements backed by sameness of normative logic and policy response across contexts. Levy's list includes: exemptions from laws—freedom of religion exempts, for instance, some persons from singing the national anthem (Sorabjee 1990: 106); assistance or affirmative action (for SCs and STs); self-government rights for minorities (in Kashmir, tribal states and autonomous district councils); external rules restricting non-members' liberty (respecting land rights of Kashmiris and tribal communities in the Northeast); internal rules for members' conduct enforced by the community (followed non-formally; not constitutionally approved); recognition/enforcement of traditional legal code (personal laws for Muslims, Christians, Parsis, and Hindus); representation of minorities (of SCs, STs, and Anglo-Indians); symbolic claims to acknowledge the worth or status of various groups (best exemplified by a comprehensive national holidays calendar that includes significant days considered holy by almost all religions).

As a compendium of various difference-sensitive rights that coexist with a common citizenship model, India's Constitution anticipates much of what gets discussed today under the broad contours of multiculturalism in contemporary liberalism. It will be interesting to observe that most of the claims made by the minorities in India during constitutional deliberations were made in the absence of a common citizenship model. By contrast, in most liberal democracies today where common citizenship rights already exist, group claims are made in the public sphere, or in other words, against the broader community. The Indian situation is not unique, but informs the constitutional process in many post-colonial multiethnic societies. But the deliberative outcome in the Indian case resulted also from the atypical and unusual precondition that trumped the case of minorities even before discussions could take place. To say that there was no Rawlsian 'veil of ignorance' would be an understatement.[19] But, as Yash Ghai (2000) astutely observes, it matters when the Constitution is framed and whether or not the time is 'ripe' for building a presumption of 'universality' into the negotiating process. 'At the time of the Indian independence,' Ghai recognises, 'there was no internationally accepted body of norms or procedures. Nor was there a consensus that constitutions had to include a bill of rights'[20] (Ghai 2000: 1135).

Although the United States Bill of Rights was a tempting exemplar for many founders, the liberal spirit that pervaded the US Constitution did not find many takers in the subcontinent.[21] In any case, a complete liberal individualist approach was a non-option given both the procedural and pragmatic compulsions to devise an inclusive political community. A quasi-liberal spirit, one that precariously balances rights of individuals with those of communities, permeates and informs the Indian constitutional experiment. Indian constitutionalism, it will be safe to concur, is deeply embedded in a 'thickly' constituted multicultural society.

In so far as norms of democratic justice apply, the collective rights of groups in the Indian case comprise a complex mix of institutional safeguards and normative protections designed as checks against political majoritarianism. But as a sine qua non of counter-majoritarian strategy, the constitutional entrenchment of group-specific rights in the Indian case must be periodically mandated by democratic procedures, chiefly by the political majority, to give it continued democratic legitimacy (e.g., the need to reaffirm group representation rights or reservations every 10 years). Whereas constitutional entrenchment would normally imply political insulation from ordinary legislative options and judicial protection, the constitutional founders did stake out a wide area for future legislative options in many matters of significance for minorities, which, of course includes the case of personal laws. Paradoxical as it may sound, it was Parliament, following the Shah Bano controversy of 1985, which restored the status quo ante in regard to personal laws after the Muslim minority felt the Supreme Court had transgressed its legitimate rights. But one needs to address whether or not, and to what degree, do rights of minorities require constitutional entrenchment.

In spite of recent theoretical support for various forms of multicultural accommodation of group-specific rights wherever applicable, a grey area that confronts political theorists is whether or not to acknowledge group differences in the Constitution itself (Kymlicka 1996, McDonald 1997). This debate plays itself out mostly in those contexts where a strong individualist strand of rights exists but where group rights also constitute a viable political option. The dilemma is whether or not some group rights should be written into the Constitution. Many scholars influenced by postmodern affections rile against difference-blind provisions in a Constitution, but are equally sceptical of entrenching group-sensitive provisions. Such scepticism is sustained by two kinds of fears: (a) an entrenchment of group-specific rights in the constitutional document will ossify differences and may exacerbate group conflict, and (b) that this mode, in not recognising the constantly mutable and contingent nature of identities, will not be flexible enough to accommodate differences that will emerge in the future. Both fears are interrelated. The first fear, in part, is related to a genuine concern that by drawing boundaries between groups the likelihood of conflicts between them will rise, rather than diminish. The second fear emerges out of a genuine concern that incorporating such group-specific rights effectively denies a level-playing field to the changing matrix of group interaction and disadvantage.

The first fear must falter in the face of evidence that any attempt to push a political agenda of common citizenship does usually turn out to be counter-productive as was proved true in the aftermath of the Shah Bano case or whenever there is a political attempt to erode the multicultural fabric of Indian society. The second objection is complex and applies more in the context of affirmative action or state support for disadvantaged groups, where what constitutes group disadvantage becomes a subject of perennial interpretation. Although this is what the constitution-makers, especially Ambedkar, also desired, recent attempts to broaden the ambit of state support for other backward classes—castes that are not similarly situated with the scheduled castes or scheduled tribes in terms of accumulated structural inequalities—has not been a particularly positive constitutional interpretation by virtue of having eroded the original intentions of the Founders to set aside support for the truly deserving.

In a certain sense, it will be appropriate (given the inconclusiveness of creative judicial and political interpretations) to conclude that the constitutional experiment is yet to see a point of closure. However, in a world that has recently woken up to value and recognise diversity, the Indian experiment will stimulate both academics and practitioners alike interested to analyse multiculturalism in a comparative context.

ENDNOTES

1 A multinational state refers to one in which ethnically heterogeneous groups coexist.

2 Separate electorates effectively meant communal representation. In such a scheme, only Muslims could elect Muslims as representatives to political offices set aside for them. The Congress and the mainstream nationalists always faulted the British for creating this institution arguing that it paved the way for the creation of Pakistan on the basis of the two-nation theory. A joint electorate with reserved seat implies a constituency of undifferentiated electorate reserved for a particular community irrespective of its relative strength in it.

3 'The dividing line was so crudely drawn that it meant the splitting of the province into two communal blocs—the one in which the Hindus were in a majority, and the other in which the Muslims predominated' (See Menon 1957: 6).

4 The then Viceroy of India, Lord Minto, recommended the Secretary of State in October 1908 that the Muslims should be granted separate electorates. While making this case he argued, 'The Indian Muhamaddans are much more than a religious body. They form in fact an absolutely separate community, distinct by marriage, food and custom, and claiming in many cases to belong to a race different from the Hindus' (Menon 1957: 10).

5 One of the innovations of the Communal Award related to the idea of *weightage*, a principle by which various minority communities granted separate electorates were given representation greater than they would normally have received on the basis of their numerical strength. For instance, although the Muslim community, according to the 1931 Census, represented 7.9 per cent of the population of Madras, it was granted 13.5 per cent of the seats in the Madras Provincial Legislative Assembly (See Retzlaff 1960: 24).

6 'The Poona Pact provided 148 seats for untouchables, instead of the 78 separately elected members given by the Communal Award. It also provided a system of primary elections for those reserved seats; a panel of four seats was to be chosen by electors from the Depressed Classes' (Galanter 1984: 32).

7 In response to Munshi's questionnaire, Kaur reasoned against political safeguards of minorities. Requiring the minorities to repose trust in the majority community, she argued: 'Axiomatically there is no reason why the interests of any individual or community should not be safe in the hands of a good person or persons, irrespective of their personal religion' (Rao Vol. II 1967: 310–11).

8 Sardar Hukam Singh's deliberation (CAD Vol. VII 1967 32: 1250). Both the Muslim League and the Sikh Panthic Party were, however, divided, fragmented, and demoralised resulting in a weakening of this demand (See Retzlaff 1963).

9 In rejecting alternative electoral systems, Rubinoff (1990) argues how the Congress rigged the electoral system in the Constituent Assembly to achieve a majoritarian FPTP system that would benefit them in national elections.

10 For an implication that Patel may have used an arms-twisting approach to secure this outcome (See Chaube 1973). In the same vein, however, Austin acknowledges the possibilities of the division in the ranks of Muslims, similar to what Retzlaff (1963) notes in another context, together with the motive of sacrifice in order to attract fair treatment from Hindus, as reasons for an increased moderation in the demands

of religious minorities that eventually paved the way for an alteration in the colonial model of representation (Austin 1966: 151).

11 See the minutes of the Sub-Committee on Fundamental Rights meetings of February–April, 1947 in Rao 1967 Vol. II: 65–198.

12 In spite of his attempts to specify particular methods of conversion—force, fraud, and those involving children—as illegal, Munshi asserted:—'So long as religion is religion, conversion by free exercise of the conscience has to be recognized' (CAD Vol. VII 1967: 837).

13 The latter reference was to Marumakkathayam law, a matriarchal law that applied to both Hindus and Muslims, in North Malabar in southern India.

14 In regard to such privately-managed community schools, Ambedkar's position was: 'The State, of course, is free to give aid, is free not to give aid; the only limitation we have placed is this, that the State shall not debar the institution from claiming aid under its grant-in-aid code merely on the ground that it is run and maintained by a community and not maintained by a public body. We have there provided also a further qualification, that while it is free to give religious instruction in the institution and the grant made by the State shall not be a bar to the giving of such instruction, it shall not give instruction to, or make it compulsory upon, the children belonging to other communities unless and until they obtain the consent of the parents of those children' (CAD Vol. VII 1967: 883).

15 Notably Retzlaff (1963), Chaube (1974), Ansari (1999) and Chirkandiyath (1999). For a recent account see Bajpai (2000).

16 As Austin observes, 'Within its limits are held the negotiations over the working of the federal system. The realignment of state boundaries on linguistic lines was done within its definition of Indian nationalism. The question of the Official Language has been debated in Parliament within the framework of a compromise designed to preserve national unity. The 'Constitution has established the accepted norms of "national" behavior' (Austin 1966: 309).

17 Of these, the guarantee of the right to property was deleted by the Constitution (44th Amendment) Act in 1978. Removed from the ambit of fundamental rights, the only protection such a right has now is contained in Article 300-A, which provides that 'no person shall be deprived of his property save by authority of law'. The remaining six rights, contained in various articles of Part III, are justiciable.

18 Although a microcosmic view of representation closely resembles

proportional representation, the sense in which it is used here suggests a rough and functional principle of proportionality attained through majoritarian representative institutions that through quotas in legislative constituencies circumscribes outcomes.

19 Given the circumstances in which the constitutional deliberations took place in India with a clear-cut precommitment to protect the interests of minority groups, the founders were guided by a prescribed goal quite unlike a situation that is presupposed by the procedure entailed in Rawls' original position.

20 By the 1990s, however, Ghai goes on to argue, there are both a substantial body of norms and consensus that favours inclusion of a bill of rights in national constitutional systems, a trait that affects the Fijian constitution of 1995 and explains the difference of approach in the Canadian context between the Bill of Rights of 1960 and the 1982 Charter (Ghai 2000: 1135). In a comparative study of a few deeply divided societies—India, Canada, South Africa, and Fiji—Ghai more generally concludes that a framework of rights provides a flexible and successful way of 'mediating competing ethnic and cultural claims' (Ghai 2000: 1099).

21 This was at the heyday of the unparalleled significance and uncritical acceptance of the US constitutional model, especially the Bill of Rights. But, as Robert Vipond (1999: 177) notes, 'The American model travels less well now, even though there has been something of a renaissance in comparative constitutional studies.' The declining significance of the US model, it needs pointing out by way of qualifying Vipond's observations, is *because* of a renaissance in comparative constitutionalism, which now finds the American model as one amongst many standards. For helpful comparisons between the Indian and American models, see Sorabjee (1990), and Jacobsohn (1996).

REFERENCES

Ansari, Iqbal A. 1999, 'Minorities and the Politics of Constitution Making in India', in D. L. Sheth and Gurpreet Mahajan (ed.), *Minority Identities and the Nation-State* New Delhi: Oxford University Press: 113–37.

Austin, Granville. 1966. *The Indian Constitution: Cornerstone of a Nation*. Oxford: Clarendon Press.

Bajpai, Rochana. 2000. 'Constituent Assembly Debates and Minority Rights'. *Economic and Political Weekly*. 27 May. 1837–45.

Chaube, Shibanikinkar. 1973. *Constituent Assembly of India: Springboard of Revolution.* New Delhi: People's Publishing House.

Chiriyankandath, James. 1999. 'Constitutional Predilections'. *Seminar.* 484: 50–55.

Conrad, Dieter. 1995. 'The Personal Law Question and Hindu Nationalism', in Vasudha Dalmia and Heinrich von Stietencron (ed.), *Representing Hinduism: The Construction of Religious Traditions and National Identity.* New Delhi: Sage: 306–337.

Constituent Assembly Debates (CAD). 1967. Vols. I–XII. Delhi: Lok Sabha Secretariat.

Coupland, R. 1944. *The Indian Problem: Report on the Constitutional Problem in India.* New York: Oxford University Press.

Galanter, Marc. 1984 [pb 1991 with new preface]. *Competing Equalities: Law and the Backward Classes in India.* Delhi: Oxford University Press.

Ghai, Yash. 2000. 'Universalism and Relativism: Human Rights as a Framework for Negotiating Interethnic Claims'. *Cardozo Law Review.* 21: 1095–1140.

Hanafin, Patrick J. and Melissa S. Williams. 2000. 'Introduction', in Patrick J. Hanafin and Melissa S. Williams (ed.), *Identity, Rights and Constitutional Transformation.* Aldershot: Ashgate.

Hardgrave, Robert L. Jr. 1993. 'India: The Dilemmas of Diversity.' *Journal of Democracy.* 4: 54–68.

Jacobsohn, Gary Jeffrey. 1996. 'Three Modes of Secular Constitutional Development: India, Israel, and the United States.' *Studies in American Political Development.* 10 (1): 1–68.

Kymlicka, Will. 1995. *Multicultural Citizenship: A Liberal Theory of Minority Rights.* Oxford: Oxford University Press.

Levy, Jacob T. 1997. 'Classifying Cultural Rights', in Ian Shapiro and Will Kymlicka (ed.), *Ethnicity and Group Rights. Nomos XXXIX.* New York: New York University Press: 22–66.

Massey, James. 1999. *Minorities in a Democracy: The Indian Experience.* New Delhi: Manohar.

McDonald, Leighton. 1997. 'Regrouping in Defence of Minority Rights: Kymlicka's *Multicultural Citizenship.*' *Osgoode Hall Law Journal.* 34: 2: 291–319.

Menon, V. P. 1957. *The Transfer of Power in India.* Princeton: Princeton University Press.

Nariman, Fali Sam. 1989. 'The Indian Constitution: An Experiment in Unity Amid Diversity', in Robert A. Goldwin, Art Kaufman, and William A. Schambra (ed.), *Forging Unity Out Of Diversity: The Approaches of Eight Nation.* Washington D.C.: American Enterprise Institute for Public Policy Research: 7–37.

Retzlaff, Ralph H. 1960. 'The Constituent Assembly of India and the Problem of Indian Unity'. Unpublished PhD. Dissertation, Cornell University.

Retzlaff, Ralph H. 1963. 'The Problem of Communal Minorities in the Drafting of the Indian Constitution', in R. N. Spann (ed.), *Constitutionalism in Asia*. New York: Asia Publishing House: 55–73.

Rubinoff, Arthur. 1990. 'India's Electoral System as a Determinant of its Party System', in Rajendra Vora (ed.), *State and Society in India*. Delhi: Chanakya Publications: 95–110.

Rudolph, Lloyd I. and Rudolph, Susanne Hoeber. 1987. *In Pursuit of Lakshmi: The Political Economy of the Indian State*. Chicago: University of Chicago Press.

Shiva Rao, B. (ed.). 1967. *The Framing of India's Constitution: Select Documents*. 5 Vols. New Delhi: Indian Institute of Public Administration.

Sorabjee, Soli J. 1990. 'Equality in the United States and India', in Louis Henkin and Albert J. Rosenthal (ed.), *Constitutionalism and Rights: The Influence of the United States Constitution Abroad*. New York: Columbia University Press: 94–124.

Stuligross, David and Ashutosh Varshney. 1999. 'Ethnic Diversities, Constitutional Designs, and Public Policies in India.' Paper presented at the Conference on Constitutional Design 2000. Kellogg Institute of International Studies: University of Notre Dame.

Tully, James. 1995. *Strange Multiplicity: Constitutionalism in an Age of Diversity*. Cambridge: Cambridge University Press.

Vipond, Robert. 1999. 'Constitutionalism as a Form of Conflict Resolution', in Patrick J. Hanafin and Melissa S. Williams (ed.), *Identity, Rights and Constitutional Transformation*. Aldershot: Ashgate: 172–85.

MATTERS OF GOVERNANCE
THEORY AND PRACTICE

3

Putting Civil Society in Its Place

Neera Chandhoke

INTRODUCTION

The arguments in this essay seek to address a question, which might well be of some significance for any discussion of state and civil society in India. The question is: what are the limits of civil society interventions? Have we, perchance, invested too heavily in the concept of civil society, or reposed far too much confidence in the ability of civil society agents to effect transformations in the lives of ordinary citizens? Are scholars and analysts of the political condition at fault inasmuch as they have, sometimes, tried to posit civil society as an alternative to the state?

I raise these questions because following the rediscovery and the reinvention of civil society in the 1970s but more particularly the 1980s, the sphere came to be seen as practically a substitute for the 'power hungry' state and the 'profit driven' market. The reasons for this development are well known by now; tremendous disenchantment with the 'overreach' of the state in the advanced capitalist, the erstwhile socialist, and the developing world. The

Originally published in *Economic and Political Weekly*, Vol. 40, No. 7, 14–20 February, 2009.

revolution 'from above' in the shape of the interventionist state: whether Keynesian, welfare, developmental or socialist had lapsed into status quoism, and the unabashed pursuit of power at the expense of the interests of citizens. The revolution 'from below', or the freedom struggle in the colonised world had trailed off into inertia. Nowhere was the sense of betrayal expressed more strongly than in the post-colonial novel, in Gabriel Garcia Marquez's *Love in the Time of Cholera*, for instance. The literary critic Jean Franco suggests that Marquez who had already begun to pillorise and parody the nation in his other writings, specifically makes the 'private' the centre of his writing in this novel. Even as the 'apocalyptic landscape of decay and cadavers bear the scars of modernisation, the 'protagonists enacting their anachronistic love story can no longer represent anything beyond their own moral passions'. *Love in the Time of Cholera*, argues Franco, 'marked the dissolution of a once totalizing myth which is now replaced by private fantasies lived out amidst private disasters' (Franco 1989: 204–12). The irony is that the novel, which during the struggle for decolonisation had constituted the nation in and for political imaginations, was now to set itself to the task of marginalising the nation.

It was around this moment that the civil society argument was propelled onto the centrestage of political imaginations, strategies, and energies. Forged initially in the context of Stalinist states in Eastern and Central Europe, the argument promised no great ruptural breaks in the lives of people. What it did suggest was that a limited and accountable state, a rule of law, constitutionalism, political and civil liberties, a free media, uncoerced associational life, and a vigilant civil society formed essential prerequisites of democracy and citizenship rights. Given the success of the 'Velvet Revolutions' against authoritarian state power in the erstwhile socialist societies, the concept as well as the practices of civil society were to attract considerable attention, as well as a fair amount of enthusiasm among democratic theorists and activists. Democratic theorists came to believe with Gouldner that 'no emancipation is possible in the modern world without a strong civil society that can strengthen the public sphere and can provide a haven from a centre of resistance to the Behemoth state' (Gouldner 1980: 355–73). And in policy circles it came to be widely felt that civil society agents, particularly the non-governmental sector could deliver social goods, empower citizens, safeguard human rights, and raise issues of public concern more effectively than traditional agents of political society such as the political party and the state. Consequently, civil society agents, particularly the non-governmental sector, were encouraged by multilateral agencies, governments, and donor organisations to play a large role in collective life. The state in the process was pluralised, sharing functions, which had traditionally fallen within its jurisdiction, with a host of agents.

The civil society argument has now been around for about twenty-five years. The problems of the world remain as intractable, even as the numbers of agents who seek to negotiate the ills of the human condition have expanded exponentially. In popular imaginations, the state still seems to occupy a central position. And it is clear that there are certain problems that only the state can resolve, and should be resolving. Is it time that we begin to reconsider the role of civil society? Is it time to once again put civil society in its place?

INDIA: THE CRISIS OF REPRESENTATION

In India the turn away from the state and to civil society could perhaps be foretold as early as the late 1960s, when political institutions began to decline rapidly. In particular, citizens began to lose confidence in the Congress party, which in its earlier avatar had mobilised millions of people in and through the freedom struggle, and which in the post-independence period dominated Indian politics. The widely respected scholar Rajni Kothari had at one point of time described Indian democracy as the 'one-party dominant system'. Indian democracy, Kothari suggested did not need an opposition party, because groups and individuals negotiated and bargained with the leadership, and with each other, within the party organisation (Kothari 1970).[1] By the late 1970s scholars began to speak of the end of the Congress system. The party was beset with what two scholars termed 'organisational atrophy', (Sisson and Roy 1990: 1–33) power came to be excessively centralised in the person of Prime Minister Indira Gandhi, and the Congress lost its capacity to either represent or negotiate popular demands. In the process the party lost touch with its constituency. In sum, individual members of the party came to be preoccupied with accessing the supreme leader more, and representing their constituents less.

Notably the decline of the Congress took place at precisely the time when popular expectations had risen dramatically. The rhetoric of Nehruvian socialism and the idea of planning for development had generated a sense of entitlement. Driven by populist imagery and radical demagoguery, the people came to expect that the state and the party in power would deliver primary education and subsidise higher education, guarantee health, remove poverty, generate jobs and incomes, institutionalise inter-group equalities, remove inequalities within the group, and protect the needy, vulnerable, and poor. But the Congress, which at that time controlled both power and resources, had not only failed to emancipate the country from poverty, illiteracy, and unemployment, it had under the leadership of PM Indira Gandhi become authoritarian. And this led to restlessness in major parts of the country.

Simmering discontent came to pervade large parts of the country, as groups mobilised to target an unresponsive state, and an equally unresponsive party system. Expectedly the politics of protest spilled over shaky political channels and took to violence. By the early 1970s, political discontent escaped all bounds and students in Gujarat and Bihar, took to the streets. Even as disgruntlement coalesced rapidly under the leadership of J. P. Narayan to mount a challenge to the political system, Prime Minister Indira Gandhi imposed internal Emergency from 1975–7. The Emergency not only suspended representative democracy, it pulverised civil liberties and froze political activism. The paradox, however, is that though the Emergency suspended constitutional democracy, an entire range of social struggles outside the political sphere of party politics erupted to question the state of democracy in the country. This development further reinforced the belief that the party system was neither here nor there when it came to representing political demands.

India was not alone in this. Analysts of Western societies were to make roughly the same complaint: that of the unresponsiveness of the state, the indifference of the bureaucracy, and the pulverisation of the party system. In the US, theorists had complained for long that elections and political parties seemed to have become the pawns of the political elite. In the 1960s the 'new left', the 'sit ins', the 'direct action' movements had already raised into question the efficacy of the system of representation. Discontent with the party system continued to mount with Walter Dean Burnham arguing that in the US, political parties had, since 1900, declined as a system of action. They won elections, and managed tensions between factions within the party, but they had not acted as forces for collective purposes and action. Indeed elections for Burnham had become 'candidate image affairs for which only the wealthy or those close to the wealthy need apply' (Burnham 1970: 176–9). In Eastern and Central Europe, from the 1970s onwards, citizens who had turned their face away from the state, parties, and trade unions, came to reinvent civil society as the locus of sociability, civility, and trust. In countries ruled by military regimes, such as Brazil, by the mid 1980s, citizen groups had come together in a space they called civil society to mount a sustained assault on unrepresentative and unresponsive governments, and to demand democracy. And the concept of civil society was catapulted onto the political scene as an alternative to non-performing governments and indifferent political parties.

In India, even as the decline of all institutions and particularly of the institutions of representative democracy gave rise to several mass-based political movements and grassroots activism; scholars were to reject political society as the arena for competition for state power, and acknowledge the significance of civil society. Since the turn of the decade of the 1980s social movements such as the anti-caste movement, the struggle for gender justice, for civil liberties, for environment, for food security, for the right to work, for the right to education, for the right to information, and movements against mega development projects that have displaced thousands of poor tribals and hill dwellers, and against child labour, have mobilised in civil society. By the year 2000, an estimated 20–30,000 grassroots movements, social movements, non-party political formations, social action groups, movement-groups and in general non-party groups, were raising issues of political significance (Seth 2004: 45–58). This turn to civil society and away from the state was reflected in government policy. From the Seventh Five Year plan (1985–90) onwards it is possible to discern a perceptible shift from government to civil society organisations in the area of service delivery.

The shift from political to civil society organisations can be seen as welcome for at least two reasons. For one, decentred and multiple civil society organisations promise an exit from centrally-controlled bureaucratic, hierarchical, and oligarchic party structures that are mainly preoccupied with winning the next election. Secondly, it is possible that a multiplicity of agents in civil society are able to respond immediately to problems and issues that require swift resolution, because they are in touch with their constituencies. Consequently NGOs have been promoted by international development institutions, the World Bank, and donor agencies because they are seen to possess certain desirable properties, such as flexibility, innovativeness and proximity on the one hand, and as possessing the capacity to deepen democracy on the other because they raise issues of livelihood and rights.

LIMITS OF CIVIL SOCIETY INTERVENTIONS

However, even as we acknowledge the important role played by civil society agents such as NGOs in foregrounding social and economic rights and thereby deepening democracy, the one question that confronts us at this juncture is the following: how much can the NGO sector achieve? What are the limits of civil society interventions? Among the other limits on civil society activism in particularly the social sector, the following are the most apparent. Firstly, civil society agents are just not in a position to summon up the kind of resources that are required to emancipate Indian citizens from poverty and deprivation. It is only the state that can do so through widening the tax net, and through monitoring the collection of revenues, so that social sector programmes can be funded. Secondly, NGOs can hardly implement schemes of redistributive justice that involve transferring of resources from the better to the worse-off sections of society. Thirdly, the non-governmental sector cannot establish and strengthen institutions that will implement social policy. These tasks simply lie outside the pale of civil society activism. NGOs can lobby for and mobilise people for social and economic rights. But ultimately the realisation of these rights depends largely upon the structures of governance, which lie outside of the ambit of civil society agents.

Across dominant streams of thought and policy prescriptions, the general consensus seems to be that the government is the problem. Instead of trying to make the state deliver what it has promised through constitutions, laws, and rhetorical flourishes, policymakers and advocates of civil society organisations would rather establish parallel systems, which can substitute for the state in areas of service delivery. And yet one significant factor inhibits the realisation of this plan, civil society agents are neither in the business of making policy, nor in the business of implementing these policies. They are in the business of creating, fostering, nurturing, and reproducing informed public opinion that can be brought to bear upon the making and implementation of policy. Citizen activism, public vigilance, informed public opinion, a free media, and a multiplicity of social associations, are a vital precondition for democracy. It is only a vibrant civil society that can prevent the political elite from lapsing on its commitments and responsibilities. Correspondingly civil society has to keep watch on the implementation of policy. In 1790, the eminent Irish orator, wit, legal luminary, and Member of British Parliament, John Curran (1750–1817) had suggested insightfully that 'the condition on which god hath given liberty to man is eternal vigilance'. It is this very task that politics entrusts to civil society.

More significantly we should not lose sight of what the state's obligations to the citizens are. The political philosopher, Thomas Nagel, has suggested that the social rules which determine the basic structure of a state are coercively imposed. Notably these rules are imposed in the name of the members. 'Without being given a choice, we are assigned a role in the collective life of a particular society. The society makes us responsible for its acts, which are taken in our name and on which, in a democracy we may even have some influence; and it holds us responsible for obeying its norms; thereby supporting the institutions through which advantages and disadvantages are created and distributed. Insofar as those institutions admit arbitrary inequalities, we are, even though the responsibility has been simply handed to us, responsible for them, and we therefore have standing to ask why we should accept them' (Nagel Vol. 111 2005: 113–47). Nagel points out that the citizens have the right to challenge the arbitrary inequalities produced and reproduced by the economic, the social, and the political order, because in a democratic state this order is constructed in the name of the citizens. Not only does the state have the power to institutionalise and mandate a just order to remedy the ills of the human condition, it also has the obligation to do so. It cannot call upon the NGO sector to bail it out of its current difficulties, which have been created by its own incompetence, corruption, and insensitivity to the needs and the aspirations of the citizens. Nor should the NGO sector believe that it can provide an alternative to the state.

More significantly this sector cannot provide such an alternative not only because it lacks the power, the responsibility, and the accountability of the state, but because till today the citizens of India continue to hold the state responsible for many things despite the pluralisation of the state to accommodate the NGO sector, and despite globalisation, which in the eyes of many scholars has waved a magic wand and shrunk the state. Scholars, activists, and donor agencies, and policymakers might just wish to create and fund organisations outside the state to perform the functions of the latter. But as various research surveys show, in India at least, the citizens show a strong preference for the state in matters ranging from social justice for the doubly disadvantaged to delivery of social goods.

An All India survey conducted in 2007 reinforces this conviction.[2] In the context of the delivery of social and economic goods, the respondents were given a choice between three options: direct government provision, cash transfers, and creation of opportunity for all. A vast majority seem to prefer that the government plays a direct role in providing these goods to the citizens. Of particular interest is the finding that citizens want the state to undertake responsibility for employment. With the advent of globalisation the nature of employment has undergone a radical change. A shift from employment from the public to the private sector as an employer, and the opening up of new sources of employment constitutes one of the main features of globalising India. Yet on five of the seven criteria related to good employment: job security, healthcare, retirement benefits, respectability, and overall job satisfaction, the majority preferred government jobs. The preferred option is for government jobs for low wages to all, rather than high wages to a few. The main motive for preferring government jobs is security of job tenure. The desire of almost 50 per cent of the respondents that the government should invest in wage employment, as against 34 per cent who preferred imparting of training and entrepreneurial skills for self-employment, and 17 per cent felt that the government should assure credit to new entrepreneurs.

Across all classifications, the majority of the respondents are of the opinion that the government should provide jobs for the underprivileged women, disabled and the weaker sections of society. Though there is no significant difference in government support for the underprivileged across respondents, the vast majority prefers reservations in government jobs and in educational institutions, 17 per cent favour cash transfers, and 21 per cent opportunities for all. Reservations for SCs and STs have the backing of all sections of the respondents, because this plays a positive role in motivating people to raise their standard of life. Yet on the issue of reservations, a majority of the respondents across economic classes and social groups felt that government's policy on assistance has to take into account both social and economic status. Assistance based on purely social status has been negated by a majority of the respondents, even those respondents who belong to the marginalised social groups. Those in high income groups believe that better access to health and education is important for the overall development of the underprivileged, and that this should be assured by the government.

Ninety per cent of our respondents felt that the government should provide low cost education compared to private and missionary schools. This response is across categories: large town, small town, and villages. The main incentives are the mid-day meals to schoolchildren provided by government schools, because these schools are recognised, because they are easily accessible, and because they provide education in the mother tongue. However, when it came to which institutions are best for their child's future, a majority of the high income group that is 77 per cent, 60 per cent of the medium income group and 50 per cent of the low income group, across locations, think that private or missionary schools compare much better to government schools. If money was not a consideration, respondents prefer sending their children to private schools as these provide higher quality of education, better sports facilities, and more qualified teachers. At the same time it was felt that it is the responsibility of the government to provide quality education, subsidise education, regulate fees, or give cash transfers to private households. These households can then choose which school to spend the cash voucher on. However, the government is held responsible for the provision of, or regulation of primary education.

The government has an extensive system of public health system in rural and in urban areas, and aims to provide adequate healthcare for all. Various health schemes and programmes targeted at specific beneficiaries such as pulse polio, and medication for tuberculosis have been launched from time to time. Yet many respondents prefer to go to private medical practitioners. The reasons for this preference range from the sub-standard quality of health provided at public healthcare centres, the paperwork required to get free treatment, inconvenient timings, and inaccessible location of these centres. A higher proportion among the low income groups—largely the scheduled castes and rural population—go to government healthcare facilities for long-term illness, because they are not able to afford private healthcare clinics. In the rural areas private healthcare facilities are not available, and for low income groups these facilities are not affordable. The data indicates a discernable shift from public to private healthcare facilities for medium and high income groups.

Yet leaving healthcare to the private providers is not what most respondents desire. When asked to choose between different possible roles that the government can play; direct provision or partial provision by the government account for almost a third of the respondents. One in every ten respondents wants the government to regulate and subsidise health services, and feels that it is the responsibility of the government to do so. The respondents who belonged to poorer households strongly desire that the government should play a direct role in the provision of health, while the richer respondents opine that the government could partially charge for this service.

Our data shows that most of the respondents from lower income groups and the scheduled castes and tribes desire that the government provides housing and shelter to all in accordance with the national agenda of Housing for All and the Indira Awas Yojana. The findings of the survey further establish that respondents do not feel that utilities should be privatised, or that specific sub tasks, such as fixing water meters, should be outsourced to private agencies in order to ensure greater efficiency. Across sections of the respondents, there seems to be a general preference for direct government provision of these facilities, with even the higher income groups less in favour of privatisation of water supply and electricity.

Clearly, political expectations that it is the responsibility of the government to provide for basic needs, is much stronger than the expectation that the government should institutionalise a system that would allow people to meet their needs, such as providing a legal framework for market transactions. The irony is manifest. Despite the poor performance of the Indian state in the social sector, despite the fact that scholars and activists have been disillusioned by the non-performance of the state, across the board, citizens continue to have high expectations of the state.

CONCLUSION

This is not to say that civil society does not matter. Citizen activism, public vigilance, informed public opinion, a free media, and a multiplicity of social associations, are a vital precondition for democracy. It is only a vibrant civil society that can prevent the political elite from lapsing on its commitments and responsibilities. 'We', writes Quentin Skinner, 'have no realistic prospects of taking direct control of the political process in any large-scale contemporary state. [But] ... there are many areas of public life, short of directly controlling the actions of the executive, where greater public participation might serve to improve the accountability of our soi distant representatives, if only by pressurizing them into taking greater account of the actual beliefs and aspirations of a majority of the citizens' (Skinner 1992: 211–24).

Yet whatever are the virtues of civil society, and these are many, we should keep in mind that civil society provides but the political and the politicised context for political society. The line between civil and political society is fuzzy, and more conceptual than real, but briefly whereas agents in political society are organised to take over political power, agents in civil society are organised to provide informed and critical political perspectives on the manner in which this power is exercised. Civil society is a companion concept/set of practices of political society. Therefore, the links between civil society actors and representatives need to be strengthened, and the domains of civil and political society have to be seen not as alternatives to each other but as prerequisites for each other. For this civil society should understand its own place in collective life, that of a vigilant caretaker, that of a monitor, and that of an initiator of policy. The responsibility for making and implementing policy remains with the state. This is what the people of India seem to desire, and in democracies, the wishes of the people should count.

ENDNOTES

[1] In 1967 Myron Weiner exploring the reasons for the success of the Congress, suggested that the reason why the party could maintain its hegemony was that it could find a place for all. It could for instance incorporate those who were dedicated to social service and who were moved by an egalitarian spirit. 'The spirit of self-sacrifice and self-abnegation' he wrote, 'which had a long honourable tradition in Hinduism and which was reformulated by Gandhi has a place in the local Congress party'. But it could also provide a place for those who wanted status and power, for people who had specific grievances and demands, for those people who were looking for conviviality,

and for those who were committed to national integration, economic development, secularism, and representative government (Kothari 1970; Weiner 1967: 472–4).

[2] The survey was conducted by Indicus for a Ford funded project titled 'Globalisation and the State in India' that Pratap B. Mehta and I directed between 2004 and 2007. The objective of the project was to evaluate state capacity during the period of globalisation. The findings have been documented. The All India survey administered a questionnaire to 7,500 citizens across 14 districts in 13 states, both rural and urban, with at least 55 responses per district. Though the focus of the survey was on the underprivileged, all segments of the population were surveyed in order to glean a comparative perspective. Male respondents formed 70 per cent of those surveyed, the Other Backward Castes constituted 28.42 per cent, and scheduled castes 27.38 per cent of those who were surveyed. The country was divided into four zones, and four districts were randomly chosen from the southern and the northern regions, and three each from east and west. Each district was broken up into three parts: large urban centre, small-urban centre, and rural. In a particular district one large town, one small town, and about 12–14 villages were chosen across four blocks. Within each cluster, in rural and urban areas, every tenth household was chosen for the survey. To investigate whether perceptions differ because of residence in a metropolis, or a small town or village, different types of places of residence were also taken into account in the sampling, and the selection process. The sampling included all types of regions: large urban, semi-rural/semi-urban and rural. This ensured the spread of respondents within the rural and the urban areas. I wish to express my gratitude to Ford Foundation and to Bishnu Mohapatra for support for the project.

REFERENCES

Burnham, Walter Dean. 1970. *Critical Elections and the Mainsprings of American Politics*. New York: Norton. 176–9.

Franco, Jean. 1989. 'The Nation as Imagined Community', in H. Aram Veeser (ed.), *The New Historicism*. New York: Routledge. 204–12.

Goulner, Alvin. 1980. 'Civil Society in Capitalism and Socialism', in Alvin Goulner (ed.), *The Two Marxisms: Contradictions and Anomalies in the Development of Theory*. London: Macmillan. 355–73.

Kothari, Rajni. 1970. *Politics in India*. New Delhi: Orient Longman.

Nagel, Thomas. 2005. 'The Problem of Global Justice'. *Philosophy and Pubic Affairs*. Vol. 33. 113–47.

Seth, D. L. 2004. 'Globalisation and New Politics of Micro-Movements'. *Economic and Political Weekly*. Vol. 39. No. 1. 45–58.

Sisson, Richard and Ramashray Roy. 1990. 'Introduction: The Congress and the Indian Party System', in Richard Sisson and Ramashray Roy (ed.), *Changing Basis of Congress Support*. Vol. No. 1. Delhi: Sage. 1–33.

Skinner, Quentin. 1992. 'On Justice, the Common Good and the Priority of Liberty', in Chantal Mouffe (ed.), *Dimensions of Radical Democracy: Pluralism, Citizenship, Community*. London: Verso. 211–4.

Weiner, Myron. 1967. *Party Building in a New Nation*. Chicago: University of Chicago Press. 472–4.

4

State, Planning and Politics of Irrigation Development: A Critique of Large Dams

Satyajit Singh

> When I walked around the site, I thought that these days, the biggest temple and mosque and gurdwara is the place where man works for the good of mankind. Which place can be greater than Bhakra Nangal, where thousands of men have worked or shed their blood and sweat and laid down their lives as well? Where can be a holier place than this; which can we regard as higher?
>
> —Pt Jawaharlal Nehru, 1954

IRRIGATION: A POLITICAL PERSPECTIVE

Of late, civil engineers, sociologists and economists have dominated the discourse on irrigation. The civil engineers have concentrated, and continue to do so, on the control, measurement and distribution of water through a centralised mechanism. This

---

This chapter draws upon some arguments presented by the author in *Taming the Waters: The Political Economy of Large Dams in India*, Oxford University Press, Delhi: 1997.

approach firmly believes that the alleviation of social problems related to water can be achieved through technological means (Buckley 1880; Cotton 1874; Clibborne 1891). The sociologists, on the other hand, have acted as a sort of a bridge between the farmers and the state in relation to problems associated with access to and distribution of water among the landed in the command area. They have emphasised farmers' participation with the irrigation bureaucracy to bring about an efficient utilisation of water (Wade 1988; Chambers 1988). The economists have also helped shape irrigation policies. Their approach has been of cost-benefit analysis, through which they have attempted to arrive at the most appropriate irrigation project for any region. As such this intervention is also of a technical nature, and has not paid due attention to the ecological impact, and in some cases to even the social aspects of irrigation (Gadgil 1948; Raj 1960; Sovani and Rath 1960; Sinha and Bhatia 1982).

These methodologies are unable to solve the problems raised by peoples' conflicts related to water. In this chapter a political approach to the irrigation question in India will be attempted. It will be emphasised that water is an important factor in the agricultural production. Though water is a common property resource, rights over the use of water are related to the changes in, and control over the production process. People's relationship to water is a dynamic one. Various social groups constantly manipulate the use of this resource in their attempt to monopolise production. Thus irrigation has to be understood in relation to the wider changes in agricultural production and to social change. A study of the role of the state, and the nature of its mediation between the different social groups in relation to water, would help us understand the rights over irrigation, and its use for specific purposes.

The political approach asserts that a theory of irrigation needs to emphasise that irrigation is an important factor in agricultural production, and thereby examine the social composition of its use, distribution, access, and its international linkages. Irrigation is analysed as a factor of agricultural production, and like other factors of production there is intense contestation over access and control over this resource. Irrigation, then, is not just the supply of water to the crops, but an important factor in agricultural production itself. Its use or abuse reflects a pattern of social relations that exist in society. Any study of irrigation, which attempts to look at irrigation technologies and management practices in isolation from the social and material relations of society, is bound to be limited. While irrigation has played the role of accentuating inequalities, it also has the potential for creating an egalitarian social structure.

This chapter also attempts to study the politics of state planning and irrigation development in post-colonial India from a political perspective. It seeks to understand the role of irrigation, particularly through large dams, in perpetuating the inequalities in Indian society. This study within a political economy framework would help us understand the instrumentality of the Indian state in the process of development and how these policies assist in the accumulation process and affect the different sections of the society.

STATE, PLANNING AND IRRIGATION

The relationship between politics and economics is a fundamental one for social scientists to study. In a seminal piece, the noted political economist Terence Byres has developed certain propositions concerning the 'intertwining of state, and class with planning' (Byres 1994). According to Byres, development planning is a form of mediation between the state and civil society. A study of development planning, according to him, must be located in a particular social formation. Attention must also be paid to how accumulation takes place as a result of a specific programme of planning. The transition and the structural changes brought about by the instrumentality of development planning should be examined. Under this political economy model, the institutions, techniques of planning and the nature of plan implementation should be discussed. Here, as elsewhere, Byres is highly critical of the study of the planning process from a purely technical viewpoint and advocates a rigorous political economy approach that is truly interdisciplinary in nature.

An analysis of planning is crucial for our study of the political economy of planned irrigation development in India. It would not only help us to highlight the nature of irrigation planning, but also point to the instrumentality of the Indian state in this process, and how the policies adopted affect different classes[1] in society. This will help us answer questions like irrigation for whom, for what purpose, and when. It will, indeed take us to examining the very nature of the Indian state itself in its moment of intervention in the planning and development of irrigation projects.

While examining irrigation development this chapter shows how these dominant classes benefit from the irrigation technology that is adopted, and in turn how they shape such policies. The rhetoric of feeding the increasing number of hungry mouths, by more than doubling productivity, might indeed sound sincere and look like a great achievement statistically speaking. However, the flip side of such a phenomenal 'development' has been to push the weaker and marginal sections of society into market relations, whose advantages have accrued to a select few. Indeed, if one were to speak in terms of the legitimate 'entitlements' (Sen 1981) of the poor, then, one would be forced to acknowledge a continuous shrinking of their meagre package. Or one might notice changed relations of production which have peripheralised them from land altogether. How irrigation planning has brought this about is being studied here.

Though in relative terms, the agricultural sector has been neglected throughout the plans, nevertheless the foundation of agricultural planning and development was laid down prior to independence. Apart from the documents of the National Planning Committee (NPC), these foundations can be traced to two other sources (National Planning Committee, 1947)—M. Visvesvaraya's book on planning, which earned him a place in the NPC (Visvesvaraya 1936), and another by an eminent nationalist economist Khagendra Sen, on economic reconstruction, which had a Foreword by Nehru (Sen 1939). The planners emphasised the use of 'stable' irrigation in the form of storage systems under medium and major projects, in other words they spoke of dams. Minor irrigation technology like tanks and wells were not given priority due to their 'uncertain' nature. At the same time, it was emphasised that the output from Indian agriculture was low in comparison to the developed countries, and there was an urgent need to learn from their modern methods of farming, fertiliser use and animal husbandry. Agricultural development for the industrial planners of modern India emerges out of the overall objective of the bourgeoisie in the process of capitalist development requiring cheap labour, cheap food, a growing surplus, and a market.

It is well-known that the technical intervention in irrigation during the colonial rule had greatly transformed social and agrarian relations. It led to the pandering of certain classes at the cost of others. Opposition to hydel power projects had begun prior to independence and there was enough evidence of water-related conflicts (Gadgil and Guha 1994). Yet the proprietary and hydraulic rights were not disturbed in independent India, as the emergent Indian state could not do without the support of the landed elite.

Irrigation planning has been high on the agenda of the builders of modern India and irrigation has made giant strides forward since independence. By 1979, we had 1,554 large dams, mostly constructed after independence, with a financial outlay of nearly Rs 70,000 crores allocated to irrigation which is nearly 10 per cent of the total public sector outlay (GOI 1992). The irrigation potential of major and medium surface irrigation projects increased from 9.7 million (m) hectares (ha) in 1950 to 34.2 m. ha. in 1991–92.[2] Foodgrains output has risen from 70 m tonnes in 1950 and climbed up to 195 m tonnes in the mid-nineties. Such figures are indeed impressive. However, these achievements have not been without their costs. The Sixth Plan document of the Planning Commission admitted that the huge investment made in irrigation has yielded disappointingly low results. The national average of food production per hectare for irrigated land is 1.7 tonnes of grains, while in some countries it is as high as 4.5 tonnes. It is suggested by some critics that the poor performance is due to an emphasis on major and medium irrigation as will be discussed in this chapter.

The allocation to irrigation and flood control through the various five-year plans has continuously increased. The expenditure has galloped, more than seventy times, from Rs 459.77 crores in the First Plan, to Rs 32,525.29 crores in the Eighth Plan. About

70 per cent of the total expenditure was earmarked for major and medium irrigation.[3] A major reason for this huge investment in irrigation is due to the desire of the Indian planners to meet the requirements of the ever rising Indian population that is expected to reach 1,350 million by the year 2015, requiring a doubling of food production to 365 million tonnes.[4] It is perceived that in an agro-climatic region like India, any increase in food production is necessarily linked to investments in irrigation. Yet, it is this rhetoric of providing food for the masses and the myth that modern science would help the state do so, has helped the state legitimise its intervention.

Just a year after independence and before the beginning of planned development in India, about 160 large-scale dams were being considered, investigated or executed (Hansen 1966). The First Plan itself emphasised the need to develop major and medium irrigation projects, allocating about 22.2 per cent of the plan outlay in the public sector for the purpose. This was in continuation with the biases expressed against minor irrigation by the NPC members. The British legacy of emphasising the 'sub-system', dominated by civil engineering continues. In this move to 'modernise', no effort whatsoever was made to go back to learn from the traditional irrigation science, which took into account sociological and ecological variables as well, apart from mechanical and technical aspects.

The Second Five Year Plan went a step further to institutionalise and codify the colonial experience in irrigation. The planners clearly pointed out the need to train more engineers, both degree and diploma holders, if India's irrigation needs were to be met. The Third Plan document highlighted the requirements of technical personnel for irrigation development, and implied that engineers—civil, electrical and mechanical—were the only professionals required for irrigation development. The total number of degree and diploma holders required in the Second and Third Plan only added up to as many as 53,200, of which 30,500 were to be civil engineers, 17,900 electrical engineers and 4,900 mechanial engineers (GOI 1961: 394). There was absolutely no mention of sociologists, political scientists, economists or historians who could have been called upon to render invaluable service in this area. The vision of the planners was to fill the irrigation departments of the country with engineers. The resultant emphasis on steel, cement, and massive designs and huge headworks dominated the irrigation map of India.

Kumar and Rajagopalan, in an interesting paper, highlighted the technological prejudice in favour of dams and canals through a survey of research work of the irrigation establishment. They pointed out that the establishment perceived the task of providing irrigation as limited to the construction of dams and canals (Kumar and Rajagopalan 1993). The irrigation establishment has not been very receptive to criticisms based on social, ecological and economic aspects of large dams and has left no stone unturned to stall moves to alter their decisions, as they did in the cases of Sardar Sarovar and Tehri projects. In his writings on irrigation development in the western parts of United States, Donald Worster has developed the notion of political alliance that helps perpetuate a particular ideology and notion of irrigation development (Worster 1985). In the following pages we will discuss the role of the irrigation bureaucracy in aligning with different classes to perpetuate the technology of large dams and the myth that irrigation by large dams is the only solution to the water needs of the country.

THE POLITICS OF COST-BENEFIT ANALYSIS

The criteria to consider the viability of a project has also changed with time and changing social concerns. The returns from irrigation, under the British rule were quite high and investment in irrigation was considered to be good business. People in Britain even bought shares in the irrigation companies that were set up. When the returns from irrigation began to decline after most of the restoration work of old irrigation systems were complete, it became necessary to follow policies that would safeguard the capital raised in the United Kingdom for the execution of irrigation projects in India. It was decided by a British Parliamentary Committee in 1879 that the 'simple interest on the capital costs of works at the beginning of a year should be less than direct or indirect receipt for the year'. Irrigation continued to be considered as an economic investment and the criterion for evaluating an irrigation project was its productivity test. It may be noted, however, that 'unproductive' works were also undertaken to provide drought relief under exceptional circumstances. These did not have to meet the strict productivity criterion.

In independent India, the financial productivity test of returns to the state, designed by the British, continued to be rigidly applied till 1964, to select irrigation projects to be undertaken by the state. However, the financial rate of return was lowered from 6 per cent per annum, prior to independence, to 3.75 per cent per annum in 1949, and was changed from time to time, rising to 4.5 per cent from 1954–60 and eventually to 5 per cent in 1960. It can be assumed that the internal rate of return was increased in an effort to maintain financial discipline. While this method of evaluation for the feasibility of a project continued, there was no strict appraisal of the returns.

This narrow monetarist approach for project evaluation in the form of internal rate of return was replaced during the Third Plan, actually in 1964, by a wider criterion of social benefit-cost analysis (GOI 1972a: 256). It took into account the monetary economics of agriculture in unirrigated land, and compared it to the monetary economics of irrigated agriculture. After deducting charges for land levelling, interest on capital, depreciation and administrative expenses, it recommended a minimum benefit-cost (BC) ratio of 1.5 for considering a project viable. This shift was facilitated with the entry of the World Bank and other international financial agencies into the irrigation and hydel power development schemes in the sixties. Theoretically, the more sophisticated concept of benefit-cost analysis took into account not only the financial costs and benefits, but also accounted for wider social, institutional, organisational and political factors as well. As Gittinger, an authority on agricultural accounting, puts it simply, cost is 'anything that reduces the objectives (and resources), while benefits is anything that contributes to the objectives (and resources)' (Gittinger 1981). In other words, the indirect costs of irrigation and benefits from it, i.e., externalities, also need to be taken into account. However, this was not reflected in the new approach that was adopted.

The benefit-cost ratio analysis as proposed by the Irrigation Commission was a step forward. However, the new method of calculation for irrigation did not carry the wide implications of social cost-benefit analysis, or say, Gittinger's definition. Understandably, economists soon challenged the newly-accepted BC method. Nilakantha Rath, a reputed irrigation economist, wrote a very important critique of the BC analysis method (Rath 1976). The new method had, in fact, been accepted so that the wider social effects could have been measured. However, Rath pointed out that, 'indirect and secondary-tertiary' effects of irrigation were excluded from these calculations, as they were considered 'extremely difficult to estimate'. This was contrary to the suggestions made by the existing literature on social costing. With the emphasis remaining on agricultural productivity and economic returns, this approach had many problems. Rath's immediate critique was, however, limited to the problems in the state accepted BC analysis method. Rath demonstrated that there were enough ways to tamper with the benefit-cost ratio, if utmost care and a uniform mode of calculation were not provided. He showed:

> One, as receipts and expenses are to be calculated from the "social point of view", opportunity cost of material imported (such as fertiliser or farm machinery) or the element of tax or subsidy in the inputs should be calculated. Two, as the net value of the produce of irrigation is being calculated, the calculation of land revenue ... would amount to double counting. Three, there are problems associated with accounting for expenditure on hired human labour ... as the "opportunity cost of hired labour is equal to its wage rate, while that of family labour has only zero opportunity cost". Four, in valuing gross receipts, the "farm harvest price" should be taken into account, after deducting taxes and including subsidies. Five, while calculating present and expected yield, an average of yields in good, bad and indifferent years needs to be taken into account; which is usually not done. Six, direct benefit/costs (flood control downstream or shortage of water to factories upstream) should be taken into account. Seven, the capital costs and value of outputs should be treated for inflationary or deflationary trends. Eight, utmost care should be taken in valuing the capital costs. For instance, costs of initial surveys and investigations should not be excluded as was being done. Nine, in

calculating the BC ratio, one should "calculate the present value of the stream of benefits over the life of the project". Ten, it is important to "highlight the costs that the economy incurs by prolonging the construction of a project ... and by the irrigation potential not being exploited at the earliest". Eleven, the rate of interest to be used, and the method of computing benefits and costs should be uniform for all projects. Twelve, project reports are at times incomplete. This can provide a favourable BC ratio, while meticulously completed ones may not get clearance (Rath 1976: 16–26).

A detailed presentation of Rath's critique indicates that not only are there problems with this prescribed BC model, but also that the calculation of the BC ratio is a tricky operation and therefore open to manipulation if the method and data of doing so is not under public scrutiny. In his painstaking critique, Rath has however failed to provide for an important variable which concern us today—ecology. In any modern irrigation scheme, taking this into account will help make better sense of the BC ratio. In addition, the use of weights and handicaps in calculating the BC ratio as it affects the different social groups (also stated in principle by the Planning Commission, but not followed) will go a long way in apportioning productive resources among different sections of the society. We have discussed that irrigation being an important factor in the production process can act both as an agent for alleviating social inequalities, as much as increasing social inequalities. As the goal of alleviating inequalities is enshrined in the Indian polity, we can argue for efforts to be made at the planning stage of irrigation projects to try to implement land reforms, through rationing irrigation, and using irrigation for rural development by providing people water rights which are not proportional to land rights. These social welfare measures should also be included in the calculations of project evaluation. Ecological variables, like submergence of genetic resources, environmental degradation, and loss of land due to waterlogging and salinity, too need to be taken into account. Further, according to this method, a given project is evaluated on its own strengths and weaknesses without even considering the possible alternatives to the project. A detailed comparative assessment needs to be done to examine the different alternatives and their potential.

Similarly, there is a great divergence between ex-ante assumptions and ex-post realities of irrigation projects. This should be kept in mind while evaluating new projects. Certain weightage should also be given to labour-intensive irrigation technologies, in comparison to capital-intensive ones, in surplus labour and capital scarce countries like India. In India today, ex-post BC calculations are not carried out, which would conclude whether a project did fulfill its goal or not. For irrigation evaluation to be truly effective, there should be a comparative social and ecological cost-benefit analysis that takes the above arguments into consideration.

While deciding on the construction of any new large irrigation project, economists have to consider certain other factors as well. One of them is the uncertainty and irreversibility of investment. Most econometric models of investment are based on the implicit assumption that investment expenditures are reversible, i.e., if the investment climate deteriorates; the project can be wound up. However, most large irrigation projects are irreversible, i.e., one cannot disinvest. This is so because the capital and equipment are location and region specific. It is in the nature of the headworks of large-scale irrigation projects, that they cannot be undone and moved to other sites. Large irrigation projects invariably incorporate an element of inflexibility; the economic environment can change, the cost of energy might rise or fall, the ecological variables might change, but large multi-purpose projects involving heavy fixed costs cannot be modified. Scarce capital can thus be tied up in a massive project producing energy or water in the wake of uncertainties. So the expenditures must be viewed as sunk costs.

Water resources are especially vulnerable to conditions of uncertainty, which arise from the unstable geophysical processes and unpredictable future economic events. Particularly important is the uncertainty concerning future societal goals. Retrospective examination shows that several large dams have been built with little acceptance of the possibility that actual conditions might turn out to be substantially different from those assumed in the plans, such as the ecological variables and water availability calculations as such projects take nearly a decade or more to construct, while the preliminary calculations are done much before the construction starts. Futurological studies cannot be accurate, but by accepting the possibility of change and thus allowing for a more complete expression of uncertainty surrounding future goals and objectives, one can opt for more flexible, less risky, and thus, more sustainable alternatives. It therefore becomes imperative to accommodate calculations that can cope with the probable and the unforeseen.

Attempts should also be made to avoid uncertainty at the level of designing development plans. To reduce uncertainty, mostly at the research and data-gathering pre-planning stages, uncertainty calculations should be built into the planning process. If an irreversible decision is made, the option of disinvesting is lost. Therefore this lost option value must be included as part of the cost of the investment. The value of the project must exceed the purchase and installation cost by an amount equal to the value of keeping the option to invest these resources elsewhere alive—an opportunity cost of investing.

The cost-benefit analysis does not take into account the energy required to build and operate a dam. A project is evaluated strictly on monetary terms and no 'energy accounting' is done, which can do more justice to ecologically controversial projects. Where such energy accounting has been carried out the results are surprising. For example, Linney and Harrison pointed out that constructing a large dam on a big river requires an enormous amount of earth to be moved to raise a structure for which access roads have to be built over long distances. Similarly, diesel and petrol is used to power the mixing plant on the site and run the heavy earthmoving equipment over the many years that are required for construction. This energy spent to construct a dam should be far less than the amount of energy a dam should release in its lifetime. However, Linney and Harison pointed out that, 'Some dams built in the past create a questionable net gain in energy' (Linney and Harrison 1981: 33).

To be more specific, Williams who studied the energy accounts of the New Melones Dam in California, USA, concluded that the dam would result in a net loss of energy. 'From the projected average year's 430 million kilowatt hours of electricity, Williams subtracted the energy costs of construction and maintenance: the loss of an existing power plant, energy for irrigation and pumping, and the energy costs of reservoir recreation. William's bottom line? A net loss of 39 million kilowatt hour per year' (*emphasis added*) (Palmer 1982: 70). Critics may argue that the New Melones Dam was an exception, or that his methodology is debatable, but there is no arguing against the notion that for a proper calculation of the BC ratio, we should conduct 'energy accounting' as done by Williams. Project evaluation should also take into account the possible 'cost escalation', 'delays' and 'targets not achieved', on the basis of past performance.

We have evidence to suggest that looking at the method of evaluating and sanctioning a large dam strictly from an economic point of view is highly inadequate, to say the least. The shift from the financial productivity test to a benefit-cost method was approved, so as to widen the ambit of evaluating irrigation projects. However, the discussion above suggests that the prescribed new method, though a step forward from the old one, was perhaps not very effective in its purpose. Why then was this criterion adopted? For an answer to that, one needs to move from a discussion on method to that of practice. The adoption of the new method had to do with the fact that perhaps it was less stringent about the financial benefits, and it is possible, that like the latter British period, new irrigation projects were failing to meet the requirements of the productivity criterion. There must have been enough pressure from vested groups like the landlords, politicians, the irrigation bureaucracy, for the adoption of a less strict evaluation criterion. The irrigation outlay rose by about 91.27 per cent annually after 1966 till the end of the Eighth Plan (projection for the latter date), compared to an increase of a mere 9.43 per cent annually during 1956–66. These figures suggest that the new method did open the 'flood-gates' for sanctioning new irrigation projects. Interestingly, along with the increased outlay, the current account losses too increased from Rs 144.80 million in 1960–1 to Rs 565.90 million in 1967–8, i.e., large-scale irrigation was promoted not only with large capital subsidies, but even the current costs were subsidised year after year. It can thus be safely said that the shift to a benefit-cost analysis, made it possible for the irrigation planners to continue to emphasise the need for large irrigation projects, in spite of the fact that the economic performance of large projects were hardly satisfactory.

GREEN REVOLUTION AND LARGE DAMS

At this stage it would be worthwhile to pause and look at the status of planned development in India at that time. By the end of the Third Plan, it was perceived that the planning process was in crisis. The draft Fourth Plan was shelved and replaced by annual plans for the period 1966–9. The neglect of agricultural development and the emphasis on industrialisation had led to the emergence of serious agrarian problems, which culminated in the most severe drought in independent India during 1966–7. Food imports to the tune of 19 metric tonne were brought in to meet the shortfall. The widespread rural hunger was also a reflection of the changing social structure triggered by the logic of accumulation of industrialisation without a change in the pattern of ownership of land, which had an impact on the agrarian structure and led to a gradual commoditisation of both land and labour. These developments in the sixties led to the designing of the NAS or the New Agricultural Strategy (Rao 1994).

Yet despite the perceived crisis in planning, the NAS did not in any way lead to a shift from the Nehru-Mahalanobis model. The New Agricultural Strategy ignored the long-standing demands of land reforms and the problems of the peasantry and the small cultivators and was an attempt to placate the kulak class through commercialisation of agriculture. In fact, it may be pointed out that the choice of green revolution, as the method of enhancing agricultural production, was undertaken to suit the needs of the industrial bourgeoisie. The green revolution led to a spurt in agro-based industry in the form of pumps, tractors, harvesters, etc., and also helped towards the expansion of certain sectors like cement and steel that were required for the construction of large irrigation projects. Land based agrarian conflicts had intensified on the eve of independence itself. Apart from the famous Telengana and Tebhaga movements, peasant insurgency and unrest was marked in Gujarat, Uttar Pradesh, Bihar, Kerala and Tamil Nadu, finally culminating in the naxalite movement (Desai 1979). The significant factor behind these conflicts was land and the associated question of livelihood. In 1982, 3.98 per cent of the rural households owned as much as 33.26 per cent of the land. The top 20 per cent of the rural households owned as much as 73.19 per cent of the land, while the bottom 40 per cent held a mere 1.2 per cent of the total landholdings. About 81.34 per cent of the rural households had either no land or less than 2 ha, amounting to 28.67 per cent of the cultivated area (Sharma 1994).

In order to tackle the leftist forces and postpone a debate on the land question, the Congress, the ruling political party of that time, had to win the support of its traditional rural allies in the freedom struggle. These could be categorised as the middle and upper peasantry, a social group below the big landlords who were the collaborators with the British. By the early sixties this social group, which had already acquired enough clout in many state governments, were able to stall all serious attempts at land reforms. The group was unhappy with the way emphasis was given to industrialisation in the development strategy adopted by the country. The state was under enormous pressure to demonstrate its support towards this section.[5]

Against this background there was also a notable shift in the United States policy towards India, whereby they specified that food imports from that country would only be against hard currency payments. In the winter of 1966, Norman Borlaug (popularly known as the father of the green revolution) harvested High Yield Varieties (HYVs) of wheat in different parts of North India and demonstrated to the Indian government that the output was far higher in comparison to the local seeds. Due to a combination of practical compulsions and political choice the NAS was born.

In many parts of India, under this scheme, an attempt was made to increase the productivity of the agro-ecosystem through highly subsidised inputs like fertilisers, diesel for pumps, tractors, irrigation, pesticides, biotechnological inputs and other agricultural machinery. The object of the NAS was to obtain self-sufficiency in foodgrain production. The package articulated a growth programme assisted by green revolution technology in better-endowed and high-productive areas. The emphasis of the NAS was in the introduction of HYVs for which an assured supply of water was required. This resulted in a renewed emphasis on irrigation, particularly in the form of large dams and tubewell development. The ability of tubewells to raise large amounts of water at a particular time was essential for the success of the HYV seeds. While public sector investment in major and medium irrigation schemes continued to grow, aided by the new method of project evaluation, the development of tubewell irrigation was left to the private sector, aided by institutional finance including finance from the World Bank. The Third Plan saw a ten-fold increase from the Second Plan in the allocation of institutional finance rising from just Rs 19.15 crores to a phenomenal Rs 115.29 crores. Institutional finance eventually shot to Rs 3,311.91 crores by the Seventh Plan. Individual farmers could take loans for the installation of motorised tubewells. The introduction of tubewells was further encouraged by the setting up of the Rural Electrification Corporation (REC) to energise the pumps and the establishment of the Agro-Industries Corporation with an objective of supplying machinery.

The green revolution was made attractive through subsidised inputs and government support of remunerative prices. The new pricing and marketing policies were effectively carried out with the setting up of Agricultural Prices Commission (APC) and Food Corporation of India (FCI). The government also set up various seed corporations and agricultural universities to provide services to farmers in their shift to and use of HYV seeds. These structural changes in agricultural strategy encouraged an increasing drift towards capitalist agriculture. Certain institutional changes were also made. Simultaneously there was a shift from the community development programme and the formation of co-operatives emphasised in the First and Second Plan, to more individualistic form of ownership and cultivation. It was argued that the panchayats were financially constrained and strongly influenced by the local elites as such the policies they followed were biased against smaller farmers. This changed in the early 1960s, largely under the influence of United States aid that favoured private capital and emphasised the need for a separate administrative set-up involving a subsidy and credit package.

Since the 1960s there has been no major change in the agrarian development strategy. Over the years the green revolution model has been consolidated and efforts have been made at its extension and wider adoption. It is important to consider whether the green revolution did achieve its objective of increasing agricultural production. Though at face value it seems that the production of foodgrains has nearly doubled from 95 mt in 1967–8, yet, the rate of growth in foodgrain production do not show any steep climb since 1967–8. The climb is gradual and continues to be marked by significant drops in bad harvest years (World Bank 1984: 93).

Wheat cultivation has been a great success in Punjab, Haryana and western Uttar Pradesh—which jointly produce two-thirds of the total wheat produced in the country. Rice cultivation has not been as much of a success, with only Andhra Pradesh, Tamil Nadu and Kerala fairing relatively well. Recent reports suggest an increase in rice cultivation in eastern India. The rate of returns is highest in wheat, rice and cash crops using the green revolution model (Acharya 1992: 112). However, if we take into account the rise in population and compare the per capita increase in foodgrain production between 1968 and 1989, then it has only risen marginally from 460 to 497 grams per person (GOI 1986). While the green revolution has increased foodgrain production in certain regions, it has far from achieved the 'miracle' that it was called to perform of eliminating hunger in the country.

The green revolution has had its critics for a number of reasons. The HYVs were initially given to the big farmers and the Economic Survey of Indian Agriculture (ESIA) considered them as 'progressive farmers' (GOI 1967). It had an inbuilt bias towards the rich farmers for they were able to take advantage of the technology with the application of the whole gamut of inputs which required considerable investment. Some studies showed that while small farmers did benefit from the new seeds (Lipton 1989), the rich benefitted more and the long-term result of this trend was a highly unequal and stratified social order. The objective of the NAS was to identify the areas with high productivity and further enhance their productive capacity through artificial inputs. As a consequence of this policy, the entire agricultural strategy for enhanced production revolved around a few highly endowed regions like Punjab and Haryana, and to a lesser extent Andhra Pradesh and Tamil Nadu at the expense of poorer states like Bihar, Orissa and Madhya Pradesh, leading to an uneven development in the country. In addition, as wheat has been more successful than rice, the western states of Punjab and Haryana had benefitted tremendously.

The postponement of the land question and the emphasis on new technology reaffirmed the government's belief in 'trickle down' theory. However, various critics have commented that this has not taken place. It has in fact been observed that at the prospect of greater returns, leased-out land has increasingly come under personal cultivation at the cost of tenant eviction (Bhalla 1977; Bardhan and Rudra 1978). The area under tenant cultivation had fallen from 20 per cent of the cultivable land in 1953–4 to only 11 per cent in 1970–1 (Dasgupta 1977). Patnaik also pointed out that the proportion of agricultural labourers rose from 28 per cent to 35 per cent between 1951 and 1971, once again indicating a differential social impact (Patnaik 1986). Gaiha in an all India survey provided evidence of increased landlessness between 1968 and 1970, a rise from 25 per cent to 35 per cent among the same set of households. At the same time there was an increasing dependence on wage income to total income (Gaiha 1981). Various studies have also pointed out to the growing dependence of the rural population on agricultural wage work between 1964–5 and 1974–5 in the first decade of the green revolution. At the same time Agarwal pointed out that there has been a decline in the average annual days of agricultural wage employment available per agricultural labourer. There has also been a decline in the annual wage income of agricultural labour households across the country, except in Uttar Pradesh (Agarwal 1986). Biplab Dasgupta aptly sums up that the major social and economic consequences of the new technology was, 'proletarianization of the peasantry and a consequent increase in the number and proportion of landless households, growing concentration of land and assets in fewer hands and widening disparity between the rich and the poor households' (Dasgupta 1977: 372).

LARGE DAMS AFTER THE FOURTH PLAN

The two significant developments in the sixties, viz., a dilution in the economic criterion of project evaluation with the introduction of the benefit-cost ratio at the instance of the World Bank, and the subsequent adoption of the NAS marked by the green revolution model which necessitated the availability of water at recurrent times for HYV seeds, resulted in a watershed in irrigation planning and development in India. Of the 1,554 large dams (including the ones under construction) in 1979, about 1,348 came up after 1952. As against Rs 1,341 crores allocated for irrigation between 1951–66, an amount of Rs 52,437 crores had been earmarked for it during the period 1966–97. The allocation in the Fourth Plan under this head alone matched the outlay in the First, Second and Third Plans together. Infact only 433 large dams existed up to 1965, and 1,121 large dams were constructed or were under construction in the next fourteen years. It may thus be fair to suggest that large dams in India got a major boost after the twin adoption of the BC ratio of evaluation and the NAS.

The construction of large dams had little to do with the adverse climatic and geographical characteristics that made agriculture difficult, but were determined more by political equations. For instance, the presence of the powerful sugarcane lobby (which required water) and the industrial bourgeoisie (which required power) in Maharashtra propelled the state to construct and plan 631 large dams between 1952 and 1979. A little more than 40 per cent of the large dams of the country are found in that state. Water continues to be diverted to the sugarcane fields of Maharashtra, which produce about 13.6 per cent of the total sugarcane in the country. The state also produces about 11 per cent of the groundnut and 19 per cent of the cotton produced in the country. At the same time, nearly 40 per cent of Maharashtra has been declared a drought-prone region. Gujarat also scores very high with 276 large dams, with its sugarcane, groundnut and cotton production amounting to 3.7, 20 and 1.3 per cent respectively of the total production in the country. In comparison, to these two states, the states of West Bengal and Bihar, which have not significantly benefitted from the green revolution, have only 17 and 31 large dams respectively (INCOLD 1979).

With the impetus provided to the green revolution technology in the NAS, along with the availability of cheap credit and indirect subsidies in electricity, another irrigation technology that has benefited is that of tubewells. Much more than canal irrigation, it is the exploitation of groundwater that has grown, almost entirely due to the widespread use of tubewell technology. However, as in the case of large dams, where rich farmers are benefitted, for a farmer with 2 to 4 ha or more land can make a profitable use of tubewell.[6] The advent of tubewells, and their capacity to drain out large amounts of water at a short notice has resulted in the lowering of the water table and the consequent drying up of the shallow wells of small farmers. Particularly important is the role of the tubewell in augmentation of water supply to meet the specific requirements of HYVs. The advent of tubewells has thus increased the disparity in income earnings. As groundwater is a common property resource, it is imperative that it is available to all social groups as against meeting the requirements of a minority with the purchasing power as it does now. Towards this endeavour, there have been calls of regulating the 'groundwater market', which aims at an equitable distribution of water and maintains a close watch on the water quality and the negative ecological impact. However, the spacing regulations of tubewells and some sort of regulation of the groundwater markets have not been implemented with success by the various state bodies (Shah 1993).

Planning and irrigation development strategy in India have created biases against traditional irrigation that have been perpetuated at the level of implementation. In India, the general belief is that the status of a minor irrigation implementation officer is lower than one involved in major projects. The existence of a market in the purchase of remunerative posts in the irrigation bureaucracy as suggested by Wade clearly demonstrates that the engineers want to be where the budgetary allocation is higher (Wade 1982). Budgets of major projects are much larger than they are for minor ones. This bias in the irrigation department gets reflected in the poor implementation of minor schemes. Moreover promotion of minor schemes usually means providing credit, which again is the responsibility of the banks, not the government. Yet despite the poor economic performance, large irrigation projects continue to dominate the irrigation map of India.

So far, the state and planning mechanism has never seriously questioned whether irrigation through the technology of large dams is the best form at all to an extent that it has now become a well-accepted policy that all river valley systems in the country have to be tapped. This target has not been set with regard to the requirements of food, as much as a deadline for the irrigation engineers to 'develop' all the river valleys by that date. As such, dam sites are chosen taking into consideration the technological and geographical implications. It is only after the site is selected that irrigation and power generation factors are taken into account. An argument is then made to irrigate 'drought-prone' and water scarce regions. Thus, the planning process is inverse of what it should be, i.e., after a concrete demand for water has been made, then a selection of irrigation technologies are made. It is once again the sub-system comprising of the headworks and canal networks rather than the main system that provides water to the crops that dictates irrigation priorities. It is thus little wonder that large irrigation projects are running at huge losses and poorly managed in planning, construction and implementation leading to targets and achievement going haywire.

RETURNS FROM IRRIGATION

Over the years returns from irrigation have been constantly falling. This fact has time and again been acknowledged by government sources. The Sixth Finance Commission agreed that there has been a 'sharp and progressive deterioration in the working results of irrigation projects' (GOI 1973a: 58). The Irrigation Commission, 1972 conceded, 'instead of a profit, the works have been showing increasing losses and imposing a growing burden on the general revenues of the States' (GOI 1972a: 261).

The losses amounted to Rs 4.84 crores in 1955–6 and steadily rose to Rs 56.59 crores in 1967–8. As against a less than two-fold increase in the area irrigated, from 7.55 m ha in 1955–6 to 14.40 m ha in 1967–8, the losses went up nearly eleven times from Rs 4.84 crores to Rs 56.59 crores respectively. The gross receipts more than doubled from Rs 16.09 crores to Rs 37 crores but working expenses registered a three-fold increase from Rs 10.59 crores to Rs 32.9 crores during the same time span (GOI 1973a: 68). This along with a five-fold increase in interest rates removed what little argument there could have been for an unqualified advocacy of widespread large-scale irrigation (Srinavasan 1976).

Four years after the adoption of the benefit-cost method in 1968, the story was not any better. The Sixth Finance Commission noted that as against a marginal loss of Rs 58 lakhs in 1950–1, the state governments sustained a loss of Rs 150 crores on major and medium irrigation projects in 1971–2. The commission further estimated that at an all India level the aggregate loss on irrigation projects, including interest charges, as projected during the Fifth Plan period, would be well over Rs 1,000 crores (GOI 1973b: 68).

The only way out seemed to be the raising of the water rate, to which the Irrigation Commission appeared to be reconciled. However, the state governments were not willing to abide by this suggestion for purely political reasons. The Finance Commission too favoured an enhancement in the water rates and suggested that it was 'imperative to fix water rates at reasonable level so as to eliminate recurring subsidies of a substantial nature from the general budget' (GOI 1973b; 59). The Committee on Taxation of Agricultural Wealth and Income went further, 'Even though in many areas, the rates vary with the nature of crop raised in hardly any case do irrigation through water rates cover interest and provision for amortisation; in a large number of cases, the amounts collected are not adequate to meet even the costs of maintenance. In fact far from being a tax on agriculture, irrigation rates carry an element of subsidy' (GOI 1972b: 98–9). The committee suggested stepping up of the rate to cover irrigation costs and to prevent the wasteful use of water and thus bring about parity between those who depend on private and public sources of irrigation.

The negative financial returns do point to the fact that irrigation through public works was being subsidised. Irrigation has largely been seen as essential for agricultural development and it is the duty of the state to take on this social role, and not make profits out of it, as the colonial state did. The debate on irrigation subsidies has only concentrated on raising water charges. However, at the same time we do need to examine the social and ecological effects of this policy of selective subsidisation of irrigation. The existence of subsidies in public irrigation works of major and medium irrigation and in the development of tubewell technology, with no complimentary support or similar assistance for traditional irrigation technology, has resulted in making the traditional irrigation technologies 'uneconomical'. The tubewell technology, that benefits rich farmers has a negative impact on environment, replaces tank irrigation, and other sustainable lift-irrigation technologies that encourages and is based upon community participation and is eco-friendly.

SMALL vs LARGE: WHICH IS 'COST EFFICIENT'?

In India except for the development of tubewell irrigation, small-scale irrigation (SSI) continues to be neglected. The emphasis on tubewells over the last few five year plans is largely due to the emphasis on green revolution. The Planning Commission, right from its inception in 1945, emphasised the benefits of small-scale irrigation to small farmers. The design of programme of traditional small-scale irrigation and its technological form not only involved water availability, but also an underlying perpetuation of politics and social relations which influenced different farming groups variously—large-scale and tubewell irrigation is biased towards the rich while the traditional and small-scale irrigation have the potential to benefit the poor more in the present socio-economic structure.

The most widespread technology of groundwater irrigation before the advent of modern tubewell technology was the *charsa*. However, in the recent years, tubewell motor pumps have left the charsa uncompetitive. Economists like Dhawan pointed out that this is because the resource cost of producing a unit of inanimate energy is much lower than the cost of providing an equivalent amount of energy through human or bullock labour (Dhawan 1975). The cost of water by charsa calculated by Mellor and Murti in Ghazipur, operated by a pair of bullocks and two persons using a leather bucket of about 50 litres turns out to be Rs 120 per thousand cubic meters. The cost with the Persian wheel is only Rs 75 per thousand cubic meters, and that through private and state tubewells is much lower at Rs 22 and Rs 33 per thousand cubic meters respectively. Moorti gave some other figures about the cost structure of different groundwater lifting devices. According to him, it costs Rs 93 to draw one thousand cubic meters with the charsa, while only Rs 1.2 to draw the same amount of water through private tubewells. For state tubewells it is Rs 1.4, and for the Persian wheel it is Rs 446 per thousand cubic meters (Moorti 1970).

This economic equation has resulted in the decline of the proportion of area irrigated by the charsa. However, this economic calculation does not take into account the subsidy provided to tubewells (in the form of low costs, access to cheap credit in addition to cheap inputs like diesel and electricity) or the ecological costs associated with tubewell technology. The continuation of traditional lift irrigation in certain pockets is due to the low opportunity cost of surplus family labour, unutilised excess bullock labour, and lack of access to credit and other subsidies. Clearly the poor peasant opts for traditional irrigation technology—as per his calculations it is the most efficient and economical technology. Rich farmers, on the other hand, opt for tubewells, except in areas where the prevalence of 'bonded labour' and usurious interest rates on capital ensure that technology does not change (Moorti 1970). Thus capitalist relations in agriculture in India, does not automatically mean new technology, but cheap technology, even if it is provided by bonded labour. The introduction of tubewells in an area drastically reduces the groundwater table and access to water through traditional water-lifts declines considerably, if not disappearing altogether. In many areas the tubewell technology also provides an impetus to rich farmers to bring about changes in the cropping pattern in accordance to the market demand. The reduction of water makes the small farmer dependent on the rich farmer for access to water through the latter's tubewells. This creates, what has been termed by Tushaar Shah as 'water markets', access to which is dependent on the purchasing power of the farmer, and needless to elaborate, the poor are further exploited and their actions get increasingly dictated by the market (Shah 1993). As a result, P. B. Ghate's belief of 1980 that a small farmer who does not already have a well on his land (which in 1980 would cost Rs 5,000 to construct) would definitely prefer tubewell to the charsa (Ghate 1980: A–162).

The fate of the charsa is met by all other traditional lift-wells. Another lift device, the don is used to lift water out of stored surface water such as tanks. A study was conducted with four operators lifting water for a field three feet above a pond. They took eight hours to transplant 18 *biswas* of paddy and their wages cost the farmer about Rs 25. For the same job the landowner could have hired a pumpset for two hours for only Rs 10. However, dhenkulis, dons, and swing baskets continue to be used in low lift conditions by small farmers irrigating their own land. Quite naturally, they suffer from a location and seasonality constraint, apart from their high labour intensity. It was estimated in 1971, that about two-fifths of the groundwater was raised by traditional water-lifts. Today, this fraction will be much smaller and thanks to the continuation of irrigation-related subsidies and agrarian development strategy it may not be altogether wrong if someone predicted that in the next decades, they will be confined to the agricultural museums.

Moving on to canal irrigation, it would be worthwhile to note that canal irrigation is not synonymous to irrigation with the help of dams. Canal irrigation has existed for a long time and has over the years provided good returns. Unfortunately, data on canal irrigation is not divided on the basis of irrigation from reservoirs of dams and more traditional forms like taking canals from rivers, building temporary bunds or weirs and barrages. However, irrigation experts accept that these practices are adequately productive and the losses from public works mentioned above are largely from dams only.

In spite of the Planning Commission being aware of the advantages of small-scale irrigation right since 1945, a reason for this meagre allocation was the cost benefit approach adopted for irrigation projects; this approach being biased against minor irrigation works (for social and ecological costs are not taken into account, and these weigh heavily against major projects as pointed out earlier) (Asopa and Tripathi 1975). Since minor irrigation works do not directly create irrigation potential and it is difficult to monitor and finance a number of such small schemes by the foreign agency, they were by and large neglected. The irrigation bureaucracy has often asserted that large projects have economies of scale, and therefore have a cost advantage over smaller irrigation projects. However, certain facts point the other way.

The link of this sort of planning with the democratic process is also a crucial one. Large irrigation projects are most 'visible' as developmental projects in the countryside and supposedly have a direct relationship to the livelihood of the majority of the rural populace. On the one hand it creates a myth of abundant food and prosperity for the majority, and on the other it appeases the beneficiaries, who are largely rich farmers. This is the rich peasantry, and is a credible votebank. Bardhan considered them as an important element in his composition of the dominant proprietary classes (Bardhan 1984).

The Planning Commission estimates that the cost to provide irrigation to one hectare of land through major and medium irrigation schemes is over Rs 2,800 in comparison to Rs 840 for an equal area by groundwater (GOI 1985). Other critics like Kanwar believe that the, 'cost of groundwater development is hardly one-fourth of surface water development in the Seventh Plan' (Kanwar 1988: 7). Others support such statistics. Talking about irrigation planning it concludes, 'The investment cost of unit irrigated area for major and minor irrigation projects was 118 per cent more than for minor irrigation' (Afro-Asian Rural Reconstruction Organisation, 1987: 82).

Yet, the cost factor between minor and major irrigation in India is not without a debate. B. D. Dhawan, a distinguished irrigation economist, believes that major works are more economical than minor ones. Contrary to the above calculations Dhawan states, 'surface irrigation works may score decisively over well irrigation, possibly by a margin of 3:2' (Dhawan 1989). His objective is to point to the flaws in processing data related to irrigation, and thereby tilt the balance in favour of major projects. He rightly points out, 'it is inappropriate to compare the irrigation projects on the basis of unit capital cost.' He points out five major drawbacks in the available estimates.

- The reported outlays are for the public sector only, thereby leaving out investments by farmers, which can be substantial in case of minor works.
- There is a lack of compatibility between outlays on irrigation in a given plan period and the resultant addition to irrigation capacity in the same plan period. The argument being that major irrigation works have a longer gestation period hence the addition to irrigation capacity is not explained by looking at the potential generated during that plan. It would be reflected only on completion of the project.
- A portion of the project outlay is not meant to result in any addition to the irrigation capacity as it may be directed towards (i) research and investigation, (ii) remodelling of headworks, lining of channels and strengthening of old irrigation system, and (iii) replacement of old ones.
- He points out that the capital saving argument is more tilted in favour of major irrigation, the reason being that the lifespan of large dams is around hundred years, while minor works need frequent replacement.
- Major works use the natural force of gravity in their operation, while minor works require energy for countering the pull of gravity. Hence the operational cost of minor schemes would be large. The equation, according to him, is about 1:10 in favour of major projects.

Dhawan has brought to light certain factors that need to be taken into consideration before any serious debate on the cost aspect of irrigation projects can take place. However, there are a number of aspects of major projects which he does not refer to, and which one can argue would tilt the balance in favour of minor projects. Before laying down his five objections to cost calculation, he emphasised the need for an exercise in terms of social costs which he saw in terms of (a) submerged land, and (b) rent. While agreeing that there is rent seeking, he intended to exclude such costs in his calculation, thus bringing down the true resource cost of major projects. Rent-seeking, after all, is part and parcel of the status quo and the technology it markets. In his detailed accounting he did not mention rent-seeking in the case of minor schemes. Clearly, he conceded that there was an inherent bias (as of now), rent-seeking being rampant in case of major projects. As such, our calculation should weigh against major projects for their inherent flaw for which public money is spent. Similarly, other social costs like inequitable distribution of water and electricity, unsatisfactory rehabilitation and improper treatment of the environment are not taken into account by Dhawan.

Indeed Dhawan's arguments can be turned against his case. He is right in pointing out that the figures quoted for minor works are public sector outlays only. However, he omits mentioning the fact that the quoted figures of benefits by major schemes should deduct the benefits by minor schemes within the command area of the project. As a Government of Punjab document points out, 'Tubewells and wells are also coming up in areas irrigated by canals. It, therefore, becomes difficult to access the net benefits accruing from these works. The old norms of area irrigated by minor irrigation works also no longer hold good and require reappraisal' (Government of Punjab, 1970: 1).

While appreciating the content of Dhawan's second argument, one can nevertheless show that long gestation periods could be a serious handicap. To cite a case, preliminary work on the Narmada Valley Project started in the 1950s (i.e., feasibility studies and paper work), at a time when the question of environment was perceived differently in India. Since then the ecological and hydrological situation had undergone considerable change when construction work on the Sardar Sarovar Project first began in 1990, and it will further change when the project will be finally completed. Thus assuming status quo in environmental and hydrological variables for such a long time and even during the life of a dam can prove disastrous.

Dhawan's argument of deleting costs other than that enhancing irrigation capacity does not hold good. These are clearly capital costs and should in all fairness be approproportioned to the respective schemes to which they belong. Dhawan later talked about replacement and operational costs of minor schemes, surely similar costs for major projects cannot be disregarded. His next argument conceded that minor schemes can at least be replaced at a cost, a large dam, alas, cannot be, as we shall see later. It may further be pointed out that the replacement costs of minor irrigation that Dhawan pointed to is perhaps related to tubewells only, for others it can be called recurring expenditure. Lastly, he dealt with operational costs and 'energy accounting' of minor projects. He, once again, did not mention the energy required to build a large dam with its innumerable channels.

The proponents of major projects also erred in their lumping up of all major projects together. However, it has been seen that different irrigation projects have different economies. The cost of irrigation of a hectare of land can differ from as little as Rs 16,300 to Rs 35,000. The cost of a project will quite obviously differ, among other things, depending on the topography of the dam site and the length of the canal networks. Therefore, if some large dams are 'cheaper', hence less problematic, we still cannot make a case for all large dams. This argument will be even more vulnerable, if we take into account the submergence area of large projects and hence the added ecological and relocation costs.

Apart from the cost of irrigating per hectare by major and minor schemes, any serious economic analysis must also look into the output per hectare by different irrigation technologies. Dhawan gave us a comparative view of foodgrain output using canals, tubewells, other groundwater lifting technologies and tanks in four different states—Punjab, Haryana, Andhra Pradesh and Tamil Nadu. And clearly, apart from foodgrain output—involving tubewell irrigation, which varies from 4.4 tonnes per ha in Punjab to 6.0 tonnes in Tamil Nadu, no other irrigation technology has any significant advantage. Dhawan's most recent data, on which he based his study, is for the year 1977–9. The output from canal irrigation varied from 1.2 tonnes per hectare in Tamil Nadu to 2.9 tonnes per hectare in Andhra Pradesh, from tanks in the range of 1.5 to 1.8 in Andhra Pradesh and Tamil Nadu respectively, and from traditional groundwater from 2.6 tonnes per hectare to 3.3 tonnes per hectare in Tamil Nadu. While there are differences in food output within canal, tank and traditional groundwater technologies, it merely points to the diversity of micro situations in which these technologies operate. More than anything, this data questioned the supposed superiority of canal irrigation in the context of enhanced food output. It can thus be said that even the 'traditional' economics that does not take into account the wider ecological and social costs which favours investment in small irrigation works.

Some other proponents of large dams, like J. F. Mistry, argued that major projects are more economical than minor ones. Again, the social and ecological costs are not taken into account in the calculation of the data below, which we have alluded to earlier. Absolutely no account of the ecological damage has been considered, neither has any provision been made against risks and uncertainty, nor any interest calculated on the high capital cost of large projects. It has also been seen that the cost of irrigating per hectare through major and medium irrigation projects has been increasing over time. The cost of irrigation in the First Plan for major and medium (1951–6) was Rs 1,520 per hectare, in the 7th (1985–90) it went up to Rs 26,873.40 per hectare. While the figures for the corresponding period in the case of minor irrigation was Rs 568.97 per hectare which rose to Rs 3,261.63 per hectare. While the cost of minor irrigation has risen by 5.73 times, that of major and medium has gone up by a steep 17.68 times. At constant prices, the cost of irrigation per hectare through major and medium projects has gone up from between Rs 3,340 to 3,940 (during the First and Fourth Plan periods) to Rs 5,830 during the Seventh Plan, as per the data provided by Mistry in the same paper (Mistry 1991: 39).

ECONOMIC AUDIT OF LARGE DAMS

The above comparative macro picture on cost aspect suggests that overall large-scale irrigation is more expensive than small-scale works in terms of ex-ante stated benefits. A limited ex-post analysis of large dams below will drive home the point that there is no question of economic superiority associated with large dams. The tabulation of benefits from irrigation and power provides the necessary credence to the project required for its sanction. As discussed earlier, the Planning Commission calls for a calculation of benefit-cost ratio and it stipulates a minimum ratio of 1.5:1. Till some time back the figures provided by the project authorities were taken for granted. With the controversy of dams hotting up, attempts have been made to scrutinise these figures and various discrepancies have emerged. Paranjpye demonstrated from his studies on the Bedthi, Tehri and Narmada projects, how the project authorities indulge in various manipulations of the figures to meet the requirements of the Planning Commission. These calculations of his, as he put it, have deliberately been on the conservative side and the social and environmental costs have not been considered. The Planning Commission procedures for weightages and handicaps on the BC ratio as it affects the various sections of the society have not been accounted for either in these calculations. Despite this, it needs to be highlighted, Paranjpye could question the economic feasibility of these projects. This, indeed reflects the malaise that has crept into the method of calculating the BC ratio.

In the Bedthi project, the number of people displaced and houses submerged exceeded 40 per cent of the government's estimate, while the submerged paddy land was thrice the government's estimate, and the submerged garden land was more than five times of the estimate (Paranjpye 1981: 32). Similarly, in the Tehri project, the benefit-cost ratio was 1.28:1 as against the government's calculation of 3.49:1. While doing this calculation, Paranjpye even pointed out that the forest area lost will be as high as 4,705 hectare as against the estimate of 1,600 hectare in the project documents. The number of prospective oustees was also disputed as 85,600 and not 46,000. Similarly, the expected life of the dam was not to be hundred years, but only sixty-two years (Paranjpye 1988: 42).

The criticism of BC ratio has been mounting. In another study, Singh and Bhatia, reviewed the Auranga project in the drought-prone Palamau district of Jharkhand. They too pointed out flaws in the traditional calculations. While the BC ratio of the Auranga project, was estimated at 3.12 in the project report, they have modified it to 1.73 after some corrections. This, according to them, can go down even further if some other neglected variables are taken into account (Sinha and Bhatia 1982).

There have been times when the Planning Commission has taken a tough stand on the BC ratio of certain dams. However, it is often easier to accept the project officials' figures than seek other evaluations. The irrigation bureaucracy is large and powerful, not allowing outsiders to enter its preserve and snoop around project-related data. It also resorts to various tactics to put pressure on the obstructing body. At times construction work on the dam starts much before the central authorities have cleared it, and then it is argued that as a considerable amount of money has been spent, it would be ridiculous to drop it at that stage. This strategy has been used in at least five projects as per the government's own admission. Work on Nagarjunasagar project in Andhra Pradesh started in 1955, while the approval was granted only on 22 September 1960, approval for the Kosi project in Bihar came in only on 25 April 1958, while here too construction work had started in 1955. Construction on the Malaprabha project in Karnataka commenced in October 1960, while the clearance was granted on 5 August 1963. Similarly, the clearance for the Tawa project in Madhya Pradesh and Kangasabati in West Bengal came after four and five years of the commencement of construction work respectively (GOI 1983: 42).

Struck with the idea that big projects are the best way to provide irrigation, the bureaucracy goes to every extent in crushing questions on the feasibility of such projects. The engineers consider such efforts as a challenge to their competence, and are often not ready for a dialogue as they may have spent a major portion of their lives in designing and executing the project. Indeed, this bureaucracy is a vested interest in the execution of large dams due to the large funds that make rent-seeking possible. As they monopolise the data concerning the project, it is extremely difficult for researchers and public interest groups to do a cost-benefit analysis of the projects. It is not surprising that till recently very little research has been done on the subject. The discussion below is an exploratory attempt to highlight the evaluation of large dams in post-independence India.

COST ESCALATION

About 32 major ongoing and initiated projects in the Fifth and Sixth Plan, which were studied by the Public Accounts Committee (PAC), showed cost overruns of 500 per cent or more. The committee clearly pointed out that not a single project had been completed within the approved cost estimates in India since independence (GOI 1983: 38). Further, according to another calculation by Chaturvedi, which is based on 30 irrigation projects, the estimated cost of Rs 913.49 crores rose to Rs 1,966.93 crores on completion—an escalation of 115.32 per cent (Chaturvedi 1976: 1). Pant put the all India cost escalation of major irrigation projects at 111 per cent and 77.94 per cent for the period 1971–81, based on figures provided by government sources. A study on Kerala showed the cost escalation for major and medium projects at about 675 per cent. With cost overruns, ranging from 78 per cent to 675 per cent, according to various estimates, the BC ratio based on estimates does seem to be a joke anyway.

The government is well aware about the steep rise in costs of irrigation and multi-purpose projects. In 1972, the Union Ministry of Irrigation and Power even appointed a Committee of Experts to probe into the matter (GOI 1973b). The experts listed four important causes for cost escalation (i) rise in prices, (ii) inadequate investigations and provisions, (iii) change in scope, design and additional requirements, and (iv) other causes like increase in land rates, rehabilitation measures, and paucity of funds and poor performance of equipment. Increase in cost due to price escalation was a major factor. Taking note of the price indices (wholesale price indices for fuel, power, light and lubricants, price indices of construction materials like cement, iron and steel; indices for labour and unit value of imports—machinery other than electrical), the committee estimated the increase in the cost of construction due to escalation of prices in six projects. As per this sample, less than half of the increase in cost, to be specific 48.33 per cent, was due to price escalation. The committee singled out increase in cost due to inadequate investigations and surveys as 'one factor that has caused significant deviation from the original estimated cost of projects' (GOI 1973b: 99). It pointed out that neither sufficient time nor adequate personnel was available to prepare accurate reports as there was always a rush for quickly preparing the feasibility report for the decision-making authority. The report pointed out that while investigations were done for the headworks, little attention was paid to the distribution system. For instance, in the Jayakwadi Project, Maharashtra, Ukai Project in Gujarat and Kangsabati Project in West Bengal, increase in expenditure due to inadequate investigations about the reservoir and lack of survey about distributaries and minors account for nearly 24 per cent, 8 per cent and 33 per cent respectively of the cost increase of the projects. The cost went up by Rs 9 crores, Rs 4.5 crores and Rs 6.7 crores respectively. Similarly, the discovery of a fault zone in the Ramganga project in UP resulted in a revision of the cost by Rs 3.2 crores in the 1961 proposal. Inadequate investigations cost an additional Rs 6.5 crores in the Kallada project in Kerala. Similarly, the Hirakud Canal turned out to be 80 miles longer than had been estimated at the stage of project report. Similar evidence is available in the case of the Beas-Sutlej link, Hidkal dam and the Pochampad project.

There is also the instance of change in scope of the project after the project has commenced. For instance in the case of the Mahanadi delta project in Orissa, about 16 per cent of the increase in costs was in lieu of changes to bring about additional area under irrigation, construction of canals and flood protection. Other projects, which were looked into by the Committee of Experts where the scope of the project underwent change are Ramganga in UP, Ukai in Gujarat, Gadak in Bihar, Kabini in Mysore, Pamba and Khitturpuzha in Kerala and in the case of the Rajasthan Canal project.

The Working Group on Irrigation, 1980 also displayed concern over the grim situation of increase in cost. In its detailed report, the Working Group was quite severe in blaming inadequate investigations and surveys at the planning stage, which led to the steep hike in price (GOI 1980a). In spite of this chronic problem of cost overruns right from 1951, the fact is that no serious attempt was made to rectify this trend. As a result, the concerned officials began to be lax about the estimates and were more concerned with getting the BC ratio to more than 1:1.5 somehow. As a result, a sharp criticism was to come from none other than the then Chairman of the CWC, who pointed out that the standards of preparation of project report are 'getting diluted', 'in many cases technical studies have not been carried out for selecting the most appropriate dam site after considering several alternatives'. There was also a need, according to him, for an, 'improvement in quality and quantity surveys of construction materials and in layout studies of the dam, based on the availability of local materials'. He further stated, 'In many cases, contour surveys of the command area are not carried out. The extent of command area is not assessed on a realistic basis. The norms for design of distribution system are not laid down in the project report. Surface and sub-surface drainage requirement of the project are not studied, and generally no provision thereof is made in the estimates. Cropping patterns are not realistic. Benefit-cost ratio is not worked out on a realistic basis. Specific problems, if any, for the project which are likely to be met during construction are not discussed' (Central Board of Irrigation and Power 1977: 5).

Despite these committees and expert opinion, cost overrun continues. It can thus be surmised that improper investigations were perhaps deliberate to ensure the clearing of the project reports. The fear that a thorough investigation may render the project cost higher than the stipulated percentage, acted against the idea of having a comprehensive and rigorous project plan. This demonstrates the mockery that the earlier exercise with the BC ratio. As the pattern is universal, it suggests that the blueprint writers deliberately underestimate the cost. Once the project is cleared and enough investment made on it, it becomes easier to get the remaining finance, as now the concern of the funding agency would be to see that the project is completed as soon as possible.

The issue of cost overrun is very important. Though the method of calculating the BC ratio is itself inadequate, it could provide some basis for assessment. However, in reality this method is totally ignored in practice. This seems to be a classic case of improper utilisation of public resources without accountability. Accountability is limited to the preparation and clearance of the project documents. Once passed, in practice it seems to become irrelevant to the ultimate decisions that are taken in the field. This structure works to the interest of the lobby of civil engineers who have the monopoly of the project data to perpetuate themselves and large dams regardless of the economic viability.

IRRIGATION PERFORMANCE

There is no doubt in the fact that large dams are primarily meant to provide irrigation. In this area also, their performance is wanting. In certain cases the project authorities do not deduct the area already under irrigation before the commencement of canal irrigation, while calculating the BC ratio as pointed out by Paranjpye and also discussed in the first section of this chapter (Paranjpye 1988). The projected benefits in respect to irrigation are not met, largely as these are magnified to ensure the clearance of the project. For instance, a micro study on the Mula dam conducted by Mitra shows that the utilisation percentage was on an average about 44.33 during 1971–82 (Mitra 1986). Bandopadhyay also indicated that the overall efficiency of water use in large dams in India is in the order of 35–40 per cent, though not indicating his source (Bandopadhyay 1987). The figures adapted from the Comptroller and Auditor General's (CAG) report is also not very impressive, and shows only 64.4 per cent achievement.

It has been pointed out that there are various discrepancies in the official irrigation statistics. Wade stated, 'Statistics are socially generated and socially appraised—their use for monitoring and control affecting both content and accuracy.' However, the errors, according to him, tend to be 'systematic' with the Revenue Department's figures being 'downward biased', while the Irrigation Department's estimates are 'upward biased' (Wade 1985). Hence we should be careful about drawing hasty conclusions using the figures that give near cent per cent utilisation. Clearly they are out of line, perhaps supplied by the Irrigation Department. In any case, it can perhaps be safely concluded that according to various estimates, the national average of irrigation actually provided would range between 35 to 65 per cent of the projections in the project reports.

It is important to get a picture of the increase in irrigated area, with the changes in cropping patterns and the relations to the market in the irrigated regions. While the area under cultivation for rice and sugarcane has doubled (both requiring large amounts of water), that of maize has gone up three times, land under cultivation of wheat has increased more than five times, between 1950–1 and 1983–4. On the other hand, the production of cereals and pulses has remained stagnant in irrigated areas. However, it is the 'poor man's crop (which require little water), jowar and bajra whose area under irrigation as a percentage of total irrigated area has declined dramatically. Clearly, the market is determining the choice of crops in irrigated agriculture.

In continuation of the discussion on the problems associated with the method of evaluation and choice of irrigation projects, the dismal economic and irrigation performance of large dams has been demonstrated. It has also been established that smaller irrigation technologies are cheaper and the actual process of project evaluation and arriving at a suitable BC ratio has little meaning left to it. Construction work on large dams quite often commences before evaluation and clearance, and even when cost overruns are nearly five to six times higher than initially estimated, there is little scrutiny or reappraisal of the planning process. Similarly, little attention paid to time and the phenomenal delays in the execution of projects have serious economic costs. And interestingly, the performance of large dams for the very purpose they are constructed, i.e., providing irrigation, is less than satisfactory. In spite of these general trends that have been observed in relation to large dams, their popularity with the irrigation bureaucracy continues.

CONCLUDING REMARKS

Planning and irrigation development strategy in India have created biases against traditional irrigation that have been perpetuated at the level of implementation. Those who believe that the status of a minor irrigation implementation officer is lower than one involved in major projects dominate the agency empowered to plan in India. The existence of a market in the purchase of remunerative posts in the irrigation bureaucracy as suggested by Wade clearly demonstrates that the engineers want to be where the budgetary allocation is higher (Wade 1982b). Budgets of major projects are much larger than for minor ones. This bias gets reflected in the poor implementation of minor schemes. Moreover promotion of minor schemes usually means credit availability, which again is the responsibility of the banks, not the government. Despite poor economic performance, due to political considerations, there continues to be an emphasis on large irrigation projects in India. This has led not only to a proliferation in subsidies, but also in a distribution of state largesse to particular groups.

The ecological challenge that is being put forward by the less endowed, therefore, is closely linked to the control of resources and production. The 'environmental movements' today relate to the demands for empowerment of the poor, decentralisation, participation, rural development and social change. The peculiar nature of irrigation development in India has generated ecological movements or more specifically, water-related conflicts. These movements question as to how a production process, involving water, is being organised. Apart from issues of displacement and ecological impact, various movements are taking up the issue of the distribution of water. This is often taken up to establish and strengthen collective institutions like *warabandi* in the command area. However, more radical proponents, for instance groups like the Pani Panchayat, espouse an alternate method of planning for irrigation and distribution of water that is linked to the choice of crops in the irrigated area. They therefore question the purpose of irrigation. As mentioned earlier, they point out that the distribution of water is not in keeping with the collective interest and sustainability of resources, rather the market, which encourages inequitable and unsustainable water management. Similarly, other groups like the Mukti Sangharsh Chalwal in the case of Baliraja dam are also opposing the statist irrigation policies of increasing monopolisation of water determined by the market forces, and its growing scarcity for others leading to drought like conditions.

As opposed to statist planning, alternative irrigation methods are being evolved by the environmental and peoples' movements in India today, which have emphasised sustainability and equitability as the principles for an alternate development model. A new attitude towards irrigation has to be central in creating agricultural prosperity based on these new principles. Critics of large dams have more often than not put their hopes on reviving traditional irrigation technologies. However, it has been emphasised here that traditional irrigation methods too have systems of exploitation and class bias built into them, and therefore, cannot on their own be an answer to all the irrigation needs of today. It is nevertheless true that as irrigation projects become more grandiose as part and parcel of the new development ideology, the levels of exploitation of both, certain groups in society, and common resources increase manifold. In this sense, smaller community based irrigation schemes indeed look attractive. Food security, alleviation of hunger and poverty, protection of ecology and environment, the need to protect threatened culture systems, all point towards the rethinking of the dominant development discourse, and with it the prevalent irrigation ideology. Making traditional irrigation systems a panacea for all our needs may not be the answer. One may still have to, at times, depend on large projects. However, these will have to be combined with smaller community based projects which would be able to tap peoples' knowledge of the environment as also empower them with wider institutional safeguards.

ENDNOTES

[1] The most sophisticated use of the term 'class' is found in Marxist literature. Though Marx never defined the term, classes can be best defined by conflicts of interests arising from the production process—the ownership of the mode of production and the social relations that emanates from it.

[2] At present the aggregate irrigation capacity for all minor irrigation works is 40 m ha and that of all major and medium irrigation is

30 m ha. See Government of India (1985), chapter on Irrigation, and also Central Water Commission (1987).

[3] As a percentage of the plan allocation, the outlay for irrigation was 22.2 per cent in the First Plan, declining to 9.2 per cent in the Second Plan when the Nehru-Mahalanobis model was adopted. After that it has hovered around 7.1 per cent in the Annual Plan period 1966–9 to 12.5 per cent during the Sixth Plan. It was 9.4 per cent during the Seventh Plan (1985–90) period (figures calculated from plan documents and Economic Surveys) (GOI 1992).

[4] These projections are based on annual nutrition requirement of 270 kg/person.

[5] Land reforms as stated in this chapter was a radical document, however, its implementation had essentially benefitted the rich peasantry. See Joshi (1975) and Frankel (1971).

[6] This chapter does not dwell upon the socio-economic impact of tubewells.

REFERENCES

Acharya, Sarthi. 1992. 'Rates of Return in Indian Agriculture'. *Economic and Political Weekly*. Vol. 28. No. 3. January 18. 111–19.

Afro-Asian Rural Reconstruction Organisation. 1987. 'Role of Irrigation in Development of Agriculture in Developing Countries'. *Rural Reconstruction.* 20(1).

Agarwal, Bina. 1986. 'Women, Poverty and Agricultural Growth in India'. *Journal of Peasant Studies.* 13 (4).

Asopa, V. N. and B. L. Tripathi. 1975. 'Irrigation Agriculture in Gujarat: Problems and Prospects'. Centre for Management in Agriculture, Indian Institute of Management. Ahmedabad. Monograph No. 53.

Bandopadhyay, Jayant. 1987. 'Political Ecology of Drought and Water Scarcity: Need for an Ecological Water Resources Policy'. *Economic and Political Weekly.* Vol. 22. No. 50. December 12. 2159–69.

Banerjee, Sumanta. 1980. *In the Wake of Naxalbari.* Kolkata: Subarnarekha Publishers.

Bardhan, Pranab. 1984. *The Political Economy of Development in India.* Oxford: Basil Blackwell.

Bardhan, Pranab and Ashok Rudra. 1978. 'Interlinkage of Land, Labour and Credit Relations: An Analysis of Village Survey Data in East India'. *Economic and Political Weekly.* Vol 13, Nos 6 and 7. February. 367–84.

Bhalla, Sheila. 1977. 'Changes in Acerage and Tenure Structure of Land Holdings in Haryana, 1962–72'. *Economic and Political Weekly*. Vol 12. No 13. March 27. A-2–A-15.

Buckley, R. B. 1880. *The Irrigation Works of India*. 42nd Edition. London: E&FNSPON.

Central Board of Irrigation and Power. 1977. *Proceedings of the First Seminar on Evolving the Strategy for Irrigation Development*. New Delhi: Central Board of Irrigation and Power. December.

Central Water Commission (CWC). 1987. *National Water Policy*. New Delhi: Government of India.

Chambers, Robert. 1988. *Managing Canal Irrigation*. New Delhi: Oxford and IBH.

Chaturvedi, A. C. 1976. 'Efficiency in Major Irrigation'. *Journal of the Institution of Engineers*. Civil Engineering Division. Vol. 57. Part C 13. November.

Clibborne, J. 1891. *Irrigation Works in India*. Roorkee. Thomason College.

Cotton, Lt. Gen. Sir Arthur. 1874. 'Lectures on Irrigation Works in India', delivered at the School of Military Engineering, Chatham, Autumn Session, Uddaraju Raman, Vijayawada: 1968.

Dasgupta, B. 1974. *The Naxalite Movement*. New Delhi: Allied Publishers.

Dasgupta, B. 1977. *Agrarian Change and the New Technology in India*. Geneva: UNRISD.

Desai, A. R. (ed.). 1979. *Peasant Struggles in India*. Mumbai: Oxford University Press.

Dhawan, B. D. 1975. 'Economics of Groundwater Utilisation: Traditional versus Modern Techniques: Review of Agriculture'. *Economic and Political Weekly*. Vol. 10. No. 22–3. June. A-31–A-42.

Dhawan, B.D. 1989. 'Major and Minor Irrigation Works: Cost Aspects of the Controversy'. *Economic and Political Weekly*. Vol. 24. No. 39. September 30. A-117–A-121.

Frankel, Francine. 1971. *India's Green Revolution: Economic Gains and Political Costs*. New Jersey: Princeton University Press.

Gadgil, D.R. 1948. *Economic Effects of Irrigation*. Poona: Gokhale Institute of Politics and Economics.

Gadgil, Madhav and Ramachandra Guha. 1994. 'Ecological Conflict and the Environmental Movement in India'. *Development and Change*. Vol. 5. No 1. January. 101–36.

Gaiha, Raghav. 1981. 'Aspects of Poverty in Rural India'. *Economics of Planning*. Vol. 17. Nos. 2–3.

Ghate, P. B. 1980. 'Irrigation for Very Small Farmers: Appropriate Technology or Appropriate Organisation?' *Economic and Political Weekly*. December. A-161–A-172.

Gittinger, J. 1981. *Economic Analysis for Agricultural Projects*. Washington DC: EDI Training Material. World Bank.

Government of India. 1961. *Third Five Year Plan*. New Delhi: Planning Commission.

Government of India. 1967. *Economic Survey of Indian Agriculture*. New Delhi: Ministry of Agriculture. viii.

Government of India. 1972a. *Report of the Irrigation Commission 1972*. Vol 1. New Delhi: Ministry of Irrigation and Power.

Government of India. 1972b. *Report of the Committee on Taxation of Agricultural Wealth and Income*. New Delhi: Ministry of Finance.

Government of India. 1973a. *Report of the Sixth Finance Commission*. New Delhi: Ministry of Finance.

Government of India. 1973b. *Report of the Expert Committee on Rise in Costs of Irrigation and Multipurpose Projects*. New Delhi. Ministry of Irrigation and Power. April.

Government of India. 1980a. *Report of the Working Group on Irrigation: Major and Medium Irrigation Programme, 1980–85*. New Delhi: Ministry of Irrigation and Power. November.

Government of India. 1983. 141st Report of the Public Accounts Committee (PAC) 1982–83. *Planning Process and Monitoring Mechanism with Reference to Irrigation Projects*. Seventh Lok Sabha. Ministry of Planning (Planning Commission). New Delhi: Lok Sabha Secretariat. April.

Government of India. 1985. *Seventh Five Year Plan: 1985–90*. New Delhi: Planning Commission.

Government of India. 1986. *Economic Survey 1985–86*. New Delhi: Ministry of Finance.

Government of India. 1992. Eighth Five Year Plan. 1992–97. New Delhi: Planning Commission.

Government of Punjab. 1970. *Report on the Survey of Minor Irrigation Works in Punjab*. Economic and Statistical Organisation. Publication No. 106.

Hansen, A. H. 1966. *The Process of Planning: A Study of India's Five Year Plans 1950–64*. Oxford: Oxford University Press.

Indian National Committee on Large Dams (INCOLD). 1979. *Register of Large Dams in India*. New Delhi: Central Board of Irrigation and Power. October.

Joshi, P.C. 1975. *Land Reforms in India: Trends and Perspectives*. New Delhi: Allied Publishers.

Kanwar, J. S. (ed.). 1988. *Water Management—The Key to Developing Agriculture*.New Delhi: Agricole Publishing Academy.

Kumar, V. Santha and R. Rajagopalan. 1993. 'Technological Prejudice: Case of Indian Irrigation'. *Economic and Political Weekly*. Vol. 28. No. 14. April. 586–96.

Linney, W. and Harrison, S. 1981. *Large Dams and the Developing World: Social and Environmental Costs and Benefits—A Look at Africa*. Kenya: Environment Liason Centre.

Lipton, Michael and Richard Longhurst. 1989. *New Seeds and Poor People*. London: Unwin Hyman.

Mistry, J. F. 1991. 'Theme Paper'. Symposium on Large Dams vs Small Dams. Vol I. New Delhi: Central Board for Irrigation and Power and Sardar Sarovar Narmada Nigam. December.

Mitra, Ashok K. 1986. 'Underutilisation Revisited Surface Irrigation in Drought Prone Areas of Western Maharashtra'. *Economic and Political Weekly*. Vol. 27. No. 17. April. 752–56.

Moorti, T. V. 1970. 'A Comparative Study of Well Irrigation in Aligarh District, India'. *Cornell International Agricultural Development Bulletin*. No 19. Ithaca: Cornell University.

National Planning Committee. 1947. *River Training and Development*. Mumbai: Vora & Co Publishers Ltd.

Palmer, Tim. 1982. *The Struggle for a River*. Berkeley: University of California.

Pant, K.C. 1973. 'Violence in a Period of Social Change'. *Young India*. Vol. 3.

Pant, Niranjan. 1986. 'Farmers Organisation in Large Irrigation Projects'. *Economic and Political Weekly*. Vol. 21. No. 52. December. A-171–5.

Paranjpye, Vijay. 1981. 'Dams Are We Damned?', in L. T. Sharma and Ravi Sharma (eds.), *Major Dams: A Second Look*. New Delhi: Gandhi Peace Foundation.

Paranjpye, Vijay. 1988. *Evaluating the Tehri Dam: Studies in Ecology and Sustainable Development*. New Delhi: Indian National Trust for Art and Cultural Heritage (INTACH). June.

Patnaik, Utsa. 1986. *The Agrarian Question and the Development of Capitalism in India*. New Delhi: Oxford University Press.

Raj, K.N. 1960. *Some Economic Aspects of the Bhakra Nangal Project*. Mumbai: Asia Publishing House.

Rao, C. Rajeswara. 1971. 'Land Struggle and its Future'. *Indian Left Review*. February.

Rao, J. Mohan. 1994. 'Agricultural Development Under State Planning', in T. J. Byres (ed.), *The State and Development Planning in India*. Delhi: Oxford University Press.

Rath, Nilakantha. 1976. 'The Current Method of Choosing Irrigation Projects in India: A Review'. *Role of Irrigation in the Development of India's Agriculture*. Seminar Series XIII. Indian Society of Agricultural Economics. 116–26.

Sen, Amartya. 1981. *Poverty and Famines*. Oxford: Blackwell. 46.

Sen, Khagendra N. 1939. *Economic Reconstruction of India*. Kolkata: The University of Calcutta Press.

Shah, Tushaar. 1993. *Groundwater Markets and Irrigation Development*. Mumbai: Oxford University Press.

Sharma, H. R. 1994. 'Distribution of Landholdings in Rural India, 1953–54 to 1981–82: Implications for Land Reforms'. *Economic and Political Weekly*. Vol. 29. No. 39. September. A-117–28.

Sinha, Baswan, and Ramesh Bhatia. 1982. *Economic Appraisal of Irrigation Project in India*. New Delhi: Agricole Publishing Academy.

Sovani, N.V. and Nilakanth Rath. 1960. *Economics of a Multiple-Purpose River Dam*. Gokhale Institute of Politics and Economics. Poona, New Delhi: Asia Publishing House.

Srinavasan, V. K. 1976. 'Returns from Investment: An Area of Increasing Concern'. *Role of Irrigation in the Development of India's Agriculture*. Seminar Series XIII. Indian Society of Agricultural Economics. 104–15.

Visvesvaraya, Sir M. 1936. *Planned Economy for India*. Bangalore: Bangalore Press.

Wade, Robert. 1982. 'The System of Administrative and Political Corruption: Canal Irrigation in South India'. *Journal of Development Studies*. Vol. 18. No. 3. April. 287–328.

Wade, Robert. 1985. 'On the Sociology of Irrigation: How do We Know the Truth about Canal Irrigation'. Discussion Paper. Report No: APU 37. Research Unit. Agriculture and Rural Development Department. Operational Policy Staff. World Bank. May.

Wade, Robert. 1988. *Village Republics: Economic Conditions for Collective Action in South India*. Cambridge: Cambridge University Press.

World Bank. 1984. *World Development Report*. New York: Oxford University Press. 93.

Worster, Donald. 1985. *Rivers of Empire: Water, Aridity and the Growth of the American West*. New York: Pantheon Books.

5

State Institutions and Poverty: A Case Study of Chittoor

N. Sukumar

INTRODUCTION

Poverty is a multidimensional and complex issue which involves one's inability to satisfy basic needs, lack of control over resources, lack of education and skills, poor health and malnutrition, lack of shelter, poor access to water and sanitation, vulnerability to violence and crime, and lack of political freedom and voice. Apart from the common causes of poverty, in the rural sector it is especially induced by agricultural stagnation. The effect of poverty is worse on the scheduled castes and scheduled tribes due to discrimination and policies of exclusion.

The chief occupation in rural Andhra Pradesh is agriculture and allied labour services—collection of non-timber forest produce and raising of livestock. The poor here have limited access to land. The marginal farmers own degraded and low-quality land. Moreover, the stranglehold of caste regulates the agricultural wages, tenancy regulations, credit facilities and share-cropping, to name a few. The shift towards more commercial cropping coupled with limited access to government credit has pushed the rural economy into debt. The shrinking agricultural sector has also forced distress migration.

Despite various poverty alleviation programmes launched by the state government, the situation has only partially improved. The Janmabhoomi Scheme, the formation of the Self Help Groups (SHGs) and a host of measures for the SCs and STs have largely failed to deliver positive results. The exclusionary decision-making process, faulty delivery mechanism, and prevalence of social discrimination further disempowered the poor. The rural poor continue to live in a precarious condition, and are deprived of access to healthcare and nutrition, education, and employment opportunities, and the common property resources are shrinking. This directly impacts the condition of women and the marginalised sections and make them more vulnerable. Their limited resources affect their strategies to cope with and mitigate risk. Moreover, they have very limited access to public or private insurance systems.

STATE INITIATIVES

In May 2000, a strategy paper on poverty reduction programmes was prepared by the Rural Poverty Task Force. Subsequently, the government set up the Poverty Eradication Mission to function as an advisory body to the state government's poverty eradication programmes. This had two objectives, (i) to promote economic mobility and (ii) to enhance social protection by reducing vulnerability of the poor. In order to minimise the risks of the vulnerable rural poor, the project worked towards widening the scope of social security, improve non-farm employment and enhance access to credit facilities. The overall strategy was to improve people's participation in the poverty alleviation programmes at the grassroot level.

This chapter examines the efficacy of the present policy initiatives in attaining the goal of poverty eradication. The study is based on the field data collected from four *mandals* of Chittoor district of Andhra Pradesh in 2004. The findings also show that the present approach of the government has failed to achieve the desired results. Although poverty has been studied extensively, however, this persisting problem needs a fresh insight. This present study locates the problem of poverty in the existing structural conditions of society.

STUDY AREA

There are three revenue sub-divisions in the district namely Madanapalle, Chittoor and Tirupati which consist of sixty-six revenue mandals. Four mandals were selected out of two revenue blocks of Madanapalle and Tirupati. Two mandals each, namely Pileru and Gangavaram, and Pakala and B.N. Kandriga were identified from Madanapalle and Tirupati subdivisions respectively. Gangavaram and B.N. Kandriga mandals are located far from the district headquarters. The Andhra Pradesh government initiated the Velugu Programme for eradication of poverty in these mandals. While this programme was implemented in its first phase in these two mandals it was not implemented in Pakala even in its third phase as it was considered to be a developed mandal. Four villages, one from each mandal were selected for field studies, i.e., Chinnagorpadu from Pakala, Parlapalli from B.N. Kandriga, Balamvaripalli from Pileru, and Bommanapalli from Gangavaram. Several government reports, newspaper reports, census reports and maps constitute the additional sources for this study.

SOCIO-ECONOMIC ANALYSIS OF THE SAMPLE HOUSEHOLDS

As per the 1991 census, Chittoor district has a population of 32.61 lakhs of which the rural population is 26.15 lakhs, and urban 6.46 lakhs. The district ranks eighth in the state with an area of 15.152 sq kms which accounts for 5.51 per cent of the total area of the state. There are five municipalities—Chittoor, Tirupati, Madanapalle, Punganur and Srikalahasti. The number of revenue villages in the district is 1,500 comprising 1,394 gram panchayats. There are thirteen towns. Chittoor district has eight medium irrigation projects. The total registered ayacut under the eight projects is 41,429 acres. There are 8,814 minor irrigation tanks with a total ayacut of 3.2 lakh acres. There are 1,29,713 irrigated wells. The dominant castes largely depend on agricultural cultivation whereas the dalits and backward castes mainly comprise the labour force.

In terms of development indicators Chittoor is poor. The literacy rate of the district is only 42.2 per cent. Industrially it is not developed as it has only a few small-scale and cottage industries. Credit facilities are made available through 67 banks, 9 agricultural credit societies, 191 non-agricultural credit societies, and also through private money-lenders. The caste composition of the district is heterogeneous. Majority of landholdings are concentrated in the hands of the Reddys and Kammas.

Out of 100 households, the other backward castes (OBCs) comprise 40, the SCs 34, STs 6 and upper castes 20. In all the four villages SCs and OBCs constitute a majority of the population (See Table 5.5).

Of 100 households, 48 are below poverty line (BPL) of which 34 (71 per cent) are landless and 12 (25 per cent) own less than 2 acres of land. Amongst the landless 3 (9 per cent) belong to the STs, 18 (53 per cent) belong to the SCs, 10 (29 per cent) belong

Table 5.1: Profile of Four Selected Mandals

Selected Mandals	Pakala	B.N. Kandriga	Pileru	Ganga-varam
Area (sq. meters)	125.49	163.87	194.58	154.74
No. of Revenue villages (inhabited)	15	24	15	16
No. of Hamlets	238	108	244	118
No. of Towns	1	0	0	0
Households	11725	7106	10972	7859
Total Population	54361	28159	48607	41843
Percentage of Urban Population	38.2	0	0	0
Percentage of Rural Population	61.8	100.00	100.00	100.00
Percentage of Scheduled Caste	21.09	31.91	9.92	19.61
Percentage of Scheduled Tribes	1.67	13.94	4.03	1.52
Sex Ratio	965	983	956	989
Density	433	178	250	270
Percentage of Male Literates	31.22	19.90	30.00	24.02
Percentage of Female Literates	18.12	7.40	16.74	11.06
Percentage of Total Literates	49.34	27.30	46.74	35.08

Source: *Handbook of Statistics 2000–1*, Chittoor District, Chief Planning Officer, Government of Andhra Pradesh.

Table 5.2: Socio-Economic Indicators of Four Selected Mandals

Selected Mandals	Pakala	B.N. Kandriga	Pileru	Ganga-varam
Hospitals	1	0	0	0
PHC	2	1	2	2
Factories (2000)	8	8	31	14
Small-scale industries (No. of units)	75	1	59	5
Banks	7	1	5	2
Primary Schools	72	53	64	75
UPS	3	6	3	6
High Schools	4	3	6	6
Junior Colleges	2	1	5	1
NGOs	2	1	10	0
Pensions (Old Age)	793	650	1220	841
Pensions (Widow)	92	54	80	69
No. of FPS	38	27	55	27
White Cards	9125	6073	9561	7096
Pink Cards	4819	1560	3785	1591

Source: *Handbook of Statistics 2000–1*, Chittoor District, Chief Planning Officer, Government of Andhra Pradesh.

Table 5.3: Profile of Four Selected Villages

Mandals	Total Population	No. of Hamlets	Percentage of Cultivated Land	Percentage of Un-cultivated Land	Percentage of Waste Land	Total Agricultural Land-Various Categories of Production: Irrigated in (acres)	Unirrigated in (acres)	Waste Land in (acres)	No. of Rainy Day's
Chinnagorpadu (Pakala Mandal)	1226 M 596 F 630	10	58	2.5	5	616	794	128	30
Balamvaripalli (Pileru Mandal)	2137 M 1050 F 1087	17	50	42	3	792	2454	NA	45
Bommanapalli (Gangavaram Mandal)	630 M 305 F 325	NA	NA	NA	NA	NA	NA	NA	48
Parlapalli (B.N. Kandriga Mandal)	851 M 425 F 426	2	NA	NA	NA	127	4	18	47

Source: Primary data collected from household survey.

*NA: Not available

Table 5.4: Land Use Pattern

Villages	Cultivated in Acres	Forest in Acres	Waste in Acres	Uncultivated in Acres	Grazing in Acres	Others
Chinnagorpadu (Pakala Mandal)	1410	80	128	234	300	370
Balamvaripalli (Pileru Mandal)	3524	382	195	1532	351	815
Bommanapalli (Gangavaram Mandal)	NA	NA	NA	NA	NA	NA
Parlapalli	486	–	18	163	188	184

Source: *Handbook of Statistics 2000–1*, Pakala, Pileru, Gangavaram and B.N. Kandriga Mandals, Assistant Statistical Officers, Chittoor, Andhra Pradesh.
*NA: Not available

Table 5.5: Social Composition of the Households

Categories	SC	ST	OBC	UC	Total
No. of Households	34	06	40	20	100

Source: Primary data collected from household survey.

Table 5.6: Landholdings and Social Composition of BPL Households

	No. of BPL	ST	SC	OBC	General
Landless	34	3	18	10	3
<2 acres	12	0	4	4	4
2–5 acres	1	0	0	1	0
5–10 acres	1	0	0	0	1
>10 acres	0	0	0	0	0
Total	48	3	22	15	8

Source: Primary data collected from household survey.

to the OBCs and 3 (9 per cent) belong to the general category. A majority of the BPL households belong to the landless category. However, households who own 5 to 10 acres of land also figure in the BPL list (See Table 5.6).

Land plays a prominent role in the livelihood of the people. Out of 100 households, 79 are landless. Majority of them belong to OBCs and SCs (87.5 per cent and 85 per cent respectively). In the general category 50 per cent of the households do not possess any land.

Table 5.7: Number of Households in Different Landholding Categories

	Landless	Less than 2 acres	2–5 acres	5–10 acre	Above 10
Chittoor	79	14	3	1	3

Source: Primary data collected from household survey.

Table 5.8: Social Categories and Landholding

	Chittoor					
	Landless	< 2 acres	2–5 acres	5–10 acres	> 10 acres	Total
SC	28	6	0	0	0	34
ST	6	0	0	0	0	6
OBC	35	4	1	0	0	40
General	10	4	2	1	3	20
Total	79	14	3	1	3	100

Source: Primary data collected from household survey.

Of the 40 households in the category of SCs/STs, 34 households are landless. None of the ST and SC households possess more than two acres of land (See Tables 5.7, 5.8 and Figure 5.1).

A majority of the landless households depend on wage labour. Among the landless households, 74 are agricultural labourers, 4 are cultivators, 4 are engaged in allied agricultural activities and 3 are non-agricultural labourers. In the category of households owning less than two acres of land 50 per cent are cultivators and the rest are engaged in wage labour, both agricultural and non-agricultural. It should be noted that one household is engaged in more than one occupation and majority of the cultivators also do agricultural and non-agricultural work (See Table 5.9).

Table 5.10 shows that out of 225 labourers, 119 are males and 106 females. Out of 176 workers engaged in other activities (construction and other occupations), 84 are males and 92 females.

Eighty per cent of the population of Chittoor depend on agriculture for their livelihood. Agriculture being seasonal, a majority of the landless remain employed for about 4 to 8 months during the year (See Table 5.11) remaining unemployed for the rest of the months. This is commonly referred to as seasonal unemployment.

Figure 5.1: Social Composition and Landholding

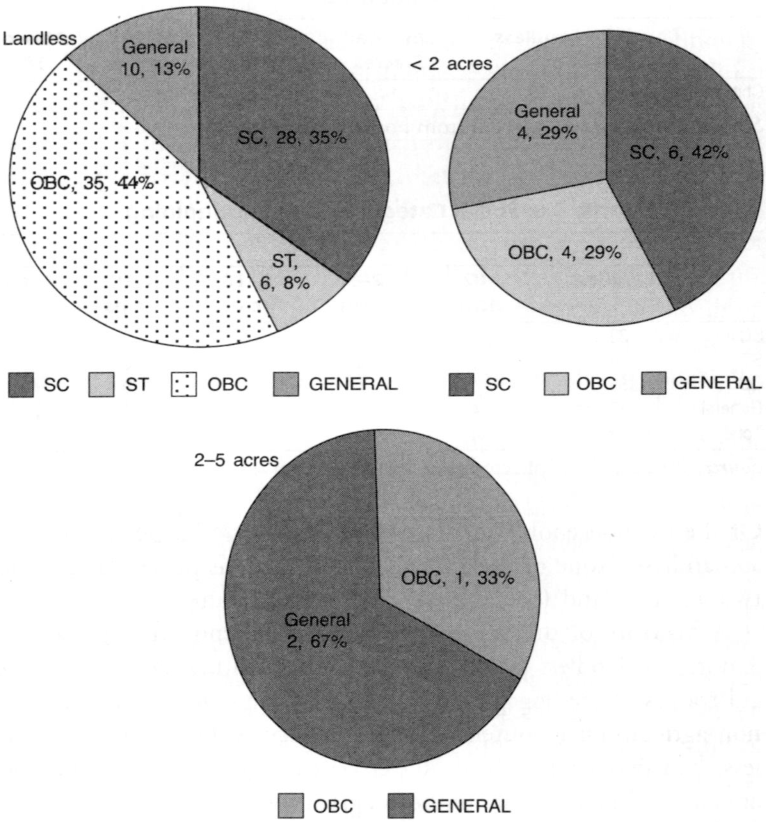

Source: Primary data collected from household survey.

Table 5.9: Occupational Patterns

	Agriculture			Non-Agriculture	Govt./ Pvt. Job
	Agri. Labour	Cultivator	Allied Agri.		
Landless	74	4	4	3	3
< 2 acres	9	10	0	1	0
2–5 acres	0	3	0	1	0
5–10 acres	0	1	0	0	0
> 10 acres	0	2	0	1	0

Source: Primary data collected from household survey.

Table 5.10: Occupational Composition

	Chittoor		
	Male	**Female**	**Total**
Service	2	2	4
Shopowners	0	0	0
Farming	9	4	13
Allied agriculture	0	3	3
Labourers	119	106	225
Household industry	1	0	1
Professionals	1	0	1
Squatters	0	0	0
Unemployed	2	1	3
Retired	0	0	0
Housewife	0	16	16
Others	84	92	176
Total (also the dependents)	221	230	451

Source: Primary data collected from household survey.

Table 5.11: Number of Days Employed

	Agriculture			
	< 4 Months	**4–8 Months**	**8–12 Months**	
Landless	14	61	3	76
< 2 acres	1	11	1	13
2–5 acres	0	3	0	3
5–10 acres	0	1	0	3
> 10 acres	0	2	1	2

Source: Primary data collected from household survey.

Table 5.12 shows that since employment opportunities are locally available, migration is less in the case of Chittoor. There are only three migrants who have moved to nearby towns in search of work, who belong to both the landless and land-owning category (See Table 5.13).

The degree of indebtedness in all the four villages studied is very high. We find that there are multiple sources of lending. A majority of the households borrowed from the banks and private money-lenders. In most cases when the borrowing is above Rs 10,000 they borrowed from banks, and if the amount borrowed is in the range of Rs 1,000 and Rs 5,000 they borrowed from the money-lenders, friends and relatives. The informal interest rates

Table 5.12: Reasons for Migration

Total Out Migration	Place of Migration	Reasons	Nature of Jobs	
	Tirupati	Lack of work	Painter	15,000
	Bangalore/Tirupati	No work in village	Contract Labour	Nil
	Hyderabad	For work	Labour	Nil

Source: Primary data collected from household survey.

Table 5.13: Migration and Social Category

Landholding Size	No. of Households Having Migration	SC	ST	OBC	General	Total
Landless	1	0	0	1	0	1
< 2 acres	1	1	0	0	0	1
2–5 acres	0	0	0	0	0	0
5–10 acres	1	0	0	0	1	1
> 10 acres	0	0	0	0	0	0
Total	3	1	0	1	1	3

Source: Primary data collected from household survey.

Table 5.14: Indebtedness, Sources of Lending

	Amount in Rs				
	< 1,000	1,000–5,000	5,000–10,000	> 10,000	Total
Banks	0	5	7	37	49
Money Lenders	1	15	7	6	29
Financial Institutions	2	2	1	3	8
Others	0	11	9	11	31
Total	3	33	24	57	117

Source: Primary data collected from household survey.

are very high varying from Rs 5 to 10 per Rs 100 per month. The interest rate goes up if the need is immediate, leading people to get caught in a debt trap. The borrowings are mostly to meet their consumption needs or purchase household goods and festival expenditure (See Table 5.14).

The majority of the borrowers are from the landless households (See Table 5.15). Unlike the landless who borrow for their consumption needs the land-owning households borrow for investments. Some

Table 5.15: Landholdings, Borrowings and Social Categories

Landholding Size	SC	ST	OBC	General	Total
Landless	17	5	30	11	63
< 2 acres	5	0	4	4	13
2–5 acres	0	0	0	2	2
5–10 acres	0	0	0	1	1
> 10 acres	0	0	0	3	3
Total	22	5	34	21	82

Source: Primary data collected from household survey.

Table 5.16: Average Annual Income

Landholding Size	No. of People	Total (Rs)	Avg/HH Income (Rs)	Per Capita Income (Rs)
Landless	346 (79)	636800	8270	1840
< 2 acres	69 (14)	246850	18988	3578
2–5 acres	17 (3)	53750	17916	3162
5–10 acres	5 (1)	25000	25000	5000
> 10 acres	14 (3)	14200	47333	10143

Figure in parenthesis shows the total number of households
Source: Primary data collected from household survey.

households borrowed from more than one source such as banks, relatives and private money-lenders.

The average annual income of the landless households is Rs 8,270 and per capita income is Rs 1,840. Households in the category of less than 2 acres of land have an average annual income of Rs 18,988, and their per capita income is double that of landless households at Rs 3,578. The average per capita income of households above 10 acres of land is Rs 10,143. It can be seen from Table 5.16 that with an increase in size of the landholdings, the average annual per capita income also increases, which shows a positive relation between the income and size of landholding.

Table 5.17 shows that out of 100 households, 81 per cent had *kutcha* houses. While in the landless household category 87 per cent had kutcha houses, none of the households above 5 acres of land had kutcha houses. Thus in terms of assets the land-owning households were better off than the landless households.

Table 5.17: Types of Houses

Landholding Size	Kutcha	Semi Pucca	Pucca
Landless	69	4	6
< 2 acres	9	4	1
2–5 acres	3	0	0
5–10 acres	0	0	1
> 10 acres	0	1	2
Total	81	9	10

Source: Primary data collected from household survey.

Livestock is considered to be a secondary source of income in rural areas. Table 5.18 shows that 54 per cent of the households possess livestock such as cows, buffaloes and sheep. However, these assets did not improve their living standards as even the households belonging to the BPL category also possess livestock. There are different schemes to provide livestock to the marginalised communities. However, most of these loans remain on paper, while the amount specified is used for paying back debts. To illustrate, a respondent stated that she availed of a loan of Rs 23,000 to purchase a Jersey cow from the SHGs. She later confessed that the money was used to pay back an earlier loan incurred for educational purpose, a common practice among the deprived communities.

Literacy is another determining factor for development. A critical dimension of poverty eradication is to create awareness among the poor sections of society by providing educational opportunities. Table 5.19 shows that out of 303 landless people, 164 are literates, whereas 139 are illiterates. Out of the 14 people in the above 10 acres of landholding households 13 are literates, and only one is illiterate. This allows them to extract maximum benefit from available

Table 5.18: Assets

Name of the District	No. of Households Having Bicycles/ Motorcycles	No. of Households Having Tractor	No. of Households Having Livestock	No. of Households Having Saving Accounts
Chittoor	15	1	53	0

Source: Primary data collected from household survey.

Table 5.19: Literacy Levels in Different Landholding Categories

Landholding Size	Literate	Illiterate	Total
Landless	164	139	303
< 2 acres	43	21	64
2–5 acres	12	4	16
5–10 acres	2	3	5
> 10 acres	13	1	14
Total	234	168	402

Source: Primary data collected from household survey.

employment opportunities. The better literacy rate also helps them to take the advantage of developmental programmes initiated by local institutions.

The male-female ratio among illiterates is 2:3. Among the literates only 7.5 per cent have crossed high school level. Studies show that the number of dropout is higher among girls than among boys and that more number of girls dropout after completing middle school. Various factors like household work (cooking and caring for their siblings), seasonal agricultural work, and location and distance of the school contribute to this dropout (See Figure 5.2).

Figure 5.2: Different Educational Levels of Male and Female

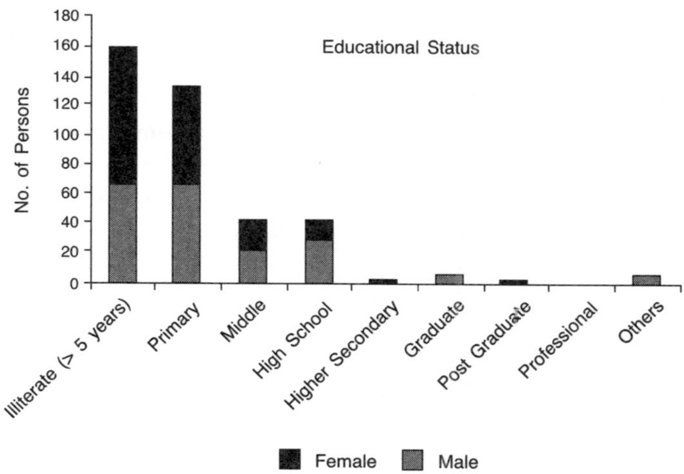

Source: Primary data collected from household survey.

Table 5.20: Educational Status and Social Categories

Educational Status	SC	ST	OBC	General	Total
Illiterate (>5 years)	59	16	66	20	161
Primary	44	16	45	31	136
Middle	16	0	12	16	44
High School	17	1	15	11	44
Higher Secondary	1	0	0	1	2
Graduate	1	0	3	2	6
Post Graduate	0	0	2	0	2
Professional	0	0	0	0	0
Others	1	0	4	2	7
Total	139	33	147	83	402

Source: Primary data collected from household survey.

The rate of illiteracy among SCs, STs, and OBCs (87.5 per cent) is much higher as compared to that of the other castes (12.5 per cent) leading to a restricted development of human capital. A number of factors create this vicious cycle. A majority of schoolchildren are first generation learners among the SCs, STs, and OBCs, and their parents lack motivation. The data reveals that due to mid-day meals, enrolment in primary schools is quite high. Lack of quality education also compel students to drop out, especially after high school. Moreover, their labour is also required to supplement household income. The high degree of illiteracy among the lower caste people acts as an impediment to their socio-economic development and traps them in the endemic cycle of poverty (See Table 5.20).

Persistence of poverty and the level of average income show their impact on the level of expenditure on food items. A majority of the poor peasants spend less than Rs 35 per week on food items, which is far below the desired average. Households owning above 5 acres of land spend above Rs 50 per week. With an increase in the size of landholdings and income the amount of expenditure on food goes up (See Table 5.21). The annual household expenditure of 20 households is Rs 80.50 on shelter. The per capita annual expense incurred on education is Rs 59.30, and on medicine is Rs 62.50.

The level of political consciousness in rural Andhra Pradesh is very high. This is quite evident from the fact that 94 per cent

Table 5.21: Consumption Expenditure in Rs Per Week

Landholding Size	< 35	35–50	> 50	Total
Landless	52	12	10	74
< 2 acres	11	1	1	13
2–5 acres	2	1	0	3
5–10 acres	0	0	1	1
> 10 acres	0	0	3	3
Govt/Pvt jobs	0	0	5	5

Source: Primary data collected from household survey.

Table 5.22: Political Party Preference of Different Social Categories

Social Categories	Congress	TDP	TOTAL
SC	2	2	34
ST	2	2	6
OBC	2	0	40
General	0	0	20
TOTAL	6	4	100

Source: Primary data collected from household survey.

Figure 5.3: Social Categories and Party Preference

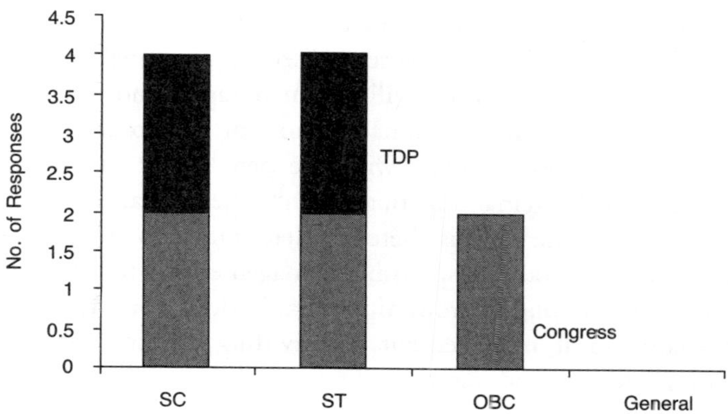

Source: Primary data collected from household survey.

of the households confirmed participating in elections, however, only 10 per cent of the households expressed their preferences for political parties. The emergence of a smaller party like the Telugu Desam Party (TDP), facilitated the pace of this political consciousness. While conducting this study we found that villagers perceived alignment with a political party as a surer way of getting benefitted from the various developmental programmes. Even the dominant communities easily avail of old age pensions, ration cards, BPL cards, etc. This reveals the close linkages between development schemes and political affiliations (See Table 5.22).

PANCHAYATS AND POVERTY ALLEVIATION SCHEMES

Despite an emphasis on employment generation and capacity-building through NGOs and Panchayati Raj Institutions (PRIs), the employment generation schemes like food-for-work programme have not been successfully implemented by the state. The approach to provide micro-credit to self help groups through NGOs and other bodies has not been successful either. The survey shows that in two villages where SHGs exist, the SHG leaders who belong to the upper castes have benefitted the most.

The state government came out with a document 'Vision 2020', which underlined that by the year 2020, Andhra Pradesh will provide a growth-conducive, de-regularised policy environment to enable market-based development. Decentralised decision-making will be the norm and local bodies will be encouraged and empowered to participate in administration. The role of the government will be to maintain close contact with the people and involve them in governance by remaining transparent, effective and responsive to their needs. The state is therefore determined to strengthen its administration through responsible management by the Panchayati Raj Institutions and community organisations. To this end, it will enable local management by dividing administrative and economic powers and responsibilities. To successfully implement this framework, any change in administrative system will be carefully managed.

In 1997, the Janmabhoomi programme was launched in the state—the focus being to involve people at the grassroots level in a sustainable developmental process. The main thrust of the programme was empowerment through people's participation by including the different marginalised sections. The gram sabhas play an important role in this programme. The district is at the apex of the three-tier structure of Panchayati Raj. This is followed by the mandal parishad—a unit where the actual implementation of the developmental programmes takes place. The gram panchayats are entrusted with the responsibility of providing civil amenities and carrying out activities like minor irrigation, watershed management and cooperative management at the village level. The Janmabhoomi programme was severely criticised as it was perceived that it was weakening the Panchayati Raj Institutions by diluting the basic objective of decentralised local governance, the cornerstone of the 73rd Amendment. The state also initiated the Development of Women and Children in Rural Areas (DWACRA) programme to promote gender empowerment and equity by providing micro-credit facilities through self help groups in rural areas. This programme was started in 1982–3 with the cooperation of the UNICEF to provide opportunities for self-employment. By gaining entrepreneurial skills villagers were expected to improve their capacity and control on labour, resources, leadership and reproductive choices.

The Velugu was executed by the Society for Elimination of Rural Poverty (SERP), which is an independent and autonomous society. The SERP, with support from the World Bank, is also responsible for the implementation of Andhra Pradesh District Poverty Initiative Project (APDPIP) in 180 backward mandals of the six districts of Adilabad, Mahaboobnagar, Anantapur, Chittoor, Srikakulam and Vijayanagaram. Between the years 2000–5, Rs 580 crores was invested to eradicate poverty. The second phase of Velugu, named Andhra Pradesh Rural Poverty Reduction Programme (APRPRP), is being implemented in the remaining districts. Velugu is the only project that covers 846 mandals across 22 districts of the state.

The anti-arrack movement in Andhra Pradesh, initiated by the women of the state challenged the powerful liquor lobby and compelled the state to initiate the DWACRA programme with an aim to provide financial assistance to women, especially the ones belonging to the dalit, tribal, economically poor community and backward castes, for employment generation. The idea was to facilitate women's participation in the decision-making process. The Andhra Pradesh government also initiated other governmental programmes like the Integrated Rural Development Programme (IRDP), Deepam, Watersheds, Chief Minister Employment Yojana (CMEY), Aapadbhandhu, Adarana, Chaitanyam, Mundadugu (for SCs, STs, OBCs, Women and Minority), Huge Allotment Schemes, Village Water Supply, Family Planning Operations, Rural Electrifications, Ration Card Distributions, Roads and Transport, Small-Scale Industries. However, the programmes are plagued by political interference, red-tapism and bureaucratic mismanagement which reduce their effectiveness.

As an ongoing experiment with direct democracy in the form of community based organisations at the local level, the Andhra Pradesh government has also implemented various welfare schemes like the Rural Employment Programme, SHGs, Joint Forest Management, Deepam Scheme, Area Development Programmes, Integrated Rural Development Programmes, Tenancy Reforms where the control over the land have been taken over by the stakeholders' association from the village sarpanches. However, increasing political and bureaucratic influence have adversely affected the functioning of these programmes.

The state government expected that all these programmes would ensure greater political participation in the gram sabhas which in turn would help the poor to focus on their demands. Despite all

Table 5.23: Panchayat Functioning

	Vote Cast in Elections			Participation in Gram/Palli Sabha			Participation in the Discussion			Sarpanch in Village		
	01	02	03	01	02	03	01	02	03	01	02	03
Chittoor	94	6	100	35	65	100	35	65	100	81	19	100

01: Yes, 02: No, 03: Total

Source: Primary data collected from household survey.

this, only 35 per cent of the respondents said that they take part in the gram sabha discussions, reflective of poor involvement of community members in the decision-making process. The sarpanchs' frequent visits to different villages do not yield any tangible result. Often, in case of a female sarpanch, the de-facto power is vested with a male family member (See Table 5.23).

Issues like roads, housing, finance, employment and other development activities are generally discussed in the palli sabha meetings. However, concerns regarding education, healthcare, access to resources, caste atrocities, gender discrimination and social audit, to name a few, are hardly raised in these meetings. The gram sabha and the palli sabha meetings are often held in the upper caste localities, indirectly ensuring spatial control, which turn out to be intimidating for the lower castes. Many a time information regarding the meetings is not properly disseminated. Often it becomes difficult for poor daily wage labourers to miss her/his day's income and attend the meetings (See Table 5.24).

Table 5.25 shows that among the landless only 33 per cent participated in the meetings whereas the involvement of households possessing more than 2 acres of land is as high as 67 per cent.

A majority of the landless households (38 per cent) participated in the political process with the hope of a better future. Personal contacts with the panchayat officials ensured participation from 29 per cent households, whereas 28 per cent households participated in order to benefit from development programmes. Only 4 per cent of the households participated in the gram sabha to exercise their

Table 5.24: Issues Discussed in Panchayat Meetings

Landholding Size	Roads	Housing and Other Loans	Employ-ment	Water	Other Devel-opment	House Allot-ments	Total
Landless	38	28	17	8	18	13	122
<2 acres	8	11	1	0	2	0	22
2–5 acres	1	3	0	1	0	0	5
5–10 acres	0	1	0	0	1	0	2
> 10 acres	3	2	0	1	1	0	7

Source: Primary data collected from household survey.

Table 5.25: Households Participating in Gram/Palli Sabha Meeting

Landholding Size	Participating	Not Participating
Landless	26	52
<2–acres	3	11
2–5–acres	2	1
5–10 acres	1	0
>10 acres	3	0
Total	35	65

Source: Primary data collected from household survey.

Figure 5.4: Participation in Gram Sabha Meetings

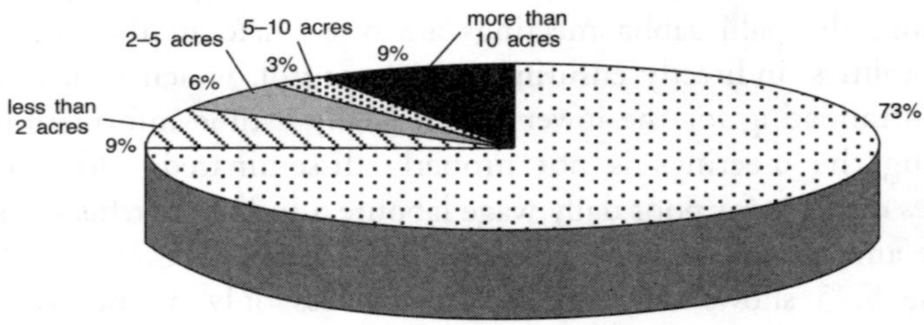

Source: Primary data collected from household survey.

Table 5.26: Issues for Participating in Election

Landholding Size	Development	Better Life	Party and Candidate Image	Political Responsibility	Others	No Response
Landless	22	30	23	3	6	15
<2 acres	2	5	0	0	1	5
2–5 acres	1	2	0	1	0	0
5–10 acres	0	0	0	0	0	1
>10 acres	2	1	0	0	0	0

Source: Primary data collected from household survey.

right to vote (See Table 5.26). Considerations of personal gains seem to be the main motivation behind political participation at the panchayat level.

In Chittoor, there are forty-three government initiated development programmes. Tables 5.27 and 5.28 show that availability of micro-

Table 5.27: Households Benefitting from Government Schemes

Landholding Size	PDS	House Loans	DWACRA	Old Age Pension	Others/ IRDP
Landless	65	9	1	30	0
<2 acres	11	3	1	6	2
2–5 acres	2	1	1	2	0
5–10 acres	0	0	0	1	0
>10 acres	2	0	0	0	0

Source: Primary data collected from household survey.

Table 5.28: Reasons for the Failure of PDS

Landholding Size	Non-Availability	Timing Improper/ Items Not Included	No Response/ No Card
Landless	69	1	9
<2 acres	13	0	0
2–5 acres	3	0	0
5–10 acres	1	0	0
>10 acres	2	0	1
Total	88	1	10

Source: Primary data collected from household survey.

credit facilities, PDS, old age and widow pensions determine people's participation in elections.

The district has not witnessed any strong social movements. Since a large majority is landless, they depend on the land-owning households. Many dalit groups have organised themselves to fight for their rights. A nascent naxalite movement exists in Srikalahasti and Pileru. Even though the district has the highest number of NGOs in the country, they play a minimal role at the grassroots level. This study, conducted in the four villages, reveals that NGOs are almost non-functional at the local level.

In the light of the above facts we can say that various developmental programmes have not yielded the desired results for the vulnerable sections of society. The World Bank initiatives to support the poor through the provision of micro-credit and capacity-building have not resulted in any tangible change in the status of the socially deprived sections. The culturally constructed socio-political structure has helped the dominant castes. The benefits of the state initiated programmes have been appropriated by the supporters of the ruling political party and their caste affiliations.

To be in touch with the constituencies, and improve governance the state government initiated video-conferencing facility. However, the situation on the ground have hardly changed as government officials remained unapproachable and continued to be perceived as highly corrupt. A family from Madanapalle region reported that they lost their land after they were cheated by an upper caste family from the same village five years ago. Slack administrative process has denied the family justice. This shows that while studying poverty one needs to address the structural-political perspective as well. So far, the policymakers have looked at poverty merely as a political and economic problem and ignored its structural dimensions. This study analyses the failure of the state in ensuring poverty eradication from a structural-political perspective.

THE CHITTOOR EXPERIENCE: A STRUCTURAL-POLITICAL PERSPECTIVE

Six decades after independence, the rural population continues to be plagued by denial of quality healthcare, access to just and equitable education, access to common property resources, and fair participation in the socio-political process regardless of caste and gender. The social and cultural control on land, water, forest resources, which are vested in a few hands, have turned the landless into deprived communities dependent on the upper castes. In turn, this dependence makes it beneficial for the upper-caste people to gain political favours. The low earning capacity of the marginalised groups increases their dependence on private money-lenders for credit at exorbitant rates of interest. The existing inequality which generates conflicts in society impoverishes the poor further. The vicious circle of poverty can only be broken by initiating structural-political reforms. Equal rights to land, forest resources, water and other endowments have to be recognised, and steps should be taken for equal distribution of natural and common resources so that human development in terms of health, employment and education can be achieved.

The People's Democratic Organisations (PDOs) must play a vital role to protect the rights of the scheduled castes and tribes, other backward castes, women, poor peasants, landless, artisans, and unorganised labourers. These developments will ensure peoples' participation in the democratic process to prepare their own plans rather than the state imposing its own policies on them. Peoples' participation in policymaking, implementation and monitoring will result in enhancement of land rights, right to natural resources, access to education, health and employment of SCs, STs, OBCs and women which will ultimately lead to social transformation and ensure development.

The pursuit of poverty eradication programmes during the past six decades show ample evidence that market-led economic development will not eradicate poverty. At present, the political system is under mounting pressure to ensure inclusive development. This prescription is based on the understanding that structural inequalities, and the power struggles they give rise to, crucially shape the efforts of poverty eradication. The socio-political and economic exclusion, as ordained and sustained by cultural norms, has led to economic exploitation of the poor and given rise to a dependency syndrome. The focus must lie on bringing about institutional changes in terms of formulation and implementation of policies. With regard to resources, it must attempt to change the basis of resource distribution and utilisation within the locality. However, these changes are constrained by the existing political process. The poverty eradication strategies are thus dependent upon the structural-political transformation.

An attempt has been made to identify the constraints in the villages surveyed in relation to the programmes like Janmabhoomi, food-for-work programme and Velugu among others. It is observed that the poor have a restricted 'political space', and as a consequence, the objectives of these programmes are not achieved in their true spirit. The political space of the poor is further constricted by the institutional channels which limit participation of the poor in policy formulation and implementation. The political discourses on poverty eradication should focus on social and political processes of the poor which form the basis for influencing decision-making, policy and programme implementations.

The poverty eradication initiatives of the government of Andhra Pradesh, which are mentioned above, have been analysed in terms of the lack of 'political space' provided to the poor in the villages surveyed, and the general observations and conclusions are summarised in the next section.

GENERAL OBSERVATIONS AND CONCLUSION

- The role of the NGOs is minimal in the implementation of the programmes.
- Widespread corruption exists in the bureaucracy.
- Funds are misutilised by the NGOs.
- The panchayats do not meet regularly. Even if panchayat meetings are held, the date and time are not advertised properly to all gram sabha members.
- A majority of SC/ST sarpanches depend on, and are influenced by the dominant politicians.
- The behaviour of government officials are marred by laziness, apathy, lack of work ethics.
- A lot of money is wasted on publicity of development programmes.
- Precious time is wasted in preparing statistics for the chief minister's video-conferencing.
- There are more than 30 welfare programmes for the poor. But due to lack of clarity about the objectives and causes of poverty the programmes are not implemented properly.
- There is a great sense of alienation among the poor, and the benefits of the various poverty eradication programmes are not easily available to them.
- Caste discrimination prevents the vulnerable groups from benefitting from development and welfare activities.

- Bank loans are not easily available to the poor as they lack minimum collateral to avail them.
- The mandal health clinics are not well-equipped and medicine distribution system is poor.
- The emergence of the Telugu Desam Party has increased political consciousness among the masses.
- Party affiliations are being used for personal purposes.
- Local politics are influenced by caste, class, family and factional rivalries.

Institutional channels like the PRIs provide 'political opportunity' for the marginalised sections. Simultaneously, the interest groups and the state have succeeded in hindering the transformation of 'political opportunities' into 'political inclusion' by creating stakeholders' associations, for example, water-users' associations, school education committees, which have no provision for reservation for the marginalised. These stakeholders have taken over the panchayat's functions, and as a consequence, marginalised sections who get elected as PRI representatives are unable to exercise their rights to manage the programmes for poverty eradication. The 'Nodal System' has made the post of the panchayat president irrelevant. The seriousness of the issue can be realised from the fact that representatives of local bodies in association with some state-level NGOs are on a collision course with the state government. Over time, the Janmabhoomi programme, which was introduced to create a spirit of participation, has been reduced to that of a forum to receive representations for loans, house-sites, ration cards, etc.

The local and political practices of the marginalised continue to reinforce patron-client relationships. The poor, who cannot afford to make sacrifices due to their economic deprivation, are excluded from the 'political stratum' which plays a dominant role in providing the vertical and horizontal linkages within the existing power structure. The irregularities in the implementation of food-for-work programmes reveal the lack of understanding of the poor, which has a direct bearing on the poverty eradication process. Dominant caste groups and interest groups with the connivance of local officials have side-tracked the benefits without any resistance from the poor. The poor and marginalised do not have any access to knowledge or information pertaining to the employment generation programmes, and hence cannot resist the actions of vested interest groups.

REFERENCES

Documents

World Bank Project Appraisal Document to the Government of Andhra Pradesh, Rural Poverty Reduction Project, 2003.

UNDP. 2001. *Human Development Report*. 2001. New Delhi: Oxford University Press.

Statistical Profile: Chittoor District. 2001 by DPO, Chittoor.

Tenth Five Year Plan. 2003. Planning Commission. Government of India.

World Bank. 2003. *World Development Report*. Washington DC: World Bank.

Books and Journals

Bhatt, Mihir R. 1997. 'Integrating Disaster Mitigating with Food Security at Panchayat Level', in P. Chaturvedi (ed.), *Food Security and Panchayati Raj*. New Delhi: Concept Publishing.

Choudhary, Anil Kumar. 2000. 'NGOs and their Role in Poverty Alleviation', in Kamta Prasad (ed.), *NGOs and Socio-Economic Development Opportunities*. New Delhi: Deep and Deep Publication.

C. H. Hanumantha Rao and S. Mahendra Dev. 2003. 'Economic Reforms and Challenges Ahead'. *Economic and Political Weekly*. Special Issue on Andhra Pradesh. Vol. 38. No. 12 and 13. 22–8 March.

Harris, Barbara. 1992. 'Rural Poverty in India: Micro-level Evidence', in Barbara Harris, S. Guha and R. H. Chossin (ed.), *India Research and Policy*. Oxford: Oxford University Press.

Kumar, Somesh. 2002. 'India: Gains and Stagnation in Bihar and Andhra Pradesh', in Deepa Narayan, Petesch Patti (ed.), *From Many Lands*. New York: World Bank.

Parthasarthy, G. 1995. 'Public Intervention and Rural Poverty: Case of Non-Sustainable Reduction in Andhra Pradesh'. *Economic and Political Weekly*. Vol 30. No: 15. 14–21 October.

Powis, Benjamin. 2003. 'Grassroots Politics and Second Wave of Decentralisation in Andhra Pradesh'. *Economic and Political Weekly*. Vol. 38. 28 June. 2617–22.

Radhakrishna, R. 1988. *Levels of Living in a State Setting: A Case of Andhra Pradesh*. Hyderabad: CESS.

Reddy, B. Sambi. 2002. 'Assessment and Identification of Rural Poor in India: A Study based on NSS Household Data'. *Journal of Rural Development*. October–December..

Reddy, Narayan. G. 2002. 'Empowering Women through Self-Help Groups and Micro Credit: The Case of NIRD Action Research Projects'. *Journal of Rural Development*. October–December.

Sainath, P. 1996. *Everybody Loves a Good Drought*. Penguin: New Delhi.

Sen, Amartya. 1982. *Poverty and Famines: An Essay on Entitlement*. New Delhi: Oxford University Press.

Sen, Biswajit. 2003. 'Understanding of Poverty and Empowerment of Poor'. *Mainstream*. Vol. XLL. No. 19. April.

Sundaram, K. and Suresh D. Tendulkar. 2003. 'Poverty in India in the 1990s: An Analysis of Changes in 15 Major States'. *Economic and Political Weekly*. Vol. XXXVIII. No. 14. 5 April.

NATIONAL RE-IMAGININGS
CLASHES OF IDENTITY

6

History, Truth and Nation: Contemporary Debates on Education in India

Nivedita Menon

Let me begin by clarifying what this chapter is not about. This chapter is not about debates on education in India—that is an area worthy of study, and raises crucial questions about pedagogy, construction of knowledge, literacy versus education and so on. But that is not what I am looking at here. What I attempt to do in this chapter is to look at one strand of these debates as they emerged in the context of the Hindu right-wing project of rewriting history textbooks, for some years before and during the NDA regime.

We see two phases when we trace this particular strand of the debate, the first during the NDA regime, when the Hindu Right was aligned against secular historians and intellectuals, and the latter a broad spectrum comprising left-of-centre liberals, to those closely linked to the CPI and CPI(M), and non-party affiliated Leftists. The

---

This chapter is based on two earlier publications, 'History and Truth, History as Truth', *Contemporary India*, Journal of the Nehru Memorial Museum and Library, Vol. 1, No. 1, January–March 2002, and 'To Accommodate the Curious Mind', *The Telegraph*, 25 August 2005.

second phase, after the defeat of the NDA in the General Elections in 2004, and the coming to power of the UPA revealed a new fault line in the secularist camp, this time arising from differing views on education, its role and purpose. While the BJP and the Hindu Right carried on its criticism along the old lines, a smaller group of nationalist historians and CPI(M)-linked intellectuals made common cause to launch an attack on the draft *National Curriculum Framework 2005* (*NCF-2005*). This document went much beyond a mere de-saffronisation move and expanded into an attempt to rethink pedagogical practices entirely. An uncommonly democratic consultative process initiated by the new Director of NCERT, Krishna Kumar, involved about three hundred people all over the country—teachers, academics and educational activists—over a period of seven months. A large number of scholars of impeccably secular credentials, including Krishna Kumar himself, participated in the process—political scientist Gopal Guru, historians Sumit Sarkar, Narayani Gupta and Neeladri Bhattacharya, to name but a few. And yet the sharp attack by the group mentioned above on the draft *NCF-2005*, termed it 'obscurantist'.

What is at stake in this debate, both phases of it? I can see two issues here. One, debates about reality and representation and claims to true or atleast truer representation of a reality are more central than ever before to public discourse all over the world. Burning questions about contemporary politics seem to turn increasingly on understandings of what constitutes acceptable difference, the particular histories that constitute such difference, and the status of 'truth' that may or may not be accorded to those histories. These issues come up in the Indian debate on education, and on history in particular quite centrally.

A second issue at stake in the Indian debate is the nation—its legitimacy in claiming paramount loyalty from its citizens at any cost. In the first part of the chapter, I focus on the first phase and the first issue, and outline some of the theoretical and philosophical issues that emerge. In the second part of the chapter, I focus on the second issue and the way it plays out in the second phase of the debate.

II

In the struggle over history during the first phase I allude to, there was little confusion on who the two sides were, and what they stood for. The Hindu Right directed rewriting of standard history textbooks produced in the 1970s by historians of worldwide repute, followed the explicit agenda of redressing what is claimed to be a distortion of the past. In this redressal, the declared aim is to valorise 'Hindu' achievements and to present the 'Hindu' community as one that has existed from time immemorial, one that has always been, and continues to be egalitarian. This community that is evoked is a homogeneous one that basically looks like the nineteenth century, North Indian, upper-caste version of Hinduism, with all its taboos and beliefs presented as eternal, but with caste inequality carefully excised. The other aspect of this project is the assimilation of all other religions other than Islam into the fold of Hinduism, and the location of Islam 'outside India', forever alien and inimical to Hindu civilisation.

On the other side in this controversy are historians and social scientists ranging from Left to liberal persuasions, but who would broadly identify themselves as secular, who lay emphasis on the need to recognise society as historically constituted, in terms of underlying structures rather than manifest appearances, and for whom therefore, power relations and conflict over power cannot be ignored while writing history. The Hindu Right's project therefore, is rejected by them as a distortion of social reality.

It is of course clear that for both sides, 'history' is the site for the struggle over the present and the future of Indian society. Locating myself on the second side, with the secular academics, I will try to identify and work through certain sorts of impasses that have been produced by this controversy.

For some years before the centrally directed project began, incidents of rewriting of history textbooks from BJP-ruled states began popping up in the newspapers—in each case, the rewriting was aimed to present the medieval period in India as one of Muslim vandalism, or at playing down the oppression of the caste system, or to present a Ram temple at Ayodhya as a 'historical fact'. Each time, the NDA central government denied responsibility by passing the buck to the state governments, or by saying that this was done by boards of private schools which the government did not control. Later, however, in a more systematic move, the CBSE, under orders from the NCERT, wrote to all schools covered by the board to delete specific sections from history textbooks written by eminent historians with worldwide recognition. These sections refer to the practice of eating beef in ancient India, point to the non-historical nature of the Puranas citing archaeological evidence, discuss Buddhist and Jain beliefs about the origin of their religions, or are critical of brahminical privilege, and of the oppression of the caste system.

Further, the NCERT introduced a National Curriculum Framework that took history out of the syllabus until Class X, integrating certain themes from history with civics and geography, to be taught as one subject. In this new 'social science' textbook, Islam is not studied under 'major religions' of India, but in a unit alongside West Asia. The HRD Minister's explanation for this was that Islam grew out of that area, and 'its history is linked with the history of the Arab civilisation'. These changes were justified by the NCERT as well as BJP spokespersons on the grounds that the old textbooks were 'one-sided', furthered a 'narrow political agenda', (that of 'Marxists'), and 'hurt the sentiments' of communities. Further, the NCERT director J. S. Rajput as well as HRD Minister Murli Manohar Joshi promised to protect such fragile sentiments in future by giving an assurance that religious experts would be consulted before making any reference to religion in textbooks. Rajput also said in an interview that there should be no disjuncture between the values a child learns at home and those she learns at school. Young minds, he held, cannot think for themselves or sift fact from fiction, and textbooks should be framed on this presumption (Hasan 2002; Habib 2002).[1]

A political argument to counter the Hindu Right's project could present an alternative view of education. We could argue that we believe that education should be subversive of the dominant values of an unjust society—that this might require in fact, the challenging of values learnt 'at home'—that we hold that the purpose of education is precisely 'to hurt sentiments', to question status quo, to destabilise order. However, this is not an argument that can be made with any hope of larger public acceptance. Indeed, it is not clear that even all of the 'us' who are opposed to the Sangh Parivar's agenda necessarily share this understanding of education.

However, if the unlikelihood of wider acceptance is the only weakness of a clearly political argument, then the arguments mobilised by historians and others who reject the politics of Hindu Right shared this weakness. These arguments generally focused on the 'scientific' and 'rational' nature of history as opposed to 'prejudice and propaganda', on the need for an 'objective' view of the past, and on 'truth' as opposed to 'falsehood' (Hasan 2002; Sen 2002; Mukherjee and Mukherjee n.d.). Sumit Sarkar wrote, 'Surely education is worthwhile only if it stimulates rational thinking and questioning, and much of inherited common sense comes under scrutiny: as when children learn that, contrary to the evidence of their eyes, the earth moves around the sun' (Sarkar 2001). A number of questions are raised by this example. Undoubtedly education should stimulate questioning, but why is it that, while challenging the Hindu Right's rewriting of history, the example that springs to Sarkar's pen is from the natural sciences? Is it because no such uncontestable 'fact' can be unproblematically produced for history? Can we and need we sustain an argument that the study of history is as 'scientific' as the study of astronomy? Or that this questioning must stop at 'science'?[2]

Underlining the struggle over the present that this controversy represented, Mridula Mukherjee and Aditya Mukherjee argued that it reflects 'two completely divergent views of the Indian nation'—that of an open, democratic, secular and civil libertarian state which was to promote a modern scientific outlook in civil society in independent India, and 'a narrow, sectarian and "Talibanised" Hindu nation' (Mukherjee and Mukherjee n.d.). Presumably, the reference to 'modern scientific outlook in civil society' is meant to emphasise the importance of such an outlook in reinforcing the 'open, democratic and secular' character of the state. In other words, there is an easy assumption here of a link between science on the one hand, and openness and democracy on the other. However, it is not clear to me that the political values of democracy and secularism have a necessary connection with 'scientific outlook', or that a sectarian society cannot mobilise 'scientific' arguments. Indeed, sexist, racist and Nazi ideologies notoriously use 'scientific' claims of natural superiority and inferiority and conversely, the ultra-scientific nuclear establishment is predicated on a brutal denial of transparency and democratic accountability. It is the discourse of science, technology and development that is used to trample the democratic rights of the thousands displaced by the Sardar Sarovar dam and other 'development' projects that coincidentally, also make the coffers of large multinational companies ring.

Conversely, 'tolerance' is entirely compatible with the absence of a 'scientific outlook', as we know from Kumar Suresh Singh's monumental project *People of India*, which documents thirty-five communities in India who traditionally have had equal faith in Islam and Hinduism, 116 who keep faith equally with Christianity and Hinduism, and seventeen communities who are Hindu, Muslim and Sikh simultaneously. It is precisely with modernity and the coming of a 'scientific outlook' that such plural identities become impossible to sustain. There is no necessary link between science on the one hand, and democracy and tolerance on the other.

It seems to me therefore, the claim to 'rationality' and 'science' here is a claim to 'truth', and the effort seems to be to establish certain accounts of the past to be true, and others, to be false. However, it is necessary to note here that, as Dominick La Capra points out, truth claims are involved at two levels in history-writing, both at the level of events (did such and such an event take place?) as well as at the level of narrative plots, interpretations and explanations (what is the meaning of the event?) (La Capra 2001: 11). Even if there is agreement on the first level, the second level is inextricably implicated within specific world-views. A striking example of an argument 'at the second level' as it were, is Amartya Sen's assertion that 'the two greatest emperors of India were Ashoka and Akbar—one was a Buddhist and the other a Muslim' (Sen 2002). Even if we assume agreement on the 'fact' that these were India's two greatest emperors, the problem at the second level remains: what Sen presents as an illustration of his argument that India was never a Hindu Rashtra but a society reflecting multiple cultural and religious influences, can as easily be used by a Sadhvi Rithambhara to prove her point that Hindus have never been able to rule in 'their own' land.

Even when 'heterodoxy' is recognised and valourised, both 'as a method' as well as 'subject matter to be studied', as Amartya Sen puts it while opposing the Hindutva version of history, it only leads to the unproblematic reassertion, 'Textbooks should contain truths rather than falsehoods' (Sen 2002). We might then ask, if heterodoxy is to be valued, both in methods of doing history as well as 'in' history, then what is the status of 'truth'? And above all, what is history?

Frantz Fanon, among others, has made the link between History and the Nation: '... it is national liberation that causes the nation to be present on the scene of history', is the way he puts it (Jewsiewicki 1992: 101). Dipesh Chakrabarty asks, 'Why cannot countries that even as late as the early 19th century did not have anything called "history" do without it today?' and answers that 'History', as one of the forms of knowledge, exported to the rest of the world by Europe in the nineteenth century, is one of the most important ways in which we learn to identify ourselves with the nation and its highest representative, the state (Chakraborty 1991: 2164). A familiar sense of grappling with 'historical consciousness' is found in other anti-imperialist contexts, where, as in Africa, historical awareness and national consciousness became inseparable, and the new history becomes a key element in the quest for national identity (Coquery-Vidrovich 1992).

History, in other words, remains intricately tied to the quest for identity, usually national identity. This is what is implied when the Mukherjees assert (in the quote above) that the difference over the approach to history is really a difference about what kind of nation we want. And conversely, it is precisely this claim to nationhood that is challenged by the provocative statement made by dalit intellectual Chandrabhan Prasad. He wrote, 'the British came too late but left too early.' The conquest of India by the British, he states baldly, 'gave the Dalits a breathing space'. Chandrabhan wonders 'how some people think that during the time of Akbar the great,' (one of India's two greatest emperors, as we have seen in one reading), India was a 'perfectly secular society' when '"we" had to carry an earthen pot hung around our neck to spit, and announce our entry to the mainstream village, lest others get polluted even by our shadow' (Prasad 2000). In Chandrabhan's history of India then, the 'secular' nation was predicated upon other exclusions. In other words, the project of history is always deeply implicated within a sharply contested political project. Thus there is an irresoluble contradiction between history as a search for identity and history as the search for objective truth.

So there is no objective truth out there—this is the argument supposedly made by 'postmodernism'. A term that has become an easy epithet of abuse within the Indian academy, its use to suggest rampant relativism, loss of moral certainty, and a helpless slide into the arms of the Hindu Right is bewildering. Moral certainty after all, is expressed as confidently by the 'bad guys' in this picture as by us. In the debate over history, the accusation that each side makes is that the other is 'tinkering with history' or 'presenting a one-sided view'. The battle is precisely over whose certainty is correct. It does not take us very far to insist that the certainty of 'their belief' must be tested by the terms set by 'our historiography', on which terrain it will be proved to be false. This is what P. K. Datta suggests in his critique of Veena Das' analysis of historians' arguments on Ayodhya. He writes, 'The recourse to historical evidence was not meant to substitute "belief" by a matching absolutism of irrefutability. On the contrary, *given the premises of historiography*, it was a coded appeal to transfer the claim from the autocratic dictates of this "belief" to the terrain of contestation, of which details provide a common, disciplinary language' (emphasis mine) (Datta 1999: 4). But in the understanding of the Hindu Right, it is *our* history that fails the test of truth on *their* terrain of belief. And where do we go from this impasse?

This question is live and painful in current debates in historiography. One striking instance is the historiography of the Holocaust. Faced with the Holocaust, even the 'radical constructivist' (in Dominick La Capra's terms) Hayden White retreated from his earlier well-known understanding that events are not in themselves meaningful, but are only retrospectively transformed into a meaningful story. La Capra suggests that the problem encountered by White is not unique to his treatment of the Holocaust, that the Holocaust raises, in an accentuated form, problems that arise with other events that he terms as embodying 'trauma'. La Capra tries to stake out a space that is different from both what he calls 'documentary' and 'radical constructivist' approaches to history-writing. Central to his reframing of the issue is the notion of 'trauma' as a 'disruptive experience that disarticulates the self and creates holes in existence', raising specific problems for representation and writing (La Capra 2001: 41).

The retreat and cautious reformulations of Hayden White and La Capra in the face of the Holocaust, but simultaneously the attempt to escape the suggestion of an unduplicatable uniqueness to the Holocaust, by generating a concept—'trauma'—that would cover a range of what one could call 'holocaust-like' events, is perplexing. What is the theoretical value in attributing a special quality to the Holocaust or Apartheid, or to the nuclear attack on Hiroshima, and terming these as 'traumatic events' constituted as such by some internal quality they possess prior to the narratives of these events which the historian and 'history' draw upon? Either we could offer more and more instances of such 'founding traumas' that become the basis of individual or group identity (the extermination of indigenous peoples in Australia and North America, the caste system in India, African slave trade, Hindu hurt at the destruction of temples by Muslim invaders) which would result in dissolving the specificity of the concept, or there would have to be a process of denying this status to some events but not to others, on the basis of some 'objectively' defined criterion, which brings us back to the positivist notion of history we are fleeing from. The instance of 'Hindu hurt' is deliberately introduced above to highlight the manner in which a trauma is retrospectively produced/recognised, precisely in order to constitute a community in the present, in the service of an ideology that both White and La Capra would recognise as anti-democratic and majoritarian, maybe even fascist. The point here is that 'trauma' is not a quality internal to the event (as indeed, we have learnt from Hayden White), but *produced* by techniques of modern history, that enable specific kinds of imagining of 'the past'.

While it is not difficult to understand the burden of guilt and responsibility generated for European intellectuals by the Holocaust, it is not at all so self-evident that the 'limits of representation' (Rorty 2000a: 2) are reached when we touch it. As scholars like Amie Cesaire and Wole Soyinka have pointed out, the Holocaust is not the first event to place a question mark on all claims of European humanism. These scholars locate the failure of European humanism centuries earlier, and that would be at the very inception of the European slave trade. There appears then, to be a parochialism involved in ascribing to the Holocaust a special status with a claim to universal validity.

It seems to me that a similar parochialism is present in the pragmatism of Richard Rorty, limiting his otherwise promising insights on the question of truth. Rorty urges that we recast what has been understood as the universal desire for 'truth' as the universal desire for 'justification' (ibid.: 1). That is, we do not need to aspire to the sublime object called truth in order to conduct democratic politics, which he defines as the attempt ultimately to bring into existence 'a planet-wide, inclusivist community' (ibid.: 9). To move towards this objective, all that we need to try to do is to justify our beliefs to a 'competent audience'—the question is 'how to persuade people to broaden the size of the audience they take to be competent, to increase the size of the relevant community of justification' (Rorty 2000b: 105).

Since I am interested here specifically in Rorty's understanding of truth, I will only quickly say that this naive inclusivism remains insensitive to the possibility that the 'Other' may resist inclusion on the terms set by the dominant discourse of universality. If the question for Rorty is posed in terms of 'how to persuade people to broaden the size of the audience *they* take to be competent' (emphasis mine), clearly, 'we' are to do the persuading, and 'they' are to be persuaded.

But to return to the question of truth, for Rorty whether or not truth consists in accurate representation of the intrinsic nature of reality is irrelevant to democratic politics. The goal of 'getting things right' (Rorty 2000a: 3) for Rorty, is not only an impossible goal, but more importantly, irrelevant to the purposes of democratic politics. What is important about being human, he says, is not the ability to grasp truth, but 'the ability to be citizens of a full-fledged democracy which is yet to come'. (Rorty 2000b: 105)

Thus, Rorty leads us to believe that he holds that 'conversation is the highest good' (Rorty 2000a: 18), that different communities are constituted on different principles, and that democratic practice requires a constant dialogue without the presumption of a context-transcendent reason, a presumption he is critical of Jürgen Habermas for holding on to (ibid.: 4). It comes as somewhat of a shock therefore, to realise that Rorty believes that this ideal value is rather more easily accessible to 'inhabitants of wealthy, secure' societies, which are axiomatically also 'tolerant and inclusivist'. These are the people 'who are brought up to bethink themselves that they might be mistaken, that there are people out there who might disagree with them, and whose disagreements need to be taken into account' (ibid.: 16–17). We realise too, that he thinks Habermas' commitment to 'universal validity' is problematic not because it is unattainable but because this presupposition plays a part only in the behaviour of 'a small minority', a minority that is 'morally superior' and 'those who belong to the liberal universalistic, inclusivist tradition of the European Enlightenment' (Appiah 1992: 231–4).

It seems then, that Rorty in his pragmatism, is simply saying that since 'we' who live in wealthy secure societies cannot take recourse to a transcendental truth to convince the rest of the world that their ways are morally inferior, 'we' should simply do our best to persuade them that inclusivism (such as 'we' have 'here') is best, but 'we' cannot really do more than that.

Here I can only gesture towards the decades of scholarship showing up precisely the non-inclusivism of the Enlightenment and the philosophical traditions associated with it, from the point of view of women, non-whites, and the non-West. Moreover, by now we are only too aware of internal critiques of contemporary western societies from a variety of sources that would not recognise it as composed entirely of people Rorty describes as having been 'brought up to bethink themselves that they might be mistaken'.

Thus, while Rorty's emphasis on the socially constructed character of truth is significant, his belief that *his* world of privilege has reached the acme of tolerance and inclusivism, and waits patiently to let others in as soon as they can be persuaded to this superior way of life, is rather disconcerting.

More fruitful to our inquiry, I think, is K. Anthony Appiah's work on this issue. Trying to face the full implications of giving up the idea of fact and values as 'radically ontologically distinct', Appiah makes two related moves. First, he proposes the notion of 'interest' as constituting areas of inquiry, or 'disciplines'. By 'interest' here he means two things: 'both in the sense in which it contrasts with disinterest, and the sense in which it contrasts with a mere lack of epistemic engagement'. Next, he takes up the notion of 'idealization' from scientific disciplines. That is, the use of idealised theories that are 'approximately true', to serve explanatory purposes. There are two major sources of idealisation as he derives them from work on physics—'one is approximate truth, the other is what we can call *truth under idealized assumptions*' (emphasis mine). Thus, in the case of ideal gas theory for instance, while the theory may be inaccurate for some specific cases because of its assumptions (i.e., in the case of a large molecule gas at high temperature the observed values deviate significantly from theory, since the theory's assumptions are that gas is composed of frictionless, perfectly inelastic point masses), the theory would still give the right answer 'in general'.

These two moves enable us to recognise whether we count a theory as false or 'approximately true' (which after all Appiah points out is just a special way of being false), is a question of *judgement*, a question that would depend on our interests. Thus, 'A chemistry whose practical focus is on the development of industrial dyes might, say, accept the idealization that river water is H_2O; a chemistry interested in energy regulation at the cellular level probably could not.' In other words, 'interests constitute areas of inquiry in part by determining what sorts of falsehoods are tolerable.' Our challenge to theories therefore, should not be on the claim of a theory as idealisation, but rather, on the basis of the *interests* by which that idealisation is judged as adequate (Menon 1992).

Such an understanding of 'truth' points to the instability of the concept as it is deployed by different disciplines, even the scientific ones, but nevertheless enables moral and ethical judgements based on 'interest'. This shifts the battle on to a different terrain—from the assumed objectivity of a transcendent truth to the subjective, *political* one of struggles to hegemonise meaning.

This does not mean that 'everything is relative', and that we are doomed to inaction and paralysis. On the contrary, denying the existence of an objective truth does not commit us to accept every interpretation to be as valid as any other (Laclau and Mouffe 1990: 109). We take positions based on our discursive universe, we affirm that within this universe 'our' interpretation is the most 'correct' or even the only one possible. We attempt to demonstrate that this particular context or discursive universe is the one that renders visible the widest range of meaning; we affirm the validity of the values that order our universe. We offer these values as a challenge to competing ones, but our boundaries are also shifted and altered by some of these challenges (as the hegemonic secular or feminist discourse might be by one kind of dalit challenge, for example). This is what the struggle to hegemonise meaning is all about.

This is a radically different project from that of, for example Richard Rorty, 'persuading people to broaden the size of the audience you take to be competent'. For Rorty, democratic politics is about trying to persuade more and more societies to adopt the (assumed) values of universalism found in (his own) 'wealthy and secure' parts of the world, which themselves have reached the point the rest of the world must now aspire to. The struggle to hegemonise meaning on the other hand, has to involve the recognition of the fundamental instability at the core of every discursive universe, including our own. As Laclau says, 'no discursive totality is absolutely self-contained ... there will always be an outside which distorts it and prevents it from fully constituting itself' (ibid.).

What are the implications of this discussion for the issue at hand? The textbooks that the Hindu Right wants to do away with have been in use for several decades. Generations of school students have read them and learnt history the secular way. And yet, every college teacher knows that the majority of students who come into her class in the first year of the undergraduate course invariably tell the story of India the way 'they' tell it. That there was a Golden Age of Hinduism, when women were respected and educated, that the Muslim invasions destroyed an egalitarian society, that 'India' has existed since the 'Vedic Age'. Tourist guides at historical monuments all over the country re-tell this story in various ways, alleging the previous existence of temples at almost every monument built by 'Muslim' rulers.

In short, 'our' history had dominated the academy and intellectual circles, 'theirs' the streets and common sense. This is not a statement of despair, rather it is one of optimism. What it means is that the battle is not on the verge of being lost, the battle is just beginning to be fought. Until now 'we' have remained unaware that a subterranean battle was raging.

Perhaps we need to make a distinction in public discourse between two senses of history—history as *a modern academic discipline* and history *as political intervention.* In the first sense, history is not 'objective truth', it is not something that can be scientifically proved. History is simply what historians do (here Rorty's idea of 'competent audience' would be useful).[3] So as far as the teaching of history is concerned, we need to build public opinion on an understanding of history as a series of conversations and mutually contested narratives, with no possibility of ultimate resolution or verifiability, based on certain disciplinary codes recognised within a 'competent community'. We have no recourse to 'truth' as opposed to 'falsehood'—indeed, if we are able to destabilise the notion of a 'true' history, we would succeed also in hitting at the foundations of the Hindu Right's attempts to appropriate the past.

And this leads us to the second sense in which we need to understand history—history as political intervention. The recognition here is that when we write history, we make history. That to tell a story about the past is to shape the story of the future. In the very effort to know, we change that which we seek to know. History in this sense is a strong political statement, and outside textbooks (where several such statements must be shown to be in collision, debate and engagement), we will defend our picture of the past precisely in terms of our 'interest' in Appiah's terms, our vision of the future.

III

In the second phase, the argument made above continues to be relevant, but the lines of difference become somewhat more difficult to delineate in simple Right/Left or secular/communal terms. The key difference between the two arguments on the secular side in this phase now has to do with what education is, what it is meant to do, and its relationship to the nation. The critics of *NCF-2005* seem to hold that education is meant to transform people steeped in ignorance and prejudice, into good modern citizens for the greater purposes of nation-building. The old Left's statism and confidence that everything 'modern' is good and everything traditional bad, and that the 'national' should always trump the 'local', is manifest in the critique of the *NCF-2005*. The latter on the other hand, is more reflective of the immense rethinking and introspection on these issues that has marked intellectual thought and political practice since the 1980s in India. It has a more self-reflexive attitude to pedagogy, and sees the task of education as that of fostering a critical consciousness. Irfan Habib thinks education should be 'geared to national development' (Habib 2005: 9–10), while Krishna Kumar argues that such education closes the mind. When education is viewed merely as a tool of national identity and economic development, he holds, it enhances intolerance. Indeed, in his opinion, education should foster critical reflection on everything, including national identity (Kumar 2005).

The two main complaints about the draft *NCF-2005*, emerging in seven essays in a booklet called *Debating Education* launched under the banner of SAHMAT were first, that the *NCF-2005* did not oppose the saffronisation of textbooks by the previous regime. This meant, it was alleged, that the *NCF-2005* was 'trying to accommodate the Sangh Parivar's views'. Second, that *NCF-2005*'s stress on 'local knowledges' and 'local belief systems' promoted regressive values and is in fact communalism in a different guise. In addition, the emphasis on the local eclipses the nation. At one of the meetings discussing the draft, a historian belonging to the critical group exclaimed, 'Are we to only hear the voices of dalits and tribals, what about the nation?'

Is it true that sufficient space and energy were not expended in the *NCF-2005* to tear apart the textbooks produced under the NDA regime? But they have by now been thoroughly exposed by some of the very scholars involved in producing the *NCF-2005*. If the draft *NCF-2005* wasted no time in reiterating well-known criticism of the previous regime, but took the initiative to outline an alternative vision of education on the assumption that this is the moment to rethink the premises on which education has been based in India then, rather than 'accommodating the Sangh Parivar', it sent out the opposite message. The Sangh Parivar will not be allowed to set our agenda any more, that it is no longer the reference point.

NCF-2005 states its commitment to secularism baldly and uncompromisingly on page 6. It reads 'India is a secular democratic state which means that all faiths are respected, but at the same time the Indian state has no preference for any particular faith.... India is a multicultural society made up of numerous regional and local cultures.... All the groups have equal rights to co-exist and flourish, and the education system needs to respond to the cultural pluralism inherent in our society.'

One of the sharpest critiques came from Irfan Habib, who attacked the idea in the *NCF-2005* that children have 'native wisdom' that educationists would do well to engage seriously with. He held quite uncompromisingly that children are a mindless mass, full of 'notions, irrational biases, superstitions, gender, caste and communal prejudices, scorn for the less privileged, etc'. Given his opinion of children, it is not surprising that he thinks the 'prime duty of school education is to eradicate such "native wisdom"'. The prime duty of education is to 'eradicate' people's beliefs. The deep and yawning chasm between the two notions of pedagogy could not be more evident.

In another essay Anil Sadgopal accuses the *NCF-2005* of valourising 'local knowledge' in such a way that everything local is valuable, including 'sati, caste, class and gender discrimination, brahminism, superstition, fatalism, child labour, lack of scientific temperament, etc'.

NCF-2005 certainly has a lot to say about local knowledge. It says, 'Unless learners can locate their individual standpoints in relation to the contexts represented in textbooks and relate this knowledge to their experiences ... knowledge is reduced to ... mere information.... Children bring to school their experiences of the world around—the trees they have climbed, the fruits they have eaten.... Yet rarely do we heed the knowledge that they ... bring into the classroom. Rarely do we ask the children to talk about or refer to the world outside the school during our teaching' (p. 27).

On page 28 a box titled 'Local Knowledge Traditions' says: 'Many communities in India also have their local knowledge traditions of naming and categorising plants, or ways of harvesting and storing water, or of practising sustainable agriculture. Sometimes these may be different from the way in which school knowledge approaches the subject.... In these situations, it could be possible that the teachers recognise and help children develop projects of study based on the local tradition, this may also involve comparing it with the school tradition. In some cases, as in the case of classification of plants, the two traditions may be simply parallel and based on different criteria considered significant. In other cases, for example, the classification and diagnosis of illnesses, it may challenge and contradict local belief systems. It is also possible to consider that there are cases where the local belief system seems more ecologically valid than the textbook opinion.'

Is this such a shocking thing to say today, when nineteenth century arrogance about Man's control over Nature has been widely acknowledged to have brought the earth to the brink of ecological disaster (Habib holds that the term 'ecologically valid' is irrelevant. 'How can a system or anything else, be ecologically valid or invalid?' he asks.)? From the eighteenth century, education and schooling have played a central role in producing the kind of population and beliefs necessary for unbridled capitalist development. Are Habib and Sadgopal votaries of such development? Is it not time that, however belatedly, we opened our ears to some of the ideas so mercilessly defeated by the relentless march of History?

As for local knowledge of the sort Sadgopal decries *NCF-2005*. Addressing it directly he says: 'The social context also calls for a much greater critical awareness and critical engagement on the part of curriculum developers and teachers. Community-based identities of gender, caste, class and religion are primary identities but they can also be oppressive and reaffirm social inequalities and hierarchies. School knowledge can also provide a lens through which children can develop a critical understanding of their social reality. It could also provide them space to talk about their experiences and anxieties within their homes (p. 29).'

However, unlike the writers in *Debating Education*, *NCF-2005* does not consider beliefs contrary to our own as something that can simply be eradicated. 'Communities may also have questions about the inclusion or exclusion of particular knowledge and experiences in the school curriculum. The school must then be prepared to listen to their concerns, and to persuade them to see the educational value of such decisions.' In other words, *NCF-2005* believes the process of social transformation to be complex and multilayered, involving the student not only in the classroom, but as located in her family and community. Most importantly, this process is understood to be uncompromisingly bound within democratic procedures like listening, persuading, mutually learning and not eradicating.

Even a quick reading of *NCF-2005* shows that it simply asserts that mere information is not knowledge. How can any serious educationist not understand or agree with this distinction? Information would be of the order of the fact that the earth goes around the sun. Knowledge construction involves understanding how this fact contradicts our everyday observation, why the otherwise valid maxim that 'theory has to be proved by empirical observation' cannot apply here, what protocols are involved when we would nevertheless say that the statement, 'The sun rises in the East' is true, why the mediaeval Church tortured Galileo for asserting what is in our lives a commonsensical fact that no one would contradict, thinking about how myths of origin and about nature evolve—a vast interdisciplinary field of knowledge opens up out of a simple bit of 'information'.

The most significant contribution of *NCF-2005* is a radical rethinking of what teaching means. Currently, at every level of education, teachers are apt to think of their work as that of 'imparting knowledge/information'. In the *NCF-2005*, teaching is understood as a process of encouraging analytical thought, debate and engagement with the world in which learners live with all its flaws and uncertainties. Students are to be led towards existing scholarship through a process of questioning and curiosity, and they should be able to engage with this scholarship not as established bodies of information but as fields of debate and discussion.

One point on which I find *NCF-2005* to be silent is the teacher's own biases to deal with uncomfortable issues like conflict and inequality. The complication here is that teachers will necessarily carry their prejudices, their class/caste privileges into the classroom. We need to recognise that the best written, most imaginatively produced textbooks and the most progressive curricula can be and are, subverted by conventional/conservative/right-wing teachers. Any curriculum would therefore have to be open-ended enough to enable the student to make her own decisions on issues, and the evaluation process would have to be such that the target of evaluation is not opinions expressed, but the analytical capacity of the student.

The most dangerous thing about *Debating Education* was that its aim was to end further debate, its critique apparently being the last word on the matter. The demand of the writers and SAHMAT was nothing less than that the *NCF-2005* be withdrawn, thus conclusively ending any further discussion. Surely there can be nothing more disastrous for education than to silence dissent against orthodoxies of the Right or Left. Eventually the *NCF-2005* was passed with a few cosmetic changes.

Interestingly at the Central Advisory Board of Education (CABE) meeting to discuss the *NCF-2005*, the CPI(M) goverrnment of West Bengal accepted the NCF, which suggests that the problems outlined by mainly CPI(M)-linked writers in *Debating Education* may be those experienced by intellectuals who have remained outside and 'above' the turbulence that political practice has involved in the last couple of decades in particular. Active radical politics produces a productive contamination of empty universalist categories, that is both creative and more ethical than a voice claiming to speak for everyone and everywhere from the standpoint of the Nation.

ENDNOTES

[1] This account has been put together from Hasan (2002) and Habib (2002).

[2] Whether 'science' itself can sustain its claim to the status of privileged access to objective knowledge is in question. The well-known debate for instance, between Einstein and Heisenberg turned on whether the outcome of an experiment would be affected by the fact of observation. Heisenberg held that it was the choice of observation that determined, for instance, whether what one was observing was a particle or a wave. Thus 'reality', according to Heisenberg, was a function of the experimental condition. However, we can set aside this debate for the duration of this chapter.

[3] There is a critique of history as made by Ashis Nandy among others, which is critical of modern history for delegitimising all other modes of comprehending the past, except those that conform to the rules of modern historiography (See Nandy 1995: Issue 34). This is an important critique, but I would argue for the need to retain the modern academic discipline of history as a valuable resource, although reconstituted now in a self-reflexive mode with the self-awareness of being only one mode of understanding the past.

REFERENCES

Appiah, K. Anthony. 1992. 'Inventing an African Practice in Philosophy: Epistemological Issues', in V. Y. Mudimbe (ed.), *The Surreptitious Speech. Presence Africaine and the Politics of Otherness 1947–87*. Chicago and London: University of Chicago Press.

Cesaire, Aime. 1972. *Discourse on Colonialism*. New York and London: Monthly Review Press.

Chakraborty, Dipesh. 1991. 'History as Critique and Critiques of History'. *Economic and Political Weekly*. 14 September. 2164.

Coquery-Vidrovich, Catherine. 1992. 'Presence Africaine: History and Historians of Africa', in V. Y. Mudimbe (ed.), *The Surreptitious Speech. Presence Africaine and the Politics of Otherness 1947–87*. Chicago and London: University of Chicago Press.

Datta, P. K. 1999. *Carving Blocs: Communal Ideology in Early Twentieth Century Bengal*. New Delhi: Oxford University Press.

Debating Education: A Critical Appraisal of National Curriculum Framework 2005. 2005. Delhi: Sahmat. August.

Delhi Historians Group. n.d. *Communalisation of Education*. New Delhi: Delhi Historians Group.

Habib, Irfan. 2002. 'Guest Column'. *The Asian Age*. 2 February.

Habib, Irfan. 2005. 'How to Evade Real Issues and Make Room for Obscurantinism', in *Social Scientist*. Vol. 33. Nos. 9–10. September–October. 5.

Hasan, Mushirul. 2002. 'Historical Disarray'. *The Indian Express*. 6 February.

Jewsiewicki, Bogumil. 1992. 'Presence Africaine as Historiography: Historicity of Societies and Specificity of Black African Culture', in V. Y. Mudimbe (ed.), *The Surreptitious Speech. Presence Africaine and the Politics of Otherness 1947–87*. Chicago and London: University of Chicago Press. 101.

Kumar, Krishna. 2005. 'Give Peace a Chance', in *Little Magazine*. Vol. 6. Issue 1 and 2.

La Capra, Dominick. 2001. 'Writing History, Writing Trauma' in Writing History, Writing Trauma. Baltimore and London: Johns Hopkins University Press.

Laclau, Ernesto and Chantal Mouffe. 1990. 'Post-Marxism without Apologies', in *New Reflections on the Revolution of Our Time*. London and New York: Verso.

Menon, Nivedita. 1992. 'Orientalism and After'. *Economic and Political Weekly*. 26 September.

Mukerjee, Mridula and Aditya Mukherjee. n.d. 'Communalisation of Education, the History Textbooks Controversy: An Overview', in *Communalisation of Education*. New Delhi: Delhi Historians Group.

Nandy, Ashis. 1995. 'History's Forgotten Doubles' History and Theory.

National Curriculum Framework. 2005. Delhi: National Council for Education Research and Training.

Prasad, Chandrabhan. 2000. 'When Dalits Walked into an Evening of The Gin Drinkers'. *The Indian Express*. 2 November.

Rorty, Richard. 2000a. 'Universalism and Truth', in Robert B. Brandom (ed.), *Rorty and his Critics*. Massachusetts and Oxford: Blackwell.

Rorty, Richard. 2000b. 'Response to Daniel Dennet', in *Rorty and his Critics*. Massachusetts and Oxford: Blackwell. 105.

Sarkar, Sumit. 2001. 'Does History Need To Be Rewritten?' *The Times of India*. 2 December.

Sen, Amartya. 2002. 'India's Two Great Emperors Were Both Non-Hindu'. *Outlook*. 21 January.

Singh, Kumar Suresh. 2006. Cited in Uday Prakash. 'The One from the Tribe'. *Tehelka*. 17 June.

Soyinka, Wole. 2002. 'Memory, Truth and Healing', in Ifi Amadiume and Abdullahi An Na'im (ed.), *The Politics of Memory, Truth, Healing and Social Justice*. London and New York: Zed Books.

7

The Conundrums of the Global-National: Using Tagore for a New Politics of the Global

P. K. Datta

Does globalisation pose a threat to the nation-state? This question has been continuously posed ever since the processes of neo-liberal globalisation, led by transnational enterprises and governments of mainly Western countries, began to put global economic and legal regimes, such as the General Agreement on Tariffs and Trade (GATT) and World Trade Organisation (WTO), into place. These treaties have reduced trade barriers, made it easier for monopolies over technology to be exercised, and for capital to be made hyper mobile. All these appear to have resulted in the weakening of the nation-state with its protective economic and cultural boundaries. This prospect has raised new theories such as Robertson's idea of the 'glocal', i.e., the elision of the global and the local, or the privileging of 'regional' powers (for example, the European Union and the North American Free Trade Association). It may be noted that the binaries of the 'global', namely the 'local' or 'regional', are terms that bypass the 'nation'. I should also add here that to the extent globalisation works up a flurry of optimism, it is due to the hope that it would see to the end of the era of international conflicts that beset the twentieth century.

Yet, despite the promise of the withering away of the nation, it has yet to begin. True, the nation-state (except for a few such as North Korea) has renounced its ideal of economic self-reliance. Against this must be reckoned the resurgence in nationalist sentiment today. The real difference seems to lie in that nationalism today locates itself in culture, normally of the majority, with little or no element of economic nationalism. This coincidence of globalisation and cultural nationalism prompts a need to look more closely at how globalisation processes culturally impact upon the 'national'. I would like to do this through a brief sketch of the ways in which promotional campaigns by transnational corporations—possibly the most visible and palpable sign of the global impact on everyday life—relate to national cultures.

It may be helpful to briefly look at the historical shifts in the culture of commodity circulation to understand this phenomenon. Truth to tell, industry did not bother itself very much with the problem of culture in the colonial period. This was given over to the state, a sphere where policymakers like Thomas Macaulay and W. W. Hunter operated. The dividing lines between the colonial powers and the colonised remained firm, buttressed by ideas of racial and civilisational difference. Consequently, cultural divisions tended to reinforce oppositions at other levels, especially that of economics and politics. Advertising and promotional campaigns by the then transnationals were not sensitive to local needs. However, the small size of the non-colonial 'native' market was not the only reason. Promotion was simply regarded as an ancillary to the quality of the commodity itself. Indeed advertisers often justified their trade by defining it as a form of imparting information to the public (Ray Chaudhury n.d.).[1] This meant that the commodity was not divorced from the factory, the workers and management, who were located in a particular country, and its publicity generally took place on the basis of qualities and images associated with the place of its origin.

This mindset persisted till the 1980s, much after decolonisation. The year 1977 was a major landmark when the Government of

India terminated the operations of Coca Cola and replaced it by a (short-lived) drink appropriately called '77'. It was not an unpopular decision for it rested on the identification of Coca Cola with American culture in a period that had inherited the anti-Americanism post the Vietnam War. The drink may have been popular, but its promotional campaign tied it to a distinctively American way of life. It was also seen as expressing the power of American culture. Conversely this posed a challenge for promotion—the commodity needed to be dissociated from the culture of its place of origin without losing its distinctiveness. The questions raised by the 1977 event found a satisfactory answer in the following decades when there was, as Klein points out, a shift from the preoccupation with creating a product to promoting a 'brand' that involved concentration on making images for the product. The product itself could now be produced anywhere in the world, as long as wages were cheap and workers could be easily disciplined. This coincided with the discovery of multiculturalism as a profitable market strategy. Thus the 'black kids' could be enthused about Adidas shoes because Michael Jordan was associated with it (Klein 2001: chap 1, 5). A new marketing strategy was then devised that could appeal to the cultural symbols of achievement of a people that had little to do with the production of the commodity. The commodity could erase its cultural otherness by appealing to cultural pride even as the omnipresent logo indicated the enterprise to be the source and guarantee of that pride.

Its success with multiculturalism has probably inspired transnational promotional campaigns in developing countries like India. The basis of this strategy, as seen in advertising campaigns, is to provide a patriotic spin to 'foreign' logos (which have originated in other countries, normally advanced Western ones, and possess an international profile). Thus the soft drinks industry becomes a major sponsor for cricket in India, the patriotic sport par excellence, an initiative that removes the memory of the rapid disappearance of soft drinks that had been produced, marketed and owned here before liberalisation. More interesting is the drive towards representing the non-global as ethnic. In such advertisements, images of local ethnic culture are shown to be actively consuming a 'foreign' product. Thus a motorcycle with a Japanese or German make kicks up dust in a Rajasthan hamlet leaving the village belles gaping in admiration, with some even breaking out in English. In these advertisements the transnational logo becomes a symbol of global culture by contrast with the ethnic image, even as the fact of sponsorship by the transnational indicates that the latter is committed to the projection of 'local' culture. Further, what is equally interesting is that the 'local' serves as an image of the national. Indeed, in various advertisements the 'local' functions interchangeably—villages of Rajasthan, backwaters of Kerala or the *mohallas* of Delhi—telescope into each other producing all of them equally as synecdoches of the nation. In short the 'local' provides a way of appealing to national pride.

The ethnicisation of the nation in order to appeal to nationalist cultural pride can be appreciated in the general context of nation (re)making in the age of globalisation. The dominant model of nation-building today in countries of the South is one in which neo-liberal policies are followed together with a fetishisation of cultural authenticity of national roots. This is a model that is being actively pursued in a number of countries of South-East Asia and China together with Islamic nations of the Middle-East. I should add here that globalisation allows for the fluidity of capital flows but immobilises labour. The confinement of labour to national boundaries is essential to regulate wages and control working conditions, which in turn, allows capital to migrate from one region to another in search for comparative advantages in labour costs. In other words, the preservation of the nation through cultural authenticity also serves a critical economic function in ensuring that national boundaries remain to freeze labour mobility. Hence, as long as nationalism legitimises itself through cultural pride, it can work comfortably with the rest of the globalising machinery.

Cultural pride seems to be the only real sphere of national autonomy and self-activity left in a world that is consciously committed to economic integration on an uneven playing field. Cultural pride allows the control of national images, spanning the spheres of self-presentation, behavioural and ritual acts to the ceremonies and objects by which the nation is presented to the 'world'. This can be extended to control the futures of minority cultures. The latter can be made to take on the burden to explain the failures of the nation that haunt it on the dark side of pride, and subordinated or even exorcised on these grounds. This pride is overtly potent, its power deriving from its ability to provide compensation to people deprived of their livelihoods or living standards by the policies of globalisation, as well as inspiring the beneficiaries of globalisation with a sense of mission and distinctiveness as they insert themselves in the fast-moving channels of global capital.

At the same time such pride can introduce a deep instability within the system of globalisation itself. Globalisation would be destroyed by the possibility of international conflict—although this eventuality seems unreal to most. It has been argued that the weakening of the nation-state has left it with only the minorities against whom they can define their boundaries and identity—(Milibank 2001). As I have argued, nationalism is not threatened by globalisation but enters into a compact with it. This means that wars between nation-states cannot be ruled out. Judging from Indo-Pakistan relationships which have become more frighteningly tense than ever before, or religio-ethnic battles that raged in Bosnia, and which take on nationalist colours, international violence seems as if not more threatening than before. Indeed there now takes place easy and rapid transitions from the oppression of minorities to wars against an external enemy: the coincidence of the anti-Muslim and Christian activities of Hindu communal nationalists and the worsening of relationships with Pakistan is revealing. It is possibly for this reason that the European Union (EU) is so alarmed by the resurgence of right-wing movements that target non-white minorities, for it is the momentum provided by such attacks that can easily translate into suspicion and hostility towards neighbouring European countries themselves.

II

It is from the context of this brittle and dangerous process of complementarity between the global and the national, that I wish to enter into Tagore's notion of an alternate global order, and the kind of identity that can be interpolated from his elaborations. Tagore provides a vision rather than a specific framework for this global order, in the sense that he sketches out some broad principles of cultural and social relationship. His concern originates from his problems with nationalism, specifically with the nationalism of cultural pride. The most significant move he makes in this direction is his novel *Gora*. Its well-known plot features an intensely nationalist Gora whose commitment to cultural pride takes the form of idealising brahmanical orthodoxy which breaks up against the revelation that he is actually the adopted son of *mleccha* white parents. Gora represents the first attempt by Tagore to problematise cultural pride by emphasing the welcome, indeed inevitable reality of cultural miscegenation that lies at the heart of nationalism itself. Further, freeing himself from cultural pride corresponds to a process whereby Gora, guided by the norms of justice and social commitment, begins to respond to a more complex reality that shows caste oppressions and prejudices as well as reveals the rich plethora of social connections, defining thereby the blindness of cultural pride to social life.

It is worth mentioning that *Gora* was produced by a deep crisis in nationalism that Tagore experienced during the Swadeshi movement. As has been shown elsewhere, his deep and creative involvement with the Swadeshi movement was rudely shaken by the outbreak of Hindu-Muslim riots that broke out in its course. After a period of six months or so when he went into a shocked and self-reflective silence, Tagore emerged with a public criticism of nationalism, observing that 'Satan cannot enter till he finds a flaw....' (Sarkar 1973:81). What he emphasised was its lack of self-reflexivity. Caught up in the celebration of itself, nationalism was unable to reflect upon its cultural biases, specifically its brahmanical contempt for Muslims. It is clear that the critique of nationalist pride developed through the writing of *Gora* deepened into the recognition of it as a mental prison, release from which involved the insertion into a many sided relationship with the world.

It is in *Ghare Baire* (*Home and the World*) that Tagore launches his most scathing critique of nationalist pride. The story features

Sandip, a ruthless Hindu nationalist, who enters into a relationship with Bimala, the wife of his friend Nikhilesh, and succeeds through the mobilisation of cultural jingoism to spark off communal riots in rural Bengal. The work is an overt fictional reflection on the Swadeshi movement. Important here is the psychic complementarity between cultural pride and the world system of colonialism (that is present in the novel by implication). Cultural pride takes the form of worshipping the nation, and in this it complements the colonial system. The latter, Tagore suggests (more elaborately in his essays on nationalism), is an outgrowth of nationalism itself, insofar as it represents the success of the people of the countries of the West in coming together as a corporate body in order to compete more efficiently against other nations. The alliance between a subject country and that of colonialism through nationalism is one that springs from commitment to greed, competition and the instrumentalism that accrues from both.

The consequences of this complementarity, it may be inferred, are analogous: the period of its publication (1915–16) as well as the theme of nationalism and violence in *Ghare Baire* clearly suggest the contextual subtext of World War I as the unavoidable culmination of colonialism The war is matched by the move towards internal cultural colonisation of minorities (blatantly in the case of Muslims, in more complex ways with women and low castes) by Sandip and the Swadeshi activists, resulting in communal conflagration. Sandip's career represents the authoritarian and repressive implications of nationalist cultural pride for the victims of the superordinate power of colonialism. The full range of Sandip's repression comes out via the contrary voice and relationships of Nikhilesh. It should be observed that Nikhilesh provides no easy alternative ethos to Sandip's, but represents a different idea of relating to the problems posed by the making of a nationalist community. These are problems that are created by the claims of justice and truth located in a web of social relationships. Specifically carrying foward the ideas of *Gora* in a more elaborate and complex direction, this assumes the need to look at the nation in terms of its different collectivities (organised around gender, caste, religion) informed by an understanding of the ways power operates in and through them; at the same time to critically examine the practices and assumptions of both nationalist activism and the subjects of the nationalist community.

Nikhilesh's loneliness and his final defeat by the communal riots that flare out around him signals the end of a long period of enquiry in Tagore that had sought to look at the problem of identities and their mutual relationships in the assumed context of a modern, globally-integrated world from the viewpoint of the nationalism of the subject country. This critique of the consequences of cultural nationalism is, however, superceded and absorbed by another set of more general concerns that Tagore had already been tackling in his prose works. This was the relationship between East and West. As such these categories emerged from what had become a commonsense conception of organising the world. Nor does Tagore depart substantially from the other commonsense notion that the West was based on the organisation principle, while the East was the domain of mutuality and co-existence. What is significant about Tagore's project is his concern with the ways whereby East and West are internally constituted.

What makes Tagore's enquiry particularly resonant is the general question of relating to the West with the asymmetrical relationship of global power that it indicates, in a way that is positive and appropriative instead of defensive cocooning within the authoritarian culturalism of nationalist pride. For Tagore the solution lies in what may be said to be a located process of mutual transformation. This involves changes in both cultures that come into contact with each other, at their separate places of location. The privileged site of his enquiry is the East, especially the culture of the Indian subcontinent.

The most exciting element of Tagore's notion of global relationship is the idea of self-division. In his letter to Thomas Sturge Moore in 1914, Tagore declared that the value of literature lay not in its fitness for 'home consumption' but 'in the fact that it is imperatively necessary for the lands where it is foreign'. Its internalisation would, he makes clear, introduce new ideas and dispositions into one's own culture, thereby producing a 'bifurcation' in the 'mental system which is so needful for all life growth' (Pal 1997:7). What this involves is a radical distancing from one's culture in order to reconstitute it. Clearly Tagore is not arguing for an embedded identity, but for a located self situated in a culture that allows for transformation. Crucial here is the fact that the other is not positioned as a presence that provides definitive boundaries with the self, but as necessary for the internal transformation of the self. Relating to the other produces a division within the self, which unlike Romantic and Modernist conceptions, is not seen as a loss or fall from a unified state, but as a necessary introduction to change. Nor is the presence of the other within the self simply additive, for it is critically engaged with the ordinary self that is reconstituted in the process.

There are two important assumptions that are involved here. The first concerns the nature of locatedness. For Tagore, locatedness is a strong proposition, which is not surprising given his intimate and creative positioning within Bengali literature. For Tagore what constitutes locatedness is not just what one inherits, but acts of deepening one's familiarity with it. For Tagore this act of familiarising is related to acquiring cultural and intellectual knowledge. When discussing the rationale for Viswa Bharati in *East and West*, Tagore dwells on the importance of bringing together the knowledge of the East first, before broadcasting it to the West (Tagore 1922, 1962: 174). Further, if one is to take into account the insights of *Gora* and *Ghare Baire*, familiarising would also involve becoming intimate with the broadening spheres of social relationships along with the problems of power that they entail.

The second aspect is the notion of the West. The idea of internal transformation through the other assumes that it is not a monolithic other that is sought to be harnessed, but a particular strand or tradition within it. This is the assumption that underlies his communication to Moore when he privileges the Romantic poets. He writes (in the letter cited above) that in India, the youth look to Byron and Shelley for what impresses a foreigner are the 'vivid and forceful' elements of English literature rather than the 'artistic'. The West is conceived as an internally differentiated entity. The axis of differentiation varies. Tagore was not an exact thinker. In another context he refers to Christianity as a spirit that goes 'counter' to the 'European temperament'. Its internalisation, resulting in a 'sharp antagonism of ... intellectual direction', had a creative impact for it stirred the vernaculars to life (Tagore 1922, 1962: 192–3). In other words, the West too is capable of fundamental changes that would alter the basis of its civilisation.

The conceptions of East and West, it is true, binarises global culture and, it may be argued, proposes a process of mutual transformation that may succeed in making both similar. However, there are other elements in Tagore's thought to suggest that these categories are really indicative of a particularly wide level of generalisation. The East would contain a variety of identities within itself. The experience of *Gora* and *Ghare Baire* is particularly apposite here, for both novels turn on the idea of a society that is made up of different collectivities which can only be reduced to a single rubric at the cost of violence. It is also significant to note that Viswa Bharati, that was set up as a university of the East to gather together its knowledge so that the West could internalise it, carried a syllabus that disaggregated 'Indian learning' according to the Vedic, the Puranic, the Buddhist, the Jain, the Islamic, the Sikh and the Zoroastrian', to which was also added the 'Chinese, Japanese and Tibetan ... for, in the past, India did not remain isolated from her own boundaries' as well as 'the Western so that it could be assimilated' (Tagore 1922, 1962: 195). One may disagree with the privileging of this broad religio-civilisational classification, but it is important to grasp the general principles through which Tagore seeks an alternate world order.

If one may crystallise Tagore's thought in a particular (and interested direction), then he may be said to propose a notion of processual identity. This may be distinguished from other notions of identity. It is different from the commitment to particular and incommensurable identities. It is not fuzzy, for it is not innocent of strong boundary markers nor does it inhabit an inherited condition of heterogeneity. It is an identity that affirms boundaries, but only to provide a location to the process of self-transformation through appropriating traditions existing within the other. This notion requires, as I have suggested, a recognition of the disaggregated nature of overarching identities (such as East and West which Tagore deploys). The attempts by Gora and Nikhilesh to relate to other collectivities, both in order to break down the exclusivism of the collective self (Gora) as well as to relate in a mutually critical manner (as Nikhilesh seeks to do), indicates Tagore's commitment to the processes of mutual transformation as one that ought to operate at all levels of identities. In other words, it is an idea of identity that is based on multiple levels possessing varying degrees of heterogeneity, with its bottom line in the commitment to self-division and transformation through relating to the other. It may be observed that this notion of identity takes into account the realities of a world where identity-making has become a conscious project and often a political and social resource. This recognition, though unstated, is a point of departure to produce a possible identity that acknowledges origins in order to go beyond them.

It may be instructive to compare the Zapatista conception with some of the current understandings of cosmopolitanism, as well as Tagore's conceptions, in order to define the challenges that face anti-globalisation movements today. A sympathetic, but critical reassessment of cosmopolitanism made recently by Craig Calhoun has defined it to be indicative of multiple belongings but lacking a hold on substantive community differences and the democratic procedures that a nation-state allows. Calhoun's argument aspires to marry cosmopolitanism with non-ethnic, civic nationalism. What Calhoun ignores in his resurrection of the relevance of the nation-state—as does much of the literature on cosmopolitanism—is the actually existing cosmopolitanism of movements such as the Zapatistas, that anchors its cosmopolitan sense of multiple belonging to a democratic movement that produces its own 'roots', an act that makes the phenomenon of rootedness a contextual act of opposition. The Zapatista identity is gathered together from various migrant linguistic and cultural groups in the Chiapas mountains of Mexico. These people have produced the Zapatista identity that is based on resistance to the policies of the Mexican government and the global agencies of the North American Free Trade Agreement (NAFTA) to which these are linked. In turn the Zapatista solidarises with other marginal identities across the world. Subcommandante Marcos, the leader of the movement (who keeps his face covered so that no charisma can coagulate around him), once said, 'Marcos is gay in San Francisco, black in South Africa, an Asian in Europe, an Anarchist in Spain, a Palestinian in Israel, a Jew in Germany ... a pacificist in Bosnia, a single woman on the Metro at 10 pm, a peasant without land ... an unemployed worker, an unhappy student and, of course, a Zapatista in the mountains' (Klein 2001). Structuring this utopian vision of multiple affiliations is the contrast and complementarity between 'Marcos' and 'Zapatista'. Marcos emerges as an identity that is a general, a generality that is undoubtedly facilitated by the facelessness of Marcos the individual. It is an ideal identity based on ideas of norms of justice and solidarity, but one that is present only in different, local contexts. At the same time 'of course, a Zapatista' indexes the locatedness of this identity. Marcos is what he is because of his moorings in the Zapatista movement, which is itself, one may be reminded, an identity carved out of several micro-identities. In short what is involved in the citation from Marcos is the notion of multiple levels of identity formation.

My reading of the Zapatista identity also points to the overlaps and distinctions with Tagore. Both have a sense of different affiliations within and without the strong boundary lines they propose for self-identification: the Zapatista in one, and the East in the other. Both Zapatista and East consist of multiple affiliations that are internal and at the same time, recognise the multiplicity of identities that lie outside its boundaries. Further, both Zapatista and East are affiliations that are linked to justice and solidarity. However, the Zapatista identity is also linked to popular movements, the value of which Tagore, for various reasons, refused to think through. On the other hand, what Tagore proposed as a mode of recognising affiliations lie outside its own boundaries of the East and exceeds the simple act of multiple identifications that marks the solidarities of Marcos. For the idea of self-division that is at the heart of the processual identity is one that recognises both the importance of difference and the impossibility of passively co-existing with it. It is the dynamic principle of change through variety, rather than simple acceptance of various identities which distinguishes Tagore's understanding.

In conclusion, I think that this conundrum produced by the imperatives of popular movement on the one hand, and of processual identity on the other hand, can be a productive one. Tagore's conception of processual identities has an important consequence for anti-globalisation movements—provided we can extend it to service the implications of popular movements in the first place. There is no reason to hope that the present phase of a happy co-existence of collective identities that have marked anti-globalisation rallies can continue. Already activists have begun to revisit earlier debates about the need for co-ordination and organisation (necessary to face the synchronised counter-offensive of globalisation), and the necessity to preserve the freedom of pluralism. The move to create tighter organisational structures, while possibly being necessary, is also a fraught enterprise. Among other things a problem that has plagued movements in the past, especially revolutionary ones, is that with coordinated organisation crops up the problem of the domination of a particular cultural bloc or group. It is here that a serious reflection on Tagore's notion of located transformation through the other may be able to address some of the problems of mutual relationships, even if it is able to preempt them. In other words, it is in this space between the imperatives of organising movement and the need for belonging to the dynamic process of identity exchange—that a popular politics of the global beckons.

ENDNOTES

An advertisement for Singer sewing machine in 1883 featured its trademark, which was an image of a recognisably Western seamstress working at the machine, at the centre of the advertisement. (Ray Chaudhury n.d.). In general the advertisements shown in this book of the late nineteenth century (and there is a representative sample) dwell on the place of production (if made by an international enterprise), and also provide the specifications of the product itself.

REFERENCES

Calhoun, Craig. 2009. 'The Class Consciousness of Frequent Travellers. Towards a Critique of Actually Existing Cosmopolitanism', in Saurabh Dube (ed.), *The Enchantments of Modernity: Empire, Nation, Globalisation*. Delhi: Routledge.

Klein, Naomi. 2001. *No Logo*. Chapters 1 and 5. London: Flamingo.

Klein, Naomi. 2001. 'The Unknown Icon', in *The Guardian*. 3 March.

Klein, Naomi. 2002. 'Farewell to The End of History: Organisation and Vision in Anti-corporate Movements', in *Socialist Register*. Vol. 38. 1–14.

Milibank, John. 2001. 'Sovereignty, Empire, Capital and Terror', in *Telos*. No. 121. Fall.

Pal, Prosanto Kumar. 1997. *Rabindrajibani*. Saptam Khanda [Vol.VII, 1321–26 1914–20]. Kolkata: Ananda Publishers Private Limited.

Ray Chaudhury, Ranabir. n.d. *Calcutta A Hundred Years Ago*. Bombay: Nachiketa Publications Ltd.

Robertson, Roland. 1990. 'Mapping the Global Condition: Globalisation as a Central Concept', in Mike Featherstone (ed.), *Nationalism, Globalisation and Modernity*. New Delhi: Sage.

Sarkar, Sumit. 1973. *Swadeshi Movement in Bengal: 1903–8*. Delhi: People's Publishing House. 81.

Tagore, Rabindranath. 1980 (f.pub 1922). 'East and West', in *Creative Unity*. Delhi: Macmillan. 93–112.

8

Contested Spaces of State and Identity Politics: Re-visiting the Relationship of Jammu & Kashmir with India

Navnita C. Behera

The countries in South Asia are undergoing a churning process. Emulating the Westphalian nation-state model in this part of the world has proved to be deeply problematic as is evident from various secessionist conflicts raging across the subcontinent. This has forced many states, especially India, to explore the creation of new, intermediate layers of state structures that are better suited to meet the divergent political aspirations of its diverse communities. In the intellectual domain too, the dominant discourse on the nation-state building has increasingly been contested by several scholars arguing in favour of re-negotiating the social contract between the state and its populace.

Located in this genre of literature, this chapter argues that the Western model of nation-state building is not a panacea, but part of the problem of state-making. It examines the concepts of state and identity in a pre-modern and modern setting, before analysing the links and relationship between state, identity and violence. This chapter concludes with an illustration of modern India's relationship with Kashmir.

The concept of state and identity, in the modern sense, is a result of the nationalist consciousness in the nineteenth century. They are not a historical given but a modern creation, an object of invention rather than discovery, to be understood by analysing the process of their historical construction. The onset of colonial rule materially changed people's perception of the collective self and place in the social and political world. The social and political formations in pre-colonial India were qualitatively different.

PRE-MODERN IDENTITY

A pre-modern identity performed a social function. People followed elaborately codified rules of social differentiation and lived among communities, but their sense of belonging and solidarity was not based on political considerations. Pre-modern identities tended to be 'fuzzy' in the sense, that the identity of an individual was distributed in several different social practices—a kind of layering in which the fact of distinctive belonging to a village, local community, caste group, religious sect, language, kinship complex and trade association would all have figured in a 'context-dependent fashion' (Kaviraj 1995: 116; Chatterjee 1994: 222).[1] Any single community did not claim to represent or exhaust all the layers of selfhood of its members and the purely social nature of links allowed an individual to belong to several communities simultaneously without coming under any pressure to clarify the identity structure in which they lived.

Not only was an individual's identity plural and flexible, but also the relationship among collective identities was very different. Unlike modern identities, where a clear and strong sense of 'we' and 'they' is the basic logic of any identity assertion, the pre-modern identity's 'self' and 'other' was very hazy and diffused, and did not have determinate boundaries. Traditional identities were not enumerated, though definable with precision for all practical purposes of social interaction (ibid.). They simply lacked the cognitive means to generate a global picture of the spaces in which social groups lived. This meant, they did not see historical processes as things, which could be bent to their collective will if people acted concertedly on a large-enough scale (Kaviraj 1992: 26). Since they did not know how many of them were there in the world, they were unaware of the tremendous potential of their collective action and lacked the means to persuade their group members to act together to shape political possibilities in their favour. They were, thus, not political in nature—a condition of modernity.

PRE-COLONIAL POLITICAL AUTHORITY

How was political authority in pre-colonial India different? The subcontinental empires, from the Mauryan (BC 312–185) and Gupta (319–540 AD) in pre-classical times to the Mughals during the medieval period accommodated intermediary levels of stale formations, viz. 'regional kingdoms' by evolving creative political mechanisms of a loosely woven web of suzerainty as distinct from a sovereign state (Renan 1990: 9).[2] The Hindu conception of society being prior to and autonomous of the state significantly circumscribed the powers of the state. Royal authorities had to work within the rules of the caste system and could not expand state powers radically, and all social demands for representation and re-distribution did not have to be routed through the state. By and large the flexible chains of political authority matched the fluidity of social boundaries. The state upheld and protected these identities and their values, rather than it constituting the highest form of identity, demanding total and complete allegiance of its subjects like the modern nation-state.

MODERN IDENTITY AND STATE

How did modernity transform the conceptions of identity and political authority and their relationship? The British brought an entirely new cognitive apparatus of figures, maps and numbers from modern Europe and imparted a sense of territoriality to identities and introduced the principle of their enumeration (Kaviraj 1995: 117). This materially changed the popular perception of the collective self. On the one hand, it made possible individuals' membership in abstract identities, based on convergence of interests[3] (Kaviraj 1992: 20–1), and on the other endowed these identities with a non-traditional capacity to undertake political action on behalf of their collective selves. In this sense, all modern identities are either directly or potentially political. For example, people were indeed Hindus or Muslims before but under conditions of modernity, their perceptions of the collective self as the majority and minority community changed fundamentally their way of being Hindu and Muslim. It forced individuals and communities to choose one aspect of their identity, in this case religion, over all others by prioritising them in an ascending order. The political scientist Don Miller pointed out:

> By their education, legislation, administration, judicial codes and procedures and even by that apparently simple operation of objective classification, the census, the British unwittingly imposed dualistic either-or oppositions as natural normative order or thought. In a multitude of ways, Indians learned that one is either this or that; that one cannot be both or neither or indifferent. The significance of identity thus became a new paramount concern.... Orthodoxy of being was gradually replacing heterodoxy of beings (Miller cited in Kakar 1995: 196).[4]

This made them self-conscious about their hitherto unrealised and untapped potential for collective action to achieve political objectives.

A third critical factor was development of vernacular language and 'print capitalism' (Anderson 1991: 44–6) introduced by colonial rule. Language, here, is not viewed as an emblem of nationhood or nationness like flags or currency but is understood in a functional sense. It is an instrument to transmit information, enabling the profile of the same identity to communicate with each other. It was print-technology that generated the capacity for people to relate to others with whom they had no direct physical interaction, but who shared the same social space. Print-language made it possible for people to imagine new bonds of affinities. It also provided the intelligentsia to get their ideas across to the masses.

The British introduced English for their administrative requirements, as the bureaucrats had to be bilingual, capable of mediating between the colonial rulers and the colonised people. The print-technology and its institutional mechanisms such as printing presses, publishing houses, newspapers and magazines that were used to spread the English language also facilitated the development of local vernacular language, Hindustani, a mixture of Hindi and Urdu. Later, this became the common medium of communication between the intelligentsia and the masses and was used as an instrument of mobilisation by the political leadership. The technological revolution along with the streamlining of education extended the reach and potential of this medium for purposes of mobilisation.

To recapitulate: a modern identity is a political historical construct based upon convergence of interests, generated by individuals and communities, to pursue common political goals. A sense of territoriality, enumeration of communities and use of a vernacular language through the print medium are the hallmark of any modern identity. The first is necessary for demanding its own sovereign space and stressing numbers through self-enumeration, and is a source of great psychological strength and immense political significance. Print-language is thus a powerful instrument for mobilising an identity for collective action.

Mass mobilisation is vital for actualising an identity's potential for collective action, but a deeply individualistic language of modernity is problematic. A political movement requires large-scale sacrifices which ordinary people are unlikely to accept if they calculate their activities in purely rational terms of individual costs and benefits (Olson 1971).[5] That is precisely why an identity must present itself as a community with an immemorial past. Since it is an imagined community with no objective past, history must be constructed anew, as a community that was lost and is to be regained. To give itself a history is not only the 'most fundamental act of self-identification of a community' (Kaviraj 1992: 16), but is integral to bestowing an emotive rationale to its political demands. Tradition through myths, memories, symbols, rituals and ideals furnishes the ingredients for psychological and social bonds of an identity. Cultural means are thus used to pursue secular political interests.

Mass mobilisation operates through selective politicisation of tradition and sensitive manipulation of popular dreams, memories, symbols and myths that appeal emotionally to an identity's social selfhood. Symbols are the optimisation of the most cherished values of an identity and arouse an emotionally powerful response from the masses. There are no standard criteria for selection of these symbols though their efficacy in mobilising the masses is a key-determining factor. Besides, the definition of *we* invariably depends on who *they* are. Subject to a given situation, an identity may seek to emphasise those symbols or features that differentiate it most critically from its 'particular other'. This situational aspect is important to understand the shifting boundaries of some identities. For instance, the Sikhs in East Punjab emphasised their religious identity in 1947 and their Punjabi language in the late 1950s. On both occasions, the situation was a critical factor in determining their choice of symbols. When India was being partitioned on the basis of religion in 1947, they projected their demand for a separate state on the grounds of Sikhs being a separate religious entity and upon linguistic reorganisation of the Indian state. They later reformulated their demand for a Punjabi Suba (Punjabi-speaking state).

Colonial rule had not only produced an image of India as a geographic and demographic entity, but also historically transformed the nature and form of political authority in a fundamental and irreversible manner. The British constructed a unitary territorial state of India with a centralised political unity based on the notion of a singular and indivisible sovereignty, eliminated the intermediary state formations and banished the indigenous concept of a multilayered sovereignty to the pages of history. It imposed a political unity rooted in the impersonal rationality of bureaucratic institutions based on Western concepts of contractual law and impersonalised sovereignty that was historically unprecedented in a society accustomed to direct personalised rule (Jalal 1995: 9–10). It ruptured the old, indigenous and creative mechanisms of compromise and collaboration between various identities and the political authority, creating a wide, unbridgeable gap between the integrative institutions of the colonial state and the complex mosaic of social and cultural diversities within Indian society.

The nature of the colonial state is critical to understand the modern state because unlike the creation of a new identity such as Indian nationalism to challenge British rule, the nationalist consciousness of the nineteenth century did not question or attempt to radically transform the colonial state. The dominant argument was that British rule was alien and unrepresentative, and hence, the demand for an independent state representing Indian nationalism. In other words, the post-colonial state in India 'only expanded and not transformed the basic institutional structures of rational authority—bureaucracy, police, courts set up by the colonial state' (Chatterjee 1994: 15).[6] Neither did they question the logic of a modern state representing one nation or that of transferring the responsibility of managing social relations among individuals and collective identities from indigenous social regulatory mechanisms such as the caste system to the state. The political leadership of modern India perceived the state as the prime mover, the key repository of political power that would act as an agency of collectively intended social change, on behalf of the Indian nation.

STATE, IDENTITY AND VIOLENCE: THE RELATIONSHIP

There is a mutually influencing social and political relationship between state, identity and violence. The logic of the modern nation-state allows recognition of only a single, determinate, demographically numerable form of nation within its jurisdiction. In a society richly endowed with diverse identities, the state's identification with only one identity is inherently problematic because it denies political space to other identities. The working of electoral democracy makes it more complicated. Democracy, as an ideology, is individual-centric, but the logic of electoral politics in a democratic system rests on the principle of majority rule.

However, a rule by a majority identity marginalises and alienates all minority identities. Since the state is the primary repository of political power, the latter are bereft of any alternative avenues for political expression. They are, therefore, forced to create political space where they constitute similar majorities, but without any fundamental transformation of the state structures, the process continues to provide the rationale for further fissure among identities. Each majority creates a minority, and its refusal to share political power with the latter politicises it and motivates it to become a majority itself, perhaps on a smaller scale or region only to practice in retribution similar inequity towards others.

There can be no doubt that checks and balances protect individual and group rights from the abuse of the majority in a democratic system. Federalism and decentralisation of power are two modern devices through which vulnerable minorities can protect themselves. However, even these can be overrun if the majority community is determined to use the state institutions only to empower itself, and to legitimise and propagate its ideology. If the ethnic character of the political majority is identifiable with a single community and remains constantly fixed, the minorities may feel permanently disenfranchised within the political system.

The modern identity's strong and determinate sense of self, inevitably leads to intolerance of others, that is, all those outside its boundaries. A dominant identity-seeking subjugation, assimilation or submergence of other identities, and on the other hand, self-assertion of a non-dominant identity which seeks a share in the state power controlled by the former, are inherently imbued with the risk of and potential for violence. For instance, the Hindu nationalists' belief that the only way to avoid large-scale (Hindu-Muslim) violence is,

> a change in the Muslim view of the community's role, traditions and institutions so that the Muslim can adapt the word meaning anything from adjustment to assimilation to the Hindu majority's national culture.... [However] to ask the Muslims to recognise themselves in the Hindu nationalist history of India, to expect them to feel their culture confirmed in Hindu symbols, rituals and celebrations

> is asking them to *renounce their cultural identity* and to erase their collective memory so that they become indistinguishable from the Hindus (Kakar 1995: 251).

As long as neither side gives in, the in-built potential of violence endures.

When the state takes on a majoritarian or sectarian character, relationship between the state and non-dominant identities turns violent. Much of this violence consists of the use of visible physical force though it may also be an indirect threat of retaliation against the recalcitrant identities. On the other hand, an identity denied political expression and alienated by the bureaucratisation of state structures, may resort to violence when political and constitutional means to achieve its objectives are either exhausted or perceived to be ineffective (ibid.: 247).[7] A judgement among the discriminated or alienated segments that 'only violence pays', abets it further as violence is perceived to be the only way of ensuring a hearing by the state.

RATIONALE OF VIOLENCE

An identity mobilises its members to commit acts of violence and justifies its use by referring to both mythological motifs and contemporary political practices. Tradition is politicised and memories of past struggles are consciously resurrected by juxtaposing historical narratives of subjugation and oppression with allusions to mythology and folklore eulogising heroic conquests and victories against the enemy. The concept of *jihad* in Islam, *dharmayudha* in Hinduism and martyrdom of *gurus* among Sikhs are examples of religion which legitimises the use of violence under certain circumstances used by these communities for a self-defined collective cause in a contemporary situation (ibid.: 248–9).[8]

Individualism is the first value to disappear in any collective violent action, and there is a kind of group coherence and solidarity which is more intensely felt and proves to be a much stronger bond than all varieties of relationships based on mere convergence of interests. The very forms of an armed struggle suggest a different vocabulary—brotherhood, comrades-in-arms, martyrdom, and inculcates a consciousness of the collective history, a common cause and a national destiny. The interest of one becomes the interest of all, for in concrete fact *everyone* will be discovered by the troops, *everyone* will be massacred or *everyone* will be saved. The motto look out for yourself is forbidden (Fanon 1970: 37, 73). The mindset changes from an individualistic thinking to that of collective goals, collective good and a collective cause. Violence is also projected as a cleansing force. It restores the self-respect of alienated members and makes them fearless. They are no longer afraid to face even death which otherwise indicates subjugation to injustice and exploitation. Because 'faced collectively and in action, death changes its countenance; now nothing seems more likely to intensify our vitality than its proximity ...' (Arendt 1970: 68). They actively seek martyrdom as that would immortalise them.

The evolution and development of this discourse may be explained by 'weaving of individual biography into social text through the use of local knowledge' (Das 1995: 134). The local knowledge of police atrocities and excesses is used to transform the individual misery into the misfortunes of the community. Examples of individual sufferings and their reiteration into the narratives of the community are important because,

> they show how the state comes to be experienced in everyday life and how this experience is transformed in the making of a violent community.... Once the community becomes the conduit through which the *individual* experience of having been violated can be seen as the experience of the *whole* community, then the next step is to explain all violence committed by the community as a response to injustice (emphasis mine) (Das 1995: 131).

A violent act committed by an individual is justified by framing it within the community's fight for justice, and is perceived as committed only on behalf of a community, for the purposes of collective good.

State violence and identities resort to violence and mutually reinforce each other in an extraordinary reciprocal homogeneity. When the state unleashes its coercive power to suppress a political movement, an entire community bears the brunt of state violence.

This not only strengthens the psychological bond of a community but also vindicates their use of violence against the state. Likewise, an identity's indiscriminate use of violence, particularly terrorism against the state as well as the general public, buttresses the government's rationale to suppress the movement by force.

Once violence comes into play, it fundamentally transforms the nature of an identity and the state, as well as narrows the space for political accommodation between the two. It significantly raises the stakes for an identity, making it more exclusive and determinate in its boundaries. The nature and tone of its demands become more stringent with emphasis shifting from negotiations with the authorities to forcing them to concede ground. Reaching a political compromise, popularly not perceived to be commensurate with the sacrifices made by the community, becomes more difficult. The state on the other hand, loses political legitimacy by excessive reliance on coercive means to manage social and political relations among various communities. The circle between state, identity and violence, and its reproduction gets completed when violence becomes a 'way of life as well as a means of both governance and redress against its excesses' (Kothari 1994: 53).

THE INDIAN NATION-STATE

The Indian nation like any modern identity is a historical construct, imagined into existence with the political objective of overthrowing colonial rule and creating an independent nation-state. The voices of anti-colonialism in the early phase emanated from the traditional communities, the older, limited and fragmented identities such as the Bengali *jati,* but lacking the skills of cognitive mapping, this 'we' was rather hazy, indeterminate and woefully inadequate to take on the might of the colonial machine. So, a new constellation had to be forged by 'breaking down the boundaries of their "natural we" and by extending their "we-ness" in different directions in an experiment in coalition-making' (Kaviraj 1992: 1–16). Eventually, this came to be known as an 'Indian we'. This was not culturally homogenous. The older, unreconstructed identities like the Rajputs, the Marathas, the Bengalis and the Sikhs had found a secure place within the new collective self. While politically they identified with the 'Indian we', they *co-existed* on the social plane.

Indian nationalism was not the only player in the political arena. From the early days of conceiving a new nation to shaping the character of the new state, other imagined communities such as the Hindu nation challenged the idea of Indian nationalism. The fact that Indian nationalism won this battle of identities was largely due to various historical and political exigencies. A critical factor was Mahatma Gandhi's politics. More than his novel technique of non-violence against the colonial military might, his construction of a 'non-monolithic, pluralist mode of consciousness had imparted a mass character to the nationalist movement' (Ahmed 1993: 126; Kaviraj 1994: 322).[9] However, while Gandhi's method of fighting for *Swaraj* won unstinted adherence from a majority of the Congress leadership, his concomitant conception of the post-colonial state, *Ramrajya,* rooted in the belief that society's *dharmically* ordered heterogeneity was prior to, and to a considerable degree autonomous of state authority and that local communities were capable of self-rule, found little support.

An alternative conceptualisation was an exclusionist Hindu nation with a monolithic unity epitomised by the centrality of the brahminical tradition with its own language and literature and myths and symbols. Golwalkar defined the ideology as 'one culture, one language, one nation-Hindu, Hindi and Hindustan' (Golwalkar 1947). In the early nineteenth century, the concept of Hindu nation and later, Hindu nation-state were out-manoeuvred by the territorial conception of Indian nationalism. The particular notion of Hindu nation being imagined and propagated was extremely narrow and rigid, incapable of extending its boundaries to include the large numbers of Muslims, Sikhs and Christians, and a vast submerged groups of lower caste Hindus and adivasis which was a historical necessity at that juncture. After independence, the proponents of Hindu state that were in a minority in the Constituent Assembly, albeit a powerful minority that may not have succeeded in securing its original objective but had a decisive influence over the state formation processes (Das 1994: 286).[10]

Nehru's brand of modernist nationalism, modelled after the European experience, finally won the day. Nehru upheld the secular, pluralist idea of the Indian nation rooted in a composite culture. Without denying the continuity of Indian tradition, it emphasised the diversity and variety, rejecting Hindu monolithicism. Nehru's difficulty was that, given the European model, the cultural unification of the Indian nation was a pre-requisite for building a modern nation-state, but did not fit the ground realities of Indian society replete with diverse social and cultural identities. The result was a paradox. Nehru insisted that conceptually the imagining of the Indian nation was an accomplished and irreversible fact that did not have to be constantly negotiated, presented and justified (Kaviraj 1994: 330). The question of cultural construction of the Indian nation was left behind in the past, rather than the future. But materially, it was in infancy, a nation-in-the-making, which needed to be protected against contending identities. Accordingly, state formation processes were geared towards constructing a strong state, capable of defending a nascent nation. This thinking dominated the mindset of the Constituent Assembly that decided to hammer out a constitutional cast within which it would be possible politically to nurture and strengthen the Indian nation (Navlakha 1996: 86).[11]

The basic contours of the Indian state's relationship with Indian nation and the sub-national identities are structurally interwoven within its Constitution. The Cabinet Mission had backed plans for a federal structure with limited compulsory central subjects of defence, foreign affairs and communications and the residuary powers to be vested in autonomous provinces. After Partition, a union with a strong centre rather than a loose federation with a weak centre was the basic objective. Partition had undoubtedly driven deep into the Indian political psyche the threat of dismemberment, but it was the future of the Indian nation at stake, as perceived by the Nehru-led Congress party, that proved to be the determining factor in opting for a quasi-federal union.

Centre-state relations, in particular, were designed after the 1935 Act. Since the Indian federation was founded by the union vesting powers in the states, 'most institutional devices for inter-governmental consultation and participation of states in national decision-making processes owed their origins to central initiatives, their authority to central statutes and their agendas and terms of reference to central ministries' (Arora and Mukerji 1992: 9). Constitutionally, the states were subordinated to the central authority and demands for more power for states were condemned as driven by parochial political considerations. The strong-state ideology fitted Nehru's programme of bolstering a national Indian identity. He believed people would no longer be required to be politically mobilised as different peoples, and they had to be encouraged to participate in national reconstruction with single-minded loyalty and devotion (ibid.: 8).

However the project of modernity, in forging an European-style Indian nation, could not be replicated totally because if the nation-state had to be culturally homogeneous by definition, it did not fit the diverse social and cultural realities of India. Recognising India's plurality, Nehru had rejected the attempt to homogenise and to impose a Hindu heartland core-culture on the Indian nation. In his vision, for any person to be Bengali or Tamil or Punjabi or Hindu or Muslim was not in contradiction with being an Indian. It was the primacy a person accorded to the regional, religious or ethnic identity and the national identity that was in question. Nehru hoped with the project of nation-building, an individual would first become an Indian and then a Bengali or Tamil or Hindu or Sikh and perhaps ultimately, the forces of modernisation would sweep away the ascriptive identities of religion, caste and ethnicity. He realised that the real challenge to the Indian nation emanated from the collective political expression of sub-national identities. Hence there is a need to build a strong central authority to manage the social relations among these identities and to ensure their allegiance to the Indian nation.

The Congress leadership had been committed to reorganisation of states on a linguistic basis since 1922, but it finally decided to maintain the status quo. The Linguistic Provinces Commission appointed by the Constituent Assembly recommended against the linguistic reorganisation of states because it would give rise to other demands for separation, and each state would still have a minority population. In reality, the nationalist leadership was afraid that 'it would bring into existence provinces with a subnational bias at a time when nationalism is yet in its infancy and is not in a position to bear any strain' (Rao cited in Navlakha 1996: 81). Nehru's response to the evidence submitted to the Linguistic Provinces Commission is revealing. He writes,

> The work of sixty years of the Indian National Congress was standing before us, face to face with centuries-old India of narrow loyalties, petty jealousies and ignorant prejudices engaged in mortal conflict and we were *simply horrified to see how thin was the ice upon which we were skating. Some of* the ablest men in the country came before us and confidentially and emphatically stated that language in the country stood for and represented culture, race, history individuality and finally a sub-nation (Harrison 1956: 621).

It beautifully reflects the paradox in Nehru's mind: Indian National Congress having constructed the Indian nation over sixty momentous years, found it incomplete, uncertain, fragile, and having to be defended against contending sub-national identities. In creating a strong centre and rejecting the principle of linguistic states, the Constituent Assembly made an obvious attempt 'to bring about a willed merger with the agencies of the state taking on the role of protecting the nation' (Navlakha 1996: 81).

MODERN INDIA AND KASHMIR

Kashmir was special because it was a Muslim-majority state and had acceded to India under extraordinary circumstances of being invaded by Pakistani raiders. It was granted a special status under Article 370 whereby no provisions of the Indian Constitution except Article I, bringing it under the territorial jurisdiction of India, was made applicable to Jammu and Kashmir (J&K). In accordance with the Instrument of Accession, Indian Parliament had legislative rights only in three areas—defence, foreign affairs and communications. The residuary powers were vested in the state, a situation unique to Jammu and Kashmir in the Indian Union.

Despite its special autonomous status, Kashmir has twice sought to break away from the Indian State. Why? We argue that it is because of imposition of larger Indian nation's political choices on Kashmir, appropriation of its political space by centralised state structures, and ultimately violent repression of local dissent. On the other hand, Kashmiris have consistently failed to achieve their objective because its leadership reproduced the hierarchical social and political structures they sought to escape by representing political aspirations of only the majority community, i.e., Kashmiri Muslims rather than all the people of J&K.

In order to understand modern India's relationship with Kashmir, let us first examine Nehru's premise of granting political autonomy to Kashmir. Nehru had granted a special status to Kashmir because its inclusion was necessary to achieve larger political objectives of scoring a victory for secular Indian nationalism vis-à-vis Pakistan's two-nation theory on the one hand, and Hindu nationalism on the other. He argued:

> It helped our thesis of nationalism not being related to religion. If the contrary thesis was proved ... it would have a powerful effect on the communal elements in India both Hindu and Muslim. That is of extreme importance to us—that we don't by taking some wrong steps in Kashmir create these terribly disruptive tendencies within India (Brecher cited in Gopal 1980: 217).

To grant special status to Kashmir was therefore a tactical move rather than acceptance of its right to autonomy in principle. While Nehru was ready to pay the price, as articulated by Sheikh Abdullah, of maximum political autonomy for Jammu and Kashmir, he would not do so at the cost of the Indian state. That is why whenever Kashmir's political aspirations came into conflict with interests of the Indian Union, the latter prevailed. For example after removing the Maharaja, Sheikh Abdullah reversed his position on the merger of Jammu and Kashmir State Forces with the Indian army to a properly organised state army (Singh 1994: 84; Bhattacharjea 1994: 177).[12] He argued that the Indian Government's powers for defence of J&K did not include the control and disposition of the state's armed forces. This directly challenged the Indian state's monopoly over military instruments of power to defend territories, and the potential of separate state army to turn hostile against the Indian state which had dangerous implications for national security. The central leadership, therefore, dismissed the National Conference's (NC) contention. It is important to note the reasons furnished by Gopalaswamy Ayyangar to grant Kashmir a special status:

> In the first place there has been a war going on ... the conditions in the state are still abnormal.... Part of the state is still in the hands of rebels and enemies. We are still entangled in the United Nations in regard to J&K.... We are also committed to ascertaining the will of the people by means of a plebiscite provided that peaceful and normal conditions can be restored and the impartiality of the plebiscite could be guaranteed (Navlakha Vol. III 1996: 78).

Clearly, neither does it appreciate Kashmiris' political aspirations nor admits its right to an autonomous status in the Indian Union. On the contrary, Article 370 was projected as a temporary provision and Ayyangar expressed the hope on behalf of 'everybody here that in due course, even J&K will become ripe for the same sort of integration as has taken place in the case of other states' (Gupta 1966: 380).

On the other hand, Sheikh Abdullah had joined India in the belief that Kashmir's political autonomy would be better protected in a secular and democratic Indian state. The relationship between Kashmir and the Indian state remained good so long as the former's expectations of an autonomous status were met. Soon fissures started appearing after the plebiscite option was dropped and J&K was declared, for all times, to be an integral part of India. The Indian state sought closer federal integration of Kashmir that was resented by the Kashmiri leadership as undue encroachment on their autonomy. The Praja Parishad agitation which demanded complete merger of J&K further compounded the situation. The Sheikh warned it would not only weaken accession but also cause suspicion among Kashmiri Muslims that 'Hindu India intended to swallow up Kashmir' (Puri 1981: 99).

The conflict was rooted in differing expectations. The Indian state viewed J&K as part of India, and Kashmiris a sub-set of the Indian nation. Despite special measures to accommodate Kashmiris' political aspirations, Nehru was ultimately bound by the logic that the Kashmiri identity like all sub-national identities—Bengali, Tamil, Punjabi identity—must be integrated in the Indian nation.

Sheikh Abdullah interpreted the Instrument of Accession literally and described the Delhi Agreement as being 'transitory and temporary', and as 'division of sovereignty whereby the state would retain complete internal sovereignty'. At a Working Committee meeting of the National Conference in May 1953, he opposed the continuation of Indo-Kashmir relations on the present basis. Sheikh's terminology of Indo-Kashmir relationship placed India and Kashmir on an equal footing—an argument not acceptable to the Indian leadership.

When Abdullah felt that Kashmir's political aspirations, as articulated by the National Conference, could not be met within the Indian Union he started exploring the idea of an independent Kashmir. In search for allies, Abdullah's attitude softened towards Pakistan and he sought international support for an independent Kashmir from the UK and US (Varshney 1992: 205).[13] This brought the Kashmiris in collision with the Indian state. So far, their disagreements were basically about the primacy of the Indian identity over the Kashmiri identity and degree of Kashmir's political autonomy. The demand for sovereign space outside the Indian state challenged its sovereignty and territorial integrity. Kashmir had also become a test case of Indian secularism. Indian leaders never accepted the two-nation theory and Kashmir's refusal to join Pakistan had undoubtedly strengthened India's secular credentials. Once Kashmir became a part of India, however provisionally, it could not break away without questioning the secular rationale of the Indian state from within and without. Kashmir had, therefore, become a hostage to the secular basis of the Indian state, and would not be allowed to secede. On 8 August 1953 Sheikh Abdullah was dismissed and arrested. The Indian state's first rupture with the Kashmiri identity was complete.

The limited and fragmented edifice of the Kashmiri identity was the most critical reason for its failure. Abdullah had increasingly distanced the Valley from Jammu and Ladakh, arguing that they could merge into the Indian Union leaving the Kashmir Valley alone to assert its independent identity. Subsequently he started differentiating between the 'Muslims and non-Muslims of the state' for the first time since 1947. He said:

> It is the Muslims who have to decide accession with India and not the non-Muslims as the latter have no place in Pakistan and because their only choice is India.... *My main concern and effort has not been to convince the Hindus and Sikhs that their future lay in India but the Muslims who form the majority.* It was Muslims who were forced to ponder whether they could rely on the Indian promises and stay within the Indian Union (emphasis added) (Cited in Puri 1981: 231).

Sheikh Abdullah's conception of the Kashmiri identity thus gradually changed from demanding self-determination for 'the people of Jammu and Kashmir State' to 'Kashmiris' and by 1953, to mainly the 'Kashmiri Muslims'. However, the plurality of J&K society exposed internal contradictions in this thesis. If Abdullah argued self-determination was the inherent right of all peoples and demanded it for Kashmiris, he could not justify denying the same to people in Jammu and Ladakh. But that was self-defeating because Jammu and Ladakh's demand for full and unconditional accession to India acted as a countervailing force to the Valley's demand for independence. Jammu and Ladakh comprised 47 per cent of the state population. Their exclusion from the Kashmiri group identity had not only caused fragmentation, but also debilitated collective strength to challenge the hegemony of the Indian nation and political dominance of the Indian state. Even Kashmiri Muslims were no longer a cohesive political force. The NC and government were divided deeply on the issue of accession. Abdullah's stance on the state's relationship with India was virtually disowned by 3 out of 4 members of cabinet (excluding him). His strategy to seek international support from the great powers proved to be counter-productive. Abdullah failed to understand that Kashmir was merely a pawn in the superpowers' global game of cold war and that support of one superpower for an independent Kashmir would be checkmated by the other. In the end, an impoverished and fragmented Kashmiri group identity without any meaningful external support was simply no match for the might of the Indian state.

After spending nearly two decades in jail, a much-chastened Sheikh Abdullah reached an accord with Mrs Indira Gandhi in

1975. Pakistan's total defeat in 1971 war had brought home the realisation that Pakistan could no longer be used as a bargaining card vis-à-vis New Delhi. The Shimla Agreement had closed the plebiscite option. Abdullah relinquished the goal of sovereign Kashmir and abandoned the demand for self-determination in favour of political autonomy. Mrs Gandhi proved to be more than a match for him. While he accepted J&K as a 'constituent unit of the Union of India', he was told clearly that the clock could not be turned back to restore Article 370 to its original form. The Kashmir Accord ratified the constitutional integration of Kashmir. Even symbolic political concessions to revert the designations of Governor to *Sadar-i-Riyasat* and Chief Minister to *Wazir-i-Azam* were not conceded. Nor was the Kashmiri leadership's plea to make Kashmir's special status permanent accepted by the central government. All that the Kashmir got in return was continuation of Article 370 on the statute book, albeit in truncated form because the promised review of all acts and ordinances passed since Abdullah's arrest never took place (Anand 1980: 112–43).

The rapprochement between Kashmir and the Indian state, however, did not last long. The undercurrents of tension rooted in differing assumptions and expectations of single nation-state and multiple identities lingered on. Although a secessionist movement by Kashmiri youth was launched only in 1989, its foundations were laid in political developments of 1970s. The changing character of the Indian state, and Mrs Indira Gandhi's politics in particular, needs to be examined in order to understand the changing contours of its relationship with Kashmir.

Under Nehru, the Indian federal structures functioned essentially within the Congress system to the extent that inner party democracy within limits of the consensual model was a reality. But Mrs Gandhi sought to create a highly personalised and centralised political system and marginalised the Congress party organisation by establishing personal control through centralised direction of the state party units. She created a federal structure constitutionally subordinating the sub-national identities to the Indian state but recognising the plural realities of a diverse society, they were allowed adequate political space to grow within the Indian polity. The institutionalised process to deal with the centre-state conflicts favoured 'inclusionary over exclusionary strategies as long as the demands were non-secessionist, secular in character and met with the approval of more than one side in the conflict' (Kohli 1988: 311). In J&K, Nehru had secured its constitutional subordination while Mrs Gandhi went one step further to erode its political autonomy. This was in keeping with the Congress politics in 1970s, when its majority at the national level was threatened by regional political parties' successful political mobilisation of sub-national identities into electoral majorities at the state level. Mrs Gandhi responded by identifying the Congress with the Indian nation thereby castigating the non-Congress parties and regional political parties, in particular, as anti-Indian and anti-national. By imposing a single Indian identity to be represented only by the Congress party, the Centre not only denied political legitimacy of sub-national identities and sought their submergence into the Indian identity but also often imposed the Congress's political choices on the states. In J&K, it meant replacement of National Conference with the Congress party, banning and debarring of Plebiscite Front from participating in state elections, refusal to roll back the erosion of J&K's autonomy in the 1975 Accord, turning down Abdullah's plea to hold fresh elections and finally, arbitrary withdrawal of support to Abdullah's government in the wake of the Congress' defeat in 1977 general elections.

By the early 1980s, Mrs Gandhi tried to harness India's Hindu majority into a political constituency and accordingly, sought to identify the Indian identity with Hindu majority populace and brand the religious minorities as anti-national. This, in league with the Congress government's policies of fomenting religious extremism by promoting the Jamaat-i-Islami to undercut the secular support base of the National Conference in J&K, contributed a great deal in communalising the political process. When the Congress failed to tame the NC leadership, it resorted to blatant strongarm tactics and abuse of central authority and arbitrarily dismissed Farooq Abdullah's popularly elected government and imposed G. M. Shah's government in Srinagar. This was the beginning of a new and much more volatile phase of Kashmiri alienation. It shook Kashmiris' faith in the Indian state and rendered the electoral process meaningless even dispensable, and sent a signal that 'any honest decision that the people may take in regard to the governance of the State could easily be set aside by the powers that be in New Delhi'. Balraj Puri observed:

> Sheikh Abdullah's dismissal [had] signaled the message that even if the Kashmiri people did not wish to remain within India, they would not be allowed to secede whereas the dismissal of Farooq conveyed the message that even if the people wished to remain within India, they would not be free to choose their own government (Puri 1993: 34).

Farooq Abdullah was never hostile to the Indian state and consistently maintained that Kashmir's accession was complete, final and irrevocable. Therefore to castigate the Kashlmiri identity as a threat and to question Farooq's patriotism, the central government did not have Indian national interests in mind but partisan political interests of the Congress party. The Congress wanted the National Conference to play second fiddle and when Farooq Abdullah, backed by the people in the Valley refused to oblige, efforts were afoot to destabilise the state government. Subsequent armtwisting to forge an electoral alliance with Congress in 1986 and blatant manipulation of 1987 elections led Kashmiris to believe that they would remain permanently disenfranchised under the present political dispensation. Kashmiris, therefore, raised the banner of revolt and started a violent political struggle to demand independence. A detailed analysis of the secessionist movement, well documented elsewhere, is beyond the task of this paper (Behera n.d.).[14] Let us, however, briefly recount the main features and turning points of the militant movement in order to throw light on its causes of failure.

The Jammu Kashmir Liberation Front (JKLF) had spearheaded the first phase of militant movement, from 1988 to 1990, demanding *azadi* (independence). Other militant groups such as Allah Tigers, Peoples League and Hizb-i-Islamia were also active. Violence was used most effectively to achieve militants' immediate political objectives to paralyse the state apparatus and de-legitimise the political institutions, which had appropriated the space to articulate the political aspirations of the Kashmiris. The militants sought to defy the state authority, and transfer peoples allegiance and loyalty to themselves from the state, attack and replace the symbols of the state with their own and render every state institution dysfunctional that could potentially meet their political challenge.

The kidnapping of Home Minister Mufti Mohammed Sayeed's daughter Rubiya Sayeed in December 1989 by JKLF militants proved to be a turning point. Stripped of political legitimacy, Farooq Abdullah's government was virtually under siege. The government's abject surrender and release of militants resulted in a mass upsurge. It was widely perceived as the ultimate proof that 'the mighty Indian State has caved in and "azadi" is round the corner'. Subsequently Jagmohan's appointment as Governor of the state, and his policy of crushing militancy finally caused it to explode and transformed the largely underground militant siege into a mass popular movement. Kalashnikovs replaced black flags and the 'boys' became 'mujahideens' overnight. The Valley witnessed a series of processions of several thousands of people demanding azadi, causing total collapse of state authority.

However, militant operations in the Valley were confined largely to urban areas. Every new 'martyr' merited a *namaz-e-janaza* (funeral prayer) from the mohalla (colony) mosque, which inevitably resulted in more firings, more martyrs and more mobs, all feeding a vicious circle. Beyond holding the security forces to ransom the militants had no long-term strategy to force the Indian state to withdraw from Kashmir. The absence of an effective state response was critical to the militants' success to paralyse the state administration throughout 1988–9. A naive belief that 'the Indian state had lost the will to govern' was backed by high hopes that once the 'uprising' started, Pakistan would invade India to secure Kashmir's liberation.[15] Both were grave miscalculations. Pakistan did not attack and India did not hand over azadi on a platter. Once the Indian state unleashed its iron fist, the militants failed to respond with an effective counter-strategy and were little match for India's massive military power. The real threat to the Indian state emanated not from militancy but from mass processions which symbolised complete rejection of state authority. It may be charitable to characterise the mass rallies purely as a product of militants' strategy but they were more in the nature of spontaneous outbursts than part of military strategy. In fact, militants were overwhelmed by the mass response but could not purposefully and effectively channelise it to achieve azadi.

Hizb-ul-Mujahideen's ascendancy in 1991 marked the beginning of the second phase of militancy, dominated by propagation of Kashmir's Islamic identity. It was a large organisation with a well-equipped, more disciplined, and highly trained cadre with considerable combat experience in Afghanistan (Amin 1995: 92; Haq 1994).[16] Its front organisations included the Jamiat-ul-Tulba, which is the students' wing and the Dukhtaran-e-Millat, which the women's wing that also ran the Islamic Relief Committee and the Islamic Blood Bank. Its organisational network spread out to the rural areas, which served as good hideouts, and village *madrasas* were a valuable source of recruitment of militants. If Azad Kashmir was the base camp of the JKLF, the Jamaat-i-Islami organised open camps throughout Pakistan to recruit mujahideen and collect funds for the Kashmiri jihad. They recruited cadres from the Valley as well because they had done systematic groundwork by introducing a Sunni Islamic culture and literature through madrasas and about 2,500–3,000 mosques teaching the Koran and Hadith (interpretation of Islam) since the 1970s. Despite being better-equipped, more disciplined and highly trained with considerable combat experience in Afghanistan, the Hizb-ul-Mujahideen cadre lacked popular support in the Valley because of its strict adherence to Islamic ideology. Kashmiri Muslims supported Hizb-ul-Mujahideen in 'the fight against India' but its pure Islamic beliefs, like offering prayers at Sufi shrines and Pirs' mazars as idolatrous soon alienated the masses.

The Hizb-ul-Mujahideen mobilised its cadre in the name of Islam and introduced the highly emotive terminology of jihad—interestingly coined in Urdu and not Kashmiri to justify political violence. A popular slogan of Hizb-ul-Mujahideen was '*Na guerrilla jang, na quami jang: al jihad, al jihad*' (It is neither a guerrilla war nor a national war: it is a holy war). Deploying the prism of religion, the problem was articulated as 'the *Muslim Valley* was waging an *Islamic Movement* against the *Hindu Indian state* in order to accede to *Islamic Pakistan*'. Its Islamist framework had significantly altered the terms of the militant movement's discourse to establish an alternative school of thought and a pro-accession lobby. However, it was precisely due to strict adherence to Islamic ideology that the Hizb found it difficult to expand its social base and lacked popular support in the Valley. Also, the ideological polarisation between the JKLF's goal of *Kashmir banega Khudmukhtar* (Kashmir will be independent) and the Hizb-ul-Mujahideen's demand of *Kashmir banega Pakistan* divided the militant ranks sharply and intensified the fragmentation of the movement. The Valley witnessed a mushrooming of groups between 1990 and 1993. Governor Jagmohan had listed forty-four active 'terrorist organisations' in January 1990 and in 1991. Ammanullah Khan put their number between sixty and seventy. At one point, the army had put the number at 157, with most of these organisations being splinter groups having only a few followers.

The Hazratbal siege and surrender of the JKLF militants in April 1993 marked the beginning of a turnaround. The Hizb-ul-Mujahideen was facing difficulties in recruiting the Kashmiri cadre. Pakistan perceived it as a sign of fatigue among the Kashmiri militants, and decided to push more Afghan veterans, Pakistani nationals and foreign mercenaries into the Valley. This trend gathered momentum around 1996 when the Taliban marched into Kabul. The rise of Taliban had also brought to the fore the Deobandi conception of jihad. The Pakistani army not only took the military bases in Afghanistan including al-Badr and gave them over to the Deobandis, Al-Qaeda and the like but also handed over the Kashmir struggle, which had thus far been managed by the Jamaat, to Deobandi groups. Important Deobandi jihadi organisations which operated in Kashmir include Harkat-ul-Ansar (later renamed as Harkat-ul-Mujahideen), Harkat-ul-Jihad-i-Islami, Al-Badr and Jaish-e-Mohammad (JeM). Lashkar-e-Taiba (LeT) is the most prominent jihadi organisation of Ahl-e-Hadith persuasion.

The induction of Pakistan-based jihadi organisations resulted in total negation of the Kashmiri component—cadre, ideology and political goals. For jihadis, Kashmiris' independence struggle and the right of self-determination are irrelevant. Kashmiriyat was debunked because Islam does not recognise territorial nationalism. They sought to forge a Pan-Islamic identity in which the Muslim-majority Kashmir Valley was only a small fry and regarded Kashmir's political struggle, a part of the world-wide religious crusade. The proponents of the transnational Islamic identity defined the *millat* to include the world's entire Muslim populace and all Islamic countries, fighting against 'various governments accused of terrorising 'true Muslims' in Islamic states and Muslim minorities in the secular states of the world. The self-professed goal was to establish a grand Islamic state which stretched from Kashmir to Pakistan through Afghanistan, Iran and Central Asia (Punjabi n.d.: 2).[17]

The key militant groups also split along the new dividing line of Kashmiri vis-à-vis non-Kashmiri cadre and leadership. Yasin Malik refused to play second fiddle to the Azad Kashmir leadership of the JKLF. At the time of his eventual split with Amanullah Khan in October 1995, Yasin asserted that, the 'movement cannot be run by remote control as Khan was doing (from Azad Kashmir). We have ended the remote control of the JKLF' (*India Today* 1995: 80). Seven years later, Hizb-ul-Mujahideen would follow suit. The decision to expel Abdul Majid Dar and other Valley-based commanders (Zafar Abdul Fateh and Asad Yazdani) by the Pakistan-based leadership headed by Syed Salauddin for favouring a dialogue with the Indian government caused a split. The bulk of the mid-level command in the Hizb-ul-Mujahideen's south and central Kashmir divisions threw their weight behind the expelled leader. Zafar Fateh said, 'Hizb is not anybody's hand-maiden.... Those who are sitting across (PoK) cannot claim to be representatives of Kashmir and the organization as they have no understanding of the ground situation' (*The Indian Express* 2002). Vice-chief Commander of the Hizb Sayedani also admitted that militant groups such as Lashkar-i-Taiba, Jaish-e-Mohammad and Harkat-ul-Mujahideen should work under local groups as 'they have no role in the policy-making of militants' (*The Times of India* 2001; *Frontline* 2004: 27–8). The Hurriyat Conference also met the same fate. When it split in 2003, Mirwaiz Umar Farooq demanded that the Muttahida (United) Jihad Council, the Muzaffarabad-based conglomeration of militant groups should stop interfering in the All Party Hurriyat Conference's (APHC) affairs (Swami 2003: 35).[18] Abdul Ghani Bhat, the former Hurriyat Chairman, fumed, 'we never thought a symbol of political unity would be broken up by its mentor'. He told a team of Pakistani journalists visiting Srinagar in November 2004 that he had torn up an earlier will in which he had expressed a desire to be buried in Pakistan (Hakim 2004: 50).

The agenda of the jihadis had marginalised the local Kashmiri voices. People strongly resented the political movement being hijacked by the Islamic warriors who had no respect for the religious beliefs of Sufi Islam and who debunked their political goal of azadi. They were disillusioned with an increasingly fragmented and criminalised militancy which had turned into a lucrative profession.

The secessionist movement was doomed owing to its internal contradictions. Politically, the Kashmiri Muslims' demand for azadi was checkmated by other communities in Jammu, Ladakh and Kashmiri Pandits in the Valley in a replay of political equations between the three regions in the 1950s. Militarily, the ideological divide between those seeking independence and others supporting accession to Pakistan depleted the limited but vital resources of the militants. The JKLF enjoyed popular support but lacked manpower and weapons, the Hizb-ul-Mujahideen had a well-trained and armed cadre but little public sympathy. Without mutual support, both failed. Denuded of its local character, the foreign militants could at best wage guerrilla warfare and bleed the Indian atate. This changed after 9/11 as Pakistan came under growing international pressure to curb their activities. Initially, the Musharraf regime sought to deflect this by focusing on Al-Qaeda and differentiating between terrorism (on its eastern borders, in Afghanistan) and the so-called freedom struggle (on its western borders, in Kashmir). It tried to protect the homegrown extremist groups because of their strategic value in securing Islamabad's regional objectives in Kashmir. Though the situation changed when many of these groups decided to side with Al-Qaeda and turned against their mentors but the Musharraf regime has not yet pulled the plug on the jihadi groups operating in Pakistan. And notwithstanding Islamabad's stand on the ongoing peace process, these groups are not likely to be amenable to any negotiated solution of Kashmir. They have debunked the dialogue process and resolved to continue jihad.

There is a military and political deadlock. The slain military commander of the Hizb-ul-Mujahideen, Abdul Majid Dar, made a perceptive comment in an interview in early December 2000. He said,

> I think the militancy has matured. General Padmanabhan has said that Indian forces can control militancy but cannot eradicate it. I agree. The militancy cannot throw out the army and the army cannot eradicate militancy. Because of this, there has to be a political solution (Faruqi 2003: 134).

On that front too, Kashmiris realise that they cannot secede forcibly and yet, they have the power to deny political legitimacy to the Indian rule unless their political aspirations are addressed. Pakistan knows it cannot liberate Kashmir by force, but continuation, at best calibration of the jihadi violence remains its only card to ensure a place on the negotiating table. The Indian leadership realises that they have warded off the threat of secession but peace will remain elusive without the consent of Pakistan and approval of the Kashmiris. The tussle between Kashmiri identity and the Indian state has once again reached a stalemate.

CONCLUSION: SEARCH FOR AN ALTERNATIVE

The problem lies essentially in applying the logic of a modern nation-state to a plural society governed through electoral democracy because the majority rule tends to get identified with the majority community's rule. Even otherwise by identifying with the majority community a modern nation-state represents a maximum number of people and not all of them. Those left out seek to construct their own identity and create alternate political space within or outside the state boundaries. But without questioning the basic logic they merely reproduce the hierarchical social conditions they seek to escape, and the state with all its instrumentalities provide the rationale for further fragmentation and politicisation of identities.

The problem cannot be tackled without a serious rethinking on the notion of Indian identity and radical restructuring of the Indian state. India's nation-building project, an inherently problematic task, has gone awry. Nehru's modernist nationalism had sought to forge 'unity in diversity', which over the years, has deteriorated to contrive 'unification of diversity'. But what needs to be questioned is not the practice and politics of the Indian modern nation-state but its very logic. Once we accept the premise of 'one state-one nation' principle, it is difficult to join issue with the operatives of its logic which acquires its own political dynamics. We need to go beyond modernity and evolve indigenous concepts, tools and mechanisms, best suited to Indian social realities. The basic notion of sub-national identities' allegiance to the national identity needs to be questioned and preferably discarded because it casts them in an inherently conflictual mould of dominant-subordinate relationship. An alternative may lie in devising a complex and multilayered matrix where all subnational identities co-exist and come together to make lip the Indian identity and not vice-versa. Decentralisation has to be conceived as providing a total model of social, economic, political and cultural arrangements, as a conception of organising civic life and reordering the whole edifice of governance. Thus, Jammu & Kashmir presents both a challenge and an opportunity for the Indian state to re-invent itself.

ENDNOTES

[1] Partha Chatterjee makes the same point by using the concept of *jati*. He argues that an individual could, without any contradiction, belong to several jati, not simultaneously but contextually, invoking in each context a collectivity in which membership is not a matter of self-interested individual choice or contractual agreement but an immediate inclusion originally as it is by birth (See Chatterjee 1994: 222; Kaviraj 1995: 116).

[2] Renan gives examples of Egypt, China and ancient Chaldea to make the same point that nations are something fairly new in the history.

Classical antiquity had republics, municipal kingdoms, confederations and local republics and empires, yet they could hardly be called nations. (See Renan 1990: 9).

3 This corresponds to Ferdinand Tonnies differentiation between the *gemeinschaften,* a community that fostered a feeling of intense solidarity and belonging, not based upon a convergence of interest, which distinguished the *gesellschaften.* Kaviraj points out an interconnected set of dichotomies between modern and traditional social forms based on this theory: solidarity based on interests and on community, the unlimited possibility of extension of *gesellschaften* associations and the naturally limited contours of *gemeinschaften,* the contractual dissolubility of societies and the indissoluble primordial nature of community belonging (See Kaviraj 1992: 20–1).

4 Don Miller as cited in Kakar 1995: 196.

5 Olson shows that if the good for which a group is mounting a collective action is indivisible, it is a rational strategy for each single individual not to work for that collective good. In this way they would avoid punishments or costs while they cannot be in the very nature of the case excluded from the benefits. Thus, individuals can 'reason that they will not actively work for say a separate and independent state, but since they cannot be excluded from independence when it comes, they would enjoy its benefits anyway' (Olson 1971).

6 He quotes M. V. Pylee, the constitutional historian, affirming, that 'India inherited the British system of government and administration in its original form. The framers of the new Constitution *could not think* of an altogether new system' (Chatterjee 1994: 15).

7 Kakar argues that for social violence to occur, the threat to an identity has to cross a certain threshold when the persecutory potential becomes fully activated and persecutory anxiety signals the annihilation of the group identity that must be combated by its forceful assertion (Kakar 1995: 247).

8 Kakar points out that violence is present in all religions as a positive and even necessary force for the realisation of religious goals. In the Semitic religions, we have the Holy War of the Christians, the Just War of the Jews and the Jihad of the Muslims where the believers are enjoined to settle and destroy evil doers. In other religions such as Hinduism and Buddhism, with their greater reputation for tolerance and non-violence, violence is elevated to the realm of the sacred, a part of the created order. In Hinduism, for instance, there is a cycle

of violence and peacefulness as the Kali Age is followed by the Golden Age. Buddhist myths talk of Seven Days of the Sword where men will look on and kill each other as beasts, after which peace will return and no life will be taken (Kakar 1995: 248–9).

[9] Kaviraj describes the 'semiotic dualism' of Gandhi's nationalism as its unique characteristic because it appealed to the modernist intelligentsia as well as reached out to the masses' (See Ahmed 1993: 126, Kaviraj 1994: 322).

[10] Suranjan Das argues that a particular method of decision-making within the Congress, the reliance on consensus, had helped the Right to continue its stranglehold on the party because from the mid-1950s onwards, Sardar Patel-led Conservatives had enjoyed a 3:1 ratio in their favour in the Congress Working Committee (Das 1994: 286).

[11] Gautam Navlakha characterises the Indian Constitution as setting out the essential characteristics of 'official nationalism' (See Navlakha 1996: 86).

[12] When Maharaja Hari Singh was reluctant to transfer the administrative control of the Jammu and Kashmir State army to the Indian army, Sheikh insisted that their separate identity should cease and they should be entirely taken over by the Indian army. But after the Maharaja was removed, Abdullah claimed that 'when the present emergency is over and the Indian forces are withdrawn, the state will be left with an army of its own to fall back upon' (See Singh 1994: 84; Bhattacharjea 1994: 177).

[13] The US Secretary of State, John Foster Dulles, had visited India and Pakistan on 24 May 1953 and reportedly canvassed for an independent Kashmir. *The New York Times* published a map, showing a plan for the partition of Jammu and Kashmir. United Kingdom also supported this stand and Prime Minister Atlee declared on 11 November 1953 that 'Kashmir should belong neither to India nor to Pakistan but be independent' (Cited in Varshney 1992: 205).

[14] I have analysed the militant movement in Kashmir in my forthcoming book (Behera n.d.).

[15] Conversations with a cross-section of active and ex-militants.

[16] Amin notes that each wing of the organisation had a leader for military and ideological training, intelligence, supplies, logistics and finances. All positions together formed the nucleus of the larger body, the *Majlis-i-Shoora*, which was the central command of the Hizb-ul-Mujahideen (See Amin 1995: 92; Haq 1994).

[17] A manifesto of Harkat-ul-Jihad-e-Islami states that 'the prime purpose of this Jamaat is dominance of Islam all over the world ... we will never rest content until we attain a three-fold objective: freedom of all occupied Muslim areas, complete protection of all Muslim minorities and the regaining of Islamic glory' and offers to serve as 'a second line of defence of each Muslim country'.

REFERENCES

Ahmed, Imtiaz. 1993. *State and Foreign Policy: India's Role in South Asia*. New Delhi: Vikas Publishing House. 126.

Amin, Tahir. 1995. *Mass Resistance in Kashmir: Origin, Evolution, Options, Islamabad.* Institute of Policy Studies. 92.

Anand. S. S. 1980. *Development of the Constitution of Jammu and Kashmir.* New Delhi: Light and Life Publishers. 112–43.

Anderson, Benedict. 1991. *Imagined Communities: Reflections on the Origin and Spread of Nationalism.* London: Verso Publishers. 44–6.

Arendt, Hannah. 1970. *On Violence*. New York: Allen Lane the Penguin Press. 68.

Arora, Balveer and Nirmal Mukerji. 1992. 'The Basic Issues', in Balveer Arora and Nirmal Mukerji (ed.), *Federalism in India: Origins and Development.* New Delhi: Vikas Publishers. 9.

Behera, Navnita. Unpublished. State, Identity & Violence: Jammu and Kashmir. New Delhi: Manohar Publishers.

Bhattacharjea, Ajit. 1994. *Kashmir: The Wounded Valley*. New Delhi: UBSPD Publishers. 177.

Brecher, Michael. 1980. In an Interview to Michael Brecher. Cited in S. Gopal. *Nehru: An Anthology*. Oxford: Oxford University Press, 1980. 217.

Chatterjee, Partha. 1994. *The Nation and its Fragments: Colonial and Postcolonial Histories.* New Delhi: Oxford University Press. 222.

Das, Suranjan. 'The Indian National Congress and the Dynamics of Nation Building; Aspects of Continuity and Change', in T. V. Sathymurthy (ed.), *State and Nation in the Context of Social Change.* Vol. I. New Delhi: Oxford University Press. 286.

Das, Veena. 1995. *Critical Events: An Anthropological Perspective on Contemporary India.* New Delhi: Oxford University Press. 134.

Fanon, Frantz. 1970. *The Wretched of the Earth.* Middlesex: Penguin Press. 37, 73.

Faruqi, Ahmad. 2003. *Rethinking the National Security of Pakistan: The Price of Strategic Myopia*. Hampshire: Ashgate. 134.

Golwalkar, M. S. 1947. *We or Our Nationhood Defined.* Nagpur: Bharat Prakashan.

Gupta, Sisir. 1966. *Kashmir: A Study in India-Pakistan Relations.* New Delhi: Asia Publishing House. 380.

Hakim, Rehana. 2004. 'Kashmir's End Less Autumn'. *Newsline*. November. 50.

Haq, Shamshul. 1994. *Hizbul Mujahideen: Its Background and Struggle* (transl. from Urdu). Rawalpindi: Markaz Matbruit Kashmir. May.

Harrison, Selig. 1956. 'The Challenge of Indian Nationalism'. *Foreign Affair*. Vol. 34. 621.

Jalal, Ayesha. 1995. *Democracy and Authoritarianism in South Asia: A Comparative and Historical Perspective*. New Delhi: Cambridge University Press 9–10.

Kakar, Sudhir. 1995. *The Colours of Violence.* New Delhi: Viking. 196.

Kaviraj, Sudipto. 1992. 'The Imaginary Institution of India', in Partha Chatterjee and Gyanendra Pandey (ed.), *Subaltern Studies VII: Writings on South Asian History and Society.* New Delhi: Oxford University Press. 26.

Kaviraj, Sudipto. 1994. 'On the Structure of Nationalist Discourse', in T. V. Sathyamurthy (ed.), *State and Nation in the Context of Social Change.* Vol. I. New Delhi: Oxford University Press. 322.

Kaviraj, Sudipto. 1995. 'Crisis of the Nation-State in India', in John Dunn (ed.), *Contemporary Crisis of the Nation-State.* Oxford: Blackwell. 116.

Kohli, Atul (ed.). 1988. *India's Democracy: An Analysis of Changing State Society Relations.* New Delhi: Orient Longman. 311.

Kothari, Rajni. 1994. 'Fragments of Discourse: Towards Conceptualization', in T. V. Sathyamurthy (ed.), *State and Nation in the Context of Social Change*, Vol. I. New Delhi: Oxford University Press. 53.

Malik, Yasin. 1995. Interview with Ramesh Vinayak. *India Today*. 15 October. 80.

Navlakha, Gautam. 1996. 'Invoking Union: Kashmir and official Nationalism of Bharat', in T. V. Sathyamurthy (ed.), *Region, Religion, Caste, Gender and Culture in Contemporary India*. Vol. 3. New Delhi: Oxford University Press. 86.

Olson, Mancur. 1971. *The Logic of Collective Action.* Boston: Harvard University Press.

Punjabi, Riyaz. n.d. 'The Concept of Islamic Caliphate: The Religious and Ethnic Pulls of Kashmir Militant Movement', in *United Kashmir Journal.* No. 2. 2.

Puri, Balraj. 1981. *Jammu and Kashmir: Triumph and Tragedy of Indian Federalization.* New Delhi: Sterling Publishers. 99.

Puri, Balraj. 1993. *Kashmir: Towards Insurgency.* New Delhi: Orient Longman. 34.

Rao, B. S. Cited in Gautam Navlakha. 1996. 'Invoking Union: Kashmir and Official Nationalism of Bharat', in T. V. Sathyamurthy (ed.), *Region, Religion, Caste, Gender and Culture in Contemporary India.* Vol. 3. New Delhi: Oxford University Press. 86.

Renan, Ernest. 1990. 'What is a Nation?', in Homi K. Bhabha (ed.), *Nation as Narration.* London: Routledge. 9.

Singh, Karan. 1994. *Autobiography*. New Delhi: Oxford University Press. 84.

Swami, Praveen. 2003. 'Danger Signals from the Valley'. *Frontline*. 20 September–10 October. 35.

Swami, Praveen. 2004. 'The Rage of the Doves'. *Frontline*. 31 January–13 February. 27–8.

The Indian Express. 2002. 6 May.

The Times of India. 2001. 23 November.

Varshney, Ashutosh. 1992. 'Three Compromised Nationalisms: Why Kashmir Has Been a Problem', in Raju G. C. Thomas (ed.), *Perspectives on Kashmir: The Roots of Conflict in South Asia*. Boulder: Westview Press. 205.

9

Military in the Power Structure of Pakistan: An Indian Perspective

Veena Kukreja

Pakistan, a typical case of praetorianism,[1] is one of the several developing countries where the military always keeps a contingency plan for a takeover ready. Pakistan's history since 1958 has been dominated by the recurring cycles of military intervention, consolidation and collapse. Pakistan has been subjected to periodic military intervention so frequently that it has become almost a regular part of that country's political process (Kukreja 2003: 44; 1991: 36). Out of its sixty-two years of post-independence history, the country had been ruled by the military for more than thirty-three years. It has continued to exercise significant influence and control even at the time of civilian rule. In the context of recent developments Shuja Nawaz succinctly remarks, 'The country is now wracked by internal divisions between provinces, and between modernist forces and the forces of militant and radical Islam, whose continuing wars in the federally administered area of the North-West Frontier Province (NWFP), Swat, and in the cities of the hinterland have created political uncertainty and chaos that has allowed the military to step in and dominate the stage yet again' (Nawaz 2008: XXVII).

In Pakistan, the army is the ultimate arbiter in the affairs of the state (Kukreja 2003; Rizvi 2000; Cohen 1984). The developments in the Pakistani state suggest that the unelected but well-entrenched military bureaucratic establishment, the bedrock of the Pakistani state structure, constitute a thinly-based edifice. This power elite has often opposed measures such as democratisation, decentralisation, accountability, land reforms, freedom of media and the independence of judiciary (Malik 1997: 94–114). Besides, as an astute scholar aptly comments, 'over time through coups and largely unfettered access to state resources, the army used its significant coercive powers with the underlying threat of its military might to challenge the authority of the state and capture power time and again, leaving the instruments of state weakened and unable to function whenever the military returned to its barracks' (Nawaz 2008: XXVIII).

To understand Pakistan, one must try to understand the Pakistan army. The objective of this chapter is to focus on the role of the military in governance and how this situation has developed. In addition, it also seeks to describe and analyse the internal dynamics of the military, and its changing role and parameters in Pakistan. Finally, it will discuss how the military in Pakistan (as the most formidable and autonomous political actor) is capable of influencing the nature and direction of political change.

THE ARMY: FINAL ARBITER IN PAKISTAN

Throughout Pakistan's history the military has remained the central locus of power. Between 1947 and 1958, the military elite had played an indirect or a 'back seat driver's role in policymaking processes and helped in the rehabilitation of refugees. It also provided aid to the civil authority during the time of natural calamities (such as flood, periodic epidemics or food shortage) and communal riots. The first instance which was of direct interest to the military in politics was the Rawalpindi Conspiracy Case in 1951, in which the Chief of General Staff, the charismatic and politically well-connected General Akbar Khan, figured as the prime accused. General Khan had earlier masterminded the invasion of Kashmir in October 1947. He was allowed to bypass the normal channels and deal directly with Prime Minister Liaquat Ali Khan. In this context, an eminent defence analyst Subramanyam aptly remarks, 'Such involvement of army officers in unconventional operations in disregard to traditional command and control was bound to encourage tendencies for political thinking and activism in the armed forces. Pakistan has had a series of court martials from the case of General Akbar Khan to the recent one on General Abbasi which illustrates that once there is an attempt at political intervention by the army, that becomes a trend' (Subramanyam 2000: 213). General Ayub Khan's evident role in preparing the blueprint of the integration of the provinces of West Pakistan was another instance of the army's increased influence in political decision-making. The declaration of limited martial law in Lahore to quell domestic disorder in 1953 engaged the army in internal security and paved the way for the military's expanding role. Powerful bureaucrats like Ghulam Muhammad, Iskander Mirza and Chaudhri Muhammad Ali helped draw the defence establishment into domestic politics, and developed a military and strategic alliance with the United States, enthusiastically supported by an ambitious army Commander-in-Chief, Ayub Khan. With the erosion of political authority, both at the central and provincial levels, the bureaucrats assumed the role of managing the state with willing feudalists ready to play a subordinate role. Eventually, the army emerged as the power broker and moved to take complete control, which was eventually consummated through a formal/direct takeover in 1958. It is now widely accepted that the military coup of Ayub Khan had the tacit support of the United States, the biggest aid donor both on economic and military fronts.

The military regime of Yahya Khan failed to adequately handle the highly politicised Bengalis of the eastern wing, which demanded their share in power after the electoral victory in 1970. The military ruler did not permit the Awami League to take over the reins of power despite the clear electoral mandate as it would have negative repercussions on the position and prerogative of the military. With the emergence of Bangladesh in 1971, the army was politically incapable to continue its rule. It temporarily assumed a low profile and allowed Z. A. Bhutto to takeover as president, who had the political mandate of the 1970 elections to his credit. He attempted to reorganise the power structures in Pakistan, but was only partially successful. He had to soon rely on the army for maintenance of law and order. Between July 1972 and June 1974, the army was called out five times to enforce law and order, the most severe case being in Baluchistan where 10,000 people were estimated killed in 17 months' operations, employing ground and air forces (Lamb 1991: 276). After the 1977 rigged elections, the situation became worse and martial law was imposed in Hyderabad, Karachi and Lahore, and the army was sent into Sindh, without even consulting Jatoi, the chief minister. In this context, Alavi writes, 'It was the military that was at the forefront of the forces that engineered the downfall of the PPP government in 1977, and the regime of Gen. Zia has the distinction of being the first unmitigated military regime in Pakistan' (Alavi 1983: 41). In sum, in 1977 Pakistani politicians both in the government, and in opposition gave the army another chance to stage a comeback as the country embraced the longest period of martial law in its history.

Under Zia-ul-Haq, the army acquired the constitutional basis to function as a legitimate political power broker in Pakistan. The Eighth Amendment was the constitutional provision to that end. Even after the restoration of democracy in 1988, the army continued to play a significant role in the politics of Pakistan. However, its style underwent a very distinct change. The army's role as a supraparty mediator in political crisis still remained acceptable to the people of Pakistan. After the 1988 elections, to become prime minister, Benazir Bhutto had to strike a deal with the then Chief of Army Staff, General Mirza Aslam Beg, that she would not meddle in the military's internal affairs such as transfers, promotions and retirements of senior army officers and nuclear and Afghan policies (Kukreja 1990: 1164–65). Thus, the army reserved its decisive role in the formulation of foreign and security policies. In sum, it retained effective power to ensure that the elected political leadership will have no power over the military itself. It continued to control the crucial levers of power and policymaking, while staying in the background. Without getting into the mess of day-to-day governance, the army determined policy in areas most important to them, like Kashmir and Afghanistan. Thus, the army's supremacy in Pakistan's politics continued, but with a significant difference. Instead of ruling directly, the army's approach was to be able to control the levers of power, defence and foreign policy while actively staying out of politics (Kukreja 1994: 1364).

After the 1997 election, Nawaz Sharif emerged as the elected Prime Minister with a two-third majority in Parliament and attained dominance over the presidency which had been the fountainhead of power for the military since the early 1980s. He repealed the notorious Eighth Amendment, tamed the judiciary and forced the Army Chief, General Karamat, to resign in October 1998. Never before in the history of Pakistan did the elected political leaders enjoy such powers. But 'this', as Jasjit Singh aptly remarks, 'itself signified the tension inherent within the power structure of Pakistan and it was inevitable that the country would be pushed toward brinkmanship by the traditional *chaudhris* of power brokerage' (Singh 1999a: 23).

INTERNAL DYNAMICS OF THE MILITARY

The organisational resources and internal dynamics of the military establishment, especially its traditions, cohesion, capabilities and disposition of the officer corps, shape the military's role in the polity. The predominant role of the military both in internal politics and in the formation of regional and foreign policies as well as ever-escalating defence expenditure in terms of resource allocation in the national exchequer, has occasionally raised questions (Kukreja 1989: 154–92).[2]

There is a common belief that since the Pakistan army was an offshoot of the British Indian Army, its conduct, especially apolitical professionalism, should be similar. But in Pakistan the army has eroded this tradition of non-involvement by intervening decisively and frequently, whereas in India the principle of civilian control over the military remains intact. The question arises why is the Pakistan army, which grew out of the Indian Army, so very different? In this context, the emphasis on the 'non-political' tradition of the British Indian Army lingering in Pakistan is not only misleading, but also a misrepresentation of facts. The concept of an apolitical military-bureaucracy may be valid to a larger extent in those countries where the democratic institutions have developed over a longer period of time. But it is fallacious to extend the same assertion to the post-colonial societies (Hashmi 1983: 149). In fact, the British Indian Army from its very inception was trained to be the custodian of law and order and to promote colonial interests at the cost of different indigenous and regional interests within the subcontinent. Besides, the emphasis on an overall civilian control over the military was subordinate to the civil authority in London. Its relationship with the civil authority in India was marked by a 'separate sphere' of military and civilian influence. It was more of an equal partner than subordinate to it (Rizvi 1976: 15–25).

It is also a gross mistake to highlight the British experience of merely twenty-nine years vis-à-vis the post-independence sixty-two years' experience. Indianisation of the Indian army (RISC Vol. II) started only in 1918. The pace improved slightly after 1932, but by 1947 only a few Indians attained the substantive rank of lieutenant colonel. The senior-most officer was only a major general.

INHERITANCE OF MILITARY TRADITION FROM MUSLIM RULERS

The creation of Pakistan on the basis of religion also led to its army having to 'adapt to Islamic principles and practices' (Cohen 1984: 34). This itself started to alter the secular moorings inherited from the Indian army. At the same time, according to Jasjit Singh, 'Pakistan and its Army have felt an overriding compulsion to detach and distance themselves from, if not actually deny, the historical linkage with their Indian past, except where Islam could be used to bolster the legitimacy of the new state formed in its name. History has often been invented for this purpose' (Singh 1995: 856). The official history of the Pakistan army focusing on the inheritance of military tradition from Muslim rulers claims that the officers and men of the army are descendents of 'the men who fought Alexander the Great, who ... established the first Muslim stronghold in India and who campaigned in the days of the great Mughal Emperors helping to *conquer and stabilise nearly the whole of the subcontinent* (emphasis added) (Khan 1963: 8). Such selective distortions have had an important role in shaping the perception of Pakistanis in general and the military men in particular (Singh 1995: 857). The implicit conclusion, of course, is that the military tradition of Pakistan is derived from their ancestors who helped establish and expand Muslim rule in the subcontinent. After independence, the Pakistani army emphasised Islam as the unifying force, though the basic structures remained largely based on the British model. In 1950 General Akbar Khan suggested the establishment of a Vietnam-like people's army, but Sandhurst remained the model at the decision-making levels (Cohen 1984: 46).

ETHNIC RECRUITMENT PATTERN: PUNJABI DOMINATION OF THE ARMY

The Pakistan army was formed virtually from scratch in 1947. The military forces were split in a proportion of 64:34 on the basis of the proportion of non-Muslims and Muslims. The actual proportion of Muslims in the British Indian Army was lower, and a significant proportion did not opt to serve with Pakistan (Singh 1995: 857). More important, the British Indian Army was organised on the basis of 'class regiments'. However, after the revolt of 1857, the British did not keep any all-Muslim units in the army; and they were the only group in the army not to have their own regiment (Cohen 1984: 37). Muslim officers and soldiers, who constituted over 25 per cent of the British Indian Army's strength in 1947, were spread among different regiments. The new Pakistan army was almost entirely Muslim. Pakistan did move on to organise class regiments based on provincial ethnicity. But this was really cosmetic, and the central role of Punjabi and Pathan officers and soldiers continued.

ETHNIC IMBALANCES

Pakistan officially discarded the British concept of 'martial races' for recruitment to the army and somewhat expanded the recruitment base. However, ethnic imbalances persist in the army. Punjab continues to provide the preponderant bulk of officers and other ranks, official estimates put its share as 65 and 70 per cent respectively. Punjab is expected to sustain its entrenched position because of its strategic importance, and it constitutes 56 per cent of Pakistan's population. The Pathans or Pashtuns are the second largest group in the army, constituting about 22–5 per cent of its officers and other ranks. The NWFP and the tribal areas are 16 per cent of Pakistan's population; if the Pathans living in Baluchistan are added, their ratio is expected to rise to about 19 per cent. The Baluch and Sindhi-speaking people (3 to 13 per cent of Pakistan's population respectively) are underrepresented in the army, especially in the higher echelons (Rizvi 2000: 240). The Urdu-speaking population is fairly represented at the officer level, but there are a very small number of *Muhajir* (Muslim migrants from India) at the soldier level. They are known to be overrepresented in the air force and the navy.

Traditionally, the Salt Range, which comprises the district/tehsils of Jhelum, Chakwal and Pinddaden Khan, and Potwar (Potohar) region of northern Punjab and the adjoining districts of NWFP are known as the army heartland, providing a large number of soldiers, both commissioned and non-commissioned officers. The Salt Range area coupled with Attock, Campbellpur, Rawalpindi and Gujarat in the Punjab and Kohat, Mardan and Peshawar in NWFP, have established their reputation as the major suppliers of manpower for the army. According to one study, the recruitment base is slowly expanding. 'Over the last three decades, other areas in the Punjab and north-western region have made manpower available for recruitment. The Punjab's districts of Sargodha, Khushab and Mianwali provide a reasonable number of recruits, especially for other ranks. Furthermore, officers and other ranks also come from urban districts like Lahore, Gujranwala, Faislabad and the Canal Colonies. In case of NWFP, the districts of Kohat, Mardan and

Bannu are still the main recruiting areas, although other regions are gradually coming up' (ibid.).

Despite the Punjabis and the Pathans continuing dominance over the army, as they have a decisive edge over the Baluch, Sindhis and Muhajirs in the population, the recruitment base within the Punjab and the NWFP has slightly expanded.

Due to the underrepresentation of the Bengalis in pre-1971 Pakistan army, the recruitment policy in East Pakistan came under much flak. The British treated the Bengalis as a non-martial race, and their recruitment was deliberately discouraged. At the time of independence, the Bengalis constituted 1 per cent of the total strength of Pakistan's armed forces, their numerical strength in the army was 155 which rose to 130,000 in 1965. First, infantry East Bengal Regiment—Senior Tigers—was set up in February 1948, but in the initial stages a number of West Pakistanis were assigned to it as officers and senior commissioned officers (SCOs). Later, Bengalis replaced them and by 1968, four such regiments were in place. However, the Bengali representation remained inadequate in the army, especially from the middle to the upper level. In 1955, according to one estimate, East Pakistan's representation was a mere 1.57 per cent. It was highest in the air force being 10 per cent (*Dawn*: 1955). By 1963, the proportion of Bengalis in the army had increased to 5 per cent for the officers (Jahan 1972: 62). At that time only 7.4 per cent of the troops were Bengalis which improved slightly after 1965. Only one Bengali attained the rank of lieutenant general and another became major general at the beginning of 1971. Their representation was much better in the air force and the navy, although it was never more than one-third (Rizvi 1976: 135–45). Considering that East Pakistan was one of the regions (along with Bihar and Uttar Pradesh) that originally fostered the idea of Pakistan, and constituted the majority population of the state, the segregation and discrimination of Bengalis was to have a serious repercussion. With the passage of time Bengali army officers and soldiers became the backbone of the armed resistance of the Pakistan army during the civil war in 1971 (Singh 1995: 857–8). Moreover, the military was always perceived by ordinary Bengalis as an outside and alien force.

In more recent years, Pakistan has maintained four major infantry regiments: the Punjab, Baluch, Frontier Force and Sindhi Regiments. But this does not suggest that other ethnic groups and communities find fairer representation in the army corresponding to their share in the national population. Some units even in the Baluch regiment have no Baluchis and a very few Pathans and Sindhis. The reason may not entirely be due to the perpetuating ethnic dominance by the Punjabi-Pathan army. Political dissent and violent disturbances have really been centred in Baluchistan and Sindh as 'both provinces had never fully accepted the foundation of Pakistan, especially in its shape that retained a Punjabi domination' (Singh 1995: 857–8).

Over the years, according to Stephen Cohen, the Punjabi-Pathan group has not merely retained its special position in the army but has strengthened it. As Cohen comments, 'In brief, the history of the Pakistan Army was the history of the Punjabi Muslim and the Pathan; this seemed entirely natural as much as there was hardly any other Muslims in the army' (Cohen 1984: 43).

Another study, considering the 1979 recruitment to the Pakistani Military Academy as a guide reveals that the officer corps has 70 per cent from the Punjab, 14 per cent from the NWFP, 9 per cent from Sindh, 3 per cent from Baluchistan and 1.9 per cent from 'Azad' Kashmir. This indicates that the proportion of Punjabis has increased notably since 1947. The recruitment within the state is also unevenly spread. For instance, by the late 1970s over 75 per cent of all ex-servicemen came from three districts of the Punjab, namely, Rawalpindi, Jhelum and Campbellpur and the two adjoining districts of the NWFP, Kohat and Mardan. The recruits mostly belong to the landowner and landless farmer classes (Singh 1995: 28). The existence of the Northern Command in Rawalpindi since the British era has left a continuing legacy in favour of the Punjab and the neighbouring frontier. Cohen, however, believes that the theory of the Punjabi domination is the product of the actual numerical imbalance between Punjab and the other provinces. Moreover, it is concerned with the 'strategic core area' that the province had obtained (Cohen 1984: 115). However, the continuing ethnic imbalance for whatever reason is perplexing and demoralising.

Ethnic imbalances generate controversy because the army has been 'instrumental in creating a centralised and authoritarian polity which ensured its dominance of state power. Whenever the ethnic and regional elite asserted their ethnic identity and regional rights, the power elite perceived it as a threat to the state and mobilised the state apparatus, especially the Army, to suppress these efforts ostensibly to protect national integrity' (Rizvi 2000; Hussain 1976: 135–45). These trends were reinforced by the establishment of military rule which curbed political participation for the ethnic and regional identities (Brown and Ganguly 1997: 83–127). Those who suffered under these political arrangements questioned the role of the military.

In addition, regional and ethnic imbalances also attract attention for other reasons. For example, the prosperity and welfare of many areas and families in the Punjab and NWFP are closely linked with the military. For the peasants, the army offers a 'safety net' against poverty. This works to the advantage of the ethnic groups and the well-represented regions. Moreover, in the wake of the military's pronounced role during the Afghanistan crisis in terms of Inter-Services Intelligence's (ISI) involvement with the Mujahideen and its total support to the Taliban operation has led the Pakistani critics to portray the army—a Punjabi institution—as aggressive, power-hungry and ruthless.

Exploring the linkage between the Punjabi-Pathan domination of the army, and the psyche of the Pakistani army, Jasjit Singh, maintains that it 'has its roots in the West Punjab North-West Frontier culture'. This culture characterises 'unwillingness to accept defeat, transferring the responsibility for it to someone else, a strong urge to dominate, a certain recklessness and a deep desire for revenge, some of the traits are represented by the Pakistan army (Singh 1999b: 17).

The Pakistani army inherited professionalism from the fighting tradition of North-West India and the new shape that the British gave to the army in India. But because of the narrow recruitment base, the clan and tribal factors play a greater role and tend to deal with professional matters from a narrow clannish perspective. Within the army, according to Singh, 'clan culture increases the pressure to prove to each other that each one is more aggressive and courageous than the other with little forethought to the consequences of the action. Kargil is but one example' (ibid.).

MILITARY'S SOCIAL BACKGROUND AND ORIENTATION

During the last five decades the socio-economic composition of the army officers has undergone a transformation. Cohen finds three distinct generational phases in the history of the Pakistan army: the British generation (1947–53), the American generation (1954–71), and the Pakistani generation (1972 onwards) (Cohen 1984).

The British Generation (1947–53)

The British generation included the pre-independence officers trained at the Royal Military Academy, Sandhurst, i.e., the King's Commissioned Officers (KCOs), and the Indian Military Academy, Dehradun, called the Indian Commissioned Officers (ICOs), and those given emergency commission during the Second World War. The British were careful in inducting Indians into the officer cadre. Those sent to Sandhurst came from loyal, prestigious and upper-class families who joined the army as a matter of prestige rather than to earn a living. The social base of recruitment slightly expanded with the start of the Dehradun Academy in 1932, but it was predominantly from upper and upper-middle class families, and families with military service tradition (Rizvi 2000: 242).

The anglicised KCOs and ICOs, in addition to the British officers, filled the senior slots in the Pakistani army at the time of Partition and set its tone in line with British training and professional orientation. However, post-Partition communal riots and the war in Kashmir had a strong bearing on their psyche and outlook and 'Pakistanized' them in their attitude towards their counterparts in India (ibid.).

The American Generation (1954–71)

The American generation refers to the period when Pakistan joined the alliance system and the military obtained US military aid, and its officers received American training. The US-military and strategic alliance with Pakistan that developed in the mid-1950s exposed them to American military equipment, training and cultural influences which eroded the British influence, especially in the case of those who joined the army in the early years of independence. However, the basic pattern of ideas and orientations of the Pakistan army, inherited from the British, survived. They could not break out of the British mould in such a decisive manner that one could talk of a distinct American generation. The air force, which relied more heavily on US aircraft and equipment, was more Americanised in social orientation. This was also partly true of the navy (ibid.: 243).

The Pakistani Generation (1972 onwards)

The post-1972 officers have been described as the Pakistani generation. The major shift began to take place as the army expanded in the 1960s, more so after the early 1970s. According to Hasan Askari Rizvi, 'Most of those who joined the officers corps in the 1970s, and later came from modest rural background and urban lower-middle and lower class backgrounds as job opportunities declined in the civilian sector. To them the army was more of a career opportunity than a family tradition or love for the profession' (ibid.). The new officers were thus more politicised and ambitious than their predecessors, who came from a relatively better social background and were not directly exposed to political pressures in their pre-military days. The new officers who are likely to occupy top staff command positions by the end of the first decade of the twenty-first century have a different orientation towards society. They are quite materialistic in their orientation and are eager to live a luxurious life. Some of them even tasted power during the Zia years.

The traditionally cautious approach towards politics and civil-society is disappearing. The junior officers freely make partisan political statements and express low, often contemptuous, opinion about civilians. The erosion of professional conduct, craving for quick material gains, and declining moral fibre of young officers have caused concern within military circles.

EXTERNAL DYNAMICS OF THE MILITARY: PAKISTAN'S SECURITY ENVIRONMENT

Since the country's creation, Pakistan's defence policy has hinged on the crucial pillar of national security. It has been compounded by hostility from its larger neighbour India. Pakistan's quarrels with India over a wide range of issues, ranging from religion to water to territorial disputes in Kashmir—has serious ramifications for Pakistan's national security.

A post-independence war over Kashmir in the wake of mass migration and little in way of defence infrastructure except for a few scattered cantonments but no ammunition factories, made Pakistan follow a rigorous policy to overcome its handicaps. The dominant elite had an obvious pro-West orientation while a bipolarised world provided incentives to enter into an alliance-based relationship.

Pakistan's preoccupation with the security threat and the attendant priority for defence partially led to the supremacy of the defence ministry and the General Headquarters (GHQ) in the wake of weakened parliamentary processes in the post-Jinnah years.

Jinnah always believed in the apolitical role of the army and always emphasised the supremacy of the civilian government. To him, the armed forces 'were the servants of the people' (Khan 1978: 10). However, at the time of formulation of security policy, the military's opinion was given due weight. For example, in October 1947, the Supreme Commander, Field Marshal Auchinleck, persuaded Jinnah to reverse his order to the Commander-in-Chief, for sending the army into Kashmir after India secured its accession and sent its troops there (Campbell-Johnson 1951: 22). Later, Pakistan's decision to induct its troops in Kashmir was also made on the advice of the Army Chief.[3] Under Liaquat Ali Khan, while he himself held the position of defence minister, and the GHQ being in Rawalpindi, the defence ministry and the army tended to be more autonomous at the behest of powerful bureaucrats. Ayub Khan, Iskander Mirza, Ghulam Muhammad and their cohorts made and pursued Pakistan's defence policy entirely according to their own biases and ambitions, mostly over and above the political authorities. Pakistan's defence needs as advocated by the establishment, and helped by the Cold

War pushed the country into closer relations with the United States (Cheema 1990: 164).[4]

COMPULSION OF HOSTILITY TOWARDS INDIA

From its very inception Pakistan has been suffering from an acute sense of insecurity vis-a-vis India. 'It projected itself not only as small and disadvantaged but as on the defensive against a real and present threat, with its survival at stake' (Harrison, Kreisberg and Kux, 1999: 171). These insecurities coupled with an identity crisis led Pakistan to assume a posture of hostility towards India. This perception is an input into the decision-making apparatus, and policy formulations which further strengthens an insecure 'national psyche' which then influences policy. This is a vicious circle. This also promoted an enemy image of each other which has created a mindset of hostility and antagonism at the elite level. Besides, the Pakistan army has a vested interest in maintaining the territorial conflict with India. There is 'an atavistic compulsion in Pakistan's power structures mindset which believes that its survival and security could only be secured by the fragmentation of India' (Dixit 1995: 244).

The insecurity in the Pakistani psyche has led to its obsession to attain parity with India's capabilities and has paved the way for militarisation of the economy at the cost of economic development. The insecurity coupled with an identity crisis that was embedded in the Pakistani nation at its commencement, is still prevalent, and have even worsened with the events in the last fifty years. Furthermore, after the separation of East Pakistan, Pakistan has adopted various strategies such as bleeding India through a thousand cuts, i.e., proxy war, as well as maintaining a nuclear first use doctrine. In this context a perceptive observer succinctly remarks, 'In many ways Pakistan needs to maintain hostility with India to justify its own existence and to define itself' (Singh 1995: 860–1). Pakistan's hostility towards India has its roots in ideology—the two-nation theory, the basis of Pakistani nationhood—but has been fostered by the military-bureaucratic axis for more than six decades. The armed forces have a stake in projecting Kashmir as a vexed territorial issue to keep filling their coffers to the brim. Without the raison d'etre of territorial dispute with India, the budgetary demands of the Pakistani armed forces will be relegated to secondary importance.

ESCALATING DEFENCE EXPENDITURE

As far as the defence expenditure is concerned, Pakistan does not provide any details and announces only the overall figure of its defence expenditure. However, it is possible to arrive at some broad trend indicators. Pakistan since its emergence braced itself for a 'political economy of defence'. From 1947–58 its defence expenditure was between 55 and 60 per cent of the country's total revenue. However, it increased after the US started giving aid to Pakistan in 1954.

Table 9.1 reveals that the most dramatic shift in Pakistan's defence expenditure had taken place following the Indo-Pak war of 1965 when the GDP jumped from 4.82 per cent to 9.86 per cent. When the army was deployed in a repressive role in East Pakistan, and later in the year due to the cost of the war, Pakistan's defence expenditure predictably escalated between 1971–2. Although with the break-up of Pakistan and emergence of Bangladesh, the defence needs reduced markedly, the defence expenditure continued to grow, increasingly by 39.7 per cent in 1974–5 over the previous year, followed by another jump of 33.07 per cent two years later. These 'repeated increases in its defence allocations were also influenced significantly by Pakistan's domestic equation between its civil-military-political leaders and interests. High levels of defence spending during the 1970s also resulted in a remarkable growth of force levels. The effect was a substantive increase in the military power, especially between January 1972 (after the war) and December 1979 (before the Soviet intervention in Afghanistan). When the size of the army nearly doubled, the navy grew three times, and the air force, combat aircraft grew one-and-a half times' (Singh 1995: 50).

Defence expenditure grew at a cumulative rate of 315.7 per cent between the year 1981–90. Pakistan's defence expenditure was maintained at a much higher level after 1980 when Pakistan resumed its proxy war against India. Moreover, from 1979 to 1992, $350 million were spent for its nuclear programme.

Table 9.1: Pakistan's Defence Expenditure, 1961–99

Year	Defex (bn Rs.)	GDP Current Prices	Popul-ation (mns)	Defence Forces	Federal Govt. Exp. (bn Rs.)	Defex/ GDP (%)	Defex/ Fed-eral Govt. Exp.
1961–2	1.109	19.139	97.5	250	1.986	5.79	55.84
1962–3	0.954	20.489	101.1	250	1.795	4.66	53.15
1963–4	1.157	22.945	104.7	253	2.337	5.04	49.51
1964–5	1.262	26.202	108.5	253	2.734	4.82	46.51
1965–6	2.855	28.969	112.5	278	4.498	9.86	63.47
1966–7	2.794	32.622	116.7	278	3.765	8.56	74.21
1967–6	2.182	35.542	121.0	351	4.077	6.14	53.52
1968–9	2.427	37.985	124.0	357	4.371	6.39	55.53
1969–70	2.749	43.347	127.0	390	5.009	6.34	53.91
1970–71	3.202	46.006	131.0	390	5.751	6.96	55.68
1971–2	3.726	49.784	135.0	404	6.926	7.48	53.80
1972–3	4.440	61.414	63.34	350	8.406	7.23	52.82
1973–4	4.949	81.690	65.89	466	11.954	6.06	41.40
1974–5	6.914	103.557	69.89	500	14.384	6.68	48.07
1975–6	6.103	119.736	72.12	502	17.709	5.10	34.46
1976–7	.121	135.982	74.33	602	20.609	5.97	39.41
1977–8	9.675	159.840	76.60	588	25.454	6.05	38.01
1978–9	10.302	177.844	78.94	518	29.861	5.79	34.50
1979–80	12.655	210.253	81.36	544	37.948	6.02	33.35
1980–1	15.300	278.196	83.84	549	46.348	5.50	33.01
1981–2	18.631	324.159	86.44	560	51.116	5.75	36.45
1982–3	23.224	364.159	89.12	588	59.076	6.37	39.91
1983–4	26.798	419.802	91.88	588	75.902	6.38	35.31
1984–5	31.794	427.157	94.73	479	90.074	6.73	35.30
1985–6	34.763	514.532	97.67	483	100.043	6.76	34.75
1986–7	41.325	572.479	100.70	483	111.856	7.22	36.94
1887–8	47.015	675.389	103.82	481	136.151	6.96	34.53
1988–9	51.053	769.745	107.04	481	156.417	6.63	32.64
1889–90	57.926	855.943	110.36	520	173.273	6.77	33.43
1990–91	64.623	1,202.600	113.78	55	183.060	6.33	34.63

(contd.)

(Table 1 contd.)

Year	Defex (bn Rs.)	GDP Current Prices	Population (mns)	Defence Forces	Federal Govt. Exp. (bn Rs.)	Defex/ GDP (%)	Defex/ Federal Govt. Exp.
1991–2	75.751	1,211.385	117.31	565	199.000	6.25	38.67
1992–3	87.461	1,341.629	120.83	580	235.000	6.52	37.91
1993–4	91.776	1,573.097	124.48	580	258.00	5.83	34.31
1994–5	104.512	1,882.071	128.08	540	295.017	5.55	34.52
1995–6	119.658	2,165.598	131.63	577	334.737	5.26	34.43
1996–7	127.441	2,404.633	135.28	587	398.209	5.30	32.00
1997–8	134.020	2,759.525	139.02	587	461.907	4.86	29.02
1998–9	145.000	2,960.000E		587	606.300	4.90	23.92
			+	513 R			

Note: Population till 1971 includes East Pakistan.
Sources: Economic Survey 1997–8, Government of Pakistan; World Military Expenditures and Arms Transfers, Arms Control and Disarmament Agency (ACDA), US Government, Washington; Pakistan Government Budget (for defence expenditure) for various years; Jasjit Singh (ed.). 1999. *Kargil 1999: Pakistan's Fourth War for Kashmir*, New Delhi: Knowledge World. 51.

MILITARY AND STRATEGIC TIES WITH THE US

Army leadership asserted the primacy of arms in politics. One of the characteristics of the army has been its desire for an external linkage and support in strategic and military terms from the very beginning. Pakistan's rulers were definitely looking for a strong reliable friend to strengthen its defence and side with it in its conflict with India. Pakistan developed a strategic alliance with the US. It is a well-known fact that General Ayub Khan played a significant role in the negotiation of Mutual Defence Assistance with the US. Moreover, the decision to participate in Southeast Asia Treaty Organisation (SEATO) and Central Treaty Organisation (CENTO) was taken on his initiative. The US military and economic aid and Pakistan's participation in SEATO and CENTO enhanced the country's military capabilities qualitatively as well as quantitatively. At the same time the US influence and involvement in Pakistan's army became pervasive. Pakistan also developed military and strategic ties with China after the Sino-Indian war of 1962 following Kautilya's dictum that the 'enemy's enemy is your friend'. At the same time the relationship with the US and China has been an important factor behind Pakistan's military adventurism, be it in 1965 and 1971, or later the proxy war against India which began in the 1980s, or the Kargil aggression in 1999.

MILITARY AID AND ARMS ACQUISITION

As a fallout of Soviet military intervention in Afghanistan, the US had provided $3.2 billion in military and security-related economic aid to Pakistan over a five-year period (1981–6). It is generally believed that nearly 60 per cent of the weapons and equipment supplied to Afghan Mujahideen between 1981 and 1991 through Pakistan was siphoned off in Pakistan. Pakistan's diversification of sources of weapon supplies has particularly intensified since 1990 when the US administration was forced to cut off aid. Even with the US, most foreign military sales (FMS) agreements were rapidly converted into commercial arrangements. As a result, US commercial arms sales to Pakistan have gone up. Despite the Pressler Amendment, therefore, American supplies more or less continued to reach Pakistan and were worth $1.03 billion in 1994. Pakistan continued to acquire substantive quantities of arms during the 1990s.

Although the US and China continued to be its most reliable suppliers, the sources of Pakistan's weapon supplies have undergone fundamental changes since the 1950s. The US arms embargo in 1965 was Pakistan's first major crisis that highlighted the urgency of diversifying the sources, especially to a more reliable supplier. It is against this backdrop that China started supply of arms to Pakistan and emerged as the most reliable supplier of weapons. 'Pakistan has continued its quest of US weapons essentially for three reasons: (i) as a symbol of strategic and political support and engagement by the United States; (ii) diversification of sources of weapons systems, and (iii) for higher-end technology weapons' (Singh 1995: 52). China, on the other hand, has been Pakistan's major and trusted supplier of weapons at a low cost for more than three decades. The comparative proportion of US weapons in Pakistan's military inventory, contrary to conventional wisdom, has been coming down over the years (ibid.).

Pakistan's defence expenditure figures do not take into account the cost of acquisition of major weapon systems. Pakistan has received substantive loans and aid from the USA, Saudi Arabia and other countries specifically for acquisition of arms. The actual resources invested in, and supporting the military power, therefore, were significantly higher than what the official defence expenditure figures reveal. Thus, high level defence expenditures naturally show an adverse impact on economic growth and development.

Of late, the high defence expenditure came under criticism for two main reasons. First, Pakistan's sinking economy in the late 1990s, and especially the pressure of bourgeoning debts made many in Pakistan look critically at the resources being made available to the military. The review proposals have ranged from suggestions for organisational changes in the military to reduction in defence expenditure to its rationalisation and for stricter control on its disbursement. There are demands that the annual budget statement should provide some details of the defence expenditure rather than the current practice of a one-line statement. Second, there is a growing realisation that more resources should be made available to the social sector (such as, healthcare, education and environment) which is not less important than the defence sector. So far Pakistan has tried to achieve external security at the cost of societal security, and allocated more resources to the military and neglected socio-economic development.

CHANGING ROLE AND PARAMETERS OF THE ARMY

The army's role and position in Pakistan's power structure has undergone changes over the years. In the 1950s and 1960s it assumed the role of an agent of modernisation and socio-economic change. In the 1970s it moved to conquer its own people in the crisis of East Pakistan and Baluchistan as a Punjabi-dominated army of an otherwise ruthless state. In the 1980s it emphasised its role as the defender of ideology.

Military as an Agent of Modernisation

Ayub Khan, in order to seek legitimacy propagated his image as that of a moderniser. His economic development and modernisation strategy won him high praise and his period (from October 1958 to March 1969) was labeled as the 'decade of development'. Pakistan became a shining example for the rest of the developing countries. Ayub's political innovation of Basic Democracies was acclaimed by many as a plausible alternative to Western democracy and the communist system. He also earned the title of 'Muslim de Gaulle' or a 'Great legislator'. Yet Ayub's regime fell in March 1969, as a result of mass movements and urban agitations. Gross quantitative indicators of economic growth supported the regime's claims regarding impressive economic development. However, behind the gross growth rates lay the stark realities of the socio-economic exploitation of the large mass of people. The policies of the Ayub regime led to an incredible concentration of wealth in a few hands. It was the deepening of regional and class inequalities during the Ayub era which provided the East Pakistani political opposition with the impetus to take themselves out of the clutches of the West Pakistani military-bureaucratic-industrial establishment.

Military as a Partisan and Ruthless Institution

Under the leadership of Yahya Khan, the army displayed an obstinate commitment to preserve a system of a strong central government and it sought to prevent the replacement of this system by a six-point autonomous order even at the risk of the break-up of the country. What made the army positively hostile to Sheikh Mujibur Rahman and his Awami League was that the latter threatened to reduce this vast and magnificent fighting machine to humbler proportions. Therefore, the military and the dominant power groups in the western wing considered transfer of power to Awami League as an even greater threat than East Pakistan's outright secession.

Military as Defender of the Ideology

Under Zia-ul-Haq's regime, organised efforts were taken to induct an Islamic dimension at the officer level. The lower middle-class, middle-rank officers accepted the army's enhanced role not only as defenders of the country, but also as soldiers of Islam. Islam replaced the symbols of the British Indian Army. Some observers have tried to conceptualise a dialectical relationship between Islam, Pakistan and the military.[5] One cannot deny the inter-relationship between Islam, Pakistan and the army, but to consider the latter as the guaranter for the others is an oversimplification, as Muslim society even under non-Muslim colonial rule produced dynamic leaders like Syed Ahmed Khan, Jinnah and Iqbal (Malik 1997: 77).

The political ethos in Pakistan (since Pakistan's first military regime in 1958) reveals that the Pakistani army has incrementally acquired an institutional identity and role which is supra-governmental and which transcends all other constitutional arrangements of governance in Pakistan (Dixit 1999: 113). The Pakistani army had declared itself, maintains Subrahmanyam, as 'the ideological guardian of the two-nation theory on which the Pakistani people believe the nation is founded. In other words, the Pakistani army considers itself above the Constitution and as the last resort of redresses when things go wrong' (Subramanyam 1999: 14). It has become the final repository for the responsibility to protect and consolidate its nationhood. Besides, in Pakistan, the sovereignty does not rest with the people as in a secular democracy, but in Almighty God, Allah, himself. The Pakistan army, according to Dixit, 'claims to be the shadow of God responsible for exercising state sovereignty for the welfare of the Pakistani people of which they claim to be the most competent judge' (Dixit 1999: 13).

A number of important developments since the 1980s have had a profound impact on the traditional balance of power inside Pakistan. In the wake of the Soviet invasion of Afghanistan, cultivation of poppy and cannabis was encouraged by Zia-ul-Haq's regime to finance terrorist activities in India. General Zia's support for poppy cultivation gave a new dimension to international drug trafficking and terrorism in India. His target was to destabilise India. The successor regimes were unable and unwilling to control the menace and power of drug barons. The second development was the growth in power and influence of the ISI directorate which conducted the proxy war in Afghanistan, and in India. The ISI, in addition to amassing weapons and waging wars in the neighbouring countries, has become a force to reckon with in domestic politics. The military also influences the political process through the intelligence agencies. The military relies on the military intelligence and the ISI to pursue its political agenda. Intelligence-gathering has become increasingly important for senior commanders pursuing behind-the-scene political intervention. This is also important for advancing the military's professional and corporate interests. The third aspect is the introduction of radical religious indoctrination of the country in general and the army in particular.

After the demise of General Zia in 1988, a new-pattern of 'soft' or 'non-takeover' intervention developed in which the emphasis shifted from assuming power directly, to playing a more subtle, but still ubiquitous role from the sidelines. The military had an important influence over foreign security and key domestic issues, and it continued to moderate confrontations among feuding politicians or state institutions. The army remained pivotal in the power structure along with the president and the prime minister under the system which was described as the Triangle of Power or the 'Troika' (Rizvi 2000: 1–2).

ISLAM AND THE MILITARY

It is worth nothing that Islam, which is integral to Pakistan military ideology, was repeatedly invoked during the wars in 1965 and 1971 to galvanise the soldiers and civilians for the defence of the country. When Zia-ul-Haq assumed command of the army in March 1976, he gave the motto of 'Iman' (faith) 'Taqwa' (piety and abstinence), and 'Jihad-fi-Sibilillah' (holy war in the name of God), which reflected his strong religious inclinations. However, this was not a major departure because Islamic principles, teachings, history and Muslim war heroes, and their battles have always been a part of military education training and ideology. Islam was emphasised as an identity and a motivational force coupled with professionalism and service discipline. Religious extremism and linkages with Islamic movements or groups were discouraged. The military represented the moderate and liberal face of Islam (Rizvi 2000: 245).

However, some developments during the Zia years had far-reaching repercussions for the role of Islam in the army. First, Zia-ul-Haq used Islam to promote conservatism and orthodoxy in the army. This fitted nicely with the transformation in the orientation of the new breed of officers who came from the middle to lower strata of society, hailing mainly from small towns and urban areas with conservative religious values. The institution of 'regimental priest' was upgraded and strengthened the bias in favour of Islamic conservatism (ibid.). According to a scholar, 'The middle level officers, recruited from more traditional sectors of Pakistani society increased the salience of Islam and of the struggle to turn Pakistan's military officers into good Muslims.... The earlier officer class who was succeeded by a "second generation" of petit bourgeois origin and "fascist" outlook' (Ahmad 1974: 425).

Some of the Islamic groups were allowed to make inroads into the army, which was something of an anathema in the past. Zia-ul-Haq had a strong inclination towards the Tableghi Jamaat, a purely religious organisation, which does not involve itself in politics, and he was the first head of state to attend its annual congregation at Raiwind. Encouraged by this, a good number of officers and men openly began to associate with the Tableghi Jamaat. Other conservative Islamic sectarian groups were also able to develop connections with the personnel of the three services, especially the army (Rizvi 2000: 246). The other group that gained access to the army and the bureaucracy was the Jamaat-i-Islami, which had a favourable disposition toward the Zia regime and was associated with the government's Afghanistan policy. The Jamaat-i-Islami, with its overtly Islamic political agenda, penetrated these institutions, and religion thus became an important part of the public profile of the in-service personnel.

The Afghanistan experience reinforced Islamic zeal among army personnel. The withdrawal of the Soviet forces from Afghanistan in 1988 created a sense of euphoria among them and the thinking process of many army personnel (including some senior officers) was frozen in the Afghanistan experience. They often argued for an Afghanistan-style armed resistance to bring an end to non-Muslim domination of the Muslims, especially in Kashmir.

The Soviet withdrawal also strengthened religious zealots inside and outside the military. A small group of religious zealots in the army were arrested in September 1995 for the planning and takeover of the Army Headquarters and the civilian government in order to establish a strict Islamic order (Abbas 1996: 89–95).

As a result of the introduction of orthodox Islamic orientation in the military, perhaps for the first time in Pakistan, military doctrine was sought to be interpreted in religious terms. General Zia in his foreword to Brigadier S. K. Malik's book *The Quranic Concept of War* states, 'the professional soldier in a Muslim army, pursuing the goals of a Muslim State cannot become "professional" if, in all his activities, he does not take on the "colour of Allah"' (Malik 1979).

STRATEGIC DOCTRINE OF TERROR

As Pakistan moved towards greater Islamisation in the 1970s and 1980s it also sought increased inspiration from religion for its strategic doctrine. General Zia encouraged such efforts. The Pakistan military believes in the 'strategic doctrine of terror' and 'total war' and links it to nuclear deterrence. Since 1990, Pakistani leaders have been using the tactic of nuclear blackmail, which succeeded in deterring India from attacking Pakistan in retaliation as exemplified in the case of the Kargil aggression and the ongoing proxy war in Jammu and Kashmir. Pakistan has considered nuclear weapons as a major means of imposing terror over a professed, but stronger enemy, i.e., India. Pakistan has threatened to use nuclear weapons against India, time and again, since they remain weapons of mass terror (Singh 1995: 46). In sum, under the nuclear umbrella, Pakistan feels more confident of waging its low-cost proxy war against India. This has also provided strategic advantage to the army vis-a-vis India.

The former Chief of Army Staff, General Pervez Musharraf, like Zia, is also a Deobandi in many ways, which symbolises the ethos and religious orientation of the present day army of Pakistan. During the Zia era, Musharraf had developed a close relationship with the ISI and Islamic fundamentalist groups like the Harkat-ul-Mujahideen (HuM) (Raman 1999).

LINKAGES BETWEEN MILITANT ISLAM, TERRORISM AND EXPORT OF JIHAD

The growing influence of Jammat-i-Islami on the army during the Bhutto period, and Islamisation of the army under Zia-ul-Haq led to its 'transition to militant Islamic orientation, therefore also acquired a nationalist character' (Singh 1999b: 17). But contrary to conventional wisdom this has not adversely affected its professionalism. On the other hand, this has provided a strong religious motivation in support of aggressive action (ibid.). The army has even interpreted the Koran since the late 1970s to justify the use of terrorism in pursuit of warfare. In 1979, it came out with an interpretation of the Koran, which argued in favour of a total war where terror was to be a central element in the run up to the war, during hostilities and for war termination (Malik 1979). Successive generations of officers have been exhorted to think in terms of the use of terror as a weapon sanctioned by the Koran. The linkages between militant Islam, terrorism, and export of jihad are exemplified through the Taliban phenomenon.

Guerrilla warfare is also a part of the army's strategic thought. From its birth, the Pakistani army has been over-sensitive to the asymmetry that existed in relation to India, which has been propagated as its enemy number one. It has, therefore, sought to merge irregular guerrilla warfare with regular organised military operations.

While most professional armies study and train to fight irregular warfare, the Pakistan army from the very beginning studied it for waging such warfare. It has also practiced it from the start. The synthesis of regular and irregular warfare was finally achieved in the Taliban operation after almost two decades of experience in Afghanistan. Unlike the Turkish armed forces, which have been a bastion of secularism, the Pakistan military, though starting with British colonial traditions, has become politicised and now Islamised, specially at the level of junior officers. This was indicated by the spectacle of bearded soldiers manning the government buildings in Pakistan after the latest military intervention. Besides, they have been nurturing militant and terrorist organisations to export Jihad to various parts of the world. Pakistan attempted to replicate the Afghan model in India. However, the same strategy failed miserably in Kargil when it came face to face with the more dedicated and professional Indian military.

In this context, commenting on the role of Islam in the army, Rizvi asserted, 'As long as Islam is coupled with professionalism and service discipline, it is a source of strength. However, whenever the imperatives of military profession are subordinated to extraneous considerations, no matter what is their source, the military faces internal problems' (Rizvi 2000: 247). Zia's policies led to the rise of religious conservatism in cross-sections of the military. One observer of military affairs comments that Islam could serve as a 'force multiplier' for a Muslim army when it was not being used for 'substituting professional hard and software in the shape of weapons and training' (Siddiqi 1995; Masood 1995). According to Rizvi, 'the major challenge the military faces in the twenty-first century is the maintenance of a professional and cohesive disposition as the new breed of officers takes over its command. The delicate balance between Islam and service discipline is going to be another important concern, especially because a number of Islamic groups continue to work on the new breed of officers and other ranks' (Rizvi 2000: 248).

ARMY AND THE 'WAR ON TERROR'

The terrorist attacks on the World Trade Centre and Pentagon in the US on 11 September 2001 had put Pakistan in the midst of the gathering storm of the US-led global war against international terrorism. It was apparent that General Musharraf was in a difficult position torn between US demands for cooperation, and demands by the Islamic clergy and terrorist organisations like Lashkar-e-Taiba, HuM, Jaish-e-Mohammad and Al-Badr and others for rejecting the same. Notwithstanding the total backing of the US in terms of military and economic aid, the Musharraf government failed to crush the Taliban and Al-Qaeda operations in enclaves of NWFP and Baluchistan. On the contrary, the armed encounters between the Taliban and their hosts in the tribal belt on the one hand, and the Pakistan security forces on the other, proliferated during 2002–7 and Islamic extremism became even stronger. The government's inept handling of the Lal Masjid crisis (2007) was a turning point for Al-Qaeda, Pakistani Taliban, and other extremist groups who now joined hands and vowed to topple the government and create an Islamic state and challenged the military with some success. In this context Shuja Nawaz rightly observes, 'Today the Pakistan army is operating in force inside its own borders again. The "enemy" this time is a growing Islamist movement known as "Talibanization" after the radical right wing and fundamentalist regime in Afghanistan.... A misdirected military approach by the Musharraf regime has given the insurgents and Islamists the upper hand. Plus, the army itself has been beset with a breakdown in its discipline, as some members of the Frontier Constabulary and Frontier Corps are reported to have balked at conducting operation against their fellow tribesmen in this area. Also, the army was neither equipped or trained for counter-insurgency warfare, and is now searching for other ways to resolve the issue' (Nawaz 2008: XXXIII).

MILITARY'S PENETRATION OF CIVILIAN INSTITUTIONS: THE ECONOMY AND SOCIETY

The long years of direct and indirect rule have enabled the military to spread out so widely into civilian institutions, the economy and society that its clout and influence no longer depend on controlling the levers of power. It is derived from its organisational strength and its significant presence in all sectors of government and society (ibid.: 233).

The military's presence is firmly established in all walks of life. It has carved out a role and position in the public and private sectors, industry, business, agriculture, education, scientific development, healthcare, communication and transportation. Such omnipresence ensures a significant role for the military in the state and society even if the generals do not directly rule. Several factors have contributed to this. First, the military regimes of Ayub Khan, and Zia-ul-Haq, respectively, included their personnel in government and semi-government jobs and civilian professions. Ayub Khan during his rule appointed senior officers, mostly retired, to senior jobs with high salaries and perks in government and semi-government corporations or autonomous bodies. General Zia in 1980 fixed a 10 per cent minimum quota for military personnel in civilian jobs which provided a basis for their induction into all government and semi-government services. Besides, the private sector was encouraged to accommodate them. General Musharraf had also inducted more than 1,200 retired and serving officers into all-civilian institutions and government departments. The military also contributed to improving their socio-economic condition by distributing agricultural land and material awards.

Second, the military has been able to translate its dominance over the state structure to become deeply entrenched in the political economy. It has expanded its role in the economy by active involvement in industry, commerce, and business, developing a stake in the government's economic policies and industrial and commercial strategies. The army's control over vast industrial and business empires has enabled it to amass sufficient clout in the economy and to develop a capacity for looking after the welfare of its personnel without relying on the civilian government (ibid.: 236–7). The most impressive result of more than five decades of dominance over the state apparatus has been the military establishment's extensive tentacles throughout the economy. Each of the three defence services of Pakistan has trusts and foundations with large investments in the national economy.

A recent study of 'Milbus' or the 'military-business interests' demonstrates how the power of the military has transformed Pakistani society to an extent that the armed forces have become an independent class (Siddiqa 2007). In this study, the Pakistan army is seen by Ayesha Siddiqa as a corporate entity that functions as the most effective political party of the country, protecting its class interests, sometimes even at the expense of national interests. She estimates that Pakistan's military-industrial complex was worth around $ 20 billion in 2007 (Siddiqa 2007: 112–18). 'It can be argued that the military's economic power correlates very closely with its political power. The three armed forces have sought to go beyond the defence budget into large-scale market activities, in addition to allocation of landed property and creation of jobs for officers and soldiers. The military's subsidiary organizations accumulated immense power. Sometimes, they gave clear signals that they did not accept civilian supremacy' (Jetly 2009: 119).

As the foregoing discussion suggests, Pakistan's army plays complex and baffling multiple roles. Cohen sums this up, 'There are armies that guard their nation's borders, there are those that are concerned with protecting their own position in society, and there are those who defend a cause or an idea. The Pakistan army does all three' (Cohen 1984: 105). It is imperative to disengage the army from its varying roles in a Pakistan which is weak, mutually-divisive, economically and politically fragile and unable to afford a huge defence establishment. In this context, the army officials reflecting 'new thinking', who feel that the army as an institution has suffered erosion in terms of professional capabilities due to its interventionist and vetoing role in domestic politics, can help politicians to evolve a common viable political culture based on plural and democratic traditions (Malik 1997: 79–80).

Despite the recent developments in Pakistan, including the formation of a new civilian government and the departure of General Musharraf, the army was too well-ensconced in the political, economic and social spheres of public life to be completely ousted from the centrestage of politics. In this context Nawaz aptly remarks, 'the army remains a key player on the political scene and will not easily relinquish its hold on power. Whatever new structure emerges over time it will have to take the army's nature and role into consideration and bring it into the equation, while, increasing the role of the civil sector. The army's leadership needs to be a willing participant in this effort to effect a smooth transition. Without such a shift, Pakistan's search for nationhood and a stable political system may remain an elusive quest' (Nawaz 2008: XLIII).

ENDNOTES

[1] Military intervention is characteristically associated with the less developed countries which are sometimes referred to as 'praetorian societies' or praetorian civil-military type, characterised by ineffective political leadership and lack of instruments and structures to channelise political support.

[2] For a review of theoretical literature on civil-military relations, see Kukreja 1989: 154–92.

[3] On 20 April 1948, General Douglas Gracey suggested in his report that if the troops were not sent to Kashmir, Pakistan's security would be jeopardised. The government of Pakistan accepted the report and formally committed the regular troops to Kashmir in early May (Ali 1967: 305–6).

[4] According to P. I. Cheema, four factors seem to have compelled Pakistan to abandon the option of non-alignment: the fear of India, the domestic political and economic problems, the ruling elite and the dictates of the international climate. But by far the most important factor was the perception that even after Partition, India was not reconciled to the establishment of Pakistan and would do everything to destroy the new state at the first opportunity (Cheema 1990: 164).

[5] Asaf Hussain maintains that without Islam, Pakistan would not have come into existence, without Pakistan the military would not be able to exist, and without the military Islam and Pakistan would be threatened. In perpetuating such a state the military was perpetuating Islam (Hussain 1979: 133).

REFERENCES

Abbas, Zafar. 1996. 'Day of Reckoning', in *The Herald*. January. 89–95.

Ahmad, Eqbal. 1974. 'Pakistan: Sign-Posts to a Police State', in *Journal of Contemporary Asia*. Vol. IV. No. 4. 425.

Ahmed, Samina. 1997. 'Centralization, Authoritarianism and the Management of Ethnic Relations in Pakistan', in Michael E. Brown and Sumit Ganguly (ed.),

Government Policies and Ethnic Relations in Asia and the Pacific. Massachusetts: The MIT Press. 83–127.

Alavi, Hamza. 1983. 'Class and State', in Hassan Gardezi and Jamil Rashid (ed.), *Pakistan: The Roots of Dictatorship*. Delhi: Oxford University Press.

Ali, Chaudhri Muhammad. 1967. *The Emergence of Pakistan*. New York: Columbia University Press. 305–06.

Amir, Ayaz. 1986. 'The Khaki Clan', in *The Herald*. Karachi: February. 40–2

Campbell-Johnson, Allen. 1951. *Mission with Mountbatten*. London: Robert Hale. 22.

Cheema, P. I. 1990. *Pakistan's Defence Policy: 1947–58*. London: Macmillan. 164.

Cohen, Stephen P. 1984. *The Pakistan Army*. New Delhi: Himalayan Books.

Dawn (Karachi), 1955. 8 January.

Dixit, J. N. 1999. 'A Difficult Neighbor', in *The Hindustan Times*. New Delhi: 27 October. 13.

Dixit. J. N. 1995. *Anatomy of a Flawed Inheritance: Indo-Pakistan Relations: 1970–94*. New Delhi: Konark Publishers. 244.

Hashmi, Bilal. 1983. 'Dragon Seed: Military in the State', in Hassan Gardezi and Jamil Rashid (ed.), *Pakistan: The Roots of Dictatorship*. Delhi: Oxford University Press. 149.

Hussain, Asaf. 1976. 'Ethnicity, National Identity and Praetorianism: The Case of Pakistan'. *Asian Survey*. Vol. XVI. No. 10. 135–45.

Hussain, Asaf. 1979. *Elite Politics in an Ideological State*. Kent, Dawson: Folkestone. 133.

Indian Statutory Commission. *Report of the Indian Statutory Commission*. Vol. 2. (Survey CMD 3568). London: His Majesty's Stationary Office.

Jahan, Rounaq. 1972. *Pakistan: Failure in National Integration*. New York: Columbia University Press. 62.

Khan, M. Asghar. 1978. 'Quaid-i-Azam on Soldiers and Politics', in *Defence Journal*. Vol. IV. No. 11. 10.

Khan, Major General Fazal Muqeem. 1963. *The Story of the Pakistan Army*. Karachi: Oxford University Press. 3.

Kukreja, Veena. 1989. 'Civil-Military Relations in Developing Countries'. *India Quarterly*. Vol. XLV. Nos. 2–3 (April–September). 154–92.

Kukreja, Veena. 1990. 'Restoration of Democracy in Pakistan: One Year of Benazir's Rule', in *Strategic Analysis*. Vol. XII. No. 9. February. 1164–65.

Kukreja, Veena. 1991. *Civil-Military Relations in South Asia: Pakistan, Bangladesh and India*. New Delhi: Sage Publications.

Kukreja, Veena. 1994. 'Pakistan's 1993 Election: Back to Square One' in *Strategic Analysis*. Vol. XVI. No. 10. January. 1364.

Kukreja, Veena. 2003. *Contemporary Pakistan: Political Processes, Conflicts and Crises*. New Delhi: Sage Publications.

Lamb, Christina. 1991. *Waiting for Allah: Pakistan's Struggle for Democracy.* New Delhi: Viking. 276.

Malik, Brig. S. K. 1979. *The Quranic Concept of War.* Lahore: Wajidalis

Malik, Iftikhar H. 1997. *State and Civil Society in Pakistan: Politics of Authority, Ideology and Ethnicity.* New York: St. Martin's Press. 77.

Malik, Iftikhar H. Malik. 1997. *State and Civil Society in Pakistan: Politics of Authority, Ideology and Ethnicity.* New York: St. Martin's Press Inc. 1997. 94–114.

Masood, Talat. 1995. 'Lessons for the Military', in *The News.* Lahore: 19 October.

Raman, B. 'Gen. Pervez Musharraf: His Past and Presenst'. *Corde@vsnl.com.* Accessed on 1 July 1999.

Rizvi, Hasan Askari. 1976. *The Military and Politics in Pakistan.* Lahore: Progressive Publishers. 15–25.

Rizvi, Hasan Askari. 2000. *Military, State and Society in Pakistan.* London: Macmillan Press Ltd.

Siddiqa, Ayesha. 2007. *Military Inc: Inside Pakistan's Military Economy.* London: Pluto Press.

Siddiqi, A. R. 1995. 'Army: Chickens are Coming Home to Roost', in *The Nation.* Lahore: 23 October.

Siddiqi, A. R. 1996. *The Military in Pakistan: Image and Reality.* Lahore: Vanguard. 64–5.

Singh, Jasjit. 1995. 'The Army in the Power Structure of Pakistan'. *Strategic Analysis.* Vol. XVIII. No. 7. 856.

Singh, Jasjit. 1999a. 'The Army in Pakistan', in Jasjit Singh (ed.), *Kargil 1999: Pakistan's Fourth War for Kashmir.* New Delhi: Knowledge World. 23.

Singh, Jasjit. 1999b. 'Nothing Uniform About Them', in *The Sunday Times of India.* New Delhi: 25 November. 17.

Subramanyam, A. 1999. 'Battle Fatigues: Predictable Replay in Pakistan', in *The Times of India.* New Delhi: 18 October. 14.

Subramanyam, A. 2000. 'Military and Governance', in V. A. Pai Panandiker (ed.), *Problems of Governance in South Asia.* New Delhi: Konark Publishers. 213.

Thornton, Thomas Perry. 1999. 'Fifty Years of Insecurity', in Seling Harrison, Paul Kreisberg and Dennis Kux (ed.), *India and Pakistan: The First Fifty Years.* New York: Cambridge University Press. 171.

Waseem, Mohammad. 2009. 'Civil-Military Relations in Pakistan', in Jashree Jetly (ed.), *Pakistan in Regional and Global Politics.* London: New York: Routledge. 119.

NEW EXPLORATIONS
SERVING THE OPPRESSED

10

How Egalitarian Are the Social Sciences in India?

Gopal Guru

A recent debate, which involved some eminent scholars, drew attention to this problems that surround the discipline of social science in this country. These interventions cover various dimensions of the social science malady. For example, Ramchandra Guha underscores absent liberals in the social sciences while Partha Chatterjee underlines the colonisation of social sciences by certain metropolitan centres in the country. These claims, particularly that of Guha's, have been contested on nuanced grounds by many scholars (e.g., Peter de Souza). The present paper argues that the introduction of the egalitarian principle into the debate seeks to extend and not undermine their criticism of social science practice in India (Guha 2001; de Souza 2002; Chatterjee 2002). The principle of egalitarianism, as we will discuss in greater detail in this chapter, becomes relevant in the context where the social sciences are divided into inferiorised empirical social sciences and the privileged abstract social sciences. As fifty years' experience shows, social science

---

Originally published in *Economic and Political Weekly*, Vol. 37, No. 51, 14 December, 2002.

practice has harboured a cultural hierarchy dividing it into the vast, inferior mass of academics who pursue empirical social science, and the privileged few who are considered the theoretical *pundits* with reflective capacity, which makes them intellectually superior to the former. To use a more familiar analogy, Indian social science represents a pernicious divide between the theoretical *brahmins* and empirical *shudras*. This pernicious dichotomy indicates the lack of egalitarian conditions in social science practice in the country.

This essay is divided into four sections. The first deals with the justification of the import of the egalitarian principle to critique the practice of social science (Hardy 1978: 87, 102). This would, of course, include a critique of the cultural hierarchies that operate through certain academic and institutional structures. The second section discusses the conditions that seem to adversely affect the growth of reflective capacity within the intellectually deprived groups such as dalits, tribals and even the other backward classes (OBCs). This section addresses the question why certain groups lack this reflective capacity as the primary condition for doing social science at a more abstract theoretical level. This would include analysis of factors that have a bearing on reflective capacity. In the third section the argument is built around moral stamina as the necessary condition for doing theory. The final section critiques the theoretical claims that have been made on behalf of dalits by non-dalits. In other words, a moral critique of the intellectual representation of dalit issues in social sciences is attempted.

EGALITARIAN PRINCIPLE AND SOCIAL SCIENCE PRACTICE

It is argued here that the egalitarian principle provides a moral opportunity and also a capacity to interrogate the exclusionary (*agrahara*) nature of social science practice in the country. Secondly, it also provides normative direction to suggest alternative modes to reorganise the boundaries of social sciences so as to make them more inclusive. The egalitarian principle is both interrogatory and suggestive. It has a capacity to bring out a sense of moral responsibility within the practitioner of social sciences, which would force the latter to offer a justification as to why she/he is talking in a particular social science language, say, of only theory. Thus egalitarianism would interrogate all kinds of intellectual mores for their arbitrariness. For example, the egalitarian principle in social sciences would not accept the following explanations: 'One has an innate ability to do only theory', 'doing theory is a part of the natural order', 'one is privileged to do only theory because one has been born from the thinking head (import from Manu) of pure bodies'.

The egalitarian import, therefore, challenges the hierarchical division which suggests that some are 'born with a theoretical spoon in their mouth and the vast majority with the empirical pot around their neck'. The egalitarian principle would also interrogate the epistemological imperialism that empowers non-dalits/tribals to launch intellectual expeditions to conquer newer epistemological territories that belong to the dalit/adivasi intellectual universe. The egalitarian principle would puncture this modernist (over)confidence by questioning, on moral grounds, the competitive element which renders every field of knowledge a free zone of investigation that can be taken over by anyone who follows the ground rules, procedures and protocols that are devised by the gatekeepers of social sciences. Thus the egalitarian principle undermines the competitive model of doing social sciences. It would put moral pressure on the modernist to keep off some fields of knowledge that might get better intellectual treatment from others. The interrogatory dimension also has a bearing on the suggestive dimension of the egalitarian principle. The interrogatory character of the principle fundamentally opposes all forms and contexts of formal exclusion from the field of intellectual inquiry.

The second aspect of egalitarian import to understand social science practice in India is suggestive for the following reasons. First, it would not 'approve of arguments like one cannot demand equal treatment in all fields of intellectual pursuit'. Similarly, it would not approve of the intellectual position that some fields of inquiry must be left free for the specialists. Secondly, the egalitarian principle would not approve of those rigid kinds of ground rules, procedures and protocols which are restrictive in nature. Further, the egalitarian principle, at least at the theoretical level, offers a promise to those cultural groups whose entry into the intellectual field has been historically prohibited by social forces in India. For example, one of its epistemological variants can render the field of knowledge (both theoretical and practical as epistemology of social action) communicable across cultural borders with persons of any cultural background in principle capable of utilising it (Thapar 2000: 25). Thirdly, this kind of egalitarianism presupposes a possibility of a common stock of concepts and categories which are equally available for use and even misuse by a person from any caste or social origin. It only suggests that the epistemological field in itself does not establish a copyright of certain cultural groups to control categories. On the contrary, it would question the politics to name categories or assign boundaries to intellectual practice in an arbitrary manner. It is in this sense that the egalitarian principle promises to undermine the dominant epistemological practices, which are not only exclusionary but also authoritarian in their intention and tend to become a force that seeks to discipline, denigrate and even deny epistemic status to certain concepts and categories that do not fall in line with the intellectual discourse which feeds on cultural hierarchy as a hegemonic necessity. In other words, without the egalitarian principle, hegemonic social science practice might make a lot of negative difference to cultural groups like dalits and advasis. As an intellectual force this kind of hegemonic practice would lead to caricaturing of the dalit/bahujans as epistemologically dumb, push them into empirical ghettos, or confine their intellectual/theoretical ambitions to the dominant methodological modes to a significant degree. Thus the lack of a genuine egalitarian principle within mainstream social science practice, as we shall argue later, would crush the confidence of the marginalised (dalits/adivasis), lower their self-esteem and humiliate them through epistemological patronage or charity. In this context it is necessary to ask the question whether we have followed the egalitarian principle in the practice of social sciences. The answer to this question cannot be given in the affirmative. One would give a very mixed answer.

Scholars have failed to address this question squarely. Instead they have lamented the falling standards of social science practice, particularly its theoretical components.[1] Thus it is suggested that there is a poverty of political theory in India. While these are valid observations, they do not comment on the authoritative and intimidating character of social science practice in the country. What is ironical is that the lamentation has been about the shrinking social base of political theory in India, not so much about the content and form of theory. The authoritarian character did not attract scholarly attention even in the recent report on social science research in India. This chapter argues that social science practice in India is still terribly exclusive, if not brahminical, and undemocratic in character. It is self-serving and self-satisfying as well. It lacks a genuine egalitarian character.

Social science discourse in India is being closely disciplined by self-appointed juries who sit in the apex court and decide the nature of practice and decide what comprises 'theory' and what is trash. It is a different matter that these canons lack authenticity as they are borrowed from the West unreservedly. The apex court in social sciences with its full bench in Delhi keeps ruling out subaltern objections as absurd and idiosyncratic at worst and emotional, descriptive-empirical and polemical at best. Among other things, 'bridgehead' methodology is deployed by the juries to silence dissenting voices which question this cultural hierarchy and threaten to offer alternative ideas of social science.[2] Most dalit-bahujans have developed only stunted ambitions that are historically and socially structured. In other words, dalits have not been able to develop the ambition for ideas and theory because of certain structural and socio-historical reasons that have provided an unprecedented advantage to the 'twice-born' in this country.

SOCIAL CONTEXT OF INTELLECTUAL HIERARCHIES

Any discourse, including the social sciences, emerges within a specific material and social context. In other words, it is the material context with appropriate conditions that shapes reflective ability among individuals or groups. What was the material context that would have prompted dalits to go for experiment, innovation and imagination? Skilled occupations do facilitate a certain degree of the innovative element among their members. Generation of knowledge takes place in the labour process (Patil 1982: 17). It is the labour process that creates the concrete possibilities for such epistemological abilities. But reflective abilities develop only in certain kinds of labour processes. For example, if the labour processes are imaginative, innovative and interesting then they provide sufficient scope for the agent to reflect continuously on the tools of production. The progressively transforming labour process unfolds umpteen opportunities for reflective capacities. The intellectual history of the West is proof enough in this regard. In India social groups, particularly the artisan castes, which were forced if not privileged to handle labour processes with innovation, could produce innovative knowledge systems. But certain groups like the dalits, who did not form part of the organic labour process, ultimately failed to develop an intellectual capacity to reflect. By and large they were always kept out of such a social context. Generation after generation, they were pushed into occupations that were completely devoid of any possibility of innovation and imagination, and hence were not impregnated with any possibility of knowledge. For example, they were pushed regularly into occupations like scavenging, sanitation and other types of manual labour which had inherent limitations in prompting them to do anything extraordinary in terms of creating knowledge. Until the arrival of modernity in India, particularly with independence, dalits were not included in the differentiated spheres of production that offer the context for imagination. In other words, ghettoisation into inferiorised manual spheres, reflecting the closed character of society, resulted in loss of confidence that is so important in developing the theoretical potential in the social sciences (Hollis and Lukes: 182). In the Indian context these occupations were more alienating and humiliating and stalled any possibility of imagination or innovation within the dalit communities. Thus before independence, the dalits lacked both the context and the conditions. But after independence labour processes did offer differentiated spheres for the dalits, but they did not create sufficient conditions that make reflectivity possible. We shall discuss this point in greater detail later. Suffice it to say that lack of conditions stalled the growth of any reflective faculty among dalits. Dalits who may have had reflective capacities could not develop them. They were denied the conditions that are necessary for the development of reflective faculties. One of the crucial conditions of reflectivity is the availability of freedom. Freedom from the immediate context that can become quite constraining is absolutely necessary for making sense of the immediate at an abstract general level. It is necessary in order to make connections through the vast number of details that are embedded into the immediate.

Freedom is also necessary to seek detachment from the immediate for illumination at the general level. If one does not enjoy that freedom and is completely trapped in the ceaseless struggle for survival, one is completely handicapped in developing any reflectivity. Ultimately it is those with economic security who can pursue philosophy and theory in the formal sense of the terms. The rest are forced to do only the empirical side of social science. Ambedkar himself had realised the need for such freedom and took time off to detach himself from the immediate 'chawl' life in Bombay and went to different places of high learning abroad. But he was not as fortunate as others to enjoy steady support from the intellectual circles that existed during his time. His reflectivity flourished almost like Ekalavya's. It is important to receive feedback from liberal interlocutors, support from institutions, with strong traditions of solid theoretical research, and financial support that would help scholars to pursue the academic agenda at a more abstract level and on more meaningful and dignified terms. Scholarship programmes are not enough to provide material security for dalits for two reasons. First, they are so meagre, and second, they do not guarantee the jobs that are so crucial for any reflectivity. Along with these conditions, the resources of the community with historically accumulated intellectual resources assure a congenial cultural context, making one's choice of theoretical research look natural. Members of the twice-born communities are fortunate to enjoy these conditions both in India and abroad. The dalits lack these community resources. The Ford Foundation deserves credit for coming forward to create some enabling conditions for dalit reflectivity.

HIERARCHICAL PAST SURVIVES IN CULTURAL PRESENT

There are historical reasons that gave a structural advantage to the top of the twice-born (TTB) in consolidating its privileged position in doing theory. Historically accumulated cultural inequalities seem to have reinforced dalit epistemological closure. This in effect left the realm of reflectivity entirely free for the TTB. Such closure has its sanction in Manu's thinking. The shudras are born from the leg and hence are deficient in terms of the capacity to think. Manu's code denied dalits and women access to formal education, which is necessary to achieve the capacity to speak in an abstract universal language. This division, with religious sanction behind it, was conveniently naturalised within folk consciousness, as is evident in the Marathi ditty:

> *Brahmanchy ghari lihina* (at the brahmin's you write and learn)
> *Kunbay ghari*; *dana* (at the tiller's you thrash)
> *Mahara ghari gana* (at the dalit's you sing)[3]

The privileged location of the TTB was further legitimised through the writing of both Indian and foreign scholars, prominent among them are P. V. Kane, who argued that brahmins were the founders of Indian philosophy (Patil 1982). In the same vein, Louis Dumont also mentions, with reservations, that brahmins as the renouncers were the creators of value and of different branches of knowledge (Dumont 1980: 275). It has also been argued by some scholars that brahmins have always pursued theoretical/pure reason with the help of intricate arguments, while Buddha was always following practical reason in order to tackle practical problems, like maintaining peace in society. However, people like Bhandarkar and Phule, Ambedkar and Sharad Patil may not accept this claim and would argue that the Buddhist philosophical tradition is the thinking tradition based on the dialogical mode which was much more democratic than the brahminical mode. Members of the TTB have consolidated cumulative advantage over dalit/bahujans for the following reasons. First, the TTB were fortunate to receive modern education from the imperialists. Many of them did not mind migrating to Western countries even though that went against the spirit of their religion. They were also the recipients of different kinds of fellowships that were showered on them by both the princely states and colonial state. Even after independence they received the attention and appreciation of the rulers. For example, a member of the TTB served as adviser to the Maratha chief minister in Maharashtra. Many prominent brahmins led intellectual-cultural bodies in the state. They have been the major beneficiaries of intellectual opportunities that are available in India and aboard. They do not mind migrating abroad, leaving the dalit/bahujan to take over the empire of empirical research. Cambridge, Oxford, Harvard and several other universities abroad and privileged institutions and premier universities at home are monopolised by the TTB. The doors of certain premier institutions in the country, like the Nehru Memorial Museum and Library (NMML) in Delhi, and Institute of Advance Studies in Shimla, were completely closed to the dalits. It is only in recent years that dalits are accommodated in these institutions, of course at the lower levels of the fellowship programmes. As far as Cambridge, Harvard and Oxford are concerned, it will take ages for the dalits to enter these educational institutions, which are known for their theoretical orientation. There is no doubt that these institutes, including the Indian ones mentioned above, have promoted quality research. But these institutions' obsession with modernity undermined the egalitarian principle which, as seen earlier, requires equal access to intellectual resources. Many urban-based scholars hold fellowships simultaneously at different places in India and abroad, seriously violating the Rawlsian justice principle that does not allow such monopoly that leads to the exclusion of a number of persons qualified for these positions. In any case dalits are the latecomers to such opportunities. They were excluded from the benefits as they could not pass the modernist test. When they are ready to compete for entry, the rules of entry have been changed from the modern to the traditional and the parochial at the NMML and more prominently at the Shimla institute.

Dalits are thus denied intellectual conditions that are necessary for developing more reflective capacities. It is frustrating, if not tragic, for dalits to languish in raw empiricism. In the absence of such opportunities, the only alternative that is available to dalits, adivasis and OBCs is to approach central bodies like the University Grants Commission (UGC) and the Indian Council of Social Science Research (ICSSR) for help. It would be interesting to know how many tribals and dalits have benefitted from the various national and international fellowship programmes that are offered by these bodies. In the absence of reliable evidence, one can hazard a guess and say that dalits and tribals are by and large out of the fellowship programmes. One of the primary reasons that can explain this exclusion from the opportunity structure is that there is active discouragement at both ends of the opportunity structure. Dalits find the UGC and ICSSR functioning more bureaucratic, and hence intimidating. We have several examples that show that dalit students were forced to give up more lucrative UGC fellowships in favour of less lucrative ones.[4] On the other hand, there is a constant flow of opportunities to the TTB. The shudras have been, as remarked earlier, left with the earthen pot full of empirical details that are thoroughly despised by the TTB as inferior. The earthen pot imagery has a grim history. During Peshawa rule in Pune the TTB forced dalits to hang earthen pots around their necks so that they could spit in it so as to avoid pollution.

Apart from the monopolisation of institutions to maintain the historical lead in epistemological status, the TTB deployed different strategies like canonising the discourse with the help of well-defined ground rules and procedures and protocols and compartmentalisation of institutions around chosen themes. For example, the high priest in theory seeks to canonise the social science discourse around ground rules that are often inhibiting protocols that are discouraging, language that is definitely frightening and procedures that cause anxiety among those who want to move away from the empirical to the theoretical. This kind of TTB professionalism strikes fear among the dalits/bahujans who then do not dare to enter the theoretical agrahara. The failure to elevate the discourse to higher levels of complexity and formulation and approximation of experience results in displeasure displayed by these gatekeepers of social sciences against the dalits, tribals and OBCs.

The creation of language becomes another effective weapon to restrict the entry of dalits into academic circles, which are based on a particular syntax, mostly Anglo-American. Some of the more nasty guards of these circles would point out the grammatical mistakes of the dalits publicly, not just for crushing the intellectual confidence of the dalits through humiliation, but also for hiding behind the language game. This restricted exchange ultimately leads to the creation of mutual admiration societies. Such societies certainly achieve a certain kind of height but hardly any depth in the social sciences. Due to their shared habitus[5] they lack imagination to invent new conceptual instruments. Thus they keep producing more of the same. We will deal with this a little later. Such societies cause epistemological isolation to the dalits. The strict observance of a language code, protocols, body language and ground rules effectively converts seminar halls into a hostile structure that very often inflict humiliation on the dalits who then feel intimidated to enter such arenas. Ultimately dalits are denied access to knowledge and its articulation. They are also denied the critical faculty to interrogate the dominant mode of thinking. For example, a dalit may have a genuinely insightful point that might challenge the big boss in social sciences, but the moment the dalit questions the premise of the big boss, immediately he is subjected to ridicule. Does not this kind of institutionalised exclusion show the dent in social science confidence? Let us look at another example, one that involves the humiliating exclusion of dalits from the established discourse in social science. If some dalits were speaking about Gramsci, suddenly the champions of Gramsci would raise objection. '*Aj kal koi bhi aira gaira nathu khaira Gramschi ke bare me bol raha hai.* Poor Gramsci must be turning in his grave'. In fact Gramsci would rest in peace in his grave seeing his thought being resurrected by the right kind of subaltern who is ridiculed as *aira gaira* by the defenders of Gramsci.

However, the high priests of theory do not mind dalits doing empirical studies. Some of them base their theoretical premises on data collected by dalits. Social science practice therefore lacks moral standing. Theory does not attract the dalit also because the latter lack internal moral reasoning based on the notion of sacrifice and endurance. Doing theory is a moral responsibility based on sacrifice that the dalits have to make in terms of pursuing spiritual rather than temporal power. It requires that one be not moved by immediate success or solution or glamour or charm. Let us see how this affects the doing capacity of reflectivity.

MORAL CONDITIONS OF REFLECTIVE CAPACITIES

Doing theory demands enduring moral stamina for successfully resisting the temptation for temporal gains that have the capacity to de-motivate a person from pursuing the spiritual. Doing serious theory also demands that one should overcome the sense of anxiety that involves an element of compulsion to perform. Performance, be it on the stage or in seminar rooms is often aimed at getting immediate recognition from the audience. In such performances what become important are body language, speech and sound, and speed of words, and not so much the careful arrangement of the content. Doing theory requires discipline, patience and endurance that go into making a theoretical statement that is made carefully and not superficially or polemically. Doing theory does not therefore bring you immediate recognition. Ambedkar's sociological, economic and jurisprudence work took a long time, and Rawls spent twenty years on his theory of justice. Against this backdrop, the temporal fetches immediate recognition.

Most dalits are vulnerable to the attraction of temporal power that does not flow from theoretical practice but from what are considered to be the more glamorous and easy spheres of mobility. This might include formal politics and networking with institutions that demand that intellectuals always be ready with data. When ambitions for the temporal grow out of proportion to the theoretical consciousness, then theoretical concerns get completely driven out from the cognitive map of the dalits. Practical reason takes precedence over theoretical reason. Along with the state, dalit politicians from both the NGO sector and formal politics promote such practical reasons because in the case of the former the empirical details come in handy to impress donor agencies, while in the case of the latter the data help in constructing the self-serving rhetoric that serves very well the everyday forms of dalit petty politics. Like the figures of atrocities are converted into such rhetoric, and are later repeated over and over again by dalits in national and international forums. One can mix some emotion to make the details more interesting.

In such an intellectual atmosphere, promoting theory requires transcending emotions and is considered a big danger, and anybody offering theory looks like a stranger to this brand of dalits who have a stake in maintaining the collective theoretical inability. The logic of the temporal dominates the academic agenda of the dalits. Thus many of them go in for soft options rather than tough courses like philosophy and theory that do not promise temporal power. It is this professionalisation of dalit interest that makes them more individualistic in their attitude and is responsible for their casualness if not callousness towards doing theory. Dalits try to compensate for theoretical deficiency by doing brilliant poetry. It is this sense of compensation that has led to the creation of brilliant poetry in Maharashtra from this class. In this regard it is really interesting to note what a dalit poet has to say about intellectual relations reversing the traditional positions of the dalits and the TTB. The poet says,

> When we were tearing you were tearing us.
> Now we tear you while you tear (Gadamar 1987: 39).

This particular ditty suggests that while the dalits skinned dead cattle, the TTB tore off the personality of the former through humiliation and intellectual exclusion. Now that the TTB skin hides in sophisticated tanneries, the dalits are deploying knowledge to tear the TTB through social auditing and intellectual intervention at various levels.

But poetry cannot be a substitute for theory. Most poetry, including the dalit ones, is based on aesthetics and metaphors and this no doubt makes things interesting. It is true that dalits have developed a good sense of aesthetics, but by definition it belongs to the particular, though it is based on rich experience, and therefore has the potential to become the guiding standard for the universal. Besides, it also generates inwardness and tends to keep some things hidden from the public imagination. But poetry has no conceptual capacity to universalise the particular and particularise the universal. It does not have that dialectical power. By contrast, theory demands clarity of concept and principle and the open examination of one's own action to see whether it is justified. Poetry helps the dalit to make connections through metaphors, but not through concepts. It is theory that is supposed to do that. It makes connections through concepts and also helps to illuminate the meaning that is embedded in complex reality. However, Gadamer would ask the question, 'Is it right to reserve the concept of truth for conceptual knowledge? Must we not also admit that the work of art possesses truth?' This is a serious question.

However, it is not entirely true that dalits turn towards either poetry or empirical research out of compulsion. On closer observation it is found that they also make a very conscious choice to do empirical research for the following reasons. They would argue that their lived experience is rich enough and can stand on its own authentic terms so that it does not require any theoretical representation. Experience for them is a sufficient condition to organise their thought and action and for ignition of everyday experience into resistance. Second, dalits argue that since they have privileged access to reality they can capture it with a full view without any theoretical representation. This claim is obviously based on ontological blindness. The assumption in such a claim is that non-dalits have an innate inability to comprehend dalit reality because of their different social location. Thus though dalits do not generate any theory, their research can always contain some valuable theoretical insights, their experience alone can illuminate aspects of human relations. Third, in defence of empiricism some of the dalits still argue that doing theory is undesirable because it makes a person intellectually arrogant, egoistic and socially alienated if not irrelevant. In this regard it is interesting to note that the critique of abstract thinking goes back to the fourteenth century in Maharashtra. The forerunner of the non-brahmin tradition, Sant Tukaram, criticises this intellectual tradition for its egoistic implication in the following *abhanga* (form of folk or devotional poetry):

> It is all to the good! O God! That you made me *kunbi*.
> Otherwise I would have been done to death through Brahminical cant and hypocrisy.
> As a Brahmin, I would have floated full of arrogance and ego
> And would have been led to the lowest of the lowest *naraka* (hell) (More n.d.)

This particular reaction of Tukaram is too self-explanatory to require any further elaboration.

These are some of the reasons that are advanced by the dalits to defend their empiricism. The question that still remains to be answered are should the dalits, tribals and the OBCs be forever lost in their unique experience? Should they not look at theory as a moral responsibility to accord respectability to their experience that otherwise is caricatured by both the snobbish theorist and politicians from TTB? Should they not move from the immediate to the abstract and restore subjectivity? Should they not stop making guest appearances in somebody else's formulations and restore to themselves the agency to reflect organically on their own experience? Thus doing theory becomes a social necessity for the dalits.

DALITS NEED THEORY AS A SOCIAL NECESSITY

It is argued here that moving away from the empirical mode to the theoretical one has become a social necessity for dalits, tribals and OBCs.

They need theory to confront the reverse orientalism that treats dalits, tribals and OBCs as the inferior empirical self and the TTB as the superior theoretical self. The descriptive mode is often deployed by the TTB in order to wrap insults and derision that is inflicted on the dalits. Thus description of the body language of the dalits and OBCs becomes an erotic need for the cultural and political satisfaction of the TTB. The theory of theatrical language offers a unique opportunity for dalit/bahujan scholars to fight this derisive description of cultural symbols. This should become a social necessity in order to become the subject of their own thinking rather than becoming the object of somebody else's thinking. To put it more crudely, the asymmetrical relationship that characterises reverse orientalism seeks to caricature dalits, tribals and OBCs as amusing objects. This kind of social sciences practice raises the issue whether social sciences in India is not reproducing the same tormenting forms of orientalism against which it had fought in the first instance? In what ways are the practioners of social sciences morally superior to the orientalists?

In view of the complete lack of theoretical intervention from dalit/bahujan scholars, some non-dalits messiahs have offered to represent dalit/bahujans theoretically. Their claim to fight this reverse orientalism on behalf of dalits looks attractive. It is argued by the TTB that they need to intervene in the dalit situation at the theoretical level only to restore voice and visibility to dalits and ultimately advance the dalit epistemological cause. But this also ends up producing reverse orientalism in a very subtle way. The claim to offer epistemological empowerment to dalits involves a charity element which by definition is condescending. This epistemological charity has several implications for dalits. First, speaking for the dalits or anybody constitutes a *jajmani* relationship, structurally involving the patron and the client. In the present case, the 'muknayak' becomes the patron and the 'dumb' becomes the client to define the patron. The patron, in a very ironical sense, tends to reproduce the brahminical mechanism of first controlling knowledge resources and then pouring them into the empty cupped palms of dalits. It happens in the same humiliating way—the TTB still pour water into the hands of the thirsty dalits. This relationship makes the 'muknayak' intellectually indispensable and the dumb almost crawl before such messiahs for rhetorical appreciation and designated empowerment rather than real theoretical elevation. We come across an umpteen number of cases of such designated empowerment when dalits publicly bask in the intellectual glory of their 'muknayaks'. This structured relationship creates legitimacy for the patrons' existence in both the dalit soul and dalit society. As a result the patron does not find it necessary to exit from the epistemological fields that are specific to the dalit and bahujan situation.

This jajmani relationship also has a third implication for the dalits. This representation tends to undervalue or underplay the discursive capacity of such groups who in favourable hermeneutic conditions can develop an epistemic stamina. But the 'muknayaks' make it a very smart move, prompting the dumb to throw up more interesting details so that the former can use these details for either grand formulation in a liberal mode or its post-modernist deconstruction. This by implication confines the dalits to the empirical and pushes them into the frozen essentialist trap.

This postmodernist construction of dalits remains blind to the hegemonic politics that would feel happy to celebrate such a construction as it replaces the need to make connections between several local experiences that belong to the same logical class of collective suffering and exploitation.

Finally, this epistemological enthusiasm of the non-dalits also suffers from another and rather serious malady. This intellectual representation remains epistemologically posterior. That is to say, the discovery of the dalit epistemological standpoint fails to explain who has arrived—whether the object (dalits) or the subject ('muknayaks'). This question becomes absolutely important because such claims have been sustained on the basis of throwing up completely new conceptual landscapes from the dalit experience. This inability to either recover or throw up an alternative concept happens because these scholars choose to theorise dalit experience standing outside the dalit experience. This representation thus remains epistemologically posterior.

In view of this posterior epistemology, its standpoint remains a mere assertion which feeds on the critique of the mainstream Marxist or feminist framework. This externality hardly enables the dalits to secure theoretical advance for their revolutionary understanding and politics. To put it more crudely, such epistemological enthusiasms may turn dalit epistemology into an exegetical horizon of difference that may radically undermine any possibility of the fusion of epistemologies that are egalitarian in nature. It is in this sense that the patronising or posterior epistemology fails to belong to the realm of social necessity. It comes up as a choice to transcend the personal intellectual frustration of those middle-class ex-radicals for whom the old frameworks have ceased to be charming options.

It is true that the old liberal or Marxist discourses tried to tighten the conceptual boundaries of social sciences in India, almost pushing the social science discipline into a state of suffocation. But these discourses did compete with one another, like the caste discourse vs class discourse for deciding protocols, procedure and ground rules for the social sciences. In the process these discourse took over the theoretical task of discovering concepts and categories for dalits, adivasis and OBCs and women. For example, the Marxist discourse introduced concepts like class, exploitation, proletariat, labour and alienation for everybody including dalits. In the liberal discourse caste, nationalism, citizenship and rights, and multiculturalism are the potent categories for everybody. This by implication suggests the dalit failure of historical imagination to do theory. Although such rendering does pose a huge theoretical challenge to provide alternative sets of categories, this is a challenge that is worth taking. Dalit theory, in order to become a social necessity, has to be vertically critical of the limitations of Marxist and liberal methods and horizontally be sensitive towards those dalit/bahujan critical impulses which may still be present in the methods as mentioned above. Thus it would be unfair to dispense with everything from Marxism or liberalism for their epistemological deficiencies. In fact doing theory is also an inner necessity for the dalits.

DALITS NEED THEORY AS INNER NECESSITY

There seem to be different factors that become the preconditions for the realisation of this inner necessity. These are the moral conditions. For dalits to realise doing theory as an inner moral necessity, they must make a conscious moral choice to use their sense of freedom for understanding and reflecting on the dalit experience. They should treat this freedom to walk out from the dalit experience as the initial condition for achieving theoretical heights in their reflections. They may go to Oxford and Cambridge to achieve height to their experience in order to accord depth to their reflections. This becomes an essential condition for doing theory. Thus the modernist theorist who is driven by individualised intellectual triumphalism of conquering newer epistemological territories becomes a morally undesirable option for the dalit. This kind of epistemological imperialism is one-sided as it shows commitment to scholarship and not to the cause. For dalits, theory comes as a double commitment both to scholarship and also to the social cause. As a part of this moral commitment the dalits should avoid walking into pure empiricism which come as alternatives in the competitive forms of tokenism in the realms of both academics and politics. Thus for dalits, theory should not begin and end with Oxford, Cambridge or the Shimla institute or the NMML. Their theory should not be caught in the self-serving professionalism and stupefaction adopted by the TTB in the country. Dalits should test the tenacity of their theory not with the certification of juries of social sciences, howsoever attractive that may be, but on the basis of how much influence these theoretical formulations enjoy in the popular mentality.

It is a Gramscian project that demands impeccable commitment on the part of the theorist to translate technical content into an ordinary idiom and common speech so that it becomes accessible to the common people and does not remain confined to seminar rooms only. In fact it should be practised from the Red Fort in Delhi. That would, by the way, resignify the fort by dispelling the deceitful rhetoric of interested parties ritually on every 15 August. Dalits are expected to take the initiative in giving a moral lead to doing theory in the country. This orientation would thus remove the cultural hierarchies that tend to divide social science practice into theoretical brahmins and empirical shudras. Ultimately social sciences in India would fulfill the fondest hopes by expanding the social base of its conceptual landscape.

ENDNOTES

[1] Many political theorists share this point, the most prominent being Bhiku Parekh who has written about the poverty of political theory in India.

[2] This is the forum called Dalit Intellectuals' Collective based in Mumbai.

[3] This is a very common saying in Maharashtra's cultural life.

[4] This is the story of a dalit who is doing PhD in social work in Chennai.

[5] This is a cue from Bourdieu.

REFERENCES

Chatterjee, Partha. 2002. 'Institutional Context of Social Science Research in South Asia'. *Economic and Political Weekly*. Vol. XXXVII. No. 35. 31 August. 3604–12.

De Souza, Peter. 2002. 'Intellectuals and Their Doman'. *Economic and Political Weekly.* Vol. XXXVII. No. 9. March.

Dumont, Louis. 1980. *Homo Hierarchicus*. London: Oxford University Press. 275.

Gadamer, H.G. 1987. *Truth and Method.* London: Sage Books. 39.

Gellne, Ernest. 1982. 'Relativism and Universalism', in Martin Hollis and Steven Lukes (ed.), *Rationality and Relativsm.* London: Basil Blackwell. 182.

Guha, Ramchandra. 2003. 'Absent Liberals: Politics and Intellectual Life in India'. *Economic and Political Weekly.* Vol. XXXVI. No. 59. December. 4663–70.

Hardy, Henry (ed.). 1978. *Concepts and Categories: Philosophical Essays*. London: Hogarh Press. 87, 102.

More, Sadanand. *Collection of Writings of Tukaram.* Philosophy Department. Pune University.

Patil, Sharad. 1982. *Satyashodhak Marxwadi* (Marathi). Vol. 5. July. 17.

Raina, Dhruv. 2000. 'The Present in the Past', in Romila Thapar (ed.), *India: New Millennium*. Delhi: Penguin. 25.

11

Social Movements in Creative Society: Of Autonomy and Interconnection

Manoranjan Mohanty

THE CENTURY OF DEMOCRATIC UPSURGE

The twentieth century has been a century of democratic upsurge. Classical forms of imperialism and colonialism were overthrown in Asia and Africa in the course of struggles for liberation. Right to independence of nations and self-determination of people acquired the status of basic human rights. The revolutions in Russia, China, Cuba, Vietnam and elsewhere challenged the foundations of class oppression by landlords and capitalists, and created visions of equality and freedom as cherished values for social reconstruction. Despite the reversals of some of those revolutions their legacies have an abiding significance.

The last three decades of this century have seen the steady emergence of new types of social movements—movements of women,

---

Originally published in Manoranjan Mohanty, Partha Mukherji with Olla Tormsquist (ed.), *People's Rights: Social Movements and the State in the Third World*, New Delhi: SAGE Publications India Pvt. Ltd., 1993.

tribals, and dalits, the environmental movements, movements of displaced people the various kinds of autonomy movements, and many others. The experience of these movements has exposed the multidimensionality of domination and oppression in society. Therefore, the struggle for liberation has also to be multidimensional. Relating class struggle with the wide spectrum of social struggle is a critical aspect of the democratic upsurge in the twentieth century.

While the struggle for democratic rights has been the principal trend of this century the persisting efforts to defend the structures of domination or create new forces of subjugation are also evident during this period of history. The phenomena of Fascism and Nazism, military dictatorships, authoritarianism, external intervention, and new forms of domination through transfer of technology, capital and modern communication are some of the indicators of the process of domination. Such trends have been visible not only at the international level but also at national and local levels.

If this is the nature of our historical movement then what is the meaning of social turbulence and upheavals which characterise contemporary society? This turbulence is visible all over the world, but more clearly discernible in the developing countries. The ruling elite views such a situation as a breakdown of order and the onset of chaos and anarchy, and invariably opts for suppressing them, only to provoke further turbulence. Seen in the context of the historical process of the twentieth century, this turbulence can be regarded as the mark of a creative society where hitherto subdued contradictions have come into the open. The upheavals may be the result of the activities of deprived groups or sections among them struggling for the realisation of their democratic rights.

The anti-colonial struggle opened up streams of democratic consciousness thus unfolding a creative society. The ideas of the great revolutions spread new visions of social transformations giving concrete socio-economic content to the agenda of the freedom struggle. The dynamics of social struggle in the post-colonial world unfolded this process still further into an expanded realm of freedom. The contemporary social movements challenged patriarchy, ethnic, racial and caste domination, and questioned the dominant model of capitalist modernisation for generating new inequalities and fresh sources of alienation. Creative society thus emerged as a theatre of intense struggle between forces of freedom and forces of domination.

In this essay, I analyse first the concept of creative society, and then take up the question of the role of the state in creative society. Thereafter, I will address some key issues concerning social movements in this context, particularly the issue of exclusiveness of contemporary social movements. This is followed by a discussion of Chinese and Indian experiences to draw some inferences. Finally, I will reflect upon how to reconcile autonomy and interconnection of social movements so as to promote fulfillment of freedom in creative society.[1]

THE CREATIVE SOCIETY

The concept of 'creative society' refers to a phase of development of a society in which a large number of potential contradictions become articulate and active.[2] This is most evident when oppressed social groups get politically mobilised and demand their rights. The upsurge of the peasants and tribals, the movements for regional autonomy and self-determination, the environmental movements and the women's movement in the developing countries are signs of emergence of creative society in contemporary times. The forms of social movements and their intensity may vary from country to country and place to place within a country. But the very presence of movements for social transformation in various spheres of a society indicates the emergence of a creative society in a country (Jan Vikas Andolan 1990; Omvedt 1994; Shah 1990; Sheth 1992).

This situation, visible in India during the last quarter of the century has been regarded by the ruling class as one of disorder leading to fissiparous tendencies in the development process in the country. Every movement for regional autonomy has been treated as disruptionist and separatist for a long period of time. Even when political compulsions forced the Government of India to make some concessions to autonomy movements, the perspective of the rulers did not change. Most of the environmental movements, especially those which question the establishment of big dams like the Sardar Sarovar dam on the river Narmada in Gujarat, Tehri in Uttar Pradesh or Indravati in Orissa are regarded as anti-development and therefore, 'against national interest'. The movement for gender justice and women's rights has been seen as disrupting the cultural milieu, being derived from Western models and creating social instability. Increased militancy of the movements of peasants and tribals is considered a problem of law and order. The civil liberty and democratic rights movement which documents the violation of human rights by the state agencies and others is often regarded as partisan and anti-state. These are some examples to indicate the governing perspective of the state in relation to the spread of demands for democratic rights in a society (Kothari 1989; Singh 1993).

The alternative view of this turbulence is to see them as expanding efforts for the creative transformation of society. These social movements seek to alter the prevailing structure of power, project values of justice, equality and freedom adding new dimensions to them. The autonomy movements challenge the existing notion of the centralised nation-state and demand restructuring of the union or the federation to facilitate fulfillment of their creative aspirations. The environment movements question the claims of the planners about the benefits of the particular development projects and point out the disruption of the harmonious relationship between nature and human beings. That the prevailing structures of patriarchy prevent the creative development of women is exposed by the feminists. Dalits would no longer tolerate the brahmanic values and institutions which have suppressed their creativity for centuries. Tribals who had enjoyed a highly creative life in the natural environment have, during the past century or so, been subjected to severe exploitation by commercial interests and agencies of the state. They have revolted against this process from time to time and there is a visible trend of their resurgence in recent years. The tribal people have been the worst victims of mining projects, big dams and location of other big projects such as steel plants. In recent years they have launched movements to assert their 'rights to earth' or the right to use and control the material and cultural resources of their area, and share it with others on mutually agreed terms. The process of disentitlement or loss of access to forest resources, water and land which has pauperised them is being challenged by many movements in various parts of the country (Mohanty 1993; Omvedt 1994).

Such a situation was regarded as a 'revolutionary situation' by many thinkers earlier. Accentuation of class contradictions providing the objective conditions and the rise of revolutionary ideology and organisation providing the subjective conditions defined the revolutionary situation (Mohanty 1977: 31–59). The notion of 'creative society' does not claim to replace it. It only refers to a wider characteristic of society in a historical phase. That characteristic is the expanded realm of democratic struggles. Moreover, the concept of a revolutionary situation traditionally focused on class contradictions whereas the creative society refers to a wider range of class and other social contradictions. The former is more oriented towards formulating strategy and tactics of revolution whereas the latter, in addition to strategy add tactics, raises many more issues related to a multidimensional transformation of society.

Creative society embodies a methodology of viewing society in terms of liberation from multiple dominations—class, caste, race, ethnicity, gender and many more yet to be discovered sources of domination—and it points at the processes already active or yet to be articulated, seeking to reconstitute society. Structures and processes of domination are shackles on human creativity, therefore they are sought to be removed.

The concept of creative society opposes any formation which suggests a terminal view of the history of society—whether an assertion that history has settled for a liberal-pluralist political economy, or a socialist command system, or a model of state-led mixed economy. None of them adequately comprehend the nature and magnitude of the creative society.

Capitalism as the dominant political economy of the world has been particularly hostile to the emergence of the creative society. The irony is that the primary postulates of capitalism—in its inception were centred on creativity and individual freedom. It had sought to dismantle the feudal shackles on human creativity. The new quest for freedom was to be based on reason, which in turn was to be based on practice in real life. In the more recent history of capitalism the accent was on pluralism to enable peaceful competition among groups, reconcile their demands and facilitate greater creativity and innovation of individuals and groups. The development of modern organisations including corporations with access to high technology and information networks is supposed to promote organisational creativity and rationality.

But all these claims—old and new—have been belied in the practice of capitalist development. They have produced an instrumental view of creativity which makes it devoid of democracy and humanism. Modern capitalism propels market homogenisation leaving little room for variety and choice. The need-multiplication drive of capitalism pulls all individuals into this market, turning them into standardised consumers of goods and services, causing alienation of humans from their cultural setting and producing newer inequalities in society. This process has pushed technology in such a direction that contrary to the claims of differentiation and specialisation, there has been considerable de-skilling of individuals and groups all over the world by standardising the labour process. Many artisans have lost their skill and many regions their art and craft. The commodification of life and social process aided by this technological trend under the auspices of monopolies and centralised public corporations has actually curbed the human urges of a creative society. This process compels homogenisation of identity groups precisely when the latter are seeking fulfillment of identities. It leads to the centralisation of the political process when they seek multiple structures of autonomy. The dynamics of high achievement sets out the parameters of politics and management. Consumerism constrains cultural creativity, and moral and ethical existence. Thus, the advanced industrial society may not be quite the example of a creative society that is fulfilling the people's democratic urges. It may actually be the picture of a system that manages instrumental creativity in a narrow framework. In developing countries this management is difficult in view of the resurgence of serious contradictions resulting from the experiments in capitalist modernisation. Thus, capitalism in modern history represents the taming of creativity and taming of reason. The creative society, therefore, is bound to break out of the capitalist process in pursuit of creativity and liberation.[3]

In the course of the socialist experiments, particularly in the erstwhile Soviet Union, the development path generally accepted the growth policies and economic targets which had similarities with those under capitalist modernisation. Essentially, it accepted the perspective of the Industrial Revolution which was organically rooted in capitalism. They were pursued through the structures of the state and the communist party which, in most cases, were centralised, bureaucratic and authoritarian. Strong leadership was sought to be justified in the name of fighting external and internal enemies. All this led to suppression of dissent, outbreak or secessionist movements and serious debates on alternative proposals for socialist construction. The Marxist vision of socialism and communism was a response to the structures of capitalism which caused alienation of men and women. Capitalist exploitation imposed constraints on human creativity. Socialism, therefore, was originally conceived as a system that would remove those constraints, promote human creativity and expand the realm of freedom. Socialism should create those material conditions which facilitated political and cultural freedom. The working class was to utilise the power it seized through the revolution to achieve material, political and cultural conditions of freedom. The revolutionary movement in Russia in the late nineteenth century had, in fact manifested the creative urges of peasants, workers, intelligentsia and youth which the Bolshevik Revolution was expected to realise. The Soviet state did provide the basic material conditions of life but did not provide channels of democratic participation. Its vision of a good society was shaped in terms of the economic objectives of the capitalist revolution. So the Soviet society instead of fulfilling the demand for a creative society created constraints on it (Mohanty 1991b).

'Creative society' is an analytical concept that captures the nature of social upsurge in the post-colonial world. Modern Western political theory is yet to come to grips with this phenomenon. Having been rooted in the post-Enlightenment history of Europe, Western political theory remains pre-occupied with the construction of a stable civil society to facilitate capitalist growth. Individual freedom is at the core of this theory which treats socialism and all forms of communitarian philosophy as passing phases. The liberation struggles which overthrew Western imperialism were never fully comprehended by mainstream Western theorists. The cold war, the collapse of the USSR and the global advance of capitalist modernisation in the early 1990s seem to have created a further hiatus between Western political theory and post-colonial societies. Concepts such as a creative society seek to grasp the multiplicity of contradictions in Asian, African and Latin American societies and at the same time ask these questions about Western societies.

In place of individual freedom—whether possessive, exclusivist or relatively more sympathetic to fellow beings—liberation (*mukti*) and fulfillment (*siddhi*) can be perceived as central values. Here, the individual is seen as a member of a class, a caste, an ethnic group, male or female—thus embodying a bundle of identities. The ordering of the identities is determined by the context. In other words, the involvement in a social movement—is explained by the person's feeling of a particular type of domination to which she has woken up, personally or as a group. It is not a problematic of individual versus society as stipulated in modern Western political theory. It is the problematic of human beings seeking conditions of freedom to realise their creativity. Individuals, groups and collectivities of all kinds treat themselves as parts of a creative society seeking liberation from all forms of domination.

SOCIAL MOVEMENTS AND MASS ORGANISATIONS

From this perspective, the political theory of the contemporary world warrants new considerations. I do not propose to take up a comprehensive study of the theory of social movements here. The attempt is to only try to understand some trends in social movements, particularly the phenomenon of exclusiveness. My argument is that this is a reaction to the 'mass organisation' approach of the political parties which denies autonomy to the social movements. This in turn is part of the general phenomenon of the elites not recognising the nature of the creative society.

The problem of exclusiveness of the social movements is fairly serious in contemporary times. Why is it that a women's movement rarely links up with an autonomy movement, an autonomy movement with the environment movement, and the latter with an agrarian struggle? Most of the social movements are preoccupied with their own particular issues of struggle. Occasionally, efforts are made for joint action, especially when state repression is severe. But that is only a temporary conjoining of the movements, which dissolves soon after the event. 'This movement is ours and that is yours'—this is a widely discernible attitude.

This phenomenon is in direct contrast to the experience of the 'mass organisations' of the political parties, including those of the communist parties. The trade unions of workers, the organisations of peasants, the associations of writers and the various cells for women, students and in some cases scheduled castes and tribes did not have much autonomy. The overall political line of the party bound them together. The strategy and tactics of these mass organisations were, by and large, determined by the central leadership of the respective parties. Mass organisations were instrumentalities of a party's mobilisation strategy. Even when they launched movements, their action originated from a party leadership's assessment of the overall situation. The movement may not necessarily have arisen from below.

The contrast is visible in three respects. First, the contemporary social movements enjoy a high degree of autonomy while the mass organisations operate under strict party leadership. Of course, the degree of control would vary according to the organisational and ideological character of the party and the prevailing state of factional conflict. Second, the social movement occurs at the grassroots level and may embody a degree of spontaneity among the local people. On the other hand, the mass organisations are assigned work from above, they recruit local cadres and may or may not generate spontaneous involvement of people. Third, the variety of local issues may lead to corresponding local movements whereas many issues may not fit the pronounced framework of the political parties. In this case, a party may at best recognise some issues as its own or 'ours', and others as being outside their agenda, or 'yours'.

The advantage of the mass organisation approach is the vertical integration of the movements and campaigns with the larger electoral or other political lines of the party. The trade union, the peasant organisation, the women's and students' wings would work actively for the electoral victory of the party's candidates. Even in the case of revolutionary struggles outside the electoral arena these wings would engage in activities in support of the main political organisation. Besides, there is usually the regional and national organisation on the mass front linking up one unit with another in different parts of the country. In other words, the mass organisations provide a cohesive integrated political framework which the social movements may lack.

But there is a serious gap in the practice of mass organisations which has been noticed in conspicuous ways in course of the upsurge of the contemporary social movements. That is the lack of recognition of the specificity and autonomy of a range of social contradictions. Their methodology of social analysis is generally based upon an aggregate view of social formations. No doubt it is necessary as a safeguard against empiricism that only took notice of parts. But most Marxists accepted the same general view as the liberals, and focused attention on the sweeping force of capitalism, the former countering it with the socialist alternative, and the latter defending and developing it. The aggregate view, especially in terms of the general trend of the social formation is essential, but it is meaningful only when it is not seen merely as an aggregate but an interconnection of specificities composing the whole.[4]

Whereas the mass organisations were inadequate responses to the multiplicity of social contradictions, the contemporary social movements are often so autonomous that there is a lack of interconnection. It has to be recognised that the spontaneity, grassroots location, innovativeness and, above all, autonomy, are the strong points of the social movements. Their methodology of social analysis is based on identification of the specificity of the social contradictions. A movement of the dalits, for example, would underline the specific caste contradiction historically and in a particular region. But this analysis, in the absence of its location in relation to other social contradictions such as the ones relating to land relations, gender inequality, etc., may turn out to be a limited exercise. Between the aggregate perspective of the party-linked mass organisations and the autonomist perspective of the contemporary social movements, politics of democratic movements (*janavadi andolan*) fail to make headway. This is the problem of 'ours and yours' which afflicts most of the movements. The parties insist on inclusiveness of their line for specific issues of society and the movements make a virtue of their exclusiveness.

As arenas of democratic struggle multiply and social movements emerge on a variety of fronts the problem of 'ours and yours' assumes serious proportions. The political parties get isolated from several social movements as their specificities are not sufficiently respected by the parties. The social movements themselves remain isolated from one another. The cumulative effect of all this is the setback to the democratic transformation of society. In this process, the movements become more and more vulnerable to repression and manipulation by the state. It is the lack of recognition of the character of this situation of expanding democratic upsurge in society which creates the exclusiveness among movements and the mechanical, all-inclusive, aggregate view of the parties.

The refusal to come to terms with this creative society pushes a state on the authoritarian path (Haragopal and Chandrasekhar 1994).

STATE AND CREATIVE SOCIETY

The post-colonial states are struggling to come to terms with the creative society. The anti-colonial movements which resulted in the countries of Asia, Africa and Latin America (ASAFLA) gaining independence were part of the upsurge of creative society. But soon after gaining independence, the post-colonial states were preoccupied with tasks of defending sovereignty and achieving economic development which were important in themselves. The modes of development and nation-building adopted by them were such that often demands of a creative society got little attention of the ruling class. What is striking is that the elites in general, including the leaders of the social movements themselves, hardly realised the implications of being placed in a creative society. Otherwise, the social movements would not be so isolated from one another, nor would they be so vulnerable to the manoeuvers by the state. On the other hand, if democratic possibilities of the post-colonial state were fully explored then the state leaders would have been positively responsive to the urgings of the creative society. They would take serious steps towards reforms in the socio-economic and political structures and respect autonomy and democratic rights of deprived groups and regions. Instead of resorting to authoritarian measures they would take responsive measures making democratic use of the relative autonomy of the state. That would be the possible role of a creative state which democratically responds to a creative society.

By putting pressure on the state to secure its positive response, the social movements play a dual role. One role involves exposing the class character, the caste, racial and patriarchal character of the state, and seeking to overthrow and replace it with a democratic state facilitating multidimensional liberation. The other role of the movements is to steadily reform it by forcing it to implement its own promises. The declarations in the Indian Constitution, especially in the chapters on Fundamental Rights and the Directive Principles of State Policy and some of the creative judicial constructions on them and also the positive political affirmations were, and still are, to a large extent, responses to the creative society in India. Social movements in contemporary India have constantly demanded their firm and just execution. Democratic rights movements in India have uniformly demanded that the agencies of the state act, according to law, reform their structures and fulfil the legitimate demands of struggling people. Duality of the state process implies constant efforts by social movements and political organisations to simultaneously try to reform and replace the state (Mohanty 1990b). But the response of the Indian state has been increasingly repressive and violent.[5] This is due to the non-recognition of the character of the creative society. Treating agrarian, tribal struggles and autonomy movements as acts of political violence only, and deploying an increased number of security forces has merely produced a vicious circle of violence. As a result, the state apparatus in India is fast losing its legitimacy and effectiveness (Haragopal and Chandrasekhar 1994).

Thus, on the one hand the self-perception of the social movements in a creative society has produced exclusiveness and reduced their effectiveness. On the other hand, the perceived role of the state by its managers as defender of peace and order has, in practice, pushed it on an authoritarian path and reduced its capacity to realise its democratic possibilities. The perception in both cases, no doubt, is rooted in the social conditions, the power structures as well as in their ideologies.

Social movements as mass-based action processes linked to social issues may have among them undemocratic and authoritarian trends as well. This is because the arena of struggle over rights encompasses both the state and civil society. Just as inspite of the dominance of ruling forces in the state process, democratic voices and actions are possible in the state, there are avenues for both the oppressed and dominant sections to be active in civil society (Chandhoke 1994; Joseph 1994). Though the very definition of creative society implies that democratic demands by the oppressed groups have salience in it, however, some political forces can also use the democratic space and democratic discourse to pursue hegemonic objectives. Communal campaigns, racial and caste agitations and other exclusivist campaigns in the name of nation, territory or a leader are examples of this trend. Further, a genuinely democratic movement for self-determination or agrarian transformation, for example, can sometimes degenerate and resort to feudal, autocratic and inhuman practices and yet justify them through the democratic idiom. That disrupts the democratic growth of a creative society and propels counterforces to align with the state to thwart even the just democratic demands of oppressed groups. Thus, rather than having a romantic notion of creative society one has to keep in mind the complexities in the dynamic environment.

Much of the present dilemma in the creative society in the developing world is the result of a dysfunction with their liberation struggles. Some important lessons in this respect can be derived from the historical experiences of the Chinese revolution and the Indian freedom struggle.

HISTORICAL LESSONS FROM INDIA AND CHINA

In both India and China there has been a decline in the memory of their freedom struggles. The post-colonial processes in both the countries led them to the paradigm of capitalist modernisation. It crystallised in China in the early 1980s and in India a decade later. Even when they celebrated anniversaries of their freedom struggle—forty-fifth anniversary of the liberation in China in 1994, Mao Zedong's birth centenary in 1993; the Golden Jubilee of the Quit India Movement in 1992, and Gandhi's 125th birth anniversary in 1994—these turned out to be a ritualistic recounting. The Swaraj (self-rule) perspective of Gandhi and the Jiefang (liberation) perspective of Mao were no longer the guiding principles of state policy or elite discourse in India and China (Mohanty 1994). The strategy of survival of the ruling class, pressures of the world political economy and their new ideologies of modernisation created discontinuities with their anti-colonial struggles of the recent past. The regimes sought legitimacy by launching new strategies of political and economic management rather than in terms of realising the values of their freedom struggle.

The emergence of creative society in modern India was evident in the nineteenth century with the voicing of the demands for abolishing social evils like untouchability, sati and child marriage. In the twentieth century, the movements for democratic government in princely states, protection of linguistic and ethnic rights, changing the colonial education system, and above all, securing freedom from British colonial rule steadily unfolded this process. The upsurge of militant peasant movements in Telangana and Bengal was one of the landmarks in the manifestation of the creative society. Similarly, the Taiping Rebellion (1850–61), the political reform movement of the 1890s, the Boxer uprising (1900), heralded the growth of the creative society in modern China. The 1911 revolution which overthrew the Manchu monarchy, the May Fourth Movement of students and workers against the Japanese and Western imperialism in 1919, the peasant movement in Hunan, the Northern Expedition to unify China, the united front against Japanese aggression involving mass mobilisation of peasants, the nationalist upsurge in literature and arts during those years, and above all, the people's democratic revolution led by the Communist Party of China demonstrated the rapid development of the creative society (Mohanty 1992). These events suggest that a series of social and political contradictions had become acute, and needed resolution.

In the course of India's freedom struggle, the people's movement in the princely states was integrated with the struggle against British imperialism. The constructive programmes of Gandhi, especially those relating to 'Harijan welfare', *Nai Talim* and cottage industries were clearly linked to the larger perspective of freedom. Whenever a peasant movement, a war mobilisation or a cultural campaign became delinked from the overall struggle against colonialism, the separation was costly. Conversely, the extent to which the anti-colonial struggle lacked a socio-economic content had its consequences. In fact, the Congress under Gandhi was so preoccupied with mobilising all sections of society against the British that its support for the peasant movement was marginal. Despite Gandhi's educational experiments the Congress did not have an alternative educational strategy. The harijan welfare programme was somewhat elaborate, but Ambedkar was not convinced about the correctness and orientation of the programme. So, Ambedkar developed his programme of dalit democratic movement (Omvedt 1994). Thus, Congress as the leading force in the Indian anti-colonial struggle did not have a full-scale response to the emerging demands of a creative society. The Communist Party of India too had only a limited perspective. Either they joined the Congress campaign against the British or took an internationalist stand, as in 1942, which alienated them from the nationalist opinion. They did launch agrarian movements and urban strikes, but these were not an integrated response to the prevailing urges of the people.

China's May Fourth Movement was a clear example of linking up specific cultural movements with wider campaigns for democracy, science and independence from colonial domination. The upsurge of cultural, literary, economic and political movements during the anti-Japan war integrated the social movements with the issue of national salvation. More importantly, the perspective of the New Democratic Revolution combined anti-colonial and anti-feudal programmes into a comprehensive framework with political, economic, social, cultural, educational and international policies in it. Whenever some campaign got isolated from this current—be it an economic project, a military initiative or a cultural effort—the consequences were negative.

It is possible to argue that the pressure of orienting all specific struggles to the overall goals of the freedom struggle was so great that autonomy of the particular struggles was limited. Perhaps contemporary rulers can substitute modernisation for independence and justify subordinating all specific social issues to it. But recent researches on the ground experiences in the anti-colonial struggle in China and India show something different. Actually there was considerable autonomy and variety in the peasant struggles, cultural campaigns and social reform drives in India to which different leaders of Congress responded differently. Outside the Congress stream, a large number of national, regional and local struggles had gone on. In China, the programme and strategies of the local movements varied according to local conditions. There was careful reconciliation between the goals and objectives of the local movements and those of the central communist leadership (Mohanty 1992).

The experiences of both India's struggle and China's revolution show that unless the dialectics of autonomy and interconnection is maintained, social movements may not achieve their objectives. In China, agrarian change, education and cultural transformation were so closely integrated with one another as components of the revolutionary movement that accomplishments in these spheres did not pose major difficulties after liberation. The New Democracy of Mao Zedong had dimensions of politics, economics and culture built into the programme. In fact, the anti-Japan campaign was a comprehensive programme on military, political, economic and cultural fronts. It illustrated the merits of autonomy and interconnection of social movements in a creative society. Revolutionary base areas, cultural groups, writers' associations and production units were autonomous. But they had a common goal of defeating Japanese imperialism and carrying forward the process of social transformation (Selden 1971). Yet, in many spheres the Communist Party of China had not yet responded to the creative urges of its people. For example, the ethnic minorities, whose support had been sought during the Long March of 1934–35, were neglected for long even after liberation. The women's question was taken up only marginally. On the whole, however, there was a dialectical integration of the overall goal of anti-imperialist revolution with specific social issues.

In contrast to the experience of the Chinese people's democratic revolution there is an exclusive preoccupation with economic construction in the policies of the Deng Xiaoping regime in post-Mao China. This perspective does not allow autonomy to social movements. All demands are subordinated to economic growth. So, the women's movement, the ethnic rights movement, the workers, etc., are not allowed to assert the autonomous rights of their respective sectors. Their organisations are called upon to help achieve production targets and make profit. The fact that the ongoing process of economic growth might adversely affect the rights of such sections is not taken into account. The Communist Party of China's mass organisation approach is implemented firmly in contemporary China. The movements are vertically linked to the parent party and are not allowed to interact horizontally lest their interconnection challenges the monopoly of the central leadership.

AUTONOMY AND INTERCONNECTION

Social movements emerged as distinct entities in reaction to processes of centralised domination. Perhaps it was necessary to assert the specificity of the demands of a social group or a region or in relation to a thus far neglected issue because the epoch of capitalist industrial revolution had disallowed such distinct existence. Liberals and most Marxists pinned their hopes on such aggregate processes as modernisation and class struggle saying that such a programme was necessary for providing the conditions for fulfilling all specific demands such as those of lower castes, women and backward areas. When the failures of such macro-strategies were evident, new social movements emerged to fight for specific issues, which was understandable. But when the centralising state, multinational capital and dominant local interests began to perceive these movements as threats, the former took full advantage of the separateness of the social movements. The liberal political parties which ordinarily spoke in the name of the whole society treated them as deviant forces. Very few of them have worked out their approaches to the new social movements. The Left parties for long treated these movements as negative forces dividing the workers' movement. Only recently have they accommodated the new issues in their framework of class struggle. The social movements themselves are so starved of resources, so preoccupied with the survival of their loose organisational strength that they have had little opportunity to establish connections with one another.

The perspective of comprehensive democratic transformation that secures ecologically sustainable development which is culturally compatible, morally satisfying, socially just and politically participative would be a perspective of the creative society. This is how the concept of development is perceived as the process of liberation or Swaraj or Jiefang. It implies struggle against multidimensional domination, and constant grappling with freshly discovered arenas of human bondage. This is the process that progressively fulfils the urges of human creativity and gradually unfolds the socialist society.

Thus, at a fundamental level every social movement embodies autonomy and interconnection. Only the socio-political situation explains as to why one of these dimensions is dominant. If either of this is missed then the problem of exclusiveness, or 'ours and yours', makes them vulnerable to pressures of the state and oppressive social forces. No doubt, the ideology and social character of movements vary, and they would be subject to a variety of political assessments. But the political imperatives of the creative society demand that social movements view one another as autonomous and interconnected at the same time.

ENDNOTES

[1] This essay carries forward the argument suggested in Mohanty 1989, 1990a.

[2] An earlier formulation of this idea appears in my paper, 'Creative Society and the Democratic State', presented at the Seminar on the Indian State at the Indian Institute of Advanced Study, Shimla (31 August–5 September 1992). I am grateful to the participants for helping me to develop this idea. Discussions with R. S. Rao at Sambalpur University have been immensely helpful.

[3] Much of the critique of the dominant development paradigm does not involve a serious critique of capitalism, thus making itself capitalism's permissible dissident (Mohanty 1991b).

[4] The *Programme Document* adopted by the Communist Party of India in its fifteenth Congress (Hyderabad, 10–16 April 1992) has sections on 'the woman question', 'the language problem', 'the nationality and tribal problem', 'protection of environment', among other things. The *Political Resolution* adopted by the fourteenth Congress (Madras, 3–9 January 1992) of the Communist Party of India (Marxist) makes references to the struggles of the scheduled castes, tribal and women. The Communist Party of India (Marxist-Leninist) groups too have recently included these dimensions in their programmes. Still, on the whole, the traditional approach of mass organisation dominates their political thinking.

[5] Reports by civil liberties organisations provide considerable evidence of the growing trends of state repressions and violence in Indian society. See the reports by the Andhra Pradesh Civil Liberties Committee (APCLC), People's Union for Democratic Rights (PUDR), People's Union for Civil Liberties (PUCL), All India Federation of Organisations of Democratic Rights (AIFODR), People's Rights Organisation (PRO), among others (also see Desai 1989).

REFERENCES

Chandhoke, N. 1994. 'Of States and Civil Societies', in Neera Chandhoke (ed.), *Understanding the Post-Colonial World: Theory and Method*. New Delhi: Sterling Publishers and Nehru Memorial Museum and Library.

Desai, A. R. (ed.). 1989. *Violations of Democratic Rights in India*. Bombay: Popular Prakashan.

Haragopal, G. and C. Chandrasekhar. 1994. 'The State Apparatus in the Third World', in Neera Chandhoke (ed.), *Understanding the Post-Colonial World: Theory and Method*. New Delhi: Sterling Publishers and Nehru Memorial Museum and Library.

Jan Vikas Andolan. 1990. 'Perspective Statement'. *Lokayan Bulletin.* Vol. 8. No. 1.

Joseph, S. 1994. 'Culture and Political Analysis in India' in Neera Chandhoke (ed.), *Understanding The Post-Colonial World: Theory and Method.* New Delhi: Sterling Publishers and Nehru Memorial Museum and Library.

Kothari, R. 1990. 'The Rise of People's Movements'. *Social Action.* Vol. 40. 3 July–September.

Kothari, R. 1988. *State Against Democracy: In Search of Humane Governance.* Delhi: Ajanta Publications.

Mohanty, M. 1977. *Revolutionary Violence: A Study of the Maoist Movement in India.* New Delhi: Sterling Publishers.

Mohanty, M. 1989. 'Changing Terms of Discount: A Poser'. *Economic and Political Weekly.* Vol. 24. No. 37.

Mohanty, M. 1990a. 'Changing Terms of Discourse and People's Democratic Movements in India', in *Indo-French Relations: History and Perspective.* New Delhi: French Cultural Centre.

Mohanty, M. 1990b. 'Duality of the State Process in India', in Ghanshyam Shah (ed.), *Capitalist Development: Critical Essays.* Bombay: Popular Prakashan.

Mohanty, M. 1990c. 'Indian State: The Emerging Trends'. *Social Action.* Vol. 40. No. 3.

Mohanty, M. 1990d. 'The Political Economy of Development in China: Socialism in the Freedom Scale'. *China Report.* Vol. 26(I).

Mohanty, M. 1990e. 'Socialism Tomorrow'. *Janata.* Annual Number. June

Mohanty, M. 1991. 'On Democratic Humanism: A Review of Rajni Kothari's Recent Works'. *Contributions to Indian Sociology* (n.s.). Vol. 25(I).

Mohanty, M. (ed.). 1992. *Chinese Revolution: Comparative Perspectives* on *Transformation of Non-Western Societies.* Delhi: Ajanta Publications.

Mohanty, M. 1993. 'Right to Earth'. *PUCL Bulletin.* December.

Mohanty, M. 1994. 'Swaraj and Jiefang: Freedom Discourse in India and China', in Neera Chandhoke (ed.), *Understanding the Post-Colonial World: Theory and Method.* New Delhi: Sterling Publishers and Nehru Memorial Museum and Library.

Omvedt, G. 1994. *Reinventing Revolution: New Social Movements and Socialist Tradition* in *India.* New York: Sharpe.

Omvedt, G. 1994. *Dalits and the Democratic Revolution: Dr Ambedkar and the Dalit Movement* in *Colonial lndia.* New Delhi: Publications India Pvt. Ltd.

Selden, M. 1971. *The Yenan Way in Revolutionary, China,* Cambridge, Massachuttes: Harvard University Press.

Shah, G. 1990. *Social Movements in India: A Review of the Literature.* New Delhi: Sage Publications India Pvt. Ltd.

Sheth, D. L. 1992. 'Movements, Intellectuals and the State: Social Policy in Nation-Building'. *Economic and Political Weekly.* Vol. 7:7. No. 8.

Singh, R. 1993. *Five Essays in the Marxian Mode.* Delhi: Ajanta Publications.

WHITHER THE INDIAN POLITY?

12

Transformation of the Indian Political Party System

M. P. Singh and Kyoung-Hee Koh

This chapter purports to analyse the transformation of the Indian political party system since the nation's independence in 1947. In doing so, this chapter does a historical review of the evolution of the party system between 1952 and 2009 Lok Sabha elections, followed by an empirical analysis of the pattern of fractionalisation of the party system and coalescence of political forces in federal Parliament. This analysis clearly demonstrates a long-term transition from one-party dominance to a multiparty configuration with coalitional governance. The latest general elections of 2004 and 2009 have confirmed that the year 1989 was indeed a turning point in Indian politics. Over half-a-century of parameter-altering changes in the society and party system discussed here have occurred under the federal Constitution that India adopted in 1949–50. This constitutional continuity in the midst of great political, social and economic changes must be rated as a rare, rather unique one for a developing polity. India joined the democratic odyssey during the 'second wave' of democracy at the end of World War II and remains committed to it. The world is now passing through a 'third wave' that set off in the mid-1970s and continued through the political upheavals of the 1980s–90s, and our own immediate neighbourhood in the early years of the twenty-first century.[1]

TRANSITION OF THE PARTY SYSTEM

The transition of India's party system since Independence may be divided into three discernible phases of evolution: (a) the period of one party consensual dominance under the aegis of the Indian National Congress (INC) during the prime ministership of Jawaharlal Nehru, Lal Bahadur Shastri and Indira Gandhi (1952–67), (b) the erosion of Congress dominance and its personalisation around Indira Gandhi's personality cult, the gradual building up of oppositional politics within the party system, mass movements in the 1970s and the return to electoral politics in 1977 following the internal 'Constitutional Emergency' (1975–7), and (c) the onset of federal politics within the political framework of fragmented multipartism

Table 12.1: Rae Index and Effective No. of Parties in Relation To Lok Sabha Elections 1952–99

Election Year	Rae Index	Effective No. of Parties
1952	0.444	1.799
1957	0.440	1.786
1962	0.463	1.862
1967	0.686	3.185
1971	0.530	2.128
1977	0.620	2.632
1980	0.537	2.160
1984	0.410	1.694
1989	0.757	4.115
1991	0.722	3.597
1996	0.830	5.882
1998	0.814	5.376
1999	0.831	5.917

Note and source: The statistical indicators are computed on election data from Arend Lijphart, *Electoral System and Party Systems*. New York: Oxford University Press, 1994, 169–72; Robert L. Hardgrave and Stanley Kochanek, *India: Government and Politics in a Developing Nation*, Fort Worth: Harcourt College Publishers, 1993, 321; and Election Commission of India Statistical Reports of General Election, 1991–9, http://www.eci.gov.in.

under the Janata Dal (JD)-led Third Front coalition governments, or Bharatiya Janata Party (BJP)-led bipolar coalition governments (1989 onwards), or the INC-led bipolar coalition governments (2004 onwards). The computed statistical properties of the phases of this periodisation are presented in Table 12.1.

CONSENSUAL ONE-PARTY DOMINANCE

Multiparty general elections in 1952, 1957 and 1962 produced one-party majority governments under the INC, the party which spearheaded post-Independence economic development in a mixed economy, with the state undertaking the lead role in a planned strategy of industrialisation. The consensual nature of the Indian political enterprise during these defining decades was maintained through a rare synergy of the 1950 Constitution, the first three five-year plans, a carryover of much of the meritocratic bureaucratic structure of the British Raj, and a pluralist approach to the party system and trade union movement under the political dominance of INC at the Centre as well as in the states. The dominant party was still led by a collective national leadership under Nehru that had fought for and won India's freedom. These were the heady days of Prometheus Unbound, despite the pains of Partition and communal riots and the largest movement of refugees in history across newly-demarcated borders in the wake of India's 'tryst with destiny' that Nehru heralded at the midnight hour on 14–15 August, 1947. During these years robust optimism was sustained with reasonable measures of political and economic development in comparison to rudimentary advances made in these respects during the British Raj. The future looked good, and what is more important within grasp, given the right perspective and perseverance. The crisis of implementation and good governance had not yet become as glaring as it did later.

In the literature on politics in India, its party system until at least the mid-1970s was variously conceptualised and hypothesised as the 'Congress system' (Kothari 1964; 1970; 1974), 'one-party dominant system' (Morris-Jones 1964, 1978) and 'predominant party system' (Sartori 1976). This means that despite legally-permitted multiparty elections, one party—the Indian National Congress—was repeatedly returned to power with an absolute majority during this period. The Congress, a colossal 'party of consensus' (in ideological as well as sociological terms) was surrounded by smaller 'parties of pressure' that functioned more like interest groups than parties due to their remote probability of coming to power singly or even as part of a coalition under the then prevailing political atmosphere. The pattern of interaction among the marginal opposition parties and the various factions in the dominant party was such that the opposition was more efficacious in concert with ideologically, regionally, and sociologically contiguous factions within the ruling party rather than in neat government-opposition demarcations. The 'middling' democratic centripetality of the dominant party also meant that die-hard right-left, centralist, regionalist, secular-communal, nationalist, communist and internationalist political forces were more distant from each other, and therefore discordant compared to the concordant/congenial factional elements within the ruling party. These qualitative features characterising the dynamics of the 'Congress system' in this phase of the Indian party system are insightfully sketched in the literature cited above. What we attempt in this chapter is to present some aggregate statistical measurements and analysis of some key political indicators pertaining to the evolution of the party system of India over half-a-century of electoral democracy. These elections were based on universal adult franchise introduced in a rush in a country lacking in the conventional socio-economic preconditions or correlations of political democracy conceptualised on the basis of the first wave of democracy in post-feudal Western Europe, North America, and Commonwealth of Nations. This we consider is a meaningful exercise and contribution to the current theoretical explorations of democratic consolidation in comparative political theory. For the party system has commonly been singled out as an important factor to explain the relatively better governmental stability in India in the early post-independence decades than in the past two decades. India is said to be slipping into a deepening crisis of governability.

Arresting this trend is crucial to democratic consolidation in the world's largest democracy and peace and stability in the South Asian region and the Afro-Asian macro-region.

Table 12.1 presents political indicators pertaining to the growth of the Indian party system since the first general elections in 1952. These are (a) effective number of parties computed by using Laakso-Taagepera index (1979) devised for this purpose, and (b) Rae index (1971) of fractionalisation of the parliamentary party system. These two measures validate our characterisation of the first phase of the Indian party system as 'consensual one-party dominance'. Even though the number of parties between 1952 and 1962 in gross terms is very large, their effective number in terms of the mean for the same period is only 1.82. The value of the Rae index of fractionalisation is also fairly low at 0.45. In other words, the party system is highly integrated and there is decisive dominance of one party, the Indian National Congress.

DOMINANCE WITH DISSENT

The fourth general elections in 1967 marked the first major electoral breach in the Congress system. This was the first post-Nehru electoral exercise after the first Prime Minister's demise on 27 May, 1964. Besides the cumulative anti-incumbency factor in place for over a period of two decades, several variables factored in to produce this first rout of the Congress in major north Indian states and Tamil Nadu, and a considerably reduced majority for the party in the Lok Sabha. In the backdrop of Nehru's failing health, the regional party bosses in the country took steps towards a kind of collective Congress leadership to take over once Nehru was gone from the political scene. The journalists nicknamed this emergent post-Nehru collective Congress leadership as the 'Syndicate'. The political atmosphere in the country at large was, however, changing fast in the backdrop of India's military debacle in the Indo-Chinese war in 1962 and a severe famine in north India a year before the 1967 elections. The war with communist China dealt a severe blow to Nehru's health as well as to the strength of the influential left-wing within the Congress Party. The Union Defence Minister, V. K. Krishna Menon, a 'cryptocommunist', was sacrificed as a scapegoat. The Congress Chief Minister of Maharashtra, Y. B. Chavan, a former Congress Socialist, was drafted into the Union Cabinet as the new defence minister. This at least partly balanced the scales in favour of the Congress right-wingers who had been cooling their heels since 1963 when the Congress president, K. Kamaraj, manoeuvred a party re-organisation plan. Under this, all Union ministers and chief ministers were prompted to resign to give the shell-shocked Prime Minister a last opportunity to reshuffle his government, in which top right-wing Union ministers had borne the brunt of retirement from the Cabinet to make them available for organisational work.

Nehru's death in May 1964 prompted the right-wing old guard to reassert itself the first time since Vallabhbhai Patel's death in December 1950 in the affairs of the government and the party, which had become Nehru's prerogative after the passing into history of what Brecher (1966) called the 'Nehru-Patel diumvirate'. But with the old guard divided among themselves over the issue of Nehru's successor party president K. Kamaraj managed to play a balancing role of the kingmaker in the emergent collective leadership conclave that decided on the successor to the first Prime Minister in 1964 and to the second prime minister in 1966. Lal Bahadur Shastri was given the nod after Nehru, and on the former's death at Tashkent, Indira Gandhi was co-opted for the job. Morarji Desai, the strong-willed Gandhian patriarch and a known right-winger among the old guards, was bypassed on both these occasions.

Shastri's unexpectedly good showing as the Prime Minister in the Indo-Pakistan war of 1965 was washed away on account of his perceived capitulation under international pressure to return the territories conquered by the Indian army in its response to Pakistani aggression, a surrender that Indira Gandhi was not to repeat in 1971–2 during the wake of the Bangladesh war. The 1967 general elections held in this backdrop proved to be a veritable wet blanket for the ruling party, resulting in its defeat in half of the states. However, the patchwork catch-all coalition governments which comprised political forces from the left through the centre to the right under the omnibus non-Congressional canopy did not offer much of an alternative to write home about.

Following Shastri's sudden death at Tashkent in the winter of 1965–6, Indira Gandhi, for her perceived amenability as a 'dumb-doll', was nominated by the party hierarchs to head the Congress parliamentary party and its government. Gandhi used the power and patronage of the premiership and the popularity of the Nehru dynasty decisively and dexterously to salvage the uncertain fortunes of the Congress and turned to populist economic policies and political ploys more appropriate to an illiberal democracy. She used the antlers of prime ministerial power and manoeuvred to force out the old guard from the party by splitting it in 1969. Two years later she registered a resounding electoral victory in the snap parliamentary elections of 1971 on the catchy slogan of *garibi hatao*. Towards the end of the same year the democratic experiment in Pakistan failed and the religion-based 'two-nation theory' on which it was founded unravelled causing an explosion of linguistic nationalism in East Bengal. India was forced to intervene militarily in the imbroglio as the Northeast came under a demographic 'aggression' due to a massive influx of refugees that exceeded the local population in Tripura and threatened to do so elsewhere.

But, despite overwhelming parliamentary and state legislative majorities, Indira Gandhi's illiberal behaviour provoked protests from the judiciary, students, party and non-party oppositional forces and socialist trade unions. The socialist-turned-Gandhian Jayaprakash Narayan was drafted from virtual political retirement to provide an overall leadership to this movement against the authoritarian Congress-Communist Party of India combine (minus Communist Party of India-Marxist that preferred to join the democratic populist thrust pitted against authoritarian populism led by Indira Gandhi). Both Gandhi and JP claimed to act democratically and invoked principles of periodicity of electoral mandate in a republican or representative democracy or recall in a participatory direct democracy. But under the specific context of the 1970s, actions of both these leaders were fraught with dangers of Third World authoritarianism or a slide into fascist populism. In the event, both of these outcomes were averted, thanks to the electoral intervention of 1977 (Chandra 2003).

The four additional landmarks of the turbulent 1980s–90s were (a) the rout of the Indira Gandhi-led Congress in the post-Emergency elections of 1977–8 in the north; (b) the emergence of the de facto Janata Party coalition government comprising five non-Congress/non-Communist opposition parties in New Delhi and major north Indian states that gradually fizzled out by 1979–80; (c) the electoral restoration of Indira Gandhi's Congress in 1980; and (d) a massive electoral landslide in favour of Rajiv Gandhi following his mother's assassination in 1984 following a police/military action to flush out Sikh terrorists from the Golden Temple in Amritsar. Riding on the 'sympathy wave' for the fallen Congress matriarch, Rajiv Gandhi was voted to power in the centenary year of the Congress with an electoral mandate which surpassed even those for Nehru and Indira Gandhi. But, as it happened, it was an electoral tide that was gained without merit and was lost by 1989. Rajiv Gandhi was assassinated by the LTTE while impressively campaigning for his party in 1991 in Tamil Nadu.

The raw number of parties between 1971 and 1984 ranged between 26 and 17, averaging at 20.75. The mean value of the effective number of parties during this phase in terms of the Laakso-Taagepapra index was 2.36. The Rae index of party system fractionalisation meaned at 0.56. This degree of fragmentation would appear to be even more magnified if we bear in mind the high level of dissent and protest as evidenced by the extra-parliamentary mass protest movement mentioned above.

FRAGMENTED MULTIPARTISM

The elections of 1989 marked India's entry into the phase of fragmented multipartism as a systemic feature. Since then coalition and/or minority governments have governed India. This period featured the Janata Dal-led Third Front, National Front and United Front governments, a Congress minority government headed by

P. V. Narasimha Rao, the BJP-led National Democratic Alliance (NDA) governments, and Congress-led United Progressive Alliance (UPA) governments. The trend so far appears to be marked by a shift from (a) one-party minority government to multi-party coalitional minority governments, and (b) from Third Front coalitions without the Congress, on the one hand, and the BJP on the other, to bipolar coalitions led by the BJP and the Congress respectively. This has reduced the Third Front to a gradually dwindling third force. The Third Front comprised the Janata Dal, the communist parties, and myriad other regional parties. With the fragmentation of all-India parties like the Congress and Janata Dal having a middle-of-the road programmatic orientation and with a right-ward lurch in the party system, regional parties have mushroomed since 1989 and forced a change in the 'go-it-alone' temperament of the two larger national parties—the Congress and BJP—making them scramble for regional allies. Even though the Congress still continues as the single largest party in the system in terms of the electoral vote share in the Lok Sabha (not necessarily in Lok Sabha seats), the BJP has been relatively more successful in building bridges with the regional parties, since in many states the regional parties face the Congress as their main opponent. The Congress being the dominant political force for so long in the past initially repelled allies both due to its stiff upper lip and also because of the antipathy of its past victims.

The much maligned Hindu majoritarian temperament of the BJP is largely a political myth. This party was politically 'untouchable' until the other day due to its political sin of practicing 'communal' politics, but has subsequently overcome this handicap by dropping the more overtly communal items from its agenda due to compulsions of coalition politics. In any case, there is difference of degree in the communalism practiced by the BJP and its cultural allies—the Rashtriya Swayamsevak Sangh (RSS), Vishwa Hindu Parishad (VHP) and Bajrang Dal. The BJP is not above the temptation to exploit to the full its Hindu communal as well as secular constitutional connections. In fact, no political party in India today can claim to be conscientiously beyond the pale of this temptation of exploiting communalism, either in its 'soft' or 'hard' versions. Security threats, the scare of 'religion in danger' among minorities as well as national provincial majorities, increasing replacement of populist politics by an Indian version of the spoils system in political as well as corporate governance, high incidence of societal violence, existence of draconian laws, and ambiguous civil rights situation at times have all tended to lend a halo of illiberality to Indian democracy in the post-Nehru phase. However, thanks to continuing multiparty elections, the pluralist rather than corporatist structure of pressure group politics, an independent mass media, a well-entrenched mass education system, excellent enclaves of natural and social science research establishments under public as well as private management, judicial independence and statutory framework of National Human Rights Commission and Minorities Commission, it would be wrong to write off India's credentials as a promising 'Third World' liberal democracy.

The raw number of parties since 1989 range between 27 in the base year (1989), 40 in 1998, and 39 in 1999. The number of effective parties computed by the Lasakso-Taagepara formula ranges between 4.115 in 1989 and 5.917 in 1999. The mean value of this index for the phase is 4.977. The Rae index of party system fractionalisation for this phase is also consistently higher, ranging from 0.757 in 1989 and 0.831 in 1999, meaning at 0.791.

Of the raw number of parties in the 1990s, seven or eight have been national parties, while there have been as many as 34 state and registered unrecognised parties in 1999 in terms of the Election Commission of India's classification. Once registered, parties fall into the category of state parties or fall into the nominal/residual category of a registered party by being denied classification as national or state parties until they qualify by virtue of electoral performance in the polls (Strangely, the commission does not weed out any party once it is registered!).

Following the two Lok Sabha elections in the 2000s—in 2004 and 2009—the ongoing pattern of the party system fragmentation more or less continued under the Congress-led UPA governing coalition, though the situation slightly improved in 2009. The raw number of parties represented in Parliament was 43 in 2004 and 34 in 2009. Between the two elections, the Congress-led

UPA consolidated itself considerably as its strength rose from 215 seats in 2004 to 261 in 2009. The position of the Congress also improved from 145 seats to 201, making it less vulnerable to internal armtwisting by its coalition partners. The BJP-led NDA continued to decline, going down from 186 seats to 159 during this period. The party's own lot went down from 138 seats to 121. Other parties outside these two major coalitions led by the two main national parties found their seats reduced from 136 in 2004 to 124 in 2009, the Left parties suffering a precipitous fall from 59 seats to 24. The effort to consolidate a third force in a Front before and during the 2009 election turned out to be infructuous. As it happened, the Third Front comprising the Left parties and some other regional players like the Bahujan Samaj Party (BSP), Biju Janata Dal, AIADMK, Telugu Desam Party (TDP), Janata Dal (Secular) won 79 seats, while a Fourth Front consisting of nine parties, mainly the Samajwadi Party and the Rashtriya Janata Dal (Bihar) bagged just 27 seats. The combined vote share of the UPA (37.22 per cent) and NDA (24.63 per cent) stood at 61.85 per cent. The vote share of the main national parties leading these alliances was 28.55 per cent for the Congress and 18.80 per cent for the BJP.

How do we explain the denouement of the system of fragmented multipartism since the 1990s, and the apparent passing into history of the earlier phases of one-party pluralist dominance in the Nehru era and the over centralised one-party dominance with mass movement dissent in the Indira Gandhi era? For one thing, it is difficult not to feel that the putative Congress dominance never really amounted to hegemony. For another, neither socio-economic nor political formations in India conform to either a mutually reinforcing cultural cleavage structure or to the polarised class structure of an advanced industrial society. Hence, with the legacy of the anti-colonial nationalist generation of leadership gone, it became increasingly difficult to aggregate the growing political differentiations and politicised identities and interests of the Indian society under the antecedently or a newly-emergent dominant party. It is not easy to quantify a discrete set of factors and values from a continuous range of causal probabilities to neatly explain how the current phase of fractionalised multipartism has come into existence.

We attempt, however, an explanatory sketch here in terms of a set of sociological and politico-economic factors in a complex web of causation at work for over half-a-century of democratic politics in the country. There was, to begin with, a concomitant decline in the capacity of the Indian National Congress to accommodate increasingly differentiated multiple societal cleavages at the same time as in its ability to reconcile the vaulting political ambition of its post-Nehru leadership. The major Congress splits of 1969 and 1978 and after may be largely understood in these terms.

Something akin to an unraveling of the organic traditional unity of the social structure has been underway without a commensurate set of electoral and party reforms to help funnel societal differentiations into a viable party system functionally consistent with the structural requirements of parliamentary and federal governance in India. We will return to this reformist theme in a subsequent section of this chapter. Meanwhile, it is important to note the cumulative effects of the political and economic rise of the predominantly Other Backward Classes (OBC) peasantry reflected in the electoral outcomes in 1967, 1977 and 1989. This was symbolically demonstrated by the appointment of the Second, Backward Classes Commission (chaired by B. P. Mandal, a neo-rich agriculturist Yadav leader of Janata Party from Bihar) in 1978, and the implementation of its recommendation for OBC reservations (besides scheduled castes/ tribes) in Central government jobs in 1990 by the Janata Dal-led National Front government in New Delhi. This decision extended a south Indian model of public reservation policy to the Union level. The Janata Party government led by Karpoori Thakur had already introduced OBC reservations in Bihar in 1978. The Janata Dal government headed by Mulayam Singh Yadav followed suit in Uttar Pradesh too in 1993. These events marked the ascendance of OBC peasant power that was to be checkmated by the mid-1990s and by the rise of Hindutva forces under the political leadership of BJP, and the assertion of dalit political power in Maharashtra, Punjab and ultimately Uttar Pradesh mainly under the BSP led by the Kanshi Ram-Mayawati duo. Important also was the articulation of linguistic, religious and tribal regionalism in Assam and Andhra Pradesh in the 1980s–90s, in addition to such previously existing political phenomenon in Tamil Nadu, Punjab, Jammu and Kashmir and the Northeast.

The shriller temper of identity politics in India today has ethnicised and regionalised the party system, which in turn has considerably held in check the earlier trend of parliamentary/executive, centralisation of power in the Union government. It instead encouraged a process of political federalisation to a degree unknown in the past. In tune with the new federal fervour in the political system, the temper of judicial behaviour has also changed to interpret the Constitution in a way that has facilitated a more autonomous functioning for state governments. The Supreme Court's ruling in the S. R. Bommai and Others v. the Union of India (1994), for instance, marked a radical departure from the past inasmuch as the Union government's decision to proclaim President's Rule in a state under Article 356 of the Constitution was made subject to judicial review. The courts had previously considered this a 'political thicket', best left to the final discretion of the Government of India.

The Supreme Court was also called upon to arbitrate on OBC reservations in the Mandal Case (1993) to rationalise this controversial public policy. It ruled that (a) more advanced sections of the OBCs ('the creamy layer') must be excluded from the benefits of reservations, and (b) in order to balance the scale between past caste-based disadvantage and current discriminations, a complete dissociation of reservation from caste criterion (i.e., for economically backward upper castes) would be inconsistent with the Constitution. The latter point is presently under political review as the erstwhile Congress Chief Minister of Rajasthan Ashok Gehlot (summer 2003) voiced support for introducing reservations for the poor among the upper castes, while the BJP-led NDA government promised to set up a constitutional commission for considering the issue of reservations for economically backward classes and review of the list of OBCs. This was finally not done. The reservation policy having grown into a sprawling federal jungle with myriad Union-State(s) variations and distortions, the judiciary may have a difficult job in its hands rationalising this.

The Hindu-Muslim row over Ayodhya has been at the hub of the Indian party system since the early 1990s and a BJP sheet-anchor in electoral mobilisation until at least the round of Assembly elections in the last quarter of the year 2003. The issue refuses to recede into the background both on account of the exacerbation of the politics of faith in South Asia, especially because of the India-Pakistan factor, which is a festering thorn in the regional flesh. But thanks to India's determined pursuit of the federal democratic option in Jammu and Kashmir and elsewhere, the People's Democratic Party (PDP)-Congress coalition government chaired by Mufti Mohammad Syed sat on the saddle in the aftermath of a free and fair election in the state towards the year-end 2002. The arrangement was that each party would alternatively head the ministry for a period of three years each. In the 2008 assembly election, the NC formed the government with the support of the Congress.

Finally since 1991, the Indian party system is adapting to a paradigm shift from a broadly Keynesian economic policy regime to a policy framework oriented towards neo-liberal economic reforms receptive to privatisation and capitalist globalisation. In the context of the deepening crisis of political or welfare liberalism of the state, the Congress government headed by P. V. Narasimha Rao accelerated the policy of enhanced business liberalism or marketisation. A broad consensus on these economic reforms is evident across party lines, and therefore the major direction of the policy has continued largely unaltered despite frequent change of guards from the centrist Congress through Janata Dal-led left-of-centre United Front to the right-of-centre BJP-led NDA and back to a Congress-led UPA coalition. The pace of reforms has, of course, varied under all these administrations, the slowdown mainly manoeuvered to trim the sails to real or apprehended electoral reprisals and disasters. The real test for the durability of the present policy consensus lies, however, in the future. Political or welfare liberalism has admittedly gone awry due to the crisis of political governability and the public sector failure in a large number of cases. Nonetheless, business liberalism may be good primarily for the market, but it tends to accentuate inequities in society and polity in terms of class, ethnic, and regional disparities over time. Whether the new policy paradigm engenders a better quality of life and human development for all, and raises the party political processes and social movements, governmental and non-governmental organisations to a higher level of political and economic integration within and among the nations of South Asia is a big question mark for the future. Indeed, the emergence of a global recession in 2008 has had some effect on India, though India with its economy, still somewhat regulated, has fared relatively well.

ELECTORAL AND PARTY SYSTEM REFORMS

The Indian electoral and party system suffers from two dysfunctionalities that got aggravated in the post-Nehru period. First, corrupt and criminal elements among the political class have cast a shadow particularly over the past few decades (Singh 2002), and second, fragmentation of party system since 1989 has made formation and maintenance of federal coalition governments, comprising nearly a dozen or two dozen parties with jumbo size ministries, extremely difficult (Singh and Saxena 2003: chap 7).

A major critique of the plural electoral law that relates to the distortion between the vote and seat shares during the Congress party's dominance in the Nehru and Indira Gandhi era is now seldom made. For with the decline of one-party dominance, social and regional diversities of India are very inadequately aggregated into larger number of parties resulting into an extreme party system fragmentation. Thus, even without formally having proportional electoral law, India has come to have, for all practical purposes, the typical effect of proportional representation. Of course, formally adopting proportionality may aggravate party system fragmentation still more.[2]

It was symptomatic of the approach of the framers of the Indian Constitution that while they made the longest basic law for the country in the world, they left the party system entirely to be evolved through convention.[3] Elections, to be sure got a chapter (Part XV), but rather a small one with only six articles that do not mention political parties at all. Even parliamentary statutes relevant in this context such as the Representation of the People Act, 1950 and 1951, the Companies Act 1956 (Section 293 A and B), the Income Tax Act, 1961 (Sections 13A and 139A and B), and Foreign Contribution (Regulation) Act, 1976 (Sections 4, 5, and 6) mention political parties incidentally in the larger framework of representation and economic laws. The Anti-Defection Act, 1985, and the related 52nd Constitutional Amendment refer to political parties directly, but only in the limited context of unprincipled floor-crossing of MPs/MLAs (Section 3). The Xth Schedule of the Constitution added by the 52nd Amendment has nothing to do with organisation and working of political parties as vital links between the state and the civil society.

Thus the founding fathers of the Indian Republic preferred not to legislate a party system. In adopting this approach, they were perhaps influenced by the British and the Commonwealth of Nations, where parties have grown as a matter of convention, without constitutional or legal fiat. The makers were also probably reassured by the vigour of the civic action which emanated from the civil society during the freedom struggle.

Given the growing pathology of the party system in India, at least two major reforms appear necessary. The first of these must address to the problem of corruption and criminality; and the second, the problem of extreme fragmentation often making governments chronically unstable. The Report of the National Commission to Review the Working of the Constitution (NCRWC Vol. I 2002: chap. 4) makes a radical departure from the previous approach to the party system as reflected in the Constituent Assembly in recommending a comprehensive legislation regulating organisations, electoral activities, and funding of political parties in a transparent, legitimate, and legally and socially accountable way. The commission also goes on to encourage political parties to adopt, on their own initiative, the national convention system for electing party leaders (as in Canada).[4] Besides being consistent with the parliamentary-federal constitution of India, the election of the prime minister and opposition party leaders in Parliament by party delegates from various states at a national party convention (rather than by party MPs) would give the leaders a larger, federal constituency and a nation-wide pre-election visibility. This will introduce a federal aggregation process in the party-political processes and arrest the extreme fragmention of parties along ethnic and regional lines.

ENDNOTES

[1] On 'waves' of democratisation in comparative politics, see Huntington (1991).

[2] Duverger (1963: 217) and Riker (1982: 762–4) theorise that plurality or first-past-the post system of electoral representation generally results in a two-party system, while a proportional system commonly produces a multiparty system. In the words of Riker, 'In short, when the definition of winning forces candidates to maximise votes in order to win (as in plurality system), they have strong motives to create a two-party system; but when the definition of winning does not require them to maximise votes (as in the runoff proportional system), then this motive for two parties is absent'. This hypothesis is largely borne out in culturally homogeneous Western liberal democracies. The Indian experience does not bear this out. For the homogenising effect of the nationalist movement against colonial rule engendered a one-party dominant system earlier, and subsequently as this legacy became weak there emerged a multiparty system. In both these phases India consistently followed plurality in electoral law. The hypothesis also needs to be tested with data from the party systems in Indian states.

[3] In his final address to the Constituent Assembly, B. R. Ambedkar, the chairman of the drafting committee, remarked that the success of the Constitution would be primarily contingent on growth of democratic culture, conventions and good administration (See the *Constituent Assembly Debates.* Book 5: 575–82). I wish he had not omitted political parties in this context. The decline of the party system today is proving to be the Achilles Heel for Indian democracy.

[4] Political parties in Canada, which is also a parliamentary-federal system much like India, adopted national leadership conventions in the early

decades of the twentieth century (See Bakvis 1990). At the national party conventions, Canadian delegates vote as individuals, while in national party conventions in the federal-presidential USA all delegates from a state vote as a bloc.

REFERENCES

Bakvis, Herman (ed.). 1990. 'Canadian Political Parties: Leaders, Candidates and Organizations in Canada'. *Research Studies for Royal Commission on Electoral Reform and Party Financing*. Toronto: Dundurn Press.

Brecher, Michael. 1966. *Political Succession in India*. Delhi: Oxford University Press.

Chandra, Bipan. 2003. *In the Name of Democracy: JP Movement and the Emergency*. New Delhi: Penguin Books.

Duverger, M. 1963. *Political Parties* (trans. from the French). New York: John Wiley Science Education.

Huntington, S. P. 1991. *The Third Wave: Democratisation in the Late Twentieth Century*. Norman and London: University of Oklahoma Press.

India (Republic). 1999. *The Constituent Assembly Debates, Official Report*. Book 5. New Delhi: Lok Sabha Secretariat (Third Reprint).

India (Republic). 2002. *Review of the Constitution: Report of The National Commission to Review the Working of the Constitution*. Website: http://Iawmin.nic.in/ncrwC/finalreport.htm. Accessed in April 2002.

Kothari, Rajni. 1964. 'The Congress System in India'. *Asian Survey*. Vol. 4(12) December.

Kothari, Rajni. 1970. *Politics in India*. New Delhi: Orient Longman.

Kothare, Rajni. 1974. 'Congress System in India Revisited'. *Asian Survey*. Vol. 4(12). December.

Laasko, M. and R. Taagepera. 1979. 'Effective Number of Parties: A Measure with Application to Western Europe'. *Comparative Political Studies*. Vo1. 12.

Mehra, A. K., D. D. Khanna, and G.W. Kueck (ed.). 2003. *Political Parties and Party Systems*. New Delhi: Sage Publications.

Morris-Jones, W. H. 1964. *The Government and Politics of lndia*. London: Hutchinson.

Morris-Jones, W. H. 1978. *Politics Mainly Indian*. New Delhi: Orient Longman.

Rae, Donglas W. 1971. *The Political Consequences of Electoral Law*. New Haven: Yale University Press.

Riker, W. H. 1982. 'The Two-Party System and Duverger's Law: An Essay on the History of Political Science'. *The American Political Science Review*. Vol. 76.

Sartori, Giovanni. 1976. *Parties and Party Systems: A Framework of Analysis*. Cambridge: Cambridge University Press.

Singh, M. P. 2002. 'Constitutionalism and Democracy in India: Electoral and Party Reforms Key to Survival', in R. N. Pal (ed.), *Indian Constitution: A Review*. Chandigarh: Centre for Rural and Industrial Development.

Singh, M. P. and Rekha Saxena. 2003. *India at the Polls: Parliamentary Elections in the Federal Phase*. New Delhi: Orient Longman.

13

The Paradoxes of Indian Politics

Achin Vanaik

Ask anyone who knows and cares about India and what its greatest achievement has been since independence, and the answer is obvious. For all the turmoil, upheavals and chaos that has taken place in an ever-changing India—the political assassinations, the social eruptions both positive and negative, the tensions created by the enormous contrasts between the rich and poor, city and village—the one seeming constant (barring the Emergency interlude) has been the remarkable endurance of its liberal-democratic political system. As the clichè goes, India is the world's largest democracy and this does mean something important.

The great British social historian, E. P. Thompson put his finger on the uniqueness of India in the world comity of nations when he said that no other country was, or is, as much of a confluence of ideas (old and new, good and bad) pertaining to politics and art, literature and science, society and economy, as India. 'All the convergent influences of the world run through this society: Hindu, Muslim, Christian, secular, Stalinist, liberal, Maoist, democratic, socialist, Gandhian. There is not a thought that is being thought in the West or East that is not active in some Indian mind. The struggle then, between the positive and the negative, between the forces of the past, the present and the future in India, held lessons for every other country and peoples. India's trajectory in the years and decades to come therefore held at least a small, but not insignificant, mirror to their own future possibilities and prospects. Every country should be interested in the ongoing Indian experiment.

Though one fully shares the belief so eloquently expressed by Thompson, this short presentation does not intend to trace that incredible variety of ideas, movements and options that so impressed the British Indophile. Even a narrative account that has the much more modest aim of simply recounting the main lines of the story of India's political development from 1947 to the turn of the new millennium would be difficult enough. Here one rests content with framing the canvas on which one might attempt such a portrayal, and to do this in the somewhat elliptical manner, perhaps, of pointing out thirteen paradoxes of Indian society. The term 'paradox' is being used in a somewhat imprecise manner to suggest not just seeming or actual contradictions but tensions, contrasts and peculiarities. In adopting this form of presentation one hopes to illuminate certain key features of the Indian political and social landscape, in particular the six ongoing processes whose complex and unpredictable interweaving are shaping the present and future. These are the forward march of the backward or intermediate castes, the slow and unsteady forward movement of Hindutva, dalit assertion, Muslim ferment, the regionalisation of the Indian polity, the emergence of what is called the Indian Middle Class (IMC) as the mass social base promoting the rise of a more clearly and explicitly right-wing politics pulling away from the country's past and traditional 'centrist' fulcrum.

Since the mid-eighties, Indian politics has entered a situation of deep flux. Of course, the Indian polity had begun this entry into uncertainty earlier on. But the pace and scale of turmoil greatly increased from the mid-eighties onwards. The more cautious turn towards economic liberalisation in the eighties gave way qualitatively to the neo-liberal turn carried out in 1991, and this through its polarising effects has played its part in creating further turbulence. But this narrative will not discuss these economic changes. Nor will it do more than cite (without further elaboration) the five landmark political events that have been signposts marking and directing the journey travelled by India so far. These are of such profound importance that they deserve separate and detailed treatment. Chronologically, these have been the Emergency (1975–77), Mandal (1990–91), Babri Masjid (1992), Pokharan II (1998), the Gujarat Pogrom (Spring–Summer 2002). Four of these landmark events have taken place after the beginning of the nineties—testimony to the dramatic 'political acceleration' that has taken place in the last fifteen years. So much so that despite the legacy of an enduring democratic polity, the future looks more unclear and open-ended in this regard than ever before. In a very real sense a battle for the 'soul of Indian nationalism' and over the persistence and substance of its democratic polity is taking place.

What then are these paradoxes? We can take the first two paradoxes together.

- From its very inception, structures appropriate to a modern political democracy were inserted into a socio-economic system of considerable backwardness.
- India after independence had a comparatively well-developed state in an underdeveloped civil society.

India faced the unique problem of implanting liberal democracy in a predominantly rural society. In the history of every other longstanding and enduring democracy, the consolidation of its structures and norms, in particular, universal suffrage to include women, racial, ethnic and religious minorities, comes only after urbanisation-industrialisation (including industrialisation of agriculture) has already substantially or fully taken place. India institutionalises a liberal-democratic society in a predominantly agricultural society. Here it is the weight not of towns or bourgeoisie but of landlords, farmers, peasants and the rural poor that plays a disproportionately greater role than anywhere else in shaping the character of that democracy.

It was not just the economy or society that created problems. Compared to the advanced industrial democracies, even India's political foundations were weak. Indian democracy was unique in many ways but perhaps its single most important dimension was the disproportionate importance played by one force. This was the

Congress as a party, as a movement, as a government-in-waiting before 1947. After independence, the Congress not only lost its character as a movement, but also became a government-within-a-government. The Congress then played a crucial role in taking over and using the administrative-political apparatuses of British rule, and its role as a system of patronage and vote-gathering, of networking and ensuring transactional exchanges and bargaining in the countryside. All this was crucial to the establishment of a functioning Indian democracy. The story of Indian democracy, of its travails, its strengths and weaknesses is therefore also in large measure the story of the Congress's post-independence evolution, of its strengths and weaknesses, its rise and decline, its changing character.

- At least since the late sixties and early seventies we have had a remarkable combination of endemic political instability at the national level yet remarkable systemic durability overall.

Why the instability? Why the durability? The sources of the first include a number of factors. There is the decline of the Congress. There is the mutation and mutilation of various democratic institutions from the bureaucracy to the judiciary to the public media. There is the rise of India's middle-upper peasantry. There is also the political volatility shown by key minority groups like dalits, tribals and Muslims. There is the extremely uneven character of economic development giving rise not only to highly unequal distribution of living standards and life opportunities but also to rising mass expectations and growing frustrations at their lack of fulfillment.

The sources of the second include the birth and institutionalisation of the structures, however flawed they may be in their practice, of democracy from the electoral system and an effective Election Commission to an independent judiciary to a lively press to a functioning bureaucracy organised on centralised and hierarchical lines. There is the spread of a democratic ethos and commitment to the preservation of a democratic polity amongst the poor and disadvantaged. There is the growing assertiveness of sections of the poorer and lower strata of society. Then also, the growing regionalisation and decentralisation of the polity, the foundations of which were laid down by two fortuitous developments. One was a conscious policy perspective—the linguistic division of states. The second was originally unanticipated but once it came about and was regularised, also proved to be a great stabilising factor—the de-synchronisation of Lok Sabha and state assembly elections.

- On the one hand we have the historic and historical decline of the Congress. On the other we have the inability of any other political formation to fully replace the Congress and its role.

The end result has been the emergence of a political and ideological vacuum or the collapse of what has been called the Nehruvian Consensus. Its four founding principles—now all under attack as never before—were socialism, secularism, democracy, non-alignment. The political forces trying their best to fill this vacuum are the BJP-RSS and the regional political formations. Neither is able to fully take over this space vacated by the Congress, while it is still an open question whether this Congress will further decline, has plateaued, or whether it will make something of a comeback. In the latest 2009 elections the Congress with a small 2 per cent increase in vote share got a very substantial increase in Lok Sabha seats of around 60. This is testimony to the vagaries of a majoritarian electoral system and the overall judgement remains that of an Indian polity in flux, still resistant to any definitive verdict concerning party trajectories. But in any case, ideologically, the centre of gravity of Indian politics has shifted decisively to the right in three crucial areas—economic outlook and policy, interpreting and institutionalising secularism, foreign policy behaviour.

- However unevenly, industrialisation is proceeding apace. This means that the economic and social weight of agricultural elites vis-à-vis urban elites is declining. But their political and cultural weight is not declining.

In a democratic set-up, those who can mobilise votes have a special importance. Rural elites have an advantage here and exercise their influence particularly through regional parties. The rising importance of regional political formations partly reflects the rising influence of such rural lobbies and vested interests. These rural elites seek upward mobility in various ways that give rise to all kinds of complicated combinations. For example, caste mobilisation expands even as the relevant and 'loyal' caste units to be identified and mobilised themselves enlarge. Cultural upward mobility of say, the middle or backward castes pushes them to connect with an encompassing 'Hindu' identity. Therefore, religious processions or *yagnas* of all kinds often obtain the patronage of these aspiring castes. This tends to favour the cultural ambitions of Hindutva. But politically the rising strength of these castes can also push against the BJP because the political vehicles they can more strongly influence and control are regional parties or more federal and loosely structured extra-regional parties rather than the more strongly centralised and internally authoritarian BJP-RSS. What seems to be emerging as a result of these intersecting developments is a 'new social bloc' of upper and higher middle castes, which socially and in terms of their aspirations are converging, and therefore are providing a more or less stable base for coalitional arrangements between certain regional parties and the BJP.

- The countryside decides which political force comes to power. The cities and towns decide the direction the polity takes.

This was true of the National Movement era. It is true today. The BJP remains limited in its rural and lower-class and lower-caste support. But it has made most of the political running in the last fifteen years precisely because it is the one force that has most effectively pursued the politics of mass mobilisation in the cities and towns of India. This was most obviously so during the notorious Ram Janmabhoomi campaign which more than any other single initiative propelled it to national prominence. Yet another obvious example is the New Economic Policy or the post-1991 economic policy changes. Whatever claims might have been made for the benefits provided by these changes to the rural masses (yet to be fulfilled) they have provided significant and immediate benefit to urban elites. India is a country overwhelmingly comprised of poor and not so-well-off people. Their aspirations influence politicking more than they influence policies, though they also have some influence on the latter.

- The politics of caste confrontation has on the whole strengthened Indian democracy and promoted integration. The politics of religious confrontation and division has weakened Indian democracy and social integration.

This is not as strange as it might first appear. Caste in India all too frequently divides along lines of oppressor and oppressed. Mobilisation by the latter to confront the former, for all its excesses, has an overall beneficial effect. It helps in ways, big and small, to redress real injustices and grievances; to give the oppressed a greater voice and stake in the existing political-democratic system and therefore to strengthen it. Division along religious lines is not a division between oppressor and oppressed. Hindus and Muslims do not exist in the same relationship as upper caste and lower caste, employer and employee, landlord and rural worker, male and female. A politics of religious mobilisation, therefore, does nothing to rectify injustices but only creates deeper hostilities and tensions between the two.

- While unfortunately there is a growing impact in Indian social and political life of the 'politics of Hinduness' or Hindutva, the relevance and impact of the 'politics of Muslimness' is limited and constrained.

With the rise of a sizeable 'middle-class' and lower middle class among Muslims to partly replace the professionals and middle-class strata of north India who migrated to Pakistan during and shortly after its formation, the hold of religious leaders and of religiously dominated and religiously influenced political parties among Muslims has, on balance, significantly weakened. Along with this declining religious influence has come a rising pre-occupation with the secular issues of seeking better education, greater women's rights and better employment prospects.

To put it another way where Muslim communal political organisations flourish (whether in Hyderabad, Moplah or elsewhere) it is possible or likely, that Hindu communal-political organisations will emerge. But the reverse does not hold. Where a Hindu communal-political organisation grows or flourishes (e.g. in Uttar Pradesh or West Bengal or Maharashtra or Gujarat) Muslims gravitate to non-BJP secular parties. Or to understand the same point from another angle: we have seen the systematic rise and consolidation on a national level of the 'politics of Hinduness'. We are as far today as at any time after Partition from the emergence of any national-level expression of the 'politics of Muslimness'. All Muslim communal-political organisations are irredeemably local or regional in character. The collective consciousness of Indian Muslims as Muslims is growing as a consequence of the rise of Hindutva, of communal riots, of the rising tide of Islamophobia generally, and as a result of greater awareness of their relative disadvantages as a community. But India is far away from providing any single or national political or electoral magnet for Muslims as Muslims.

The cultural similarities between local Hindus and Muslims are still strong enough that the religious similarities amongst geographically dispersed and linguistically different Hindus or Muslims cannot compensate for the much stronger cultural differences amongst them, though they belong to the same religious 'community'. What is more, there is a growing gap between elite Muslims and the Muslim masses that has weakened the hold of parties like the Congress operating through such elite loyalties. There is also the growing connection of Muslims to occupationally adjacent communities like dalits and lower castes that makes the political formations representing them (like the Bahujan Samaj Party) more attractive to these local Muslim communities.

- While the economic and social status of the 'Indian Middle Class' (petty bourgeoisie/professionals) is growing, their

> political influence though strong is not quite commensurate. The IMC though huge in absolute numbers is not, as in the advanced industrialised democracies, a median category.

Government policies usually (but not always) favour these groups but the democratic system does not. The contrast in this respect with Western democracies is striking. In the West, the poor and lower classes are electorally apathetic. Abstention rates in voting are much higher among them than in the case of the middle classes and upper strata of society.

It is no surprise, therefore, that in the United States poor blacks (and whites) hardly bother to vote because they know it will make no difference to their lives. In India, the reverse holds. Abstention rates are higher among the upper sections of society. The poor in India do vote because it makes some difference to their lives and they know it. In contrast to Western democracies (where the reverse holds) the percentage size of voter turnouts in India declines as one moves from local to state-wise to national-level elections but remains high at all levels.

In the United States, the Clinton administration could talk of bringing about a 'middle-class bill of rights'. In India, there is much more likely to be government talk of bringing about a 'dalit bill of rights'. In the West, the middle classes and professionals dominate not just the professions, the corporate sector, the public media and the upper echelons of the civil and military bureaucracy. They also dominate the political process and system. In India the 'middle classes' dominate most all that their Western equivalents dominate, but not however, the Indian political process or system. Since the IMC belongs at best to the top 15 per cent to 20 per cent of the population they are not a median category that can act as a powerful social buffer vis-à-vis the working class, the working poor and the underclass, as in the advanced democracies. Indeed, the social pressure from below upon them is much greater and the need of the governing elite to periodically appeal to these more numerous social forces below them creates a greater sense of insecurity amongst the IMC. This 'middle class' has a one-sided hostility to corruption—they rail against the corrupted but rarely against the corruptors who all too often come from their own elite ranks. They all tend to be strongly attracted to themes like 'discipline' and the 'strong hand' or to the view that there should be minimal educational qualifications before being entitled to vote or stand for public office.

There is a more general theoretical issue that also needs to be addressed here. Much if not most of conventional democratic theory holds that the middle class is the crucial social foundation for stabilising democratic political rule. This viewpoint is contested from the Left in the writings of Marx and Trotsky where the former saw the middle strata of his time as a vacillating category which cannot lead but can only follow either of the two classes—the bourgeoisie proper or the proletariat—who alone can direct society along capitalist or socialist lines. Trotsky even more perceptively pointed out that far from being the crucial social anchor for political democracy it is the self-consciousness of the middle strata of his time (the petty bourgeoisie) that most importantly influences the form taken by bourgeois rule, whether authoritarian or democratic. Trotsky's insight can be extended to our times even after allowing for the growth in size of, and the internal differentiation of the contemporary middle class. Thus the middle class can be just as easily the crucial social foundation for fascism as for liberal democracy. Certainly, in India the IMC is not the most important social anchor for the sustenance of liberal democracy/bourgeois democracy but is in fact the most important social base for right-wing Hindutva politics. This is true not just of the lower middle-class and petty bourgeoisie but of other and higher sections of the IMC. Indeed, the expansion of the Sangh's electoral and political base amongst urban 'professionals' and amongst middle and upper businesses has been, relatively speaking, significantly greater than its expansion downwards amongst the rural Other Backward Classes.

- In determining the formation of national governments the electoral weight of regional parties has become of crucial importance. In determining national/international policies the political weight of regional parties has been largely marginal.

The growing regionalisation of the Indian polity over the decades has been a source of greater coherence and stability nationally. In its earlier phase this process allowed for the emergence of a variety of regional political parties better able to represent and address the state and local level concerns of the populace. In its more recent phase it has enabled the emergence of coalition politics at the national level giving regional parties a greater stake than ever in deepening and sustaining the federal character of the Indian polity while maintaining a strong Centre. However, the regional parties have been of two types, those that cannot and do not have extra-regional ambitions, and those that do. In neither case so far have either type succeeded in becoming significant extra-regional forces. They have remained limited regional formations with specific and parochial programmes and political projects and perspectives reflecting the limitations of their geographical and/or social bases. Their involvement in governments at the Centre has so far always been in tandem with a direction-setting 'national' political formation as the hub of the governing coalition that has had a corresponding national/international agenda. This 'national' aspirant has then been able to deal fairly easily through standard bargaining processes with the more parochial demands of these regional forces, and therefore, to push through with its own national/international policies.

The three examples so far of a governing coalition have been the United Front (UF) government of 1996–8, the National Democratic Alliance (NDA) government of 1998/99–2004, and the United Progressive Alliance (UPA) government of 2004 and 2009. The UF government had the main rump of the Janata Dal as its 'national' hub and this JD was the main legatee of the 'nationally' formed Janata Party formed during, first the immediate post-Emergency period, and second, of the Janata Dal again forged from the beginning as a 'national' party by V. P. Singh, and which governed at the mercy of the Left and Right parties in the Centre during the interregnum of 1989–91. For the NDA the 'national' hub was the BJP, which could and did set the national/international agenda. When during the Gujarat pogrom and its aftermath, signs of unease over the communalism of the Sangh surfaced, a determined BJP was easily able to bring to heel the 'secular' regional parties, that in the final analysis were far more concerned to remain in power for narrow parochial ends than to fight vigorously for more principled politics of much wider scope and importance. For the UPA the 'national' hub is the Congress party. The only regional political formations that do have a genuine nationalist/internationalist orientation, programmatically speaking, are the two mainstream Left parties—the CPI and CPM, which though not formally so, can be taken as a united political force. Their impact on a Congress determined to pursue neo-liberal economic policies, a soft Hindutva at home, and a strategic partnership with the US internationally, has been minimal. In the 2009 elections the Congress has emerged much stronger within the new governing coalition and there is even less likelihood that the regional partners can exercise significant influence on its national and international policies.

- The most resolute and principled defenders of a 'bourgeois' but secular-liberal and welfarist democracy in India are the purportedly 'anti-bourgeois' mainstream communist parties, not the parties of the Centre or the right, regional or national.

Domestically, the CPI and CPM are the fiercest opponents of Hindutva and therefore recognised by the Sangh as their most hostile and relentless opponents. As for the Congress, it has moved dramatically away from its own political legacy and past programmatic vision of an Indian version of humane, social democratic capitalism at home and strong nationalist independence abroad. What we have had is not the 'Congressisation' of the BJP but rather the 'BJPisation' of the Congress. The mainstream Left parties have long since shed their revolutionary or even seriously Left-radical character. They do not represent by their practice the most oppressed sections of Indian society and pose no threat whatsoever to the Indian bourgeoisie, big or small, regional or national. Their orientation towards foreign capital is pragmatic not hostile. They seek the best, i.e., 'nationalist', terms of engagement with such capital rather than the absence of any such engagement. It is not the Congress but this mainstream Left (to be sharply distinguished from the Maoist Left) that is actually the main political legatee of Nehruvianism today. It is this Left that is most determined to defend the essential character of the Indian Constitution, not to attack its 'bourgeois' character.

- Socially-electorally, the Congress today is, proportionately speaking, more than ever before in its post-independence history, a party of the lower castes and lower classes. Yet in its policy orientation and behaviour it has never before been so Right-wing!

In the course of the nineties, the all-India electoral haemorrhage of the Congress from the top was so much greater than from below. Its upper caste Hindu vote as a proportion of all upper castes fell from 36 per cent in 1991 to 21 per cent in 2004 while its proportion of dalit (39 per cent and 37 per cent) and adivasi votes (45 per cent and 42 per cent) remained relatively stable between the two election periods. The proportion of Muslims voting Congress actually rose from 38 per cent to 50 per cent. In short, the Congress is the party of the poor and lower castes more than ever before in its history, but is also now decisively and determinedly right-wing in its policy orientation and behaviour. Three interconnected factors explain this extraordinary disjunction.

First, the emergence of a 'middle class' of mass proportions comprising the top 20 per cent or more of Indian society provided the professional recruiting ground and the social base for explicitly right-wing, self-serving elite-driven policies. Second, the emergence of a totally new kind of Congress leadership highly compatible with the values, preoccupations and interests of this burgeoning layer of elites and middle class and very different in its political culture, reflexes and commitment from that of the Congress past. It is this Congress leadership (starting from Rajiv Gandhi as the 'face of modern India'), which in a context of internal organisational decay, is most responsible for the systematic-cumulative programmatic shift of the party to the right that eventually passed beyond the point of no return. Finally, there is the enormous pressure exerted by the remarkable rise of the BJP-RSS in large part also explained by its expanding support amidst this middle class.

In a more comparative survey, the most important contribution of the rise of the New Right in the three democracies of United States, United Kingdom and India, from the beginning of the eighties onwards, was its contribution to the decisive transformation of the main alternative party contender. This ensured the longer-term right-wing transformation of governmental policy. But where Reaganism and Thatcherism could only debouch into the eventual emergence of the Clinton 'New Democrats' and Blair's 'New Labour' after provoking the rise and resistance of a 'New Left' in both parties (Jesse Jackson and Tony Benn), that then had to be crushed within the parties through a fierce internal struggle, the Congress witnessed no such process. This Congress long ago shed the rooted organisational structure, which could have been the source and terrain of such a struggle to retain the party's historical character.

It is now a right-wing party, decisively transformed from its historical past. But one that is outflanked to its right (the BJP-RSS) by a formation that is not the Indian equivalent of say, Christian Democracy, but is more dangerously authoritarian, anti-secular/anti-democratic, and communal-racist than either the Republicans or the British Conservatives. This relatively sharper contrast of the two right-wing parties dominating Indian politics today, misleads many into still believing that the Congress party is basically a 'centrist' force, albeit leaning more to the right than before. It also prevents many from recognising the obvious. For at least the next decade or more, the overall profile is clear—the normalisation of right-wing politics at the Centre at all levels, social, economic, cultural, the external—as two coalition groupings, led by the Congress and BJP, with some degree of interchangeability of junior regional partners, compete with each other.

- Indian democracy is a seemingly strange combination. It is extraordinarily violent and authoritarian at the micro-level. Yet it is extremely difficult to institutionalise such authoritarianism at the macro-level.

At the level of face-to-face transactions and contact in ordinary life among the poor and not-so-well-off, things are all too often hard, brutal and highly undemocratic. At the level of slums, villages, mohallas, districts, and even broader spaces, authoritarian practices are so routinised as to make something of a mockery of the notion of democratic life, existence and opportunities. But despite this and despite frequent outbreaks of violence, the other contrasting side of the picture is the enormous difficulty in institutionalising macro-level structures of authoritarianism. Not only was the Emergency a much milder form of 'national authoritarianism' than most African, Latin American and Asian dictatorial variants, its very collapse indicated the great difficulties involved in setting up structures conducive to long-term authoritarian rule in India.

But lest we draw too much solace from this unusual paradox or contradiction, we also need to remind ourselves that India today faces the continuing threat of Hindutva forces. But there are two more challenges that also need to be mentioned. Neo-liberalism as economic doctrine, policy and practice demands, and always gets in some form or the other a rightwards and anti-democratic shift at the levels of politics and ideology. This is a functional necessity. In its foreign policy the Indian elites and the Indian state is subordinating itself to the US imperial project—the most profoundly authoritarian and anti-democratic international project conceivable, albeit one sought to be justified in the name of promoting global democracy! The price, therefore, for maintaining the single most precious fruit of India's history as an independent nation-state—its democratic dignity—is the exercise of utmost public vigilance.

Note on the Contributors

ASHOK ACHARYA is Associate Professor at Department of Political Science, Delhi University. He writes on multiculturalism, affirmative action, issues of egalitarianism, diversity and liberty in political theory.

NAVNITA C. BEHERA is Professor at Department of Political Science, Delhi University. She writes on Kashmir, South Asia and on various theories concerning international relations.

RAJEEV BHARGAVA is currently Director, Centre for the Study of Developing Societies (CSDS), New Delhi. He writes widely on issues of secularism, Indian Constitution, methodological individualism and on key issues in political theory.

NEERA CHANDHOKE is Professor at Department of Political Science, Delhi University, and is Director, Developing Countries Research Centre (DCRC). She writes on contemporary political theory, comparative politics, civil society and democratic institutions.

P. K. DATTA is Professor at Department of Political Science, Delhi University. He writes on Tagore, Indian political thought and Indian literature and culture, as well as on the history of colonial India.

GOPAL GURU is Chairperson, Centre for Political Studies, Jawaharlal Nehru University. He writes on Ambedkar, dalit politics and theoretical issues concerning social deprivation and exclusion.

KYOUNG-HEE KOH teaches at the Hankuk University, Seoul, South Korea. She was a postdoctoral fellow in the Department of Political Science, Delhi University.

VEENA KUKREJA is Associate Professor at Department of Political Science, Delhi University. She writes on South Asian politics with a particular focus on Pakistan and India-Pakistan relations.

NIVEDITA MENON is Professor at Centre for Political Studies, Jawaharlal Nehru University. She writes on feminist politics, social movements in India and issues pertaining to equality, liberty, diversity, methodologies in political theory.

MANORANJAN MOHANTY is former Head, Department of Political Science, Delhi University. He is currently associated with the Institute of Chinese Studies and with Council for Social Development (CSD). His areas of interest are Third World politics, social movements of caste, class and gender, and comparative studies of India and China.

M. P. SINGH is former Head, Department of Political Science, Delhi University. He writes widely on the Indian Constitution, federalism, the party system and other matters pertaining to Indian government and politics.

SATYAJIT SINGH is Professor and is currently Dean of the School of Development Studies, Ambedkar University, Delhi. His area of specialisation is public policy and he writes widely on issues of governance, water management and rural development.

N. SUKUMAR is Assistant Professor at Department of Political Science, Delhi University. He writes widely on Indian political thinkers, social inclusion and exclusion, Ambedkar and poverty.

ACHIN VANAIK is Head, Department of Political Science, Delhi University. He writes widely on the political economy of India, international relations, nuclear disarmament, secularism and communalism.

Index